CHRISTOPHER COLUMBUS.

FRONTISPIECE—Irving, Vol. **Seven.**

THE WORKS OF

WASHINGTON IRVING

THE LIFE AND VOYAGES

OF

CHRISTOPHER COLUMBUS

PART TWO

A TOUR ON THE PRAIRIES

WITH FRONTISPIECE

NEW YORK AND LONDON
THE CO-OPERATIVE PUBLICATION SOCIETY, Inc.

CONTE

VOLUME SEVEN

THE LIFE AND VOYAGES

OF

CHRISTOPHER COLUMBUS

(3)

Contents

4

BOOK XVI.

BOOK XVII.

BOOK XVIII.

APPENDIX.

Contents

5

A TOUR ON THE PRAIRIES

6   Contents

LIFE AND VOYAGES OF

CHRISTOPHER COLUMBUS

THE LIFE AND VOYAGES

OF

CHRISTOPHER COLUMBUS

BOOK THIRTEEN
(*Continued*)

CHAPTER THREE

COLUMBUS SUMMONED TO APPEAR BEFORE BOBADILLA
[1500]

WHEN the tidings reached Columbus at Fort Conception of the high-handed proceedings of Bobadilla, he considered them the unauthorized acts of some rash adventurer like Ojeda. Since government had apparently thrown open the door to private enterprise, he might expect to have his path continually crossed, and his jurisdiction infringed by bold intermeddlers, feigning or fancying themselves authorized to interfere in the affairs of the colony. Since the departure of Ojeda another squadron had touched upon the coast, and produced a transient alarm, being an expedition under one of the Pinzons, licensed by the sovereigns to make discoveries. There had also been a rumor of another squadron hovering about the island, which proved, however, to be unfounded.*

The conduct of Bobadilla bore all the appearance of a lawless usurpation of some intruder of the kind. He had possessed himself forcibly of the fortress, and consequently cf the town. He had issued extravagant licenses injurious to

---

* Letter of Columbus to the Nurse of Prince Juan.

the government, and apparently intended only to make partisans among the people; and had threatened to throw Columbus himself in irons.   That this man could really be sanctioned by government in such intemperate measures was repugnant to belief.   The admiral's consciousness of his own services, the repeated assurances he had received of high consideration on the part of the sovereigns, and the perpetual prerogatives granted to him under their hand and seal, with all the solemnity that a compact could possess, all forbade him to consider the transactions at San Domingo otherwise than as outrages on his authority by some daring or misguided individual.

To be nearer to San Domingo, and obtain more correct information, he proceeded to Bonao, which was now beginning to assume the appearance of a settlement, several Spaniards having erected houses there and cultivated the adjacent country.   He had scarcely reached the place when an alcalde, bearing a staff of office, arrived there from San Domingo, proclaiming the appointment of Bobadilla to the government, and bearing copies of his letters patent.   There was no especial letter or message sent to the admiral, nor were any of the common forms of courtesy and ceremony observed in superseding him in the command; all the proceedings of Bobadilla toward him were abrupt and insulting.

Columbus was exceedingly embarrassed how to act.   It was evident that Bobadilla was intrusted with extensive powers by the sovereigns, but that they could have exercised such a sudden, unmerited, and apparently capricious act of severity, as that of divesting him of all his commands, he could not believe.   He endeavored to persuade himself that Bobadilla was some person sent out to exercise the functions of chief judge, according to the request he had written home to the sovereigns, and that they had intrusted him likewise with provisional powers to make an inquest into the late troubles of the island.   All beyond these powers he tried to believe were mere assumptions and exaggerations of authority, as in the case of Aguado.   At all events, he was determined to act upon such presumption, and to endeavor to gain time. If the monarchs had really taken any harsh measures with respect to him, it must have been in consequence of misrepresentations. The least delay might give them an opportunity of ascertaining their error and making the necessary amends.

He wrote to Bobadilla, therefore, in guarded terms, welcoming him to the island; cautioning him against precipitate measures, especially in granting licenses to collect gold; informing him that he was on the point of going to Spain, and in a little time would leave him in command, with everything fully and clearly explained. He wrote at the same time to the like purport to certain monks who had come out with Bobadilla, though he observes that these letters were only written to gain time.* He received no replies; but while an insulting silence was observed toward him, Bobadilla filled up several of the blank letters, of which he had a number signed by the sovereigns, and sent them to Roldan, and other of the admiral's enemies, the very men whom he had been sent out to judge. These letters were full of civilities and promises of favor.†

To prevent any mischief which might arise from the licenses and indulgences so prodigally granted by Bobadilla, Columbus published by word and letter that the powers assumed by him could not be valid, nor his licenses availing, as he himself held superior powers granted to him in perpetuity by the crown, which could no more be superseded in this instance than they had been in that of Aguado.

For some time Columbus remained in this anxious and perplexed state of mind, uncertain what line of conduct to pursue in so singular and unlooked-for a conjuncture. He was soon brought to a decision. Francisco Velasquez, deputy treasurer, and Juan de Trasierra, a Franciscan friar, arrived at Bonao, and delivered to him the royal letter of credence, signed by the sovereigns on the 26th of May, 1499, command-

---

* Letter of Columbus to the Nurse of Prince Juan.
† Ibid. Herrera, decad. i., lib. iv.

ing him to give implicit faith and obedience to Bobadilla; and they delivered, at the same time, a summons from the latter to appear immediately before him.

This laconic letter from the sovereigns struck at once at the root of all his dignity and power. He no longer made hesitation or demur, but complying with the peremptory summons of Bobadilla, departed, almost alone and unattended, for San Domingo.*

CHAPTER FOUR

COLUMBUS AND HIS BROTHERS ARRESTED AND SENT TO SPAIN IN CHAINS

[1500]

THE tidings that a new governor had arrived, and that Columbus was in disgrace, and to be sent home in chains, circulated rapidly through the Vega, and the colonists hastened from all parts to San Domingo to make interest with Bobadilla. It was soon perceived that there was no surer way than that of vilifying his predecessor. Bobadilla felt that he had taken a rash step in seizing upon the government, and that his own safety required the conviction of Columbus. He listened eagerly, therefore, to all accusations, public or private; and welcome was he who could bring any charge, however extravagant, against the admiral and his brothers.

Hearing that the admiral was on his way to the city, he made a bustle of preparation, and armed the troops, affecting to believe a rumor that Columbus had called upon the caciques of the Vega to aid him with their subjects in a resistance to the commands of government. No grounds appear for this absurd report, which was probably invented to give a coloring of precaution to subsequent measures of violence

---

* Herrera, decad. i., lib. iv., cap. 9. Letter to the Nurse of Prince Juan.

and insult. The admiral's brother, Don Diego, was seized, thrown in irons, and confined on board of a caravel, without any reason being assigned for his imprisonment.

In the meantime Columbus pursued his journey to San Domingo, traveling in a lonely manner, without guards or retinue. Most of his people were with the adelantado, and he had declined being attended by the remainder. He had heard of the rumors of the hostile intentions of Bobadilla; and although he knew that violence was threatened to his person, he came in this unpretending manner to manifest his pacific feelings and to remove all suspicion.*

No sooner did Bobadilla hear of his arrival than he gave orders to put him in irons and confine him in the fortress. This outrage to a person of such dignified and venerable appearance and such eminent merit seemed for the time to shock even his enemies. When the irons were brought, every one present shrank from the task of putting them on him, either from a sentiment of compassion at so great a reverse of fortune or out of habitual reverence for his person. To fill the measure of ingratitude meted out to him, it was one of his own domestics, "A graceless and shameless cook," says Las Casas, "who, with unwashed front, riveted the fetters with as much readiness and alacrity as though he were serving him with choice and savory viands. I knew the fellow," adds the venerable historian, "and I think his name was Espinosa." †

Columbus conducted himself with characteristic magnanimity under the injuries heaped upon him. There is a noble scorn which swells and supports the heart, and silences the tongue of the truly great, when enduring the insults of the unworthy. Columbus could not stoop to deprecate the arrogance of a weak and violent man like Bobadilla. He looked beyond this shallow agent and all his petty tyranny to the sovereigns who had employed him. Their injustice or

---

* Las Casas, Hist. Ind., lib. i., cap. 180.
† Ibid., lib. i., cap. 180.

ingratitude alone could wound his spirit; and he felt assured that when the truth came to be known they would blush to find how greatly they had wronged him. With this proud assurance he bore all present indignities in silence.

Bobadilla, although he had the admiral and Don Diego in his power, and had secured the venal populace, felt anxious and ill at ease. The adelantado, with an armed force under his command, was still in the distant province of Xaragua, in pursuit of the rebels. Knowing his soldier-like and determined spirit, he feared he might take some violent measure when he should hear of the ignominious treatment and imprisonment of his brothers. He doubted whether any order from himself would have any effect, except to exasperate the stern Don Bartholomew. He sent a demand, therefore, to Columbus, to write to his brother, requesting him to repair peaceably to San Domingo, and forbidding him to execute the persons he held in confinement; Columbus readily complied. He exhorted his brother to submit quietly to the authority of his sovereigns, and to endure all present wrongs and indignities, under the confidence that when they arrived at Castile everything would be explained and redressed.*

On receiving this letter, Don Bartholomew immediately complied. Relinquishing his command, he hastened peacefully to San Domingo, and on arriving experienced the same treatment with his brothers, being put in irons and confined

---

* P. Martyr mentions a vulgar rumor of the day, that the admiral, not knowing what might happen, wrote a letter in cipher to the adelantado, urging him to come with arms in his hands to prevent any violence that might be contrived against him; that the adelantado advanced, in effect, with his armed force, but having the imprudence to proceed some distance ahead of it, was surprised by the governor before his men could come to his succor, and that the letter in cipher had been sent to Spain. This must have been one of the groundless rumors of the day, circulated to prejudice the public mind. Nothing of the kind appears among the charges in the inquest made by Bobadilla, and which was seen, and extracts made from it, by Las Casas, for his history. It is, in fact, in total contradiction to the statements of Las Casas, Herrera and Fernando Columbus.

on board of a caravel. They were kept separate from each other, and no communication permitted between them. Bobadilla did not see them himself, nor did he allow others to visit them, but kept them in ignorance of the cause of their imprisonment, the crimes with which they were charged, and the process that was going on against them.*

It has been questioned whether Bobadilla really had authority for the arrest and imprisonment of the admiral and his brothers,† and whether such violence and indignity was in any case contemplated by the sovereigns. He may have fancied himself empowered by the clause in the letter of instructions, dated March 21, 1499, in which, speaking of the rebellion of Roldan, "he is authorized to *seize the persons and sequestrate the property* of those who appeared to be culpable, and then to proceed against them and against the absent, with the highest civil and criminal penalties." This evidently had reference to the persons of Roldan and his followers, who were then in arms, and against whom Columbus had sent home complaints; and this, by a violent construction, Bobadilla seems to have wrested into an authority for seizing the person of the admiral himself. In fact, in the whole course of his proceedings, he reversed and confounded the order of his instructions. His first step should have been

---

* Charlevoix, in his History of San Domingo (lib. iii., p. 199), states that the suit against Columbus was conducted in writing; that written charges were sent to him, to which he replied in the same way. This is contrary to the statements of Las Casas, Herrera and Fernando Columbus. The admiral himself, in his letter to the Nurse of Prince Juan, after relating the manner in which he and his brothers had been thrown into irons and confined separately, without being visited by Bobadilla or permitted to see any other persons, expressly adds, "I make oath that I do not know for what I am imprisoned." Again, in a letter written some time afterward from Jamaica, he says, "I was taken and thrown, with two of my brothers, in a ship, loaded with irons, with little clothing and much ill-treatment, without being summoned or convicted by justice."

† Herrera, decad. i., lib. iv., cap. 10. Oviedo Cronica, lib. iii., cap. 6.

to proceed against the rebels; this he made the last. His last step should have been, in case of ample evidence against the admiral, to have superseded him in office; and this he made the first, without waiting for evidence. Having predetermined, from the very outset, that Columbus was in the wrong, by the same rule he had to presume that all the opposite parties were in the right. It became indispensable to his own justification to inculpate the admiral and his brothers; and the rebels he had been sent to judge became, by this singular perversion of rule, necessary and cherished evidences, to criminate those against whom they had rebelled.

The intentions of the crown, however, are not to be vindicated at the expense of its miserable agent. If proper respect had been felt for the rights and dignities of Columbus, Bobadilla would never have been intrusted with powers so extensive, undefined, and discretionary; nor would he have dared to proceed to such lengths, with such rudeness and precipitation, had he not felt assured that it would not be displeasing to the jealous-minded Ferdinand.

The old scenes of the time of Aguado were now renewed with tenfold virulence, and the old charges revived, with others still more extravagant. From the early and never-to-be-forgotten outrage upon Castilian pride, of compelling hidalgos, in time of emergency, to labor in the construction of works necessary to the public safety, down to the recent charge of levying war against the government, there was not a hardship, abuse, nor sedition in the island, that was not imputed to the misdeeds of Columbus and his brothers. Besides the usual accusations of inflicting oppressive labor, unnecessary tasks, painful restrictions, short allowances of food, and cruel punishments upon the Spaniards, and waging unjust wars against the natives, they were now charged with preventing the conversion of the latter, that they might send them slaves to Spain, and profit by their sale. This last charge, so contrary to the pious feelings of the admiral, was founded on his having objected to the baptism of certain Indians of mature age, until they could be instructed in the

doctrines of Christianity; justly considering it an abuse of
that holy sacrament to administer it thus blindly.*

Columbus was charged, also, with having secreted pearls,
and other precious articles, collected in his voyage along the
coast of Paria, and with keeping the sovereigns in ignorance
of the nature of his discoveries there, in order to exact new
privileges from them; yet it was notorious that he had sent
home specimens of the pearls and journals and charts of his
voyage, by which others had been enabled to pursue his
track.

Even the late tumults, now that the rebels were admitted
as evidence, were all turned into matters of accusation.
They were represented as spirited and loyal resistances to
tyranny exercised upon the colonists and the natives. The
well-merited punishments inflicted upon certain of the ringleaders were cited as proofs of a cruel and revengeful disposition, and a secret hatred of Spaniards. Bobadilla believed,
or affected to believe, all these charges. He had, in a manner, made the rebels his confederates in the ruin of Columbus. It was become a common cause with them. He could
no longer, therefore, conduct himself toward them as a judge.
Guevara, Requelme, and their fellow convicts, were discharged almost without the form of a trial, and it is even
said were received into favor and countenance. Roldan,
from the very first, had been treated with confidence by
Bobadilla, and honored with his correspondence. All the
others, whose conduct had rendered them liable to justice,
received either a special acquittal or a general pardon. It
was enough to have been opposed in any way to Columbus
to obtain full justification in the eyes of Bobadilla.

The latter had now collected a weight of testimony, and
produced a crowd of witnesses, sufficient, as he conceived, to
insure the condemnation of the prisoners and his own continuance in command. He determined, therefore, to send the
admiral and his brothers home in chains, in the vessels ready

---

* Muñoz, Hist. N. Mundo, part unpublished.

for sea, transmitting at the same time the inquest taken in their case, and writing private letters, enforcing the charges made against them, and advising that Columbus should on no account be restored to the command, which he had so shamefully abused.

San Domingo now swarmed with miscreants just delivered from the dungeon and the gibbet. It was a perfect jubilee of triumphant villainy and dastard malice. Every base spirit, which had been awed into obsequiousness by Columbus and his brothers when in power now started up to revenge itself upon them when in chains. The most injurious slanders were loudly proclaimed in the streets; insulting pasquinades and inflammatory libels were posted up at every corner; and horns were blown in the neighborhood of their prisons, to taunt them with the exultings of the rabble.*
When these rejoicings of his enemies reached him in his dungeon, and Columbus reflected on the inconsiderate violence already exhibited by Bobadilla, he knew not how far his rashness and confidence might carry him, and began to entertain apprehensions for his life.

The vessels being ready to make sail, Alonzo de Villejo was appointed to take charge of the prisoners and carry them to Spain. This officer had been brought up by an uncle of Fonseca, was in the employ of that bishop, and had come out with Bobadilla. The latter instructed him, on arriving at Cadiz, to deliver his prisoners into the hands of Fonseca, or of his uncle, thinking thereby to give the malignant prelate a triumphant gratification. This circumstance gave weight with many to a report that Bobadilla was secretly instigated and encouraged in his violent measures by Fonseca, and was promised his protection and influence at court, in case of any complaints of his conduct.†

Villejo undertook the office assigned him, but he discharged it in a more generous manner than was intended.

---

* Hist. del Almirante, cap. 86.
† Las Casas, Hist. Ind., lib. i., cap. 180, MS.

"This Alonzo de Villejo," says the worthy Las Casas, "was a hidalgo of honorable character, and my particular friend." He certainly showed himself superior to the low malignity of his patrons. When he arrived with a guard to conduct the admiral from the prison to the ship, he found him in chains in a state of silent despondency. So violently had he been treated, and so savage were the passions let loose against him, that he feared he should be sacrificed without an opportunity of being heard, and his name go down sullied and dishonored to posterity. When he beheld the officer enter with the guard, he thought it was to conduct him to the scaffold. "Villejo," said he, mournfully, "whither are you taking me?" "To the ship, your Excellency, to embark," replied the other. "To embark!" repeated the admiral, earnestly; "Villejo, do you speak the truth?" "By the life of your Excellency," replied the honest officer, "it is true!" With these words the admiral was comforted, and felt as one restored from death to life. Nothing can be more touching and expressive than this little colloquy, recorded by the venerable Las Casas, who doubtless had it from the lips of his friend Villejo.

The caravels set sail early in October, bearing off Columbus shackled like the vilest of culprits, amid the scoffs and shouts of a miscreant rabble, who took a brutal joy in heaping insults on his venerable head, and sent curses after him from the shores of the island he had so recently added to the civilized world. Fortunately the voyage was favorable, and of but moderate duration, and was rendered less disagreeable by the conduct of those to whom he was given in custody. The worthy Villejo, though in the service of Fonseca, felt deeply moved at the treatment of Columbus. The master of the caravel, Andreas Martin, was equally grieved: they both treated the admiral with profound respect and assiduous attention. They would have taken off his irons, but to this he would not consent. "No," said he proudly, "their majesties commanded me by letter to submit to whatever Bobadilla should order in their name; by their authority he has put upon me these chains; I will wear them until they shall order them to be taken off, and I will preserve them afterward as relics and memorials of the reward of my services."*

"He did so," adds his son Fernando; "I saw them always hanging in his cabinet, and he requested that when he died they might be buried with him!"†

BOOK FOURTEEN

CHAPTER ONE

SENSATION IN SPAIN ON THE ARRIVAL OF COLUMBUS IN IRONS—HIS APPEARANCE AT COURT

[1500]

THE arrival of Columbus at Cadiz, a prisoner and in chains, produced almost as great a sensation as his triumphant return from his first voyage. It was one of those striking and obvious facts which speak to the feelings of the multitude, and preclude the necessity of reflection. No one stopped to inquire into the case. It was sufficient to be told that Columbus was brought home in irons from the world he had discovered. There was a general burst of indignation in Cadiz, and in the powerful and opulent Seville, which was echoed throughout all Spain. If the ruin of Columbus had been the intention of his enemies, they had defeated their object by their own violence. One of those reactions took place, so frequent in the public mind, when persecution is pushed to an unguarded length. Those of the populace who had recently been loud in their clamor against Columbus were now as loud in their reprobation of his treatment, and a

---

* Las Casas, Hist. Ind., lib. i., cap. 180, MS.
† Hist. del Almirante, cap. 86.

strong sympathy was expressed, against which it would have been odious for the government to contend.

The tidings of his arrival, and of the ignominious manner in which he had been brought, reached the court at Granada, and filled the halls of the Alhambra with murmurs of astonishment. Columbus, full of his wrongs, but ignorant how far they had been authorized by the sovereigns, had forborne to write to them. In the course of his voyage, however, he had penned a long letter to Dona Juana de la Torre, the aya of Prince Juan, a lady high in favor with Queen Isabella. This letter, on his arrival at Cadiz, Andreas Martin, the captain of the caravel, permitted him to send off privately by express. It arrived, therefore, before the protocol of the proceedings instituted by Bobadilla, and from this document the sovereigns derived their first intimation of his treatment.* It contained a statement of the late transactions of the island, and of the wrongs he had suffered, written with his usual artlessness and energy. To specify the contents would be but to recapitulate circumstances already recorded. Some expressions, however, which burst from him in the warmth of his feelings, are worthy of being noted. "The slanders of worthless men," says he, "have done me more injury than all my services have profited me." Speaking of the misrepresentations to which he was subjected, he observes: "Such is the evil name which I have acquired, that if I were to build hospitals and churches, they would be called dens of robbers." After relating in indignant terms the conduct of Bobadilla, in seeking testimony respecting his administration from the very men who had rebelled against him, and throwing himself and his brothers in irons, without letting them know the offenses with which they were charged, "I have been much aggrieved," he adds, "in that a person should be sent out to investigate my conduct, who knew that if the evidence which he could send home should appear to be of a serious nature, he would remain in the government." He complains that,

---

* Las Casas, Hist. Ind., lib. i., cap. 182.

in forming an opinion of his administration, allowances had
not been made for the extraordinary difficulties with which he
had to contend, and the wild state of the country over which
he had to rule. "I was judged," he observes, "as a governor
who had been sent to take charge of a well-regulated city,
under the dominion of well-established laws, where there was
no danger of everything running to disorder and ruin; but
I ought to be judged as a captain, sent to subdue a numerous
and hostile people, of manners and religion opposite to ours,
living not in regular towns, but in forests and mountains. It
ought to be considered that I have brought all these under
subjection to their majesties, giving them dominion over another world, by which Spain, heretofore poor, has suddenly
become rich. Whatever errors I may have fallen into, they
were not with an evil intention; and I believe their majesties
will credit what I say. I have known them to be merciful
to those who have willfully done them disservice; I am convinced that they will have still more indulgence for me, who
have erred innocently, or by compulsion, as they will hereafter be more fully informed; and I trust they will consider
my great services, the advantages of which are every day
more and more apparent."

When this letter was read to the noble-minded Isabella,
and she found how grossly Columbus had been wronged and
the royal authority abused, her heart was filled with mingled
sympathy and indignation. The tidings were confirmed by
a letter from the alcalde or corregidor of Cadiz, into whose
hands Columbus and his brothers had been delivered, until
the pleasure of the sovereigns should be known;* and by another letter from Alonzo de Villejo, expressed in terms accordant with his humane and honorable conduct toward his
illustrious prisoner.

However Ferdinand might have secretly felt disposed
against Columbus, the momentary tide of public feeling was
not to be resisted. He joined with his generous queen in her

---

* Oviedo, Cronica, lib. iii., cap. 6.

reprobation of the treatment of the admiral, and both sovereigns hastened to give evidence to the world that his imprisonment had been without their authority, and contrary to their wishes. Without waiting to receive any documents that might arrive from Bobadilla, they sent orders to Cadiz that the prisoners should be instantly set at liberty, and treated with all distinction. They wrote a letter to Columbus, couched in terms of gratitude and affection, expressing their grief at all that he had suffered, and inviting him to court. They ordered, at the same time, that two thousand ducats should be advanced to defray his expenses.*

The loyal heart of Columbus was again cheered by this declaration of his sovereigns. He felt conscious of his integrity, and anticipated an immediate restitution of all his rights and dignities. He appeared at court in Granada on the 17th of December, not as a man ruined and disgraced, but richly dressed, and attended by an honorable retinue. He was received by the sovereigns with unqualified favor and distinction. When the queen beheld this venerable man approach, and thought on all he had deserved and all he had suffered, she was moved to tears. Columbus had borne up firmly against the rude conflicts of the world—he had endured with lofty scorn the injuries and insults of ignoble men; but he possessed strong and quick sensibility. When he found himself thus kindly received by his sovereigns, and beheld tears in the benign eyes of Isabella, his long-suppressed feelings burst forth; he threw himself on his knees, and for some time could not utter a word for the violence of his tears and sobbings.†

Ferdinand and Isabella raised him from the ground, and endeavored to encourage him by the most gracious expressions. As soon as he regained self-possession he entered into

---

* Las Casas, lib. i., cap. 182. Two thousand ducats, or two thousand eight hundred and forty-six dollars, equivalent to eight thousand five hundred and thirty-eight dollars of the present day.

† Herrera, decad. i., lib. iv., cap. 10.

an eloquent and high-minded vindication of his loyalty, and the zeal he had ever felt for the glory and advantage of the Spanish crown, declaring that if at any time he had erred, it had been through inexperience in government, and the extraordinary difficulties by which he had been surrounded.

There needed no vindication on his part. The intemperance of his enemies had been his best advocate. He stood in presence of his sovereigns a deeply-injured man, and it remained for them to vindicate themselves to the world from the charge of ingratitude toward their most deserving subject. They expressed their indignation at the proceedings of Bobadilla, which they disavowed as contrary to their instructions, and declared that he should be immediately dismissed from his command.

In fact, no public notice was taken of the charges sent home by Bobadilla, nor of the letters written in support of them. The sovereigns took every occasion to treat Columbus with favor and distinction, assuring him that his grievances should be redressed, his property restored, and he reinstated in all his privileges and dignities.

It was on the latter point that Columbus was chiefly solicitous. Mercenary considerations had scarcely any weight in his mind. Glory had been the great object of his ambition, and he felt that, as long as he remained suspended from his employments, a tacit censure rested on his name. He expected, therefore, that the moment the sovereigns should be satisfied of the rectitude of his conduct, they would be eager to make him amends; that a restitution of his viceroyalty would immediately take place, and he should return in triumph to San Domingo. Here, however, he was doomed to experience a disappointment which threw a gloom over the remainder of his days. To account for this flagrant want of justice and gratitude in the crown, it is expedient to notice a variety of events which had materially affected the interests of Columbus in the eyes of the politic Ferdinand.

CHAPTER TWO

CONTEMPORARY VOYAGES OF DISCOVERY

THE general license granted by the Spanish sovereigns in 1495, to undertake voyages of discovery, had given rise to various expeditions by enterprising individuals, chiefly persons who had sailed with Columbus in his first voyages. The government, unable to fit out many armaments itself, was pleased to have its territories thus extended, free of cost, and its treasury at the same time benefited by the share of the proceeds of these voyages, reserved as a kind of duty to the crown. These expeditions had chiefly taken place while Columbus was in partial disgrace with the sovereigns. His own charts and journal served as guides to the adventurers; and his magnificent accounts of Paria and the adjacent coasts had chiefly excited their cupidity.

Besides the expedition of Ojeda, already noticed, in the course of which he touched at Xaragua, one had been undertaken at the same time by Pedro Alonzo Nino, native of Moguer, an able pilot, who had been with Columbus in the voyages to Cuba and Paria. Having obtained a license, he interested a rich merchant of Seville in the undertaking, who fitted out a caravel of fifty tons burden, under condition that his brother Christoval Guerra should have the command. They sailed from the bar of Saltes, a few days after Ojeda had sailed from Cadiz, in the spring of 1499, and arriving on the coast of Terra Firma, to the south of Paria, ran along it for some distance, passed through the gulf, and thence went one hundred and thirty leagues along the shore of the present republic of Colombia, visiting what was afterward called the Pearl Coast. They landed in various places; disposed of their European trifles to immense profit, and returned with a large store of gold and pearls; having made, in their diminutive bark, one of the most extensive and lucrative voyages yet accomplished.

About the same time the Pinzons, that family of bold and opulent navigators, fitted out an armament of four caravels at Palos, manned in a great measure by their own relations and friends. Several experienced pilots embarked in it who had been with Columbus to Paria, and it was commanded by Vicente Yañez Pinzon, who had been captain of a caravel in the squadron of the admiral on his first voyage.

Pinzon was a hardy and experienced seaman, and did not, like the others, follow closely in the track of Columbus. Sailing in December, 1499, he passed the Canary and Cape de Verde Islands, standing southwest until he lost sight of the polar star. Here he encountered a terrible storm, and was exceedingly perplexed and confounded by the new aspect of the heavens. Nothing was yet known of the southern hemisphere, nor of the beautiful constellation of the cross, which in those regions has since supplied to mariners the place of the north star. The voyagers had expected to find at the south pole a star correspondent to that of the north. They were dismayed at beholding no guide of the kind, and thought there must be some prominent swelling of the earth, which hid the pole from their view.*

Pinzon continued on, however, with great intrepidity. On the 26th of January, 1500, he saw, at a distance, a great headland, which he called Cape Santa Maria de la Consolacion, but which has since been named Cape St. Augustine. He landed and took possession of the country in the name of their Catholic majesties; being a part of the territories since called the Brazils. Standing thence westward, he discovered the Maragnon, since called the River of the Amazons; traversed the Gulf of Paria, and continued across the Caribbean Sea and the Gulf of Mexico, until he found himself among the Bahamas, where he lost two of his vessels on the rocks, near the island of Jumeto. He returned to Palos in Septem-

---

* Peter Martyr, decad. i., lib. ix.

ber, having added to his former glory that of being the first
European who had crossed the equinoctial line in the western
ocean, and of having discovered the famous kingdom of
Brazil, from its commencement at the river Maragnon to
its most eastern point. As a reward for his achievements
power was granted to him to colonize and govern the lands
which he had discovered, and which extended southward
from a little beyond the river of Maragnon to Cape St.
Augustine.*

The little port of Palos, which had been so slow in furnishing the first squadron for Columbus, was now continually
agitated by the passion for discovery. Shortly after the sailing of Pinzon, another expedition was fitted out there, by
Diego Lepe, a native of the place, and manned by his adventurous townsmen. He sailed in the same direction with
Pinzon, but discovered more of the southern continent than
any other voyager of the day, or for twelve years afterward.
He doubled Cape St. Augustine, and ascertained that the
coast beyond ran to the southwest. He landed and performed the usual ceremonies of taking possession in the
name of the Spanish sovereigns, and in one place carved
their names on a magnificent tree, of such enormous magnitude that seventeen men with their hands joined could not
embrace the trunk. What enhanced the merit of his discoveries was that he had never sailed with Columbus. He had
with him, however, several skillful pilots, who had accompanied the admiral in his voyage.†

Another expedition of two vessels sailed from Cadiz, in
October, 1500, under the command of Rodrigo Bastides of
Seville. He explored the coast of Terra Firma, passing
Cape de la Vela, the western limits of the previous discov-
eries on the mainland, continuing on to a port since called
The Retreat, where afterward was founded the seaport of

---

* Herrera, decad. i., lib. iv., cap. 12.   Muñoz, Hist. N. Mundo, part
unpublished.

† Las Casas, Hist. Ind., lib. ii., cap. 2.   Muñoz, part unpublished.

Nombre de Dios. His vessels being nearly destroyed by the
teredo, or worm which abounds in those seas, he had great
difficulty in reaching Xaragua in Hispaniola, where he lost
his two caravels, and proceeded with his crew by land to San
Domingo. Here he was seized and imprisoned by Bobadilla,
under pretext that he had treated for gold with the natives
of Xaragua.*

Such was the swarm of Spanish expeditions immediately
resulting from the enterprises of Columbus; but others were
also undertaken by foreign nations. In the year 1497, Sebastian Cabot, son of a Venetian merchant resident in Bristol, sailing in the service of Henry VII. of England, navigated to the northern seas of the New World. Adopting the
idea of Columbus, he sailed in quest of the shores of Cathay,
and hoped to find a northwest passage to India. In this voyage he discovered Newfoundland, coasted Labrador to the
fifty-sixth degree of north latitude, and then returning, ran
down southwest to the Floridas, when, his provisions beginning to fail, he returned to England.† But vague and scanty
accounts of this voyage exist, which was important, as including the first discovery of the northern continent of the
New World.

The discoveries of rival nations, however, which most excited the attention and jealousy of the Spanish crown, were
those of the Portuguese. Vasco de Gama, a man of rank
and consummate talent and intrepidity, had, at length, accomplished the great design of the late Prince Henry of
Portugal, and, by doubling the Cape of Good Hope in the
year 1497, had opened the long-sought-for route to India.

Immediately after Gama's return a fleet of thirteen sail
was fitted out to visit the magnificent countries of which he
brought accounts. This expedition sailed on the 9th of March,
1500, for Calicut, under the command of Pedro Alvarez de
Cabral. Having passed the Cape de Verde Islands, he

---

* Las Casas, Hist. Ind., lib. ii., cap. 2.   Muñoz, part unpublished.
† Hakluyt's Collection of Voyages, Vol. III., p. 7.

sought to avoid the calms prevalent on the coast of Guinea, by stretching far to the west. Suddenly, on the 25th of April, he came in sight of land unknown to any one in his squadron; for, as yet, they had not heard of the discoveries of Pinzon and Lepe. He at first supposed it to be some great island; but after coasting it for some time he became persuaded that it must be part of a continent. Having ranged along it somewhat beyond the fifteenth degree of southern latitude, he landed at a harbor which he called Porto Securo, and taking possession of the country for the crown of Portugal, dispatched a ship to Lisbon with the important tidings.* In this way did the Brazils come into the possession of Portugal, being to the eastward of the conventional line settled with Spain as the boundaries of their respective territories. Dr. Robertson, in recording this voyage of Cabral, concludes with one of his just and elegant remarks:

"Columbus's discovery of the New World was," he observes, "the effort of an active genius, guided by experience, and acting upon a regular plan, executed with no less courage than perseverance. But from this adventure of the Portuguese it appears that chance might have accomplished that great design, which it is now the pride of human reason to have formed and perfected. If the sagacity of Columbus had not conducted mankind to America, Cabral, by a fortunate accident, might have led them, a few years later, to the knowledge of that extensive continent."†

---

* Lafiteau, Conquetes des Portugais, lib. ii.
† Robertson, Hist. America, Book II.

CHAPTER THREE

NICHOLAS DE OVANDO APPOINTED TO SUPERSEDE BOBADILLA

[1501]

THE numerous discoveries briefly noticed in the preceding chapter had produced a powerful effect upon the mind of Ferdinand. His ambition, his avarice, and his jealousy were equally inflamed. He beheld boundless regions, teeming with all kinds of riches, daily opening before the enterprises of his subjects; but he beheld at the same time other nations launching forth into competition, emulous for a share of the golden world which he was eager to monopolize. The expeditions of the English and the accidental discovery of the Brazils by the Portuguese caused him much uneasiness. To secure his possession of the continent, he determined to establish local governments or commands in the most important places, all to be subject to a general government, established at San Domingo, which was to be the metropolis.

With these considerations, the government, heretofore granted to Columbus, had risen vastly in importance; and while the restitution of it was the more desirable in his eyes, it became more and more a matter of repugnance to the selfish and jealous monarch. He had long repented having vested such great powers and prerogatives in any subject, particularly in a foreigner. At the time of granting them he had no anticipation of such boundless countries to be placed under his command. He appeared almost to consider himself outwitted by Columbus in the arrangement; and every succeeding discovery, instead of increasing his grateful sense of the obligation, only made him repine the more at the growing magnitude of the reward. At length, however, the affair of Bobadilla had effected a temporary exclusion of Columbus from his high office, and that without any odium to the crown, and the wary monarch secretly determined that the door thus closed between him and his dignities should never again be opened.

Perhaps Ferdinand may really have entertained doubts as to the innocence of Columbus, with respect to the various charges made against him. He may have doubted also the sincerity of his loyalty, being a stranger, when he should find himself strong in his command, at a great distance from the parent country, with immense and opulent regions under his control. Columbus himself, in his letters, alludes to reports circulated by his enemies, that he intended either to set up an independent sovereignty, or to deliver his discoveries into the hands of other potentates; and he appears to fear that these slanders might have made some impression on the mind of Ferdinand. But there was one other consideration which had no less force with the monarch in withholding this great act of justice—Columbus was no longer indispensable to him. He had made his great discovery; he had struck out the route to the New World, and now any one could follow it. A number of able navigators had sprung up under his auspices, and acquired experience in his voyages. They were daily besieging the throne with offers to fit out expeditions at their own cost, and to yield a share of the profits to the crown. Why should he, therefore, confer princely dignities and prerogatives for that which men were daily offering to perform gratuitously?

Such, from his after-conduct, appears to have been the jealous and selfish policy which actuated Ferdinand in forbearing to reinstate Columbus in those dignities and privileges so solemnly granted to him by treaty, and which it was acknowledged he had never forfeited by misconduct.

This deprivation, however, was declared to be but temporary; and plausible reasons were given for the delay in his reappointment. It was observed that the elements of those violent factions, recently in arms against him, yet existed in the island; his immediate return might produce fresh exasperation; his personal safety might be endangered, and the island again thrown into confusion. Though Bobadilla, therefore, was to be immediately dismissed from command, it was deemed advisable to send out some officer of talent and discretion to supersede him, who might dispassionately investigate the recent disorders, remedy the abuses which had arisen, and expel all dissolute and factious persons from the colony. He should hold the government for two years, by which time it was trusted that all angry passions would be allayed, and turbulent individuals removed; Columbus might then resume the command with comfort to himself and advantage to the crown. With these reasons, and the promise which accompanied them, Columbus was obliged to content himself. There can be no doubt that they were sincere on the part of Isabella, and that it was her intention to reinstate him in the full enjoyment of his rights and dignities, after his apparently necessary suspension. Ferdinand, however, by his subsequent conduct, has forfeited all claim to any favorable opinion of the kind.

The person chosen to supersede Bobadilla was Don Nicholas de Ovando, commander of Lares, of the order of Alcantara. He is described as of the middle size, fair complexioned, with a red beard, and a modest look, yet a tone of authority. He was fluent in speech, and gracious and courteous in his manners. A man of great prudence, says Las Casas, and capable of governing many people, but not of governing the Indians, on whom he inflicted incalculable injuries. He possessed great veneration for justice, was an enemy to avarice, sober in his mode of living, and of such humility that when he rose afterward to be grand commander of the order of Alcantara he would never allow himself to be addressed by the title of respect attached to it.* Such is the picture drawn of him by historians; but his conduct in several important instances is in direct contradiction to it. He appears to have been plausible and subtle, as well as

---

* Las Casas, Hist. Ind., lib. ii., cap. 3.

fluent and courteous; his humility concealed a great love of command, and in his transactions with Columbus he was certainly both ungenerous and unjust.

The various arrangements to be made, according to the new plan of colonial government, delayed for some time the departure of Ovando. In the meantime every arrival brought intelligence of the disastrous state of the island under the maladministration of Bobadilla. He had commenced his career by an opposite policy to that of Columbus. Imagining that rigorous rule had been the rock on which his pred ecessors had split, he sought to conciliate the public by all kinds of indulgence. Having at the very outset relaxed the reins of justice and morality, he lost all command over the community; and such disorder and licentiousness ensued that many, even of the opponents of Columbus, looked back with regret upon the strict but wholesome rule of himself and the adelantado.

Bobadilla was not so much a bad as an imprudent and a weak man. He had not considered the dangerous excesses to which his policy would lead. Rash in grasping authority, he was feeble and temporizing in the exercise of it; he could not look beyond the present exigency. One dangerous indulgence granted to the colonists called for another; each was ceded in its turn, and thus he went on from error to error—showing that in government there is as much danger to be apprehended from a weak as from a bad man.

He had sold the farms and estates of the crown at low prices, observing that it was not the wish of the monarchs to enrich themselves by them, but that they should redound to the profit of their subjects. He granted universal permission to work the mines, exacting only an eleventh of the produce for the crown. To prevent any diminution in the revenue, it became necessary, of course, to increase the quantity of gold collected. He obliged the caciques, therefore, to furnish each Spaniard with Indians, to assist him both in the labors of the field and of the mine. To carry this into more complete effect, he made an enumeration of the natives of the island, reduced them into classes, and distributed them, according to his favor or caprice, among the colonists. The latter, at his suggestion, associated themselves in partnerships of two persons each, who were to assist one another with their respective capitals and Indians, one superintending the labors of the field and the other the search for gold. The only injunction of Bobadilla was to produce large quantities of ore. He had one saying continually in his mouth, which shows the pernicious and temporizing principle upon which he acted: "Make the most of your time," he would say; "there is no knowing how long it will last," alluding to the possibility of his being speedily recalled. The colonists acted up to his advice, and so hard did they drive the poor natives that the eleventh yielded more revenue to the crown than had ever been produced by the third under the government of Columbus. In the meantime the unhappy natives suffered under all kinds of cruelties from their inhuman taskmasters. Little used to labor, feeble of constitution, and accustomed in their beautiful and luxuriant island to a life of ease and freedom, they sank under the toils imposed upon them, and the severities by which they were enforced. Las Casas gives an indignant picture of the capricious tyranny exercised over the Indians by worthless Spaniards, many of whom had been transported convicts from the dungeons of Castile. These wretches, who in their own countries had been the vilest among the vile, here assumed the tone of grand cavaliers. They insisted upon being attended by trains of servants. They took the daughters and female relations of caciques for their domestics, or rather for their concubines, nor did they limit themselves in number. When they traveled, instead of using the horses and mules with which they were provided, they obliged the natives to transport them upon their shoulders in litters or hammocks, with others attending to hold umbrellas of palm-leaves over their heads to keep off the sun, and fans of feathers to cool them; and Las Casas affirms that he has seen the backs and shoulders of the unfortunate Indians who bore these litters raw and bleeding from the task. When these arrogant upstarts arrived at an Indian village they consumed and lavished away the provisions of the inhabitants, seizing upon whatever pleased their caprice, and obliging the cacique and his subjects to dance before them for their amusement. Their very pleasures were attended with cruelty. They never addressed the natives but in the most degrading terms, and on the least offense, or the least freak of ill-humor, inflicted blows and lashes, and even death itself.*

Such is but a faint picture of the evils which sprang up under the feeble rule of Bobadilla, and are sorrowfully described by Las Casas from actual observation, as he visited the island just at the close of his administration. Bobadilla had trusted to the immense amount of gold, wrung from the miseries of the natives, to atone for all errors and secure favor with the sovereigns; but he had totally mistaken his course. The abuses of his government soon reached the royal ear, and, above all, the wrongs of the natives reached the benevolent heart of Isabella. Nothing was more calculated to arouse her indignation, and she urged the speedy departure of Ovando, to put a stop to these enormities.

In conformity to the plan already mentioned, the government of Ovando extended over the islands and Terra Firma, of which Hispaniola was to be the metropolis. He was to enter upon the exercise of his powers immediately upon his arrival, by procuration, sending home Bobadilla by the return of the fleet. He was instructed to inquire diligently into the late abuses, punishing the delinquents without favor or partiality, and removing all worthless persons from the island. He was to revoke immediately the license granted by Bobadilla for the general search after gold, it having been given without royal authority. He was to require, for the crown, a third of what was already collected, and one half of all that should be collected in future. He was empowered to build towns, granting them the privileges enjoyed by mu-

---

* Las Casas, Hist. Ind., lib. ii., cap. 1, MS.

nicipal corporations of Spain, and obliging the Spaniards, and particularly the soldiers, to reside in them, instead of scattering themselves over the island. Among many sage provisions there were others injurious and illiberal, characteristic of an age when the principles of commerce were but little understood, but which were continued by Spain long after the rest of the world had discarded them as the errors of dark and unenlightened times. The crown monopolized the trade of the colonies. No one could carry merchandises there on his own account. A royal factor was appointed, through whom alone were to be obtained supplies of European articles. The crown reserved to itself not only exclusive property in the mines, but in precious stones, and like objects of extraordinary value, and also in dyewoods. No strangers, and, above all, no Moors nor Jews, were permitted to establish themselves in the island, nor to go upon voyages of discovery. Such were some of the restrictions upon trade which Spain imposed upon her colonies, and which were followed up by others equally illiberal. Her commercial policy has been the scoff of modern times; but may not the present restrictions on trade, imposed by the most intelligent nations, be equally the wonder and the jest of future ages?

Isabella was particularly careful in providing for the kind treatment of the Indians. Ovando was ordered to assemble the caciques, and declare to them that the sovereigns took them and their people under their especial protection. They were merely to pay tribute like other subjects of the crown, and it was to be collected with the utmost mildness and gentleness. Great pains were to be taken in their religious instruction; for which purpose twelve Franciscan friars were sent out, with a prelate named Antonio de Espinal, a venerable and pious man. This was the first formal introduction of the Franciscan order into the New World.*

All these precautions with respect to the natives were defeated by one unwary provision. It was permitted that the

---

* Las Casas, Hist. Ind., lib. ii., cap. 3, MS.

Indians might be compelled to work in the mines, and in other employments; but this was limited to the royal service. They were to be engaged as hired laborers, and punctually paid. This provision led to great abuses and oppressions, and was ultimately as fatal to the natives as could have been the most absolute slavery.

But, with that inconsistency frequent in human conduct, while the sovereigns were making regulations for the relief of the Indians, they encouraged a gross invasion of the rights and welfare of another race of human beings. Among their various decrees on this occasion, we find the first trace of negro slavery in the New World. It was permitted to carry to the colony negro slaves born among Christians;* that is to say, slaves born in Seville and other parts of Spain, the children and descendants of natives brought from the Atlantic coast of Africa, where such traffic had for some time been carried on by the Spaniards and Portuguese. There are signal events in the course of history, which sometimes bear the appearance of temporal judgments. It is a fact worthy of observation that Hispaniola, the place where this flagrant sin against nature and humanity was first introduced into the New World, has been the first to exhibit an awful retribution.

Amid the various concerns which claimed the attention of the sovereigns, the interests of Columbus were not forgotten. Ovando was ordered to examine into all his accounts, without undertaking to pay them off. He was to ascertain the damages he had sustained by his imprisonment, the interruption of his privileges, and the confiscation of his effects. All the property confiscated by Bobadilla was to be restored; or if it had been sold, to be made good. If it had been employed in the royal service, Columbus was to be indemnified out of the treasury; if Bobadilla had appropriated it to his own use, he was to account for it out of his private purse. Equal care was to be taken to indemnify the brothers of the

---

* Herrera, Hist. Ind., decad. i., lib. iv., cap. 12.

admiral for the losses they had wrongfully suffered by their arrest.

Columbus was likewise to receive the arrears of his revenues, and the same were to be punctually paid to him in future. He was permitted to have a factor resident in the island, to be present at the melting and marking of the gold, to collect his dues, and in short to attend to all his affairs. To this office he appointed Alonzo Sanchez de Carvajal; and the sovereigns commanded that his agent should be treated with great respect.

The fleet appointed to convey Ovando to his government was the largest that had yet sailed to the New World. It consisted of thirty sail, five of them from ninety to one hundred and fifty tons burden, twenty-four caravels from thirty to ninety, and one bark of twenty-five tons.* The number of souls embarked in this fleet was about twenty-five hundred; many of them persons of rank and distinction, with their families.

That Ovando might appear with dignity in his new office he was allowed to use silks, brocades, precious stones, and other articles of sumptuous attire, prohibited at that time in Spain, in consequence of the ruinous ostentation of the nobility. He was permitted to have seventy-two esquires as his body-guard, ten of whom were horsemen. With this expedition sailed Don Alonzo Maldonado, appointed as alguazil mayor or chief-justice, in place of Roldan, who was to be sent to Spain. There were artisans of various kinds: to these were added a physician, surgeon, and apothecary; and seventy-three married men † with their families, all of respectable character, destined to be distributed in four towns, and to enjoy peculiar privileges, that they might form the basis of a sound and useful population. They were to displace an equal number of the idle and dissolute who were to

---

* Muñoz, part inedit. Las Casas says the fleet consisted of thirty-two sail. He states from memory, however; Muñoz from documents.

† Muñoz, Hist. N. Mundo, part inedit.

be sent from the island: this excellent measure had been especially urged and entreated by Columbus. There was also live stock, artillery, arms, munitions of all kinds; everything, in short, that was required for the supply of the island.

Such was the style in which Ovando, a favorite of Ferdinand, and a native subject of rank, was fitted out to enter upon the government withheld from Columbus. The fleet put to sea on the 13th of February, 1502. In the early part of the voyage it was encountered by a terrible storm; one of the ships foundered, with one hundred and twenty passengers; the others were obliged to throw overboard everything on deck, and were completely scattered. The shores of Spain were strewed with articles from the fleet, and a rumor spread that all the ships had perished. When this reached the sovereigns, they were so overcome with grief that they shut themselves up for eight days and admitted no one to their presence. The rumor proved to be incorrect: but one ship was lost. The others assembled again at the island of Gomera in the Canaries, and pursuing their voyage, arrived at San Domingo on the 15th of April.*

CHAPTER FOUR

PROPOSITION OF COLUMBUS RELATIVE TO THE RECOVERY OF THE HOLY SEPULCHER

[1500–1501]

COLUMBUS remained in the city of Granada upward of nine months, endeavoring to extricate his affairs from the confusion into which they had been thrown by the rash conduct of Bobadilla, and soliciting the restoration of his offices and dignities. During this time he constantly experienced the smiles and attentions of the sovereigns, and promises were repeatedly made him that he should ultimately be rein-

---

* Las Casas, Hist. Ind., lib. ii., cap. 3, MS.

stated in all his honors. He had long since, however, ascertained the great interval that may exist between promise and performance in a court. Had he been of a morbid and repining spirit, he had ample food for misanthropy. He beheld the career of glory which he had opened thronged by favored adventurers; he witnessed preparations making to convey with unusual pomp a successor to that government from which he had been so wrongfully and rudely ejected; in the meanwhile his own career was interrupted, and as far as public employ is a gauge of royal favor he remained apparently in disgrace.

His sanguine temperament was not long to be depressed; if checked in one direction it broke forth in another. His visionary imagination was an internal light, which, in the darkest times, repelled all outward gloom, and filled his mind with splendid images and glorious speculations. In this time of evil, his vow to furnish, within seven years from the time of his discovery, fifty thousand foot soldiers, and five thousand horse, for the recovery of the holy sepulcher, recurred to his memory with peculiar force. The time had elapsed, but the vow remained unfulfilled, and the means to perform it had failed him. The New World, with all its treasures, had as yet produced expense instead of profit; and so far from being in a situation to set armies on foot by his own contributions, he found himself without property, without power, and without employ.

Destitute of the means of accomplishing his pious intentions, he considered it his duty to incite the sovereigns to the enterprise; and he felt emboldened to do so, from having originally proposed it as the great object to which the profits of his discoveries should be dedicated. He set to work, therefore, with his accustomed zeal, to prepare arguments for the purpose. During the intervals of business, he sought into the prophecies of the holy Scriptures, the writings of the fathers, and all kinds of sacred and speculative sources, for mystic portents and revelations which might be construed to bear upon the discovery of the New World, the conversion of the Gentiles, and the recovery of the holy sepulcher: three great events which he supposed to be predestined to succeed each other. These passages, with the assistance of a Carthusian friar, he arranged in order, illustrated by poetry, and collected into a manuscript volume, to be delivered to the sovereigns. He prepared, at the same time, a long letter, written with his usual fervor of spirit and simplicity of heart. It is one of those singular compositions which lay open the visionary part of his character, and show the mystic and speculative reading with which he was accustomed to nurture his solemn and soaring imagination.

In this letter he urged the sovereigns to set on foot a crusade for the deliverance of Jerusalem from the power of the unbelievers. He entreated them not to reject his present advice as extravagant and impracticable, nor to heed the discredit that might be cast upon it by others; reminding them that his great scheme of discovery had originally been treated with similar contempt. He avowed in the fullest manner his persuasion that, from his earliest infancy, he had been chosen by Heaven for the accomplishment of those two great designs, the discovery of the New World and the rescue of the holy sepulcher. For this purpose, in his tender years, he had been guided by a Divine impulse to embrace the profession of the sea, a mode of life, he observes, which produces an inclination to inquire into the mysteries of nature; and he had been gifted with a curious spirit, to read all kinds of chronicles, geographical treatises, and works of philosophy. In meditating upon these, his understanding had been opened by the Deity, "as with a palpable hand," so as to discover the navigation to the Indies, and he had been inflamed with ardor to undertake the enterprise. "Animated as by a heavenly fire," he adds, "I came to your highnesses: all who heard of my enterprise mocked at it; all the sciences I had acquired profited me nothing; seven years did I pass in your royal court disputing the case with persons of great authority and learned in all the arts, and in the end they decided that all was vain. In your highnesses alone remained faith and constancy. Who will doubt that this light was from the holy Scriptures, illumining you as well as myself with rays of marvelous brightness?"

These ideas, so repeatedly, and solemnly, and artlessly expressed, by a man of the fervent piety of Columbus, show how truly his discovery arose from the working of his own mind, and not from information furnished by others. He considered it a Divine intimation, a light from Heaven, and the fulfillment of what had been foretold by our Saviour and the Prophets. Still he regarded it but as a minor event, preparatory to the great enterprise, the recovery of the holy sepulcher. He pronounced it a miracle effected by Heaven, to animate himself and others to that holy undertaking; and he assured the sovereigns that, if they had faith in his present as in his former proposition, they would assuredly be rewarded with equally triumphant success. He conjured them not to heed the sneers of such as might scoff at him as one unlearned, as an ignorant mariner, a worldly man; reminding them that the Holy Spirit works not merely in the learned, but also in the ignorant; nay, that it reveals things to come, not merely by rational beings, but by prodigies in animals, and by mystic signs in the air and in the heavens.

The enterprise here suggested by Columbus, however idle and extravagant it may appear in the present day, was in unison with the temper of the times and of the court to which it was proposed. The vein of mystic erudition by which it was enforced, likewise, was suited to an age when the reveries of the cloister still controlled the operations of the cabinet and the camp. The spirit of the crusades had not yet passed away. In the cause of the church, and at the instigation of its dignitaries, every cavalier was ready to draw his sword; and religion mingled a glowing and devoted enthusiasm with the ordinary excitement of warfare. Ferdinand was a religious bigot; and the devotion of Isabella went as near to bigotry as her liberal mind and magnanimous spirit would permit. Both the sovereigns were under the influence of ecclesiastical politicians, constantly guiding their enter-

prises in a direction to redound to the temporal power and
glory of the church. The recent conquest of Granada had
been considered a European crusade, and had gained to the
sovereigns the epithet of Catholic. It was natural to think
of extending their sacred victories still further, and retaliat-
ing upon the Infidels their domination of Spain and their long
triumphs over the cross. In fact, the Duke of Medina Si-
donia had made a recent inroad into Barbary, in the course
of which he had taken the city of Melilla, and his expedition
had been pronounced a renewal of the holy wars against the
Infidels in Africa.*

There was nothing, therefore, in the proposition of Columbus that could be regarded as preposterous, considering
the period and circumstances in which it was made, though
it strongly illustrates his own enthusiastic and visionary character. It must be recollected that it was meditated in the
courts of the Alhambra, among the splendid remains of Moorish grandeur, where, but a few years before, he had beheld
the standard of the faith elevated in triumph above the sym-
bols of infidelity. It appears to have been the offspring of
one of those moods of high excitement, when, as has been
observed, his soul was elevated by the contemplation of his
great and glorious office; when he considered himself under
Divine inspiration, imparting the will of Heaven, and fulfilling the high and holy purposes for which he had been
predestined.†

---

* Garibay, Hist. España, lib. xix., cap. 6. Among the collections
existing in the library of the late Prince Sebastian, there is a folio which,
among other things, contains a paper or letter, in which is a calculation
of the probable expenses of an army of twenty thousand men, for the
conquest of the Holy Land. It is dated in 1509 or 1510, and the handwriting appears to be of the same time.

† Columbus was not singular in this belief; it was entertained by
many of his zealous and learned admirers. The erudite lapidary, Jayme
Ferrer, in the letter written to Columbus in 1495, at the command of
the sovereigns, observes: "I see in this a great mystery: the divine and
infallible Providence sent the great St. Thomas from the west into the
east, to manifest in India our holy and Catholic faith; and you, Señor,

CHAPTER FIVE

PREPARATIONS OF COLUMBUS FOR A FOURTH VOYAGE OF DISCOVERY

[1501-1502]

THE speculation relative to the recovery of the holy sepulcher held but a temporary sway over the mind of Columbus. His thoughts soon returned, with renewed ardor, to their wonted channel. He became impatient of inaction, and soon conceived a leading object for another enterprise of discovery. The achievement of Vasco de Gama, of the long attempted navigation to India by the Cape of Good Hope, was one of the signal events of the day. Pedro Alvarez Cabral, following in his track, had made a most successful voyage, and returned with his vessels laden with the precious commodities of the East. The riches of Calicut were now the theme of every tongue, and the splendid trade now opened in diamonds and precious stones from the mines of Hindostan; in pearls, gold, silver, amber, ivory, and porcelain; in silken stuffs, costly woods, gums, aromatics, and spices of all kinds. The discoveries of the savage regions of the New World, as yet, brought little revenue to Spain; but this route, suddenly opened to the luxurious countries of the East, was pouring immediate wealth into Portugal.

He sent in an opposite direction, from the east into the west, until you have arrived in the Orient, into the extreme part of Upper India, that the people may hear that which their ancestors neglected of the preaching of St. Thomas. Thus shall be accomplished what was written, *in omnem terram exibit sonus eorum*." . . . . And again, "The office which you hold, Señor, places you in the light of an apostle and embassador of God, sent by His divine judgment, to make known His holy name in unknown lands."—Letra de Mossen Jayme Ferrer, Navarrete Coleccion, tom. ii., decad. 68. See also the opinion expressed by Agostino Ginstiniani, his contemporary, in his Polyglot Psalter.

Columbus was roused to emulation by these accounts. He now conceived the idea of a voyage, in which, with his usual enthusiasm, he hoped to surpass not merely the discovery of Vasco de Gama, but even those of his own previous expeditions. According to his own observations in his voyage to Paria, and the reports of other navigators who had pursued the same route to a greater distance, it appeared that the coast of Terra Firma stretched far to the west. The southern coast of Cuba, which he considered a part of the Asiatic continent, stretched onward toward the same point. The currents of the Caribbean Sea must pass between those lands. He was persuaded, therefore, that there must be a strait existing somewhere thereabout, opening into the Indian Sea. The situation in which he placed his conjectural strait was somewhere about what at present is called the Isthmus of Darien.* Could he but discover such a passage, and thus link the New World he had discovered with the opulent Oriental regions of the old, he felt that he should make a magnificent close to his labors, and consummate this great object of his existence.

When he unfolded his plan to the sovereigns, it was listened to with great attention. Certain of the royal council, it is said, endeavored to throw difficulties in the way, observing that the various exigencies of the times, and the low state of the royal treasury, rendered any new expedition highly inexpedient. They intimated also that Columbus ought not to be employed until his good conduct in Hispaniola was satisfactorily established by letters from Ovando. These narrow-minded suggestions failed in their aim; Isabella had implicit confidence in the integrity of Columbus. As to the expense, she felt that while furnishing so powerful a fleet and splendid retinue to Ovando, to take possession of his government, it would be ungenerous and ungrateful to refuse a few ships to the discoverer of the New World, to enable him to prose-

---

* Las Casas, lib. ii., cap. 4. Las Casas specifies the vicinity of Nombre de Dios as the place.

cute his illustrious enterprises. As to Ferdinand, his cupidity was roused at the idea of being soon put in possession of a more direct and safe route to those countries with which the crown of Portugal was opening so lucrative a trade. The project also would occupy the admiral for a considerable time, and, while it diverted him from claims of an inconvenient nature, would employ his talents in a way most beneficial to the crown. However the king might doubt his abilities as a legislator, he had the highest opinion of his skill and judgment as a navigator. If such a strait as the one supposed were really in existence, Columbus was, of all men in the world, the one to discover it. His proposition, therefore, was promptly acceded to; he was authorized to fit out an armament immediately; and repaired to Seville in the autumn of 1501 to make the necessary preparations.

Though this substantial enterprise diverted his attention from his romantic expedition for the recovery of the holy sepulcher, it still continued to haunt his mind. He left his manuscript collection of researches among the prophecies in the hands of a devout friar of the name of Gaspar Gorricio, who assisted to complete it. In February, also, he wrote a letter to Pope Alexander VII., in which he apologizes on account of indispensable occupations, for not having repaired to Rome, according to his original intention, to give an account of his grand discoveries. After briefly relating them, he adds that his enterprises had been undertaken with intent of dedicating the gains to the recovery of the holy sepulcher. He mentions his vow to furnish, within seven years, fifty thousand foot and five thousand horse for the purpose, and another of like force within five succeeding years. This pious intention, he laments, had been impeded by the arts of the devil, and he feared, without Divine aid, would be entirely frustrated, as the government which had been granted to him in perpetuity had been taken from him. He informs his Holiness of his being about to embark on another voyage, and promises solemnly, on his return, to repair to Rome, without delay, to relate everything by word of mouth, as well as to present him with an account of his voyages, which he had kept from the commencement to the present time, in the style of the Commentaries of Cæsar.*

It was about this time, also, that he sent his letter on the subject of the sepulcher to the sovereigns, together with the collection of prophecies.† We have no account of the manner in which the proposition was received. Ferdinand, with all his bigotry, was a shrewd and worldly prince. Instead of a chivalrous crusade against Jerusalem, he preferred making a pacific arrangement with the Grand Soldan of Egypt, who had men cheated destruction of the sacred edifice. He dispatched, therefore, the learned Peter Martyr, so distinguished for his historical writings, as embassador to the soldan, by whom all ancient grievances between the two powers were satisfactorily adjusted, and arrangements made

---

* Navarrete, Colec. Viag., tom. ii., p. 145.

† A manuscript volume containing a copy of this letter and of the collection of prophecies is in the Columbian Library, in the Cathedral of Seville, where the author of this work has seen and examined it, since publishing the first edition. The title and some of the early pages of the work are in the handwriting of Fernando Columbus, the main body of the work is by a strange hand, probably by the Friar Gaspar Gorricio, or some brother of his convent. There are trifling marginal notes or corrections, and one or two trivial additions in the handwriting of Columbus, especially a passage added after his return from his fourth voyage and shortly before his death, alluding to an eclipse of the moon which took place during his sojourn in the island of Jamaica. The handwriting of this last passage, like most of the manuscript of Columbus which the author has seen, is small and delicate, but wants the firmness and distinctness of his earlier writing, his hand having doubtless become unsteady by age and infirmity.

This document is extremely curious as containing all the passages of Scripture and of the works of the fathers which had so powerful an influence on the enthusiastic mind of Columbus, and were construed by him into mysterious prophecies and revelations. The volume is in good preservation, excepting that a few pages have been cut out. The writing, though of the beginning of the fifteenth century, is very distinct and legible. The library mark of the book is Estante Z. Tab. 138, No. 25.

for the conservation of the holy sepulcher, and the protection of all Christian pilgrims resorting to it.

In the meantime Columbus went on with the preparations for his contemplated voyage, though but slowly, owing, as Charlevoix intimates, to the artifices and delays of Fonseca and his agents. He craved permission to touch at the island of Hispaniola for supplies on his outward voyage. This, however, the sovereigns forbade, knowing that he had many enemies in the island, and that the place would be in great agitation from the arrival of Ovando and the removal of Bobadilla. They consented, however, that he should touch there briefly on his return, by which time they hoped the island would be restored to tranquillity. He was permitted to take with him, in this expedition, his brother the adelantado, and his son Fernando, then in his fourteenth year; also two or three persons learned in Arabic, to serve as interpreters, in case he should arrive at the dominions of the Grand Khan, or of any other eastern prince where that language might be spoken, or partially known. In reply to letters relative to the ultimate restoration of his rights, and to matters concerning his family, the sovereigns wrote him a letter, dated March 14, 1502, from Valencia de Torre, in which they again solemnly assured him that their capitulations with him should be fulfilled to the letter; and the dignities therein ceded enjoyed by him, and his children after him; and if it should be necessary to confirm them anew, they would do so and secure them to his son. Besides which, they expressed their disposition to bestow further honors and rewards upon himself, his brothers, and his children. They entreated him, therefore, to depart in peace and confidence, and to leave all his concerns in Spain to the management of his son Diego.*

This was the last letter that Columbus received from the sovereigns, and the assurances it contained were as ample and absolute as he could desire. Recent circumstances, however, had apparently rendered him dubious of the future. During

---

* Las Casas, Hist. Ind., lib. ii., cap. 4.

the time that he passed in Seville, previous to his departure, he took measures to secure his fame, and preserve the claims of his family, by placing them under the guardianship of his native country. He had copies of all the letters, grants, and privileges from the sovereigns, appointing him admiral, viceroy, and governor of the Indies, copied and authenticated before the alcaldes of Seville. Two sets of these were transcribed, together with his letter to the nurse of Prince Juan, containing a circumstantial and eloquent vindication of his rights; and two letters to the Bank of St. George, at Genoa, assigning to it the tenth of his revenues, to be employed in diminishing the duties on corn and other provisions—a truly benevolent and patriotic donation, intended for the relief of the poor of his native city. These two sets of documents he sent by different individuals to his friend, Doctor Nicolo Oderigo, formerly embassador from Genoa to the court of Spain, requesting him to preserve them in some safe deposit, and to apprise his son Diego of the same. His dissatisfaction at the conduct of the Spanish court may have been the cause of this precautionary measure, that an appeal to the world, or to posterity, might be in the power of his descendants, in case he should perish in the course of his voyage.*

---

* These documents lay unknown in the Oderigo family until 1670, when Lorenzo Oderigo presented them to the government of Genoa, and they were deposited in the archives. In the disturbances and revolutions of after times one of these copies was taken to Paris and the other disappeared. In 1816 the latter was discovered in the library of the deceased Count Michel Angelo Cambiaso, a senator of Genoa. It was procured by the king of Sardinia, then sovereign of Genoa, and given up by him to the city of Genoa in 1821. A custodia, or monument, was erected in that city for its preservation, consisting of a marble column supporting an urn, surmounted by a bust of Columbus. The documents were deposited in the urn. These papers have been published, together with a historical memoir of Columbus, by D. Gio. Battista Spotorno, Professor of Eloquence, etc., in the University of Genoa.

BOOK FIFTEEN

CHAPTER ONE

DEPARTURE OF COLUMBUS ON HIS FOURTH VOYAGE—RE-
FUSED ADMISSION TO THE HARBOR OF SAN DOMINGO
—EXPOSED TO A VIOLENT TEMPEST

[1502]

AGE was rapidly making its advances upon Columbus when he undertook his fourth and last voyage of discovery. He had already numbered sixty-six years, and they were years filled with care and trouble, in which age outstrips the march of time. His constitution, originally vigorous in the extreme, had been impaired by hardships and exposures in every clime, and silently preyed upon by the sufferings of the mind. His frame, once powerful and commanding, and retaining a semblance of strength and majesty even in its decay, was yet crazed by infirmities and subject to paroxysms of excruciating pain. His intellectual forces alone retained their wonted health and energy, prompting him, at a period of life when most men seek repose, to sally forth with youthful ardor on the most toilsome and adventurous of expeditions.

His squadron for the present voyage consisted of four caravels, the smallest of fifty tons burden, the largest not exceeding seventy, and the crews amounting in all to one hundred and fifty men. With this little armament and these slender barks did the venerable discoverer undertake the search after a strait, which, if found, must conduct him into the most remote seas, and lead to a complete circumnavigation of the globe.

In this arduous voyage, however, he had a faithful counselor, and an intrepid and vigorous coadjutor, in his brother

Don Bartholomew, while his younger son Fernando cheered him with his affectionate sympathy. He had learned to appreciate such comforts, from being too often an isolated stranger, surrounded by false friends and perfidious enemies.

The squadron sailed from Cadiz on the 9th of May, and passed over to Ercilla, on the coast of Morocco, where it anchored on the 13th. Understanding that the Portuguese garrison was closely besieged in the fortress by the Moors, and exposed to great peril, Columbus was ordered to touch there and render all the assistance in his power. Before his arrival the siege had been raised, but the governor lay ill, having been wounded in an assault. Columbus sent his brother, the adelantado, his son Fernando, and the captains of the caravels on shore, to wait upon the governor, with expressions of friendship and civility, and offers of the services of his squadron. Their visit and message gave high satisfaction, and several cavaliers were sent to wait upon the admiral in return, some of whom were relatives of his deceased wife, Dona Felippa Munoz. After this exchange of civilities, the admiral made sail on the same day, and continued his voyage.* On the 25th of May he arrived at the Grand Canary, and remained at that and the adjacent islands for a few days, taking in wood and water. On the evening of the 25th he took his departure for the New World. The trade winds were so favorable that the little squadron swept gently on its course, without shifting a sail, and arrived on the 15th of June at one of the Caribbee Islands, called by the natives Mantinino.† After stopping here for three days, to take in wood and water, and allow the seamen time to wash their clothes, the squadron passed to the west of the island and sailed to Dominica, about ten leagues distant.‡ Columbus continued

---

* Hist. del Almirante, cap. 88.

† Señor Navarrete supposes this island to be the same at present called Santa Lucia. From the distance between it and Dominica, as stated by Fernando Columbus, it was more probably the present Martinica.

‡ Hist. del Almirante, cap. 88.

hence along the inside of the Antilles, to Santa Cruz, then
along the south side of Porto Rico, and steered for San Domingo. This was contrary to the original plan of the admiral,
who had intended to steer to Jamaica,* and thence to take a
departure for the continent, and explore its coasts in search
of the supposed strait. It was contrary to the orders of the
sovereigns also, prohibiting him on his outward voyage to
touch at Hispaniola. His excuse was that his principal vessel sailed extremely ill, could not carry any canvas, and continually embarrassed and delayed the rest of the squadron.†
He wished, therefore, to exchange it for one of the fleet which
had recently conveyed Ovando to his government, or to purchase some other vessel at San Domingo; and he was persuaded that he would not be blamed for departing from his
orders, in a case of such importance to the safety and success
of his expedition.

It is necessary to state the situation of the island at this
moment. Ovando had reached San Domingo on the 15th of
April. He had been received with the accustomed ceremony
on the shore, by Bobadilla, accompanied by the principal
inhabitants of the town. He was escorted to the fortress,
where his commission was read in form, in presence of all the
authorities. The usual oaths were taken, and ceremonials
observed; and the new governor was hailed with great
demonstrations of obedience and satisfaction. Ovando entered upon the duties of his office with coolness and prudence,
and treated Bobadilla with a courtesy totally opposite to the
rudeness with which the latter had superseded Columbus.
The emptiness of mere official rank, when unsustained by
merit, was shown in the case of Bobadilla. The moment his
authority was at an end all his importance vanished. He
found himself a solitary and neglected man, deserted by
those whom he had most favored, and he experienced the
worthlessness of the popularity gained by courting the preju-

---

* Letter of Columbus from Jamaica. Journal of Porras, Navarrete,
tom. i.

† Hist. del Almirante, cap. 88. Las Casas, lib. ii., cap. 5.

dices and passions of the multitude. Still there is no record
of any suit having been instituted against him; and Las
Casas, who was on the spot, declares that he never heard
any harsh thing spoken of him by the colonists.*

The conduct of Roldan and his accomplices, however,
underwent a strict investigation, and many were arrested to
be sent to Spain for trial. They appeared undismayed, trusting to the influence of their friends in Spain to protect them,
and many relying on the well-known disposition of the Bishop
Fonseca to favor all who had been opposed to Columbus.

The fleet which had brought out Ovando was now ready
for sea; and was to take out a number of the principal delinquents, and many of the idlers and profligates of the island.
Bobadilla was to embark in the principal ship, on board of
which he put an immense amount of gold, the revenue collected for the crown during his government, and which he
confidently expected would atone for all his faults. There
was one solid mass of virgin gold on board of this ship which
is famous in the old Spanish chronicles. It had been found
by a female Indian in a brook, on the estate of Francisco de
Garay and Miguel Diaz, and had been taken by Bobadilla
to send to the king, making the owners a suitable compen-
sation. It was said to weigh three thousand six hundred
castellanos.†

Large quantities of gold were likewise shipped in the fleet
by the followers of Roldan, and other adventurers, the wealth
gained by the sufferings of the unhappy natives. Among
the various persons who were to sail in the principal ship
was the unfortunate Guarionex, the once powerful cacique of
the Vega. He had been confined in Fort Conception ever
since his capture after the war of Higuey, and was now to
be sent a captive in chains to Spain. In one of the ships,
Alonzo Sanchez de Carvajal, the agent of Columbus, had
put four thousand pieces of gold, to be remitted to him,
being part of his property, either recently collected or recovered from the hands of Bobadilla.‡

---

* Las Casas, Hist. Ind., lib. ii., cap. 8. † Ibid., cap. 5. ‡ Ibid.

The preparations were all made, and the fleet was ready to put to sea, when, on the 29th of June, the squadron of Columbus arrived at the mouth of the river. He immediately sent Pedro de Terreros, captain of one of the caravels, on shore to wait on Ovando, and explain to him that the purpose of his coming was to procure a vessel in exchange for one of his caravels, which was extremely defective. He requested permission also to shelter his squadron in the harbor; as he apprehended, from various indications, an approaching storm. This request was refused by Ovando. Las Casas thinks it probable that he had instructions from the sovereigns not to admit Columbus, and that he was further swayed by prudent considerations, as San Domingo was at that moment crowded with the most virulent enemies of the admiral, many of them in a high state of exasperation, from recent proceedings which had taken place against them.*

When the ungracious refusal of Ovando was brought to Columbus, and he found all shelter denied him, he sought at least to avert the danger of the fleet, which was about to sail. He sent back the officer, therefore, to the governor, entreating him not to permit the fleet to put to sea for several days, assuring him that there were indubitable signs of an impending tempest. This second request was equally fruitless with the first. The weather, to an inexperienced eye, was fair and tranquil; the pilots and seamen were impatient to depart. They scoffed at the prediction of the admiral, ridiculing him as a false prophet, and they persuaded Ovando not to detain the fleet on so unsubstantial a pretext.

It was hard treatment of Columbus, thus to be denied the relief which the state of his ships required, and to be excluded in time of distress from the very harbor he had discovered. He retired from the river full of grief and indignation. His crew murmured loudly at being shut out from a port of their own nation, where even strangers, under similar circumstances, would be admitted. They repined at having

---

* Las Casas, ubi sup.

embarked with a commander liable to such treatment, and
anticipated nothing but evil from a voyage in which they
were exposed to the dangers of the sea and repulsed from the
protection of the land.

Being confident, from his observations of those natural
phenomena in which he was deeply skilled, that the anticipated storm could not be distant, and expecting it from the
land side, Columbus kept his feeble squadron close to the
shore, and sought for secure anchorage in some wild bay or
river of the island.

In the meantime the fleet of Bobadilla set sail from San
Domingo, and stood out confidently to sea. Within two days
the predictions of Columbus were verified. One of those tremendous hurricanes, which sometimes sweep those latitudes,
had gradually gathered up. The baleful appearance of the
heavens, the wild look of the ocean, the rising murmur of the
winds, all gave notice of its approach. The fleet had scarcely
reached the eastern point of Hispaniola when the tempest
burst over it with awful fury, involving everything in wreck
and ruin. The ship on board of which were Bobadilla, Roldan, and a number of the most inveterate enemies of Columbus, was swallowed up with all its crew, and with the celebrated mass of gold, and the principal part of the ill-gotten
treasure, gained by the miseries of the Indians. Many of
the ships were entirely lost, some returned to San Domingo,
in shattered condition, and only one was enabled to continue
her voyage to Spain. That one, according to Fernando Columbus, was the weakest of the fleet, and had on board the
four thousand pieces of gold, the property of the admiral.

During the early part of this storm the little squadron of
Columbus remained tolerably well sheltered by the land. On
the second day the tempest increased in violence, and the
night coming on with unusual darkness, the ships lost sight
of each other and were separated. The admiral still kept
close to the shore, and sustained no damage. The others,
fearful of the land in such a dark and boisterous night, ran
out for sea-room, and encountered the whole fury of the

elements. For several days they were driven about at the
mercy of wind and wave, fearful each moment of shipwreck,
and giving up each other as lost. The adelantado, who commanded the ship already mentioned as being scarcely sea-
worthy, ran the most imminent hazard, and nothing but his
consummate seamanship enabled him to keep her afloat. At
length, after various vicissitudes, they all arrived safe at
Port Hermoso, to the west of San Domingo. The adelantado had lost his long-boat; and all the vessels, with the
exception of that of the admiral, had sustained more or less
injury.

When Columbus learned the signal destruction that had
overwhelmed his enemies, almost before his eyes, he was
deeply impressed with awe, and considered his own preservation as little less than miraculous. Both his son Fernando
and the venerable historian Las Casas looked upon the event
as one of those awful judgments which seem at times to deal
forth temporal retribution. They notice the circumstance
that, while the enemies of the admiral were swallowed up by
the raging sea, the only ship of the fleet which was enabled
to pursue her voyage, and reach her port of destination, was
the frail bark freighted with the property of Columbus. The
evil, however, in this, as in most circumstances, overwhelmed
the innocent as well as the guilty. In the ship with Bobadilla and Roldan perished the captive Guarionex, the unfortunate cacique of the Vega.*

CHAPTER TWO

VOYAGE ALONG THE COAST OF HONDURAS
[1502]

FOR several days Columbus remained in Port Hermoso,
to repair his vessels and permit his crews to repose and refresh themselves after the late tempest. He had scarcely left

---

* Las Casas, Hist. Ind., lib. ii., cap. 5. Hist. del Almirante, cap. 88.

this harbor when he was obliged to take shelter from another storm in Jacquemel, or, as it was called by the Spaniards, Port Brazil. Hence he sailed on the 14th of July, steering for Terra Firma. The weather falling perfectly calm, he was borne away by the currents until he found himself in the vicinity of some little islands near Jamaica,* destitute of springs, but where the seamen obtained a supply of water by digging holes in the sand on the beach.

The calm continuing, he was swept away to the group of small islands, or keys, on the southern coast of Cuba, to which, in 1494, he had given the name of The Gardens. He had scarcely touched there, however, when the wind sprang up from a favorable quarter, and he was enabled to make sail on his destined course. He now stood to the southwest, and after a few days discovered, on the 30th of July, a small but elevated island, agreeable to the eye from the variety of trees with which it was covered. Among these was a great number of lofty pines, from which circumstance Columbus named it Isla de Pinos. It has always, however, retained its Indian name of Guanaja,† which has been extended to a number of smaller islands surrounding it. This group is within a few leagues of the coast of Honduras, to the east of the great bay or gulf of that name.

The adelantado, with two launches full of people, landed on the principal island, which was extremely verdant and fertile. The inhabitants resembled those of other islands, excepting that their foreheads were narrower. While the adelantado was on shore, he beheld a great canoe arriving, as from a distant and important voyage. He was struck with its magnitude and contents. It was eight feet wide, and as long as a galley, though formed of the trunk of a single tree. In the center was a kind of awning or cabin of palm-leaves, after the manner of those in the gondolas of Venice, and sufficiently close to exclude both sun and rain. Under this sat a

---

* Supposed to be the Morant Keys.
† Called in some of the English maps Bonacca.

cacique with his wives and children. Twenty-five Indians rowed the canoe, and it was filled with all kinds of articles of the manufacture and natural production of the adjacent countries. It is supposed that this bark had come from the province of Yucatan, which is about forty leagues distant from this island.

The Indians in the canoe appeared to have no fear of the Spaniards and readily went alongside of the admiral's caravel. Columbus was overjoyed at thus having brought to him at once, without trouble or danger, a collection of specimens of all the important articles of this part of the New World. He examined with great curiosity and interest the contents of the canoe. Among various utensils and weapons similar to those already found among the natives, he perceived others of a much superior kind. There were hatchets for cutting wood, formed not of stone but copper; wooden swords, with channels on each side of the blade, in which sharp flints were firmly fixed by cords made of the intestines of fishes; being the same kind of weapon afterward found among the Mexicans. There were copper bells, and other articles of the same metal, together with a rude kind of crucible in which to melt it; various vessels and utensils neatly formed of clay, of marble, and of hard wood; sheets and mantles of cotton, worked and dyed with various colors; great quantities of cacao, a fruit as yet unknown to the Spaniards, but which, as they soon found, the natives held in great estimation, using it both as food and money. There was a beverage also extracted from maize or Indian corn, resembling beer. Their provisions consisted of bread made of maize, and roots of various kinds, similar to those of Hispaniola. From among these articles Columbus collected such as were important to send as specimens to Spain, giving the natives European trinkets in exchange, with which they were highly satisfied. They appeared to manifest neither astonishment nor alarm when on board of the vessels, and surrounded by people who must have been so strange and wonderful to them. The woman wore mantles, with which they wrapped themselves, like the female Moors of Granada, and the men had cloths of cotton round their loins. Both sexes appeared more particular about these coverings, and to have a quicker sense of personal modesty than any Indians Columbus had yet discovered.

These circumstances, together with the superiority of their implements and manufactures, were held by the admiral as indications that he was approaching more civilized nations. He endeavored to gain particular information from these Indians about the surrounding countries; but as they spoke a different language from that of his interpreters he could understand them but imperfectly. They informed him that they had just arrived from a country, rich, cultivated, and industrious, situated to the west. They endeavored to impress him with an idea of the wealth and magnificence of the regions, and the people in that quarter, and urged him to steer in that direction. Well would it have been for Columbus had he followed their advice. Within a day or two he would have arrived at Yucatan; the discovery of Mexico and the other opulent countries of New Spain would have necessarily followed; the Southern Ocean would have been disclosed to him, and a succession of splendid discoveries would have shed fresh glory on his declining age, instead of its sinking amid gloom, neglect, and disappointment.

The admiral's whole mind, however, was at present intent upon discovering the strait. As the countries described by the Indians lay to the west, he supposed that he could easily visit them at some future time, by running with the trade-winds along the coast of Cuba, which he imagined must continue on, so as to join them. At present he was determined to seek the mainland, the mountains of which were visible to the south, and apparently not many leagues distant;* by keeping along it steadfastly to the east, he must at length arrive to where he supposed it to be severed from the coast of Paria by an intervening strait; and passing through

---

* Journal of Porras, Navarrete, tom. i.

this, he should soon make his way to the Spice Islands and the richest parts of India.*

He was encouraged the more to persist in his eastern course by information from the Indians that there were many places in that direction which abounded with gold. Much of the information which he gathered among these people was derived from an old man more intelligent than the rest, who appeared to be an ancient navigator of these seas. Columbus retained him to serve as a guide along the coast, and dismissed his companions with many presents.

Leaving the island of Guanaja, he stood southwardly for the mainland, and after sailing a few leagues discovered a cape, to which he gave the name of Caxinas, from its being covered with fruit trees, so called by the natives. It is at present known as Cape Honduras. Here, on Sunday the 14th of August, the adelantado landed with the captains of the caravels and many of the seamen, to attend mass, which was performed under the trees on the seashore, according to the pious custom of the admiral, whenever circumstances would permit. On the 17th the adelantado again landed at a river about fifteen miles from the point, on the bank of which he displayed the banners of Castile, taking possession of the country in the name of their Catholic majesties; from which circumstances he named this the River of Possession.†

At this place they found upward of a hundred Indians assembled, laden with bread and maize, fish and fowl, vegetables, and fruits of various kinds. These they laid down as presents before the adelantado and his party, and drew back to a distance without speaking a word. The adelantado distributed among them various trinkets, with which they were well pleased, and appeared the next day in the same place, in greater numbers, with still more abundant supplies of provisions.

The natives of this neighborhood, and for a considerable

---

* Las Casas, lib. ii., cap. 20. Letter of Columbus from Jamaica.
† Journal of Porras, Navarrete, Colec., tom. i.

distance eastward, had higher foreheads than those of the
islands. They were of different languages, and varied from
each other in their decorations. Some were entirely naked;
and their bodies were marked by means of fire with the figures of various animals. Some wore coverings about the
loins; others short cotton jerkins without sleeves; some wore
tresses of hair in front. The chieftains had caps of white or
colored cotton. When arrayed for any festival, they painted
their faces black, or with stripes of various colors, or with circles round the eyes. The old Indian guide assured the admiral that many of them were cannibals. In one part of
the coast the natives had their ears bored, and hideously
distended; which caused the Spaniards to call that region
la Costa de la Oreja, or "The Coast of the Ear." *

From the River of Possession, Columbus proceeded along
what is at present called the coast of Honduras, beating
against contrary winds, and struggling with currents, which
swept from the east like the constant stream of a river. He
often lost in one tack what he had laboriously gained in two,
frequently making but two leagues in a day, and never more
than five. At night he anchored under the land, through
fear of proceeding along an unknown coast in the dark, but
was often forced out to sea by the violence of the currents.†
In all this time he experienced the same kind of weather that
had prevailed on the coast of Hispaniola, and had attended
him more or less for upward of sixty days. There was, he
says, almost an incessant tempest of the heavens, with heavy
rains, and such thunder and lightning that it seemed as if the
end of the world was at hand. Those who know anything
of the drenching rains and rending thunder of the tropics
will not think his description of the storms exaggerated. His
vessels were strained so that their seams opened; the sails
and rigging were rent, and the provisions were damaged by
the rain and by the leakage. The sailors were exhausted

---

* Las Casas, lib. ii., cap. 21.   Hist. del Almirante, cap. 90.
† Hist. del Almirante, cap. 80.

with labor and harassed with terror. They many times confessed their sins to each other, and prepared for death. "I
have seen many tempests," says Columbus, "but none so
violent or of such long duration." He alludes to the whole
series of storms for upward of two months, since he had been
refused shelter at San Domingo. During a great part of this
time he had suffered extremely from the gout, aggravated by
his watchfulness and anxiety. His illness did not prevent
his attending to his duties; he had a small cabin or chamber
constructed on the stern, whence, even when confined to his
bed, he could keep a lookout and regulate the sailing of the
ships. Many times he was so ill that he thought his end approaching. His anxious mind was distressed about his brother
the adelantado, whom he had persuaded against his will to
come on this expedition, and who was in the worst vessel of
the squadron. He lamented also having brought with him
his son Fernando, exposing him at so tender an age to such
perils and hardships, although the youth bore them with the
courage and fortitude of a veteran. Often, too, his thoughts
reverted to his son Diego, and the cares and perplexities into
which his death might plunge him.* At length, after struggling for upward of forty days since leaving the Cape of
Honduras, to make a distance of about seventy leagues, they
arrived on the 14th of September at a cape where the coast,
making an angle, turned directly south, so as to give them
an easy wind and free navigation. Doubling the point, they
swept off with flowing sails and hearts filled with joy; and
the admiral, to commemorate this sudden relief from toil and
peril, gave to the Cape the name of Gracias a Dios, or Thanks
to God.†

---

* Letter from Jamaica. Navarrete, Colec., tom. i.
† Las Casas, lib. ii., cap. 21 Hist. del Almirante, cap. 91.

CHAPTER THREE

VOYAGE ALONG THE MOSQUITO COAST, AND TRANSACTIONS AT CARIARI

[1503]

AFTER doubling Cape Gracias a Dios, Columbus sailed directly south, along what is at present called the Mosquito shore. The land was of varied character, sometimes rugged, with craggy promontories and points stretching into the sea, at other places verdant and fertile, and watered by abundant streams. In the rivers grew immense reeds, sometimes of the thickness of a man's thigh: they abounded with fish and tortoises, and alligators basked on the banks. At one place Columbus passed a cluster of twelve small islands, on which grew a fruit resembling the lemon, on which account he called them the Limonares.*

After sailing about sixty-two leagues along this coast, being greatly in want of wood and water, the squadron anchored on the 16th of September, near a copious river, up which the boats were sent to procure the requisite supplies. As they were returning to their ships, a sudden swelling of the sea, rushing in and encountering the rapid current of the river, caused a violent commotion, in which one of the boats was swallowed up, and all on board perished. This melancholy event had a gloomy effect upon the crews, already dispirited and careworn from the hardships they had endured, and Columbus, sharing their dejection, gave the stream the sinister name of El rio del Desastre, or the River of Disaster.†

Leaving this unlucky neighborhood, they continued for

---

* P. Martyr, decad. iii., lib. iv. These may have been the lime, a small and extremely acid species of the lemon.

† Las Casas, lib. ii., cap. 21. Hist. del Almirante, cap. 91. Journal of Porras.

several days along the coast, until finding both his ships and
his people nearly disabled by the buffetings of the tempests,
Columbus, on the 25th of September, cast anchor between a
small island and the mainland, in what appeared a commodious and delightful situation.   The island was covered with
groves of palm-trees, cocoanut-trees, bananas, and a delicate
and fragrant fruit, which the admiral continually mistook
for the mirabolane of the East Indies.   The fruits and flowers and odoriferous shrubs of the island sent forth grateful
perfumes, so that Columbus gave it the name of La Huerta,
or The Garden.   It was called by the natives, Quiribiri.   Immediately opposite, at a short league's distance, was an Indian village named Cariari, situated on the bank of a beautiful river.   The country around was fresh and verdant, finely
diversified by noble hills and forests, with trees of such height
that Las Casas says they appeared to reach the skies.

When the inhabitants beheld the ships, they gathered together on the coast, armed with bows and arrows, war-clubs
and lances, and prepared to defend their shores.   The Spaniards, however, made no attempt to land during that or the
succeeding day, but remained quietly on board repairing the
ships, airing and drying the damaged provisions, or reposing
from the fatigues of the voyage.   When the savages perceived that these wonderful beings, who had arrived in this
strange manner on their coast, were perfectly pacific, and
made no movement to molest them, their hostility ceased,
and curiosity predominated.   They made various pacific sig·
nals, waving their mantles like banners, and inviting the
Spaniards to land.   Growing still more bold, they swam to
the ships, bringing off mantles and tunics of cotton, and ornaments of the inferior sort of gold called guanin, which they
wore about their necks.   These they offered to the Spaniards.
The admiral, however, forbade all traffic, making them presents, but taking nothing in exchange, wishing to impress
them with a favorable idea of the liberality and disinterested-
ness of the white men.   The pride of the savages was touched
at the refusal of their proffered gifts, and this supposed con-

tempt for their manufactures and productions. They endeavored to retaliate by pretending like indifference. On returning to shore, they tied together all the European articles which had been given them, without retaining the least trifle, and left them lying on the strand, where the Spaniards found them on a subsequent day.

Finding the strangers still declined to come on shore, the natives tried in every way to gain their confidence, and dispel the distrust which their hostile demonstrations might have caused. A boat approaching the shore cautiously one day, in quest of some safe place to procure water, an ancient Indian, of venerable demeanor, issued from among the trees, bearing a white banner on the end of a staff, and leading two girls, one about fourteen years of age, the other about eight, having jewels of guanin about their necks. These he brought to the boat and delivered to the Spaniards, making signs that they were to be detained as hostages while the strangers should be on shore. Upon this the Spaniards sallied forth with confidence and filled their water-casks, the Indians remaining at a distance, and observing the strictest care, neither by word nor movement to cause any new distrust. When the boats were about to return to the ships, the old Indian made signs that the young girls should be taken on board, nor would he admit of any denial. On entering the ships the girls showed no signs of grief nor alarm, though surrounded by what to them must have been uncouth and formidable beings. Columbus was careful that the confidence thus placed in him should not be abused. After feasting the young females, and ordering them to be clothed and adorned with various ornaments, he sent them on shore. The night, however, had fallen, and the coast was deserted. They had to return to the ship, where they remained all night under the careful protection of the admiral. The next morning he restored them to their friends. The old Indian received them with joy, and manifested a grateful sense of the kind treatment they had experienced. In the evening, however, when the boats went on

shore, the young girls appeared, accompanied by a multitude
of their friends, and returned all the presents they had received, nor could they be prevailed upon to retain any of
them, although they must have been precious in their eyes;
so greatly was the pride of these savages piqued at having
their gifts refused.

On the following day, as the adelantado approached the
shore, two of the principal inhabitants, entering the water,
took him out of the boat in their arms, and carrying him to
land, seated him with great ceremony on a grassy bank.   Don
Bartholomew endeavored to collect information from them
respecting the country, and ordered the notary of the squadron to write down their replies.   The latter immediately prepared pen, ink, and paper, and proceeded to write; but no
sooner did the Indians behold this strange and mysterious
process, than, mistaking it for some necromantic spell, intended to be wrought upon them, they fled with terror.
After some time they returned, cautiously scattering a fragrant powder in the air, and burning some of it in such a
direction that the smoke should be borne toward the Spaniards by the wind.   This was apparently intended to counteract any baleful spell, for they regarded the strangers as
beings of a mysterious and supernatural order.

The sailors looked upon these counter-charms of the Indians with equal distrust, and apprehended something of
magic; nay, Fernando Columbus, who was present, and
records the scene, appears to doubt whether these Indians
were not versed in sorcery, and thus led to suspect it in
others.*

Indeed, not to conceal a foible, which was more characteristic of the superstition of the age than of the man, Columbus himself entertained an idea of the kind, and assures
the sovereigns, in his letter from Jamaica, that the people of
Cariari and its vicinity are great enchanters, and he intimates that the two Indian girls who had visited his ship had

* Hist. del Almirante, cap. 91.

magic powder concealed about their persons. He adds that the sailors attributed all the delays and hardships experienced on that coast to their being under the influence of some evil spell, worked by the witchcraft of the natives, and that they still remained in that belief.*

For several days the squadron remained at this place, during which time the ships were examined and repaired, and the crews enjoyed repose and the recreation of the land. The adelantado, with a band of armed men, made excursions on shore to collect information. There was no pure gold to be met with here, all their ornaments were of guanin; but the natives assured the adelantado that, in proceeding along the coast, the ships would soon arrive at a country where gold was in great abundance.

In examining one of the villages, the adelantado found, in a large house, several sepulchers. One contained a human body embalmed; in another, there were two bodies wrapped in cotton, and so preserved as to be free from any disagreeable odor. They were adorned with the ornaments most precious to them when living; and the sepulchers were decorated with rude carvings and paintings representing various ani-

---

* Letter from Jamaica.

NOTE.—We find instances of the same kind of superstition in the work of Marco Polo, and as Columbus considered himself in the vicinity of the countries described by that traveler, he may have been influenced in this respect by his narrations. Speaking of the island of Soccotera (Socotra), Marco Polo observes: "The inhabitants deal more in sorcery and witchcraft than any other people, although forbidden by their archbishop, who excommunicates and anathematizes them for the sin. Of this, however, they make little account, and if any vessel belonging to a pirate should injure one of theirs, they do not fail to lay him under a spell, so that he cannot proceed on his cruise until he has made satisfaction for the damage; and even although he should have a fair and leading wind, they have the power of causing it to change, and thereby obliging him, in spite of himself, to return to the island. They can in like manner cause the sea to become calm, and at their will can raise tempests, occasion shipwrecks, and produce many other extraordinary effects that need not be particularized.—Marco Polo, book iii., cap. 35, Eng. translation by W. Marsden.

mals, and sometimes what appeared to be intended for por-
traits of the deceased.* Throughout most of the savage tribes
there appears to have been great veneration for the dead, and
an anxiety to preserve their remains undisturbed.

When about to sail, Columbus seized seven of the people,
two of whom, apparently the most intelligent, he selected
to serve as guides; the rest he suffered to depart. His late
guide he had dismissed with presents at Cape Gracias a Dios.
The inhabitants of Cariari manifested unusual sensibility at
this seizure of their countrymen. They thronged the shore,
and sent off four of their principal men with presents to the
ships, imploring the release of the prisoners.

The admiral assured them that he only took their companions as guides, for a short distance along the coast, and
would restore them soon in safety to their homes. He ordered various presents to be given to the embassadors; but
neither his promises nor gifts could soothe the grief and apprehension of the natives at beholding their friends carried
away by beings of whom they had such mysterious apprehensions.†

CHAPTER FOUR

VOYAGE ALONG COSTA RICA—SPECULATIONS CONCERNING
THE ISTHMUS AT VERAGUA

[1502]

ON the 5th of October the squadron departed from Cariari,
and sailed along what is at present called Costa Rica (or the
Rich Coast), from the gold and silver mines found in after
years among its mountains. After sailing about twenty-two
leagues the ships anchored in a great bay, about six leagues
in length and three in breadth, full of islands, with channels

---

* Las Casas, lib. ii., cap. 21. Hist. del Almirante, cap. 91.
† Las Casas, lib. ii., cap. 21. Hist. del Almirante, cap. 91. Letter
of Columbus from Jamaica.

opening between them, so as to present three or four entrances.
It was called by the natives Caribaro,* and had been pointed
out by the natives of Cariari as plentiful in gold.

The islands were beautifully verdant, covered with groves,
and sent forth the fragrance of fruits and flowers. The channels between them were so deep and free from rocks that the
ships sailed along them as if in canals in the streets of a city,
the spars and rigging brushing the overhanging branches of
the trees. After anchoring, the boats landed on one of the
islands, where they found twenty canoes. The people were
on shore among the trees. Being encouraged by the Indians
of Cariari, who accompanied the Spaniards, they soon advanced with confidence. Here, for the first time on this
coast, the Spaniards met with specimens of pure gold; the
natives wearing large plates of it suspended round their necks
by cotton cords; they had ornaments likewise of guanin,
rudely shaped like eagles. One of them exchanged a plate
of gold, equal in value to ten ducats, for three hawks' bells.†

On the following day the boats proceeded to the mainland
at the bottom of the bay. The country around was high and
rough, and the villages were generally perched on the heights.
They met with ten canoes of Indians, their heads decorated
with garlands of flowers, and coronets formed of the claws
of beasts and the quills of birds; ‡ most of them had plates
of gold about their necks, but refused to part with them. The
Spaniards brought two of them to the admiral to serve as
guides. One had a plate of pure gold worth fourteen ducats,
another an eagle worth twenty-two ducats. Seeing the great
value which the strangers set upon this metal, they assured
them it was to be had in abundance within the distance of
two days' journey; and mentioned various places along the

---

* In some English maps this bay is called Almirante, or Carnabaco
Bay. The channel by which Columbus entered is still called Boca del
Almirante, or the Mouth of the Admiral.

† Journal of Porras, Navarrete, tom. i.

‡ P. Martyr, decad. iii., lib. v.

coast whence it was procured, particularly Veragua, which was about twenty-five leagues distant.*

The cupidity of the Spaniards was greatly excited, and they would gladly have remained to barter, but the admiral discouraged all disposition of the kind. He barely sought to collect specimens and information of the riches of the country, and then pressed forward in quest of the great object of his enterprise, the imaginary strait.

Sailing on the 17th of October, from this bay, or rather gulf, he began to coast this region of reputed wealth, since called the coast of Veragua; and after sailing about twelve leagues arrived at a large river, which his son Fernando calls the Guaig. Here, on the boats being sent to land, about two hundred Indians appeared on the shore, armed with clubs, lances, and swords of palm-wood. The forests echoed with the sound of wooden drums, and the blasts of conch-shells, their usual war signals. They rushed into the sea up to their waists, brandishing their weapons, and splashing the water at the Spaniards in token of defiance; but were soon pacified by gentle signs and the intervention of the interpreters, and willingly bartered away their ornaments, giving seventeen plates of gold, worth one hundred and fifty ducats, for a few toys and trifles.

When the Spaniards returned the next day to renew their traffic, they found the Indians relapsed into hostility, sounding their drums and shells, and rushing forward to attack the boats. An arrow from a crossbow, which wounded one of them in the arm, checked their fury, and on the discharge of a cannon they fled with terror. Four of the Spaniards sprang on shore, pursuing and calling after them. They threw down their weapons and came, awestruck and gentle as lambs, bringing three plates of gold, and meekly and thankfully receiving whatever was given in exchange.

Continuing along the coast, the admiral anchored in the mouth of another river called the Catiba. Here likewise the

---

* Columbus's Letter from Jamaica.

sound of drums and conchs from among the forests gave notice that the warriors were assembling. A canoe soon came
off with two Indians, who, after exchanging a few words
with the interpreters, entered the admiral's ship with fearless
confidence; and being satisfied of the friendly intentions of
the strangers, returned to their cacique with a favorable
report. The boats landed, and the Spaniards were kindly
received by the cacique. He was naked like his subjects,
nor distinguished in any way from them, except by the great
deference with which he was treated, and by a trifling attention paid to his personal comfort, being protected from a
shower of rain by an immense leaf of a tree. He had a large
plate of gold, which he readily gave in exchange and permitted his people to do the same. Nineteen plates of pure
gold were procured at this place. Here, for the first time in
the New World, the Spaniards met with signs of solid archi-
tecture; finding a great mass of stucco, formed of stone and
lime, a piece of which was retained by the admiral as a specimen,* considering it an indication of his approach to countries
where the arts were in a higher state of cultivation.

He had intended to visit other rivers along this coast,
but the wind coming on to blow freshly, he ran before it,
passing in sight of five towns, where his interpreters assured
him he might procure great quantities of gold. One they
pointed out as Veragua, which has since given its name to
the whole province. Here, they said, were the richest mines,
and here most of the plates of gold were fabricated. On the
following day they arrived opposite a village called Cubiga,
and here Columbus was informed that the country of gold
terminated.† He resolved not to return to explore it, considering it as discovered, and its mines secured to the crown,
and being anxious to arrive at the supposed strait, which he
flattered himself could be at no great distance.

In fact, during his whole voyage along the coast he had
been under the influence of one of his frequent delusions.

---

* Hist. del Almirante, cap. 92.   † Ibid.

From the Indians met with at the island of Guanaja, just arrived from Yucatan, he had received accounts of some great, and, as far as he could understand, civilized nation in the interior. This intimation had been corroborated, as he imagined, by the various tribes with which he had since communicated. In a subsequent letter to the sovereigns he informs them that all the Indians of this coast concurred in extolling the magnificence of the country of Ciguare, situated at ten days' journey, by land, to the west. The people of that region wore crowns, and bracelets, and anklets of gold, and garments embroidered with it. They used it for all their domestic purposes, even to the ornamenting and embossing of their seats and tables. On being shown coral, the Indians declared that the women of Ciguare wore bands of it about their heads and necks. Pepper and other spices being shown them, were equally said to abound there. They described it as a country of commerce, with great fairs and seaports, in which ships arrived armed with cannon. The people were warlike also, armed like the Spaniards with swords, bucklers, cuirasses, and crossbows, and they were mounted on horses. Above all, Columbus understood from them that the sea continued round to Ciguare, and that ten days beyond it was the Ganges.

These may have been vague and wandering rumors concerning the distant kingdoms of Mexico and Peru, and many of the details may have been filled up by the imagination of Columbus. They made, however, a strong impression on his mind. He supposed that Ciguare must be some province belonging to the Grand Khan, or some other eastern potentate, and as the sea reached it, he concluded it was on the opposite side of a peninsula, bearing the same position with respect to Veragua that Fontarabia does with Tortosa in Spain, or Pisa with Venice in Italy. By proceeding further eastward, therefore, he must soon arrive at a strait, like that of Gibraltar, through which he could pass into another sea, and visit this country of Ciguare, and, of course, arrive at the banks of the Ganges. He accounted for the circumstance of his having

arrived so near to that river by the idea which he had long
entertained, that geographers were mistaken as to the circumference of the globe; that it was smaller than was generally imagined, and that a degree of the equinoctial line was
but fifty-six miles and two-thirds.*

With these ideas Columbus determined to press forward,
leaving the rich country of Veragua unexplored. Nothing
could evince more clearly his generous ambition than hurrying in this brief manner along a coast where wealth was to
be gathered at every step, for the purpose of seeking a strait
which, however it might produce vast benefit to mankind,
could yield little else to himself than the glory of the discovery.

CHAPTER FIVE

DISCOVERY OF PUERTO BELLO AND EL RETRETE—COLUM-
BUS ABANDONS THE SEARCH AFTER THE STRAIT

[1502]

ON the 2d of November the squadron anchored in a spacious and commodious harbor, where the vessels could approach close to the shore without danger. It was surrounded
by an elevated country; open and cultivated, with houses
within bowshot of each other, surrounded by fruit-trees,
groves of palms, and fields producing maize, vegetables, and
the delicious pineapple, so that the whole neighborhood had
the mingled appearance of orchard and garden. Columbus
was so pleased with the excellence of the harbor and the
sweetness of the surrounding country that he gave it the
name of Puerto Bello.† It is one of the few places along
this coast which retain the appellation given by the illustrious discoverer. It is to be regretted that they have so gen-

---

* Letter of Columbus from Jamaica. Navarrete, Colec., tom. i.
† Las Casas, lib. ii., cap. 23. Hist. del Almirante.

erally been discontinued, as they were so often records of his feelings, and of circumstances attending the discovery.

For seven days they were detained in this port by heavy rain and stormy weather. The natives repaired from all quarters in canoes, bringing fruits and vegetables and balls of cotton, but there was no longer gold offered in traffic. The cacique and seven of his principal chieftains had small plates of gold hanging in their noses, but the rest of the natives appear to have been destitute of all ornaments of the kind. They were generally naked and painted red; the cacique alone was painted black.*

Sailing hence, on the 9th of November, they proceeded eight leagues to the eastward, to the point since known as Nombre de Dios; but being driven back for some distance, they anchored in a harbor in the vicinity of three small islands. These, with the adjacent country of the mainland, were cultivated with fields of Indian corn, and various fruits and vegetables, whence Columbus called the harbor Puerto de Bastimentos, or Port of Provisions. Here they remained until the 23d, endeavoring to repair their vessels, which leaked excessively. They were pierced in all parts by the teredo or worm which abounds in the tropical seas. It is of the size of a man's finger, and bores through the stoutest planks and timbers, so as soon to destroy any vessel that is not well coppered. After leaving this port they touched at another called Guiga, where above three hundred of the natives appeared on the shore, some with provisions, and some with golden ornaments, which they offered in barter. Without making any stay, however, the admiral urged his way forward; but rough and adverse winds again obliged him to take shelter in a small port, with a narrow entrance, not above twenty paces wide, beset on each side with reefs of rocks, the sharp points of which rose above the surface. Within, there was not room for more than five or six ships; yet the port was so deep that they had no good anchorage, unless they approached near enough to the land for a man to leap on shore.

* Peter Martyr, decad. iii., lib. iv.

From the smallness of the harbor, Columbus gave it the name of El Retrete, or The Cabinet. He had been betrayed into this inconvenient and dangerous port by the misrepresentations of the seamen sent to examine it, who were always eager to come to anchor and have communication with the shore.*

The adjacent country was level and verdant, covered with herbage, but with few trees. The port was infested with alligators, which basked in the sunshine on the beach, filling the air with a powerful and musky odor. They were timorous, and fled on being attacked, but the Indians affirmed that if they found a man sleeping on the shore they would seize and drag him into the water. These alligators Columbus pronounced to be the same as the crocodiles of the Nile. For nine days the squadron was detained in this port by tempestuous weather. The natives of this place were tall, well proportioned, and graceful; of gentle and friendly manners, and brought whatever they possessed to exchange for European trinkets.

As long as the admiral had control over the actions of his people, the Indians were treated with justice and kindness, and everything went on amicably. The vicinity of the ships to land, however, enabled the seamen to get on shore in the night without license. The natives received them in their dwellings with their accustomed hospitality; but the rough adventurers, instigated by avarice and lust, soon committed excesses that roused their generous hosts to revenge. Every night there were brawls and fights on shore, and blood was shed on both sides. The number of the Indians daily augmented by arrivals from the interior. They became more powerful and daring as they became more exasperated; and seeing that the vessels lay close to the shore, approached in a great multitude to attack them.

The admiral thought at first to disperse them by discharging cannon without ball, but they were not intimidated by the sound, regarding it as a kind of harmless thunder. They replied to it by yells and howlings, beating their lances and

---

* Las Casas, lib. ii., cap. 23.   Hist. del Almirante, cap. 92.
* * *4 —VOL. VII.

clubs against the trees and bushes in furious menace. The situation of the ships so close to the shore exposed them to assaults, and made the hostility of the natives unusually formidable. Columbus ordered a shot or two, therefore, to be discharged among them. When they saw the havoc made, they fled in terror, and offered no further hostility.*

The continuance of stormy winds from the east and the northeast, in addition to the constant opposition of the currents, disheartened the companions of Columbus, and they began to murmur against any further prosecution of the voyage. The seamen thought that some hostile spell was operating, and the commanders remonstrated against attempting to force their way in spite of the elements, with ships crazed and worm-eaten, and continually in need of repair. Few of his companions could sympathize with Columbus in his zeal for mere discovery. They were actuated by more gainful motives, and looked back with regret on the rich coast they had left behind, to go in search of an imaginary strait. It is probable that Columbus himself began to doubt the object of his enterprise. If he knew the details of the recent voyage of Bastides he must have been aware that he had arrived from an opposite quarter to about the place where that navigator's exploring voyage from the east had terminated; consequently that there was but little probability of the existence of the strait he had imagined.†

---

* Las Casas, lib. ii., cap. 23. Hist. del Almirante, cap. 92.

† It appears doubtful whether Columbus was acquainted with the exact particulars of that voyage, as they could scarcely have reached Spain previously to his sailing. Bastides had been seized in Hispaniola by Bobadilla, and was on board of that very fleet which was wrecked at the time that Columbus arrived off San Domingo. He escaped the fate that attended most of his companions and returned to Spain, where he was rewarded by the sovereigns for his enterprise. Though some of his seamen had reached Spain previous to the sailing of Columbus, and had given a general idea of the voyage, it is doubtful whether he had transmitted his papers and charts. Porras, in his journal of the voyage of Columbus, states that they arrived at the place where the discoveries of Bastides terminated; but this information he may have obtained subsequently at San Domingo.

At all events, he determined to relinquish the further prosecution of his voyage eastward for the present, and to return to the coast of Veragua, to search for those mines of which he had heard so much and seen so many indications. Should they prove equal to his hopes, he would have wherewithal to return to Spain in triumph, and silence the reproaches of his enemies, even though he should fail in the leading object of his expedition.

Here, then, ended the lofty anticipations which had elevated Columbus above all mercenary interests; which had made him regardless of hardships and perils, and given a heroic character to the early part of this voyage. It is true, he had been in pursuit of a mere chimera, but it was the chimera of a splendid imagination and a penetrating judgment. If he was disappointed in his expectation of finding a strait through the Isthmus of Darien, it was because Nature herself had been disappointed, for she appears to have attempted to make one, but to have attempted it in vain.

CHAPTER SIX

RETURN TO VERAGUA—THE ADELANTADO EXPLORES
THE COUNTRY

[1502]

ON the 5th of December Columbus sailed from El Retrete, and relinquishing his course to the east, returned westward, in search of the gold mines of Veragua. On the same evening he anchored in Puerto Bello, about ten leagues distant; whence departing on the succeeding day, the wind suddenly veered to the west, and began to blow directly adverse to the new course he had adopted. For three months he had been longing in vain for such a wind, and now it came merely to contradict him. Here was a temptation to resume his route to the east, but he did not dare trust to the continuance of the wind, which, in these parts, appeared but seldom to blow from that quarter. He resolved, therefore, to keep on in the present direction, trusting that the breeze would soon change again to the eastward.

In a little while the wind began to blow with dreadful violence, and to shift about in such manner as to baffle all seamanship. Unable to reach Veragua, the ships were obliged to put back to Puerto Bello, and when they would have entered that harbor, a sudden veering of the gale drove them from the land. For nine days they were blown and tossed about, at the mercy of a furious tempest, in an unknown sea, and often exposed to the awful perils of a lee-shore. It is wonderful that such open vessels, so crazed and decayed, could outlive such a commotion of the elements. Nowhere is a storm so awful as between the tropics. The sea, according to the description of Columbus, boiled at times like a caldron; at other times it ran in mountain waves, covered with foam. At night the raging billows resembled great surges of flame, owing to those luminous particles which cover the surface of the water in these seas, and throughout the whole course of the Gulf Stream. For a day and night the heavens glowed as a furnace with the incessant flashes of lightning; while the loud claps of thunder were often mistaken by the affrighted mariners for signal guns of distress from their foundering companions. During the whole time, says Columbus, it poured down from the skies, not rain, but as it were a second deluge. The seamen were almost drowned in their open vessels. Haggard with toil and affright, some gave themselves over for lost; they confessed their sins to each other, according to the rites of the Catholic religion, and prepared themselves for death; many, in their desperation, called upon death as a welcome relief from such overwhelming horrors. In the midst of this wild tumult of the elements, they beheld a new object of alarm. The ocean in one place became strangely agitated. The water was whirled up into a kind of pyramid or cone, while a livid cloud, tapering to a point, bent down to meet it. Joining together, they formed

a vast column, which rapidly approached the ships, spinning
along the surface of the deep, and drawing up the waters
with a rushing sound. The affrighted mariners, when they
beheld this waterspout advancing toward them, despaired of
all human means to avert it, and began to repeat passages
from St. John the Evangelist. The waterspout passed close
by the ships without injuring them, and the trembling mariners attributed their escape to the miraculous efficacy of
their quotations from the Scriptures.*

In this same night they lost sight of one of the caravels,
and for three dark and stormy days gave it up for lost. At
length, to their great relief, it rejoined the squadron, having
lost its boat, and been obliged to cut its cable, in an attempt
to anchor on a boisterous coast, and having since been driven
to and fro by the storm. For one or two days there was an
interval of calm, and the tempest-tossed mariners had time
to breathe. They looked upon this tranquillity, however, as
deceitful, and in their gloomy mood beheld everything with
a doubtful and foreboding eye. Great numbers of sharks, so
abundant and ravenous in these latitudes, were seen about
the ships. This was construed into an evil omen; for among
the superstitions of the seas it is believed that these voracious
fish can smell dead bodies at a distance; that they have a
kind of presentiment of their prey, and keep about vessels
which have sick persons on board, or which are in danger
of being wrecked. Several of these fish they caught, using
large hooks fastened to chains, and sometimes baited merely
with a piece of colored cloth. From the maw of one they took
out a living tortoise, from that of another the head of a
shark, recently thrown from one of the ships; such is the
indiscriminate voracity of these terrors of the ocean. Notwithstanding their superstitious fancies, the seamen were
glad to use a part of these sharks for food, being very short
of provisions. The length of the voyage had consumed the
greater part of their sea-stores; the heat and humidity of the

* Las Casas, lib. ii., cap. 24. Hist. del Almirante, cap. 90.

climate and the leakage of the ships had damaged the remainder, and their biscuit was so filled with worms that, notwithstanding their hunger, they were obliged to eat it in the dark, lest their stomachs should revolt at its appearance.*

At length, on the 17th, they were enabled to enter a port resembling a great canal, where they enjoyed three days' repose. The natives of this vicinity built their cabins in trees on stakes or poles laid from one branch to another. The Spaniards supposed this to be through the fear of wild beasts, or of surprisals from neighboring tribes; the different nations of these coasts being extremely hostile to one another. It may have been a precaution against inundations caused by floods from the mountains. After leaving this port they were driven backward and forward by the changeable and tempestuous winds until the day after Christmas, when they sheltered themselves in another port, where they remained until the 3d of January, 1503, repairing one of the caravels, and procuring wood, water, and a supply of maize or Indian corn. These measures being completed, they again put to sea, and on the day of Epiphany, to their great joy, anchored at the mouth of a river called by the natives Yebra, within a league or two of the river Veragua, and in the country said to be so rich in mines. To this river, from arriving at it on the day of Epiphany, Columbus gave the name of Belen or Bethlehem.

For nearly a month he had endeavored to accomplish the voyage from Puerto Bello to Veragua, a distance of about thirty leagues, and had encountered so many troubles and adversities, from changeable winds and currents, and boisterous tempests, that he gave this intermediate line of seaboard the name of La Costa de los Contrastes, or the Coast of Contradictions.†

Columbus immediately ordered the mouths of the Belen, and of its neighboring river of Veragua, to be sounded. The latter proved too shallow to admit his vessels, but the Belen

---

* Hist. del Almirante, cap. 94.   † Ibid.

was somewhat deeper, and it was thought they might enter it with safety. Seeing a village on the banks of the Belen, the admiral sent the boats on shore to procure information. On their approach the inhabitants issued forth with weapons in hand to oppose their landing, but were readily pacified. They seemed unwilling to give any intelligence about the gold mines; but, on being importuned, declared that they lay in the vicinity of the river of Veragua. To that river the boats were dispatched on the following day. They met with the reception so frequent along this coast, where many of the tribes were fierce and warlike, and are supposed to have been of Carib origin. As the boats entered the river, the natives sallied forth in their canoes, and others assembled in menacing style on the shores. The Spaniards, however, had brought with them an Indian of that coast, who put an end to this show of hostility by assuring his countrymen that the strangers came only to traffic with them.

The various accounts of the riches of these parts appeared to be confirmed by what the Spaniards saw and heard among these people. They procured in exchange for the veriest trifles twenty plates of gold, with several pipes of the same metal, and crude masses of ore. The Indians informed them that the mines lay among distant mountains; and that when they went in quest of it they were obliged to practice rigorous fasting and continence.*

The favorable report brought by the boats determined the admiral to remain in the neighborhood. The river Belen having the greatest depth, two of the caravels entered it on

---

* A superstitious notion with respect to gold appears to have been very prevalent among the natives. The Indians of Hispaniola observed the same privations when they sought for it, abstaining from food and from sexual intercourse. Columbus, who seemed to look upon gold as one of the sacred and mystic treasures of the earth, wished to encourage similar observances among the Spaniards; exhorting them to purify themselves for the research of the mines by fasting, prayer, and chastity. It is scarcely necessary to add that his advice was but little attended to by his rapacious and sensual followers.

the 9th of January, and the two others on the following day at high tide, which on that coast does not rise above half a fathom.* The natives came to them in the most friendly manner, bringing great quantities of fish, with which that river abounded. They brought also golden ornaments to traffic, but continued to affirm that Veragua was the place whence the ore was procured.

The adelantado, with his usual activity and enterprise, set off on the third day, with the boats well armed, to ascend the Veragua about a league and a half, to the residence of Quibian, the principal cacique. The chieftain, hearing of his intention, met him near the entrance of the river, attended by his subjects in several canoes. He was tall, of powerful frame and warlike demeanor; the interview was extremely amicable. The cacique presented the adelantado with the golden ornaments which he wore, and received as magnificent presents a few European trinkets. They parted mutually well pleased. On the following day Quibian visited the ships, where he was hospitably entertained by the admiral. They could only communicate by signs, and as the chieftain was of a taciturn and cautious character the interview was not of long duration. Columbus made him several presents; the followers of the cacique exchanged many jewels of gold for the usual trifles, and Quibian returned, without much ceremony, to his home.

On the 24th of January there was a sudden swelling of the river. The waters came rushing from the interior like a vast torrent; the ships were forced from their anchors, tossed from side to side, and driven against each other; the foremast of the admiral's vessel was carried away, and the whole squadron was in imminent danger of shipwreck. While exposed to this peril in the river, they were prevented from running out to sea by a violent storm and by the breakers which beat upon the bar. This sudden rising of the river Columbus attributed to some heavy fall of rain among the range of dis-

---

* Hist. del Almirante, cap. 95.

tant mountains, to which he had given the name of the mountains of San Christoval. The highest of these rose to a peak far above the clouds.*

The weather continued extremely boisterous for several days. At length, on the 6th of February, the sea being tolerably calm, the adelantado, attended by sixty-eight men well armed, proceeded in the boats to explore the Veragua, and seek its reputed mines. When he ascended the river and drew near to the village of Quibian, situated on the side of a hill, the cacique came down to the bank to meet him, with a great train of his subjects, unarmed, and making signs of peace. Quibian was naked, and painted after the fashion of the country. One of his attendants drew a great stone out of the river, and washed and rubbed it carefully, upon which the chieftain seated himself as upon a throne.† He received the adelantado with great courtesy; for the lofty, vigorous, and iron form of the latter, and his look of resolution and command, were calculated to inspire awe and respect in an Indian warrior. The cacique, however, was wary and politic. His jealousy was awakened by the intrusion of these strangers into his territories; but he saw the futility of any open attempt to resist them. He acceded to the wishes of the adelantado, therefore, to visit the interior of his dominions, and furnished him with three guides to conduct him to the mines.

Leaving a number of his men to guard the boats, the adelantado departed on foot with the remainder. After penetrating into the interior about four leagues and a half, they slept for the first night on the banks of a river, which seemed to water the whole country with its windings, as they had crossed it upward of forty times. On the second day they proceeded a league and a half further, and arrived among thick forests, where their guides informed them the mines were situated. In fact, the whole soil appeared to be im-

---

* Las Casas, lib. ii., cap. 25. Hist. del Almirante, cap. 95.
† Peter Martyr, decad. iii., lib. iv.

pregnated with gold. They gathered it from among the roots of the trees, which were of an immense height and magnificent foliage. In the space of two hours each man had collected a little quantity of gold, gathered from the surface of the earth. Hence the guides took the adelantado to the summit of a high hill, and showing him an extent of country as far as the eye could reach, assured him that the whole of it, to the distance of twenty days' journey westward, abounded in gold, naming to him several of the principal places.* The adelantado gazed with enraptured eye over a vast wilderness of continued forest, where only here and there a bright column of smoke from amid the trees gave sign of some savage hamlet, or solitary wigwam, and the wild, unappropriated aspect of this golden country delighted him more than if he had beheld it covered with towns and cities, and adorned with all the graces of cultivation. He returned with his party, in high spirits, to the ships, and rejoiced the admiral with the favorable report of his expedition. It was soon discovered, however, that the politic Quibian had deceived them. His guides, by his instructions, had taken the Spaniards to the mines of a neighboring cacique, with whom he was at war, hoping to divert them into the territories of his enemy. The real mines of Veragua, it was said, were nearer and much more wealthy.

The indefatigable adelantado set forth again on the 16th of February, with an armed band of fifty-nine men, marching along the coast westward, a boat with fourteen men keeping pace with him. In this excursion he explored an extensive tract of country, and visited the dominions of various caciques, by whom he was hospitably entertained. He met continually with proofs of abundance of gold; the natives generally wearing great plates of it suspended round their necks by cotton cords. There were tracts of land, also, cultivated with Indian corn—one of which continued for the extent of six leagues; and the country abounded with excellent

---

* Letter of the Admiral from Jamaica.

fruits. He again heard of a nation in the interior, advanced in arts and arms, wearing clothing, and being armed like the Spaniards. Either these were vague and exaggerated rumors concerning the great empire of Peru, or the adelantado had misunderstood the signs of his informants. He returned, after an absence of several days, with a great quantity of gold, and with animating accounts of the country. He had found no port, however, equal to the river of Belen, and was convinced that gold was nowhere to be met with in such abundance as in the district of Veragua.*

CHAPTER SEVEN

COMMENCEMENT OF A SETTLEMENT ON THE RIVER BELEN
—CONSPIRACY OF THE NATIVES—EXPEDITION OF
THE ADELANTADO TO SURPRISE QUIBIAN

[1503]

THE reports brought to Columbus, from every side, of the wealth of the neighborhood; the golden tract of twenty days' journey in exent, shown to his brother from the mountain; the rumors of a rich and civilized country at no great distance, all convinced him that he had reached one of the most favored parts of the Asiatic continent. Again his ardent mind kindled up with glowing anticipations. He fancied himself arrived at a fountain-head of riches, at one of the sources of the unbounded wealth of King Solomon. Josephus, in his work on the antiquities of the Jews, had expressed an opinion that the gold for the building of the temple of Jerusalem had been procured from the mines of the Aurea Chersonesus. Columbus supposed the mines of Veragua to be the same. They lay, as he observed, "within the same distance from the pole and from the line"; and if the information which he fancied he had received from the In-

* Las Casas, lib. ii., cap. 25. Hist. del Almirante, cap. 95.

dians was to be depended on, they were situated about the same distance from the Ganges.*

Here, then, it appeared to him, was a place at which to found a colony, and establish a mart that should become the emporium of a vast tract of mines. Within the two first days after his arrival in the country, as he wrote to the sovereigns, he had seen more signs of gold than in Hispaniola during four years. That island, so long the object of his pride and hopes, had been taken from him, and was a scene of confusion; the pearl coast of Paria was ravaged by mere adventurers; all his plans concerning both had been defeated; but here was a far more wealthy region than either, and one calculated to console him for all his wrongs and deprivations.

On consulting with his brother, therefore, he resolved immediately to commence an establishment here, for the purpose of securing the possession of the country, and exploring and working the mines. The adelantado agreed to remain with the greater part of the people while the admiral should return to Spain for re-enforcements and supplies. The greatest dispatch was employed in carrying this plan into immediate operation. Eighty men were selected to remain. They were separated into parties of about ten each, and commenced building houses on a small eminence, situated on the bank of a creek, about a bow-shot within the mouth of the river Belen. The houses were of wood, thatched with the leaves of palm-trees. One larger than the rest was to serve as a magazine, to receive their ammunition, artillery, and a part of their provisions. The principal part was stored, for greater security, on board of one of the caravels, which was to be left for the use of the colony. It was true they had but a scanty supply of European stores remaining, consisting chiefly of biscuit, cheese, pulse, wine, oil, and vinegar; but the country produced bananas, plantains, pineapples, cocoanuts, and other fruit. There was also maize in abundance, together with various roots, such as were found in Hispan-

---

* Letter of Columbus from Jamaica.

iola. The rivers and seacoast abounded with fish. The natives, too, made beverages of various kinds. One from the juice of the pineapple, having a vinous flavor; another from maize, resembling beer; and another from the fruit of a species of palm-tree.* There appeared to be no danger, therefore, of suffering from famine. Columbus took pains to conciliate the good-will of the Indians, that they might supply the wants of the colony during his absence, and he made many presents to Quibian, by way of reconciling him to this intrusion into his territories.†

The necessary arrangements being made for the colony, and a number of the houses being roofed, and sufficiently finished for occupation, the admiral prepared for his departure, when an unlooked-for obstacle presented itself. The heavy rains which had so long distressed him during this expedition had recently ceased. The torrents from the mountains were over, and the river, which had once put him to such peril by its sudden swelling, had now become so shallow that there was not above half a fathom of water on the bar. Though his vessels were small, it was impossible to draw them over the sands which choked the mouth of the river, for there was a swell rolling and tumbling upon them enough to dash his worm-eaten barks to pieces. He was obliged, therefore, to wait with patience, and pray for the return of those rains which he had lately deplored.

In the meantime Quibian beheld, with secret jealousy and indignation, these strangers erecting habitations and manifesting an intention of establishing themselves in his territories. He was of a bold and warlike spirit, and had a great force of warriors at his command; and, being ignorant of the vast superiority of the Europeans in the art of war, thought it easy, by a well-concerted artifice, to overwhelm and destroy them. He sent messengers round, and ordered all his fighting men to assemble at his residence on the river Veragua, under pretext of making war upon a neighboring prov-

---

* Hist. del Almirante, cap. 96.   † Letter from Jamaica.

ince. Numbers of the warriors, in repairing to his headquarters, passed by the harbor. No suspicions of their real design were entertained by Columbus or his officers; but their movements attracted the attention of the chief notary, Diego Mendez, a man of a shrewd and prying character, and zealously devoted to the admiral. Doubting some treachery, he communicated his surmises to Columbus, and offered to coast along in an armed boat to the river Veragua and reconnoiter the Indian camp. His offer was accepted, and he sallied from the river accordingly, but had scarcely advanced a league when he descried a large force of Indians on the shore. Landing alone, and ordering that the boat should be kept afloat, he entered among them. There were about a thousand, armed and supplied with provisions, as if for an expedition. He offered to accompany them with his armed boat; his offer was declined, with evident signs of impatience. Returning to his boat, he kept watch upon them all night, until, seeing they were vigilantly observed, they returned to Veragua.

Mendez hastened back to the admiral, and gave it as his opinion that the Indians had been on their way to surprise the Spaniards. The admiral was loth to believe in such treachery, and was desirous of obtaining clearer information, before he took any step that might interrupt the apparently good understanding that existed with the natives. Mendez now undertook, with a single companion, to penetrate by land to the headquarters of Quibian, and endeavor to ascertain his intentions. Accompanied by one Rodrigo de Escobar, he proceeded on foot along the seaboard, to avoid the tangled forests, and arriving at the mouth of the Veragua, found two canoes with Indians, whom he prevailed on, by presents, to convey him and his companion to the village of the cacique. It was on the bank of the river; the houses were detached and interspersed among trees. There was a bustle of warlike preparation in the place, and the arrival of the two Spaniards evidently excited surprise and uneasiness. The residence of the cacique was larger than the others, and situ-

ated on a hill which rose from the water's edge. Quibian
was confined to the house by indisposition, having been
wounded in the leg by an arrow. Mendez gave himself out
as a surgeon come to cure the wound: with great difficulty
and by force of presents he obtained permission to proceed.
On the crest of the hill and in front of the cacique's dwelling
was a broad, level, open place, round which, on posts, were
the heads of three hundred enemies slain in battle. Undismayed by this dismal array, Mendez and his companion
crossed the place toward the den of this grim warrior. A
number of women and children about the door fled into the
house with piercing cries. A young and powerful Indian,
son of the cacique, sallied forth in a violent rage, and struck
Mendez a blow which made him recoil several paces. The
latter pacified him by presents and assurances that he came
to cure his father's wound, in proof of which he produced a
box of ointment. It was impossible, however, to gain access
to the cacique, and Mendez returned with all haste to the
harbor to report to the admiral what he had seen and learned.
It was evident there was a dangerous plot impending over
the Spaniards, and as far as Mendez could learn from the Indians who had taken him up the river in their canoe, the
body of a thousand warriors which he had seen on his previous reconnoitering expedition had actually been on a hostile
enterprise against the harbor, but had given it up on finding
themselves observed.

This information was confirmed by an Indian of the
neighborhood, who had become attached to the Spaniards
and acted as interpreter. He revealed to the admiral the
designs of his countrymen, which he had overheard. Quibian intended to surprise the harbor at night with a great
force, burn the ships and houses, and make a general massacre. Thus forewarned, Columbus immediately set a double
watch upon the harbor. The military spirit of the adelantado suggested a bolder expedient. The hostile plan of Quibian was doubtless delayed by his wound, and in the meantime he would maintain the semblance of friendship. The

adelantado determined to march at once to his residence, capture him, his family, and principal warriors, send them prisoners to Spain, and take possession of his village.

With the adelantado to conceive a plan was to carry it into immediate execution, and, in fact, the impending danger admitted of no delay. Taking with him seventy four men, well armed, among whom was Diego Mendez, and being accompanied by the Indian interpreter who had revealed the plot, he set off on the 30th of March, in boats, to the mouth of the Veragua, ascended it rapidly, and, before the Indians could have notice of his movements, landed at the foot of the hill on which the house of Quibian was situated.

Lest the cacique should take alarm and fly at the sight of a large force, he ascended the hill, accompanied by only five men, among whom was Diego Mendez; ordering the rest to come on, with great caution and secrecy, two at a time, and at a distance from each other. On the discharge of an arquebuse, they were to surround the dwelling and suffer no one to escape.

As the adelantado drew near to the house, Quibian came forth, and seating himself in the portal, desired the adelantado to approach singly. Don Bartholomew now ordered Diego Mendez and his four companions to remain at a little distance, and when they should see him take the cacique by the arm to rush immediately to his assistance. He then advanced with his Indian interpreter, through whom a short conversation took place, relative to the surrounding country. The adelantado then adverted to the wound of the cacique, and pretending to examine it, took him by the arm. At the concerted signal four of the Spaniards rushed foward, the fifth discharged the arquebuse. The cacique attempted to get loose, but was firmly held in the iron grasp of the adelantado. Being both men of great muscular power, a violent struggle ensued. Don Bartholomew, however, maintained the mastery, and Diego Mendez and his companions coming to his assistance, Quibian was bound hand and foot. At the report of the arquebuse, the main body of the Spaniards surrounded the house, and seized most of those who were within, consisting of fifty persons, old and young. Among these were the wives and children of Quibian, and several of his principal subjects. No one was wounded, for there was no resistance, and the adelantado never permitted wanton bloodshed. When the poor savages saw their prince a captive, they filled the air with lamentations, imploring his release, and offering for his ransom a great treasure, which they said lay concealed in a neighboring forest.

The adelantado was deaf to their supplications and their offers. Quibian was too dangerous a foe to be set at liberty; as a prisoner he would be a hostage for the security of the settlement. Anxious to secure his prize, he determined to send the cacique and other prisoners on board of the boats, while he remained on shore with a part of his men to pursue the Indians who had escaped. Juan Sanchez, the principal pilot of the squadron, a powerful and spirited man, volunteered to take charge of the captives. On committing the chieftain to his care, the adelantado warned him to be on his guard against any attempt at rescue or escape. The sturdy pilot replied that if the cacique got out of his hands he would give them leave to pluck out his beard, hair by hair; with this vaunt he departed, bearing off Quibian bound hand and foot. On arriving at the boat, he secured him by a strong cord to one of the benches. It was a dark night. As the boat proceeded down the river, the cacique complained piteously of the painfulness of his bonds. The rough heart of the pilot was touched with compassion, and he loosened the cord by which Quibian was tied to the bench, keeping the end of it in his hand. The wily Indian watched his opportunity, and when Sanchez was looking another way plunged into the water and disappeared. So sudden and violent was his plunge that the pilot had to let go the cord lest he should be drawn in after him. The darkness of the night and the bustle which took place in preventing the escape of the other prisoners rendered it impossible to pursue the cacique, or even to ascertain his fate. Juan Sanchez hastened to the ships with the residue of the captives, deeply mortified at being thus outwitted by a savage.

The adelantado remained all night on shore. The following morning, when he beheld the wild, broken, and mountainous nature of the country, and the scattered situation of the habitations perched on different heights, he gave up the search after the Indians, and returned to the ships with the spoils of the cacique's mansion. These consisted of bracelets, anklets, and massive plates of gold, such as were worn round the neck, together with two golden coronets. The whole amounted to the value of three hundred ducats.* One-fifth of the booty was set apart for the crown. The residue was shared among those concerned in the enterprise. To the adelantado one of the coronets was assigned as a trophy of his exploit.†

CHAPTER EIGHT

DISASTERS OF THE SETTLEMENT

[1503]

IT was hoped by Columbus that the vigorous measure of the adelantado would strike terror into the Indians of the neighborhood, and prevent any further designs upon the settlement. Quibian had probably perished. If he survived, he must be disheartened by the captivity of his family, and

-----

* Equivalent to one thousand two hundred and eighty-one dollars at the present day.

† Hist. del Almirante, cap. 98. Las Casas, lib. ii., cap. 27. Many of the particulars of this chapter are from a short narrative given by Diego Mendez, and inserted in his last will and testament. It is written in a strain of simple egotism, as he represents himself as the principal and almost the sole actor in every affair. The facts, however, have all the air of veracity, and being given on such a solemn occasion, the document is entitled to high credit. He will be found to distinguish himself on another hazardous and important occasion in the course of this history.—Vide Navarrete, Colec., tom. i.

several of his principal subjects, and fearful of their being made responsible for any act of violence on his part. The heavy rains, therefore, which fall so frequently among the mountains of this isthmus, having again swelled the river, Columbus made his final arrangements for the management of the colony, and having given much wholesome counsel to the Spaniards who were to remain, and taken an affectionate leave of his brother, got under way with three of the caravels, leaving the fourth for the use of the settlement. As the water was still shallow at the bar, the ships were lightened of a great part of their cargoes, and towed out by the boats in calm weather, grounding repeatedly. When fairly released from the river, and their cargoes reshipped, they anchored within a league of the shore, to await a favorable wind. It was the intention of the admiral to touch at Hispaniola, on his way to Spain, and send thence supplies and re-enforcements. The wind continuing adverse, he sent a boat on shore on the 6th of April, under the command of Diego Tristan, captain of one of the caravels, to procure wood and water, and make some communications to the adelantado. The expedition of this boat proved fatal to its crew, but was providential to the settlement.

The cacique Quibian had not perished as some had supposed. Though both hands and feet were bound, yet in the water he was as in his natural element. Plunging to the bottom, he swam below the surface until sufficiently distant to be out of view in the darkness of the night, and then emerging made his way to shore. The desolation of his home and the capture of his wives and children filled him with anguish; but when he saw the vessels in which they were confined leaving the river, and bearing them off, he was transported with fury and despair. Determined on a signal vengeance, he assembled a great number of his warriors and came secretly upon the settlement. The thick woods by which it was surrounded enabled the Indians to approach unseen within ten paces. The Spaniards, thinking the enemy completely discomfited and dispersed, were perfectly off their guard. Some had strayed to the seashore to take a farewell look at the ships; some were on board of the caravel in the river; others were scattered about the houses; on a sudden the Indians rushed from their concealment with yells and howlings, lanched their javelins through the roofs of palm-leaves, hurled them in at the windows, or thrust them through the crevices of the logs which composed the walls. As the houses were small several of the inhabitants were wounded. On the first alarm the adelantado seized a lance and sallied forth with seven or eight of his men. He was joined by Diego Mendez and several of his companions, and they drove the enemy into the forest, killing and wounding several of them. The Indians kept up a brisk fire of darts and arrows from among the trees, and made furious sallies with their war-clubs; but there was no withstanding the keen edge of the Spanish weapons, and a fierce bloodhound being let loose upon them completed their terror. They fled howling through the forest, leaving a number of dead on the field, having killed one Spaniard and wounded eight. Among the latter was the adelantado, who received a slight thrust of a javelin in the breast.

Diego Tristan arrived in his boat during the contest, but feared to approach the land, lest the Spaniards should rush on board in such numbers as to sink him. When the Indians had been put to flight he proceeded up the river in quest of fresh water, disregarding the warnings of those on shore, that he might be cut off by the enemy in their canoes.

The river was deep and narrow, shut in by high banks and overhanging trees. The forests on each side were thick and impenetrable, so that there was no landing-place excepting here and there where a footpath wound down to some fishing-ground, or some place where the natives kept their canoes.

The boat had ascended about a league above the village, to a part of the river where it was completely overshadowed by lofty banks and spreading trees. Suddenly yells and war-whoops and blasts of conch-shells rose on every side. Light canoes darted forth in every direction from dark hollows and overhanging thickets, each dexterously managed by a single savage, while others stood up brandishing and hurling their lances. Missiles were lanched also from the banks of the river and the branches of the trees. There were eight sailors in the boat, and three soldiers. Galled and wounded by darts and arrows, confounded by the yells and blasts of conchs and the assaults which thickened from every side, they lost all presence of mind, neglected to use either oars or firearms, and only sought to shelter themselves with their bucklers. Diego Tristan had received several wounds, but still displayed great intrepidity, and was endeavoring to animate his men when a javelin pierced his right eye and struck him dead. The canoes now closed upon the boat, and a general massacre ensued. But one Spaniard escaped, Juan de Noya, a cooper of Seville. Having fallen overboard in the midst of the action, he dived to the bottom, swam under water, gained the bank of the river unperceived, and made his way down to the settlement, bringing tidings of the massacre of his captain and comrades.

The Spaniards were completely dismayed, were few in number, several of them were wounded, and they were in the midst of tribes of exasperated savages, far more fierce and warlike than those to whom they had been accustomed. The admiral, being ignorant of their misfortunes, would sail away without yielding them assistance, and they would be left to sink beneath the overwhelming force of barbarous foes, or to perish with hunger on this inhospitable coast. In their despair they determined to take the caravel which had been left with them, and abandon the place altogether. The adelantado remonstrated with them in vain; nothing would content them but to put to sea immediately. Here a new alarm awaited them. The torrents having subsided, the river was again shallow, and it was impossible for the caravel to pass over the bar.

They now took the boat of the caravel to bear tidings of their danger to the admiral, and implore him not to abandon them; but the wind was boisterous, a high sea was rolling, and a heavy surf, tumbling and breaking at the mouth of the river, prevented the boat from getting out. Horrors increased upon them. The mangled bodies of Diego Tristan and his men came floating down the stream, and drifting about the harbor, with flights of crows, and other carrion birds, feeding on them, and hovering, and screaming, and fighting about their prey. The forlorn Spaniards contemplated this scene with shuddering; it appeared ominous of their own fate.

In the meantime the Indians, elated by their triumph over the crew of the boat, renewed their hostilities. Whoops and yells answered each other from various parts of the neighborhood. The dismal sound of conchs and war-drums in the deep bosom of the woods showed that the number of the enemy was continually augmenting. They would rush forth occasionally upon straggling parties of Spaniards, and make partial attacks upon the houses. It was considered no longer safe to remain in the settlement, the close forest which surrounded it being a covert for the approaches of the enemy. The adelantado chose, therefore, an open place on the shore, at some distance from the wood. Here he caused a kind of bulwark to be made of the boat of the caravel, and of chests, casks, and similar articles. Two places were left open as embrasures, in which were placed a couple of falconets, or small pieces of artillery, in such a manner as to command the neighborhood.

In this little fortress the Spaniards shut themselves up; its walls were sufficient to screen them from the darts and arrows of the Indians, but mostly they depended upon their firearms, the sound of which struck dismay into the savages, especially when they saw the effect of the balls, splintering and rending the trees around them, and carrying havoc to such a distance. The Indians were thus kept in check for the present, and deterred from venturing from the forest; but the Spaniards, exhausted by constant watching and incessant alarms, anticipated all kinds of evil when

their ammunition should be exhausted, or they should be
driven forth by hunger to seek for food.*

CHAPTER NINE

DISTRESS OF THE ADMIRAL ON BOARD OF HIS SHIP—ULTI-
MATE RELIEF OF THE SETTLEMENT

[1503]

WHILE the adelantado and his men were exposed to such
imminent peril on shore, great anxiety prevailed on board of
the ships. Day after day elapsed without the return of Diego
Tristan and his party, and it was feared some disaster had
befallen them. Columbus would have sent on shore to make
inquiries, but there was only one boat remaining for the service of the squadron, and he dared not risk it in the rough
sea and heavy surf. A dismal circumstance occurred to
increase the gloom and uneasiness of the crews. On board
of one of the caravels were confined the family and household of the cacique Quibian. It was the intention of Columbus to carry them to Spain, trusting that as long as they remained in the power of the Spaniards their tribe would be
deterred from further hostilities. They were shut up at night
in the forecastle of the caravel, the hatchway of which was
secured by a strong chain and padlock. As several of the
crew slept upon the hatch, and it was so high as to be considered out of reach of the prisoners, they neglected to fasten
the chain. The Indians discovered their negligence. Collecting a quantity of stones from the ballast of the vessel they
made a great heap directly under the hatchway. Several of
the most powerful warriors mounted upon the top, and bending their backs, by a sudden and simultaneous effort, forced

---

* Hist. del Almirante, cap. 98. Las Casas, lib. ii. Letter of Columbus from Jamaica. Relation of Diego Mendez, Navarrete, tom. i.
Journal of Porras, Navarrete, tom. i.

up the hatch, flinging the seamen who slept upon it to the opposite side of the ship. In an instant the greater part of the Indians sprang forth, plunged into the sea, and swam for shore. Several, however, were prevented from sallying forth; others were seized on the deck and forced back into the forecastle; the hatchway was carefully chained down, and a guard was set for the rest of the night. In the morning, when the Spaniards went to examine the captives, they were all found dead. Some had hanged themselves with the ends of ropes, their knees touching the floor; others had strangled themselves by straining the cords tight with their feet. Such was the fierce, unconquerable spirit of these people and their horror of the white men.*

The escape of the prisoners occasioned great anxiety to the admiral, fearing they would stimulate their countrymen to some violent act of vengeance, and he trembled for the safety of his brother. Still this painful mystery reigned over the land. The boat of Diego Tristan did not return, and the raging surf prevented all communication. At length, one Pedro Ledesma, a pilot of Seville, a man of about forty-five years of age, and of great strength of body and mind, offered, if the boat would take him to the edge of the surf, to swim to shore and bring off news. He had been piqued by the achievement of the Indian captives, in swimming to land at a league's distance, in defiance of sea and surf. "Surely," he said, "if they dare venture so much to procure their individual liberties, I ought to brave at least a part of the danger, to save the lives of so many companions." His offer was gladly accepted by the admiral, and was boldly accomplished. The boat approached with him as near to the surf as safety would permit, where it was to await his return. Here, stripping himself, he plunged into the sea, and after buffeting for some time with the breakers, sometimes rising upon their surges, sometimes buried beneath them and dashed upon the sand, he succeeded in reaching the shore.

---

* Hist. del Almirante, cap. 99.

He found his countrymen shut up in their forlorn fortress, beleaguered by savage foes, and learned the tragical fate of Diego Tristan and his companions.   Many of the Spaniards, in their horror and despair, had thrown off all subordination, refused to assist in any measure that had in view a continuance in this place, and thought of nothing but escape.   When they beheld Ledesma, a messenger from the ships, they surrounded him with frantic eagerness, urging him to implore the admiral to take them on board, and not abandon them on a coast where their destruction was inevitable.   They were preparing canoes to take them to the ships, when the weather should moderate, the boat of the caravel being too small, and swore that, if the admiral refused to take them on board, they would embark in the caravel, as soon as it could be extricated from the river, and abandon themselves to the mercy of the seas, rather than remain upon that fatal coast.

Having heard all that his forlorn countrymen had to say, and communicated with the adelantado and his officers, Ledesma set out on his perilous return.   He again braved the surf and the breakers, reached the boat which was waiting for him, and was conveyed back to the ships.   The disastrous tidings from the land filled the heart of the admiral with grief and alarm.   To leave his brother on shore would be to expose him to the mutiny of his own men and the ferocity of the savages.   He could spare no re-enforcement from his ships, the crews being so much weakened by the loss of Tristan and his companions.   Rather than the settlement should be broken up, he would gladly have joined the adelantado with all his people; but in such case how could intelligence be conveyed to the sovereigns of this important discovery, and how could supplies be obtained from Spain?   There appeared no alternative, therefore, but to embark all the people, abandon the settlement for the present, and return at some future day, with a force competent to take secure possession of the country.*   The state of the weather rendered the

---

* Letter of Columbus from Jamaica.

practicability even of this plan doubtful. The wind continued high, the sea rough, and no boat could pass between the squadron and the land. The situation of the ships was itself a matter of extreme solicitude. Feebly manned, crazed by storms, and ready to fall to pieces from the ravages of the teredo, they were anchored on a lee shore, with a boisterous wind and sea, in a climate subject to tempests, and where the least augmentation of the weather might drive them among the breakers. Every hour increased the anxiety of Columbus for his brother, his people, and his ships, and each hour appeared to render the impending dangers more imminent. Days of constant perturbation and nights of sleepless anxiety preyed upon a constitution broken by age, by maladies, and hardships, and produced a fever of the mind, in which he was visited by one of those mental hallucinations deemed by him mysterious and supernatural. In a letter to the sovereigns he gives a solemn account of a kind of vision by which he was comforted in a dismal night, when full of despondency and tossing on a couch of pain:

"Wearied and sighing," says he, "I fell into a slumber, when I heard a piteous voice saying to me, 'O fool, and slow to believe and serve thy God, who is the God of all! What did He more for Moses, or for His servant David, than He has done for thee? From the time of thy birth He has ever had thee under His peculiar care. When He saw thee of a fitting age He made thy name to resound marvelously throughout the earth, and thou wert obeyed in many lands, and didst acquire honorable fame among Christians. Of the gates of the Ocean Sea, shut up with such mighty chains, He delivered thee the keys; the Indies, those wealthy regions of the world, He gave thee for thine own, and empowered thee to dispose of them to others, according to thy pleasure. What did He more for the great people of Israel when He led them forth from Egypt? Or for David, whom, from being a shepherd, He made a king in Judea? Turn to Him, then, and acknowledge thine error; His mercy is infinite. He has many and vast inheritances yet in reserve. Fear not to seek them. Thine age shall be no impediment to any great undertaking. Abraham was above a hundred years when he begat Isaac; and was Sarah youthful? Thou urgest despondingly for succor. Answer! who hath afflicted thee so much, and so many times?—God, or the world? The privileges and promises which God hath made thee He hath never broken; neither hath He said, after having received thy services, that His meaning was different, and to be understood in a different sense. He performs to the very letter. He fulfills all that He promises, and with increase. Such is His custom. I have shown thee what thy Creator hath done for thee, and what He doeth for all. The present is the reward of the toils and perils thou hast endured in serving others.' I heard all this," adds Columbus, "as one almost dead, and had no power to reply to words so true, excepting to weep for my errors. Whoever it was that spake to me, finished by saying, 'Fear not! Confide! All these tribulations are written in marble, and not without cause.'"

Such is the singular statement which Columbus gave to the sovereigns of his supposed vision. It has been suggested that this was a mere ingenious fiction, adroitly devised by him to convey a lesson to his prince; but such an idea is inconsistent with his character. He was too deeply imbued with awe of the Deity, and with reverence for his sovereign, to make use of such an artifice. The words here spoken to him by the supposed voice are truths which dwelt upon his mind and grieved his spirit during his waking hours. It is natural that they should recur vividly and coherently in his feverish dreams; and in recalling and relating a dream one is unconsciously apt to give it a little coherency. Besides, Columbus had a solemn belief that he was a peculiar instrument in the hands of Providence, which, together with a deep tinge of superstition common to the age, made him prone to mistake every striking dream for a revelation. He is not to be measured by the same standard with ordinary men in ordinary circumstances. It is difficult for the mind to realize his situation, and to conceive the exaltations of spirit to which he must have been subjected. The artless manner in which, in his letter to the sovereigns, he mingles up the rhapsodies and dreams of his imagination, with simple facts, and sound practical observations, pouring them forth with a kind of scriptural solemnity and poetry of language, is one of the most striking illustrations of a character richly compounded of extraordinary and apparently contradictory elements.

Immediately after this supposed vision, and after a duration of nine days, the boisterous weather subsided, the sea became calm, and the communication with the land was restored. It was found impossible to extricate the remaining caravel from the river; but every exertion was made to bring off the people and the property before there should be a return of bad weather. In this the exertions of the zealous Diego Mendez were eminently efficient. He had been for some days preparing for such an emergency. Cutting up the sails of the caravel, he made great sacks to receive the biscuit. He lashed two Indian canoes together with spars, so that they could not be overturned by the waves, and made a platform on them capable of sustaining a great burden. This kind of raft was laden repeatedly with the stores, arms, and ammunition, which had been left on shore, and with the furniture of the caravel, which was entirely dismantled. When well freighted, it was towed by the boat to the ships. In this way, by constant and sleepless exertions, in the space of two days, almost everything of value was transported on board the squadron, and little else left than the hull of the caravel, stranded, decayed, and rotting in the river. Diego Mendez superintended the whole embarkation with unwearied watchfulness and activity. He and five companions were the last to leave the shore, remaining all night at their perilous post, and embarking in the morning with the last cargo of effects.

Nothing could equal the transports of the Spaniards, when they found themselves once more on board of the ships, and saw a space of ocean between them and those forests which had lately seemed destined to be their graves. The joy of their comrades seemed little inferior to their own, and the perils and hardships which yet surrounded them were forgotten for a time in mutual congratulations. The admiral was so much impressed with a sense of the high services rendered by Diego Mendez, throughout the late time of danger and disaster, that he gave him the command of the caravel, vacant by the death of the unfortunate Diego Tristan.*

CHAPTER TEN

DEPARTURE FROM THE COAST OF VERAGUA—ARRIVAL AT JAMAICA—STRANDING OF THE SHIPS

[1503]

THE wind at length becoming favorable, Columbus set sail, toward the end of April, from the disastrous coast of Veragua. The wretched condition of the ships, the enfeebled state of the crews, and the scarcity of provisions, determined him to make the best of his way to Hispaniola, where he might refit his vessels and procure the necessary supplies for the voyage to Europe. To the surprise of his pilot and crews, however, on making sail, he stood again along the coast to the eastward, instead of steering north, which they considered the direct route to Hispaniola. They fancied that he intended to proceed immediately for Spain, and murmured loudly at the madness of attempting so long a voyage with ships destitute of stores and consumed by the worms. Columbus and his brother, however, had studied the navigation of those seas with a more observant and experienced eye. They considered it advisable to gain a considerable distance to the east, before standing across for Hispaniola, to avoid being swept away, far below their destined

---

* Hist. del Almirante, cap. 99, 100. Las Casas, lib. ii., cap. 29. Relacion por Diego Mendez. Letter of Columbus from Jamaica. Journal of Porras, Navarrete, Colec., tom. i.

port, by the strong currents setting constantly to the west.*
The admiral, however, did not impart his reasons to the pilots,
being anxious to keep the knowledge of his routes as much to
himself as possible, seeing that there were so many adventurers crowding into the field, and ready to follow on his
track. He even took from the mariners their charts,† and
boasts, in a letter to the sovereigns, that none of his pilots
would be able to retrace the route to and from Veragua, nor
to describe where it was situated.

Disregarding the murmurs of his men, therefore, he continued along the coast eastward as far as Puerto Bello. Here
he was obliged to leave one of the caravels, being so pierced
by worms that it was impossible to keep her afloat. All the
crews were now crowded into two caravels, and these were
little better than mere wrecks. The utmost exertions were
necessary to keep them free from water; while the incessant
labor of the pumps bore hard on men enfeebled by scanty diet
and dejected by various hardships. Continuing onward, they
passed Port Retrete, and a number of islands to which the
admiral gave the name of Las Barbas, now termed the Mu-
latas, a little beyond Point Blas. Here he supposed that he
had arrived at the province of Mangi in the territories of the
Grand Khan, described by Marco Polo as adjoining to Cathay.‡
He continued on about ten leagues further, until he approached
the entrance of what is at present called the Gulf of Darien.
Here he had a consultation with his captains and pilots, who
remonstrated at his persisting in this struggle against contrary winds and currents, representing the lamentable plight
of the ships and the infirm state of the crews.§ Bidding farewell, therefore, to the mainland, he stood northward on the
1st of May, in quest of Hispaniola. As the wind was easterly, with a strong current setting to the west, he kept as

---

* Hist. del Almirante. Letter from Jamaica.
† Journal of Porras, Navarrete, Colec., tom. i.
‡ Letter from Jamaica.
§ Testimony of Pedro de Ledesma. Pleito de los Colones.

near the wind as possible. So little did his pilots know of their situation that they supposed themselves to the east of the Caribbee Islands, whereas the admiral feared that, with all his exertions, he should fall to the westward of Hispaniola.* His apprehensions proved to be well founded; for, on the 10th of the month, he came in sight of two small low islands to the northwest of Hispaniola, to which, from the great quantities of tortoises seen about them, he gave the name of the Tortugas; they are now known as the Caymans. Passing wide of these, and continuing directly north, he found himself, on the 30th of May, among the cluster of islands on the south side of Cuba, to which he had formerly given the name of the Queen's Gardens; having been carried between eight and nine degrees west of his destined port. Here he cast anchor near one of the keys, about ten leagues from the main island. His crews were suffering excessively through scanty provisions and great fatigue; nothing was left of the sea-stores but a little biscuit, oil, and vinegar; and they were obliged to labor incessantly at the pumps to keep the vessels afloat. They had scarcely anchored at these islands when there came on, at midnight, a sudden tempest of such violence that, according to the strong expression of Columbus, it seemed as if the world would dissolve.† They lost three of their anchors almost immediately, and the caravel "Bermuda" was driven with such violence upon the ship of the admiral that the bow of the one and the stern of the other were greatly shattered. The sea running high, and the wind being boisterous, the vessels chafed and injured each other dreadfully, and it was with great difficulty that they were separated. One anchor only remained to the admiral's ship, and this saved him from being driven upon the rocks; but at daylight the cable was found nearly worn asunder. Had the darkness continued an hour longer he could scarcely have escaped shipwreck.‡

---

* Letter from Jamaica.　　　　　　† Letter from Jamaica.
‡ Hist. del Almirante, cap. 100.　Letter of Columbus from Jamaica.

At the end of six days, the weather having moderated, he resumed his course, standing eastward for Hispaniola: "His people," as he says, "dismayed and down-hearted; almost all his anchors lost, and his vessels bored as full of holes as a honeycomb." After struggling against contrary winds and the usual currents from the east, he reached Cape Cruz, and anchored at a village in the province of Macaca,* where he had touched in 1494, in his voyage along the southern coast of Cuba. Here he was detained by head winds for several days, during which he was supplied with cassava bread by the natives. Making sail again, he endeavored to beat up to Hispaniola; but every effort was in vain. The winds and currents continued adverse; the leaks continually gained upon his vessels, though the pumps were kept incessantly going, and the seamen even bailed the water out with buckets and kettles. The admiral now stood, in despair, for the island of Jamaica, to seek some secure port; for there was imminent danger of foundering at sea. On the eve of St. John, the 23d of June, they put into Puerto Bueno, now called Dry Harbor, but met with none of the natives from whom they could obtain provisions, nor was there any fresh water to be had in the neighborhood. Suffering from hunger and thirst, they sailed eastward, on the following day, to another harbor, to which the admiral on his first visit to the island had given the name of Port Santa Gloria.

Here, at last, Columbus had to give up his long and arduous struggle against the unremitting persecution of the elements. His ships, reduced to mere wrecks, could no longer keep the sea, and were ready to sink even in port. He ordered them, therefore, to be run aground, within a bowshot of the shore, and fastened together, side by side. They soon filled with water to the decks. Thatched cabins were then erected at the prow and stern for the accommodation of the crews, and the wreck was placed in the best possible state of defense. Thus castled in the sea, he trusted to be able to re-

---

* Hist. del Almirante. Journal of Porras.

pel any sudden attack of the natives, and at the same time
to keep his men from roving about the neighborhood and indulging in their usual excesses. No one was allowed to go
on shore without especial license, and the utmost precaution
was taken to prevent any offense being given to the Indians.
Any exasperation of them might be fatal to the Spaniards in
their present forlorn situation. A firebrand thrown into their
wooden fortress might wrap it in flames, and leave them defenseless amid hostile thousands.

BOOK SIXTEEN

CHAPTER ONE

ARRANGEMENT OF DIEGO MENDEZ WITH THE CACIQUES FOR
SUPPLIES OF PROVISIONS—SENT TO SAN DOMINGO
BY COLUMBUS IN QUEST OF RELIEF

[1503]

THE island of Jamaica was extremely populous and fertile, and the harbor soon swarmed with Indians, who brought
provisions to barter with the Spaniards. To prevent any disputes in purchasing or sharing these supplies, two persons
were appointed to superintend all bargains, and the provisions thus obtained were divided every evening among the
people. This arrangement had a happy effect in promoting
a peaceful intercourse. The stores thus furnished, however,
coming from a limited neighborhood of improvident beings,
were not sufficient for the necessities of the Spaniards, and
were so irregular as often to leave them in pinching want.
They feared, too, that the neighborhood might soon be exhausted, in which case they should be reduced to famine. In
this emergency, Diego Mendez stepped forward with his ac-

customed zeal, and volunteered to set off, with three men, on a foraging expedition about the island. His offer being gladly accepted by the admiral, he departed with his comrades well armed. He was everywhere treated with the utmost kindness by the natives. They took him to their houses, set meat and drink before him and his companions, and performed all the rites of savage hospitality. Mendez made an arrangement with the cacique of a numerous tribe that his subjects should hunt and fish, and make cassava bread, and bring a quantity of provisions every day to the harbor. They were to receive in exchange knives, combs, beads, fish-hooks, hawks' bells, and other articles, from a Spaniard, who was to reside among them for that purpose. The agreement being made, Mendez dispatched one of his comrades to apprise the admiral. He then pursued his journey three leagues further, when he made a similar arrangement, and dispatched another of his companions to the admiral. Proceeding onward, about thirteen leagues from the ships, he arrived at the residence of another cacique, called Huarco, where he was generously entertained. The cacique ordered his subjects to bring a large quantity of provisions, for which Mendez paid him on the spot, and made arrangements for a like supply at stated intervals. He dispatched his third companion with this supply to the admiral, requesting, as usual, that an agent might be sent to receive and pay for the regular deliveries of provisions.

Mendez was now left alone, but he was fond of any enterprise that gave individual distinction. He requested of the cacique two Indians to accompany him to the end of the island; one to carry his provisions and the other to bear the hammac or cotton net in which he slept. These being granted, he pushed resolutely forward along the coast until he reached the eastern extremity of Jamaica. Here he found a powerful cacique of the name of Ameyro. Mendez had buoyant spirits, great address, and an ingratiating manner with the savages. He and the cacique became great friends, exchanged names, which is a kind of token of brotherhood, and Mendez engaged him to furnish provisions to the ships.

He then bought an excellent canoe of the cacique, for which he gave a splendid brass basin, a short frock or cassock, and one of the two shirts which formed his stock of linen. The cacique furnished him with six Indians to navigate his bark, and they parted mutually well pleased. Diego Mendez coasted his way back, touching at the various places where he had made his arrangements. He found the Spanish agents already arrived at them, loaded his canoe with provisions, and returned in triumph to the harbor, where he was received with acclamations by his comrades, and with open arms by the admiral. The provisions he brought were a most seasonable supply, for the Spaniards were absolutely fasting; and thenceforward Indians arrived daily, well laden, from the marts which he had established.* The immediate wants of his people being thus provided for, Columbus revolved, in his anxious mind, the means of getting from this island. His ships were beyond the possibility of repair, and there was no hope of any chance sail arriving to his relief, on the shores of a savage island, in an unfrequented sea. The most likely measure appeared to be to send notice of his situation to Ovando, the governor at San Domingo, entreating him to dispatch a vessel to his relief. But how was this message to be conveyed? The distance between Jamaica and Hispaniola was forty leagues, across a gulf swept by contrary currents; there were no means of transporting a messenger, except in the light canoes of the savages; and who would undertake so hazardous a voyage in a frail bark of the kind? Suddenly the idea of Diego Mendez, and the canoe he had recently purchased, presented itself to the mind of Columbus. He knew the ardor and intrepidity of Mendez, and his love of distinction by any hazardous exploit. Taking him aside, therefore, he addressed him in a manner calculated both to stimulate his zeal and flatter his self-love. Mendez himself gives an artless account of this interesting conversation, which is full of character.

---

* Relacion por Diego Mendez. Navarrete, tom. i.

"Diego Mendez, my son," said the venerable admiral, "none of those whom I have here understand the great peril in which we are placed, excepting you and myself. We are few in number, and these savage Indians are many, and of fickle and irritable natures. On the least provocation they may throw firebrands from the shore, and consume us in our straw-thatched cabins. The arrangement which you have made with them for provisions, and which at present they fulfill so cheerfully, to-morrow they may break in their caprice, and may refuse to bring us anything; nor have we the means to compel them by force, but are entirely at their pleasure. I have thought of a remedy, if it meets with your views. In this canoe, which you have purchased, some one may pass over to Hispaniola, and procure a ship, by which we may all be delivered from this great peril into which we have fallen. Tell me your opinion on the matter."

"To this," says Diego Mendez, "I replied: 'Señor, the danger in which we are placed I well know is far greater than is easily conceived. As to passing from this island to Hispaniola, in so small a vessel as a canoe, I hold it not merely difficult, but impossible; since it is necessary to traverse a gulf of forty leagues, and between islands where the sea is extremely impetuous and seldom in repose. I know not who there is would adventure upon so extreme a peril.' "

Columbus made no reply, but from his looks and the nature of his silence, Mendez plainly perceived himself to be the person whom the admiral had in view. "Whereupon," continues he, "I added: 'Señor, I have many times put my life in peril of death to save you and all those who are here, and God has hitherto preserved me in a miraculous manner. There are, nevertheless, murmurers who say that your Excellency intrusts to me all affairs wherein honor is to be gained, while there are others in your company who would execute them as well as I do. Therefore I beg that you would summon all the people, and propose this enterprise to them, to see if among them there is any one who will undertake it, which I doubt. If all decline it, I will then come forward and risk my life in your service, as I many times have done.' " *

The admiral gladly humored the wishes of the worthy Mendez, for never was simple egotism accompanied by more generous and devoted loyalty. On the following morning the crew was assembled and the proposition publicly made. Every one drew back at the thoughts of it, pronouncing it the height of rashness. Upon this, Diego Mendez stepped forward. "Señor," said he, "I have but one life to lose, yet I am willing to venture it for your service and for the good of all here present, and I trust in the protection of God, which I have experienced on so many other occasions."

Columbus embraced this zealous follower, who immediately set about preparing for his expedition. Drawing his canoe on shore, he put on a false keel, nailed weather-boards along the bow and stern to prevent the sea from breaking over it; payed it with a coat of tar; furnished it with a mast and sail; and put in provisions for himself, a Spanish comrade, and six Indians.

In the meantime Columbus wrote letters to Ovando, requesting that a ship might be immediately sent to bring him and his men to Hispaniola. He wrote a letter likewise to the sovereigns; for, after fulfilling his mission at San Domingo, Diego Mendez was to proceed to Spain on the admiral's affairs. In the letter to the sovereigns Columbus depicted his deplorable situation, and entreated that a vessel might be dispatched to Hispaniola to convey himself and his crew to Spain. He gave a comprehensive account of his voyage, most particulars of which have already been incorporated in this history, and he insisted greatly on the importance of the discovery of Veragua. He gave it as his opinion that here were the mines of the Aurea Chersonesus, whence Solomon had derived such wealth for the building of the Temple. He entreated that this golden coast might not, like other places which he had discovered, be abandoned to adventurers, or placed under the

---

* Relacion por Diego Mendez. Navarrete, Colec., tom. i.

government of men who felt no interest in the cause. "This is not a child," he adds, "to be abandoned to a stepmother. I never think of Hispaniola and Paria without weeping. Their case is desperate and past cure; I hope their example may cause this region to be treated in a different manner." His imagination becomes heated. He magnifies the supposed importance of Veragua, as transcending all his former discoveries; and he alludes to his favorite project for the deliverance of the holy sepulcher: "Jerusalem," he says, "and Mount Sion are to be rebuilt by the hand of a Christian. Who is he to be? God, by the mouth of the Prophet, in the fourteenth Psalm, declares it. The abbot Joachim * says that he is to come out of Spain." His thoughts then revert to the ancient story of the Grand Khan, who had requested that sages might be sent to instruct him in the Christian faith. Columbus, thinking that he had been in the very vicinity of Cathay, exclaims, with sudden zeal, "Who will offer himself for this task? If our Lord permit me to return to Spain, I engage to take him there, God helping, in safety."

Nothing is more characteristic of Columbus than his earnest, artless, at times eloquent, and at times almost incoherent letters. What an instance of soaring enthusiasm and irrepressible enterprise is here exhibited! At the time that he was indulging in these visions, and proposing new and romantic enterprises, he was broken down by age and infirmities, racked by pain, confined to his bed, and shut up in a

---

* Joachim, native of the burgh of Celico, near Cozenza, traveled in the Holy Land. Returning to Calabria, he took the habit of the Cistercians in the monastery of Corazzo, of which he became prior and abbot, and afterward rose to higher monastic importance. He died in 1202, having attained seventy-two years of age, leaving a great number of works; among the most known are commentaries on Isaiah, Jeremiah, and the Apocalypse. There are also prophecies by him, "which" (says the Dictionnaire Historique), "during his life, made him to be admired by fools and despised by men of sense; at present the latter sentiment prevails. He was either very weak or very presumptuous, to flatter himself that he had the keys of things of which God reserves the knowledge to Himself."—Dict. Hist., tom. 5, Caen, 1785.

wreck on the coast of a remote and savage island. No stronger picture can be given of his situation than that which shortly follows this transient glow of excitement; when with one of his sudden transitions of thought, he awakens, as it were, to his actual condition.

"Hitherto," says he, "I have wept for others; but now, have pity upon me, Heaven, and weep for me, O earth! In my temporal concerns, without a farthing to offer for a mass; cast away here in the Indies; surrounded by cruel and hostile savages; isolated, infirm, expecting each day will be my last; in spiritual concerns, separated from the holy sacraments of the church, so that my soul, if parted here from my body, must be forever lost! Weep for me, whoever has charity, truth, and justice! I came not on this voyage to gain honor or estate, that is most certain, for all hope of the kind was already dead within me. I came to serve your majesties with a sound intention and an honest zeal, and I speak no falsehood. If it should please God to deliver me hence, I humbly supplicate your majesties to permit me to repair to Rome, and perform other pilgrimages."

The dispatches being ready, and the preparations of the canoe completed, Diego Mendez embarked, with his Spanish comrade and his six Indians, and departed along the coast to the eastward. The voyage was toilsome and perilous. They had to make their way against strong currents. Once they were taken by roving canoes of Indians, but made their escape, and at length arrived at the end of the island, a distance of thirty-four leagues from the harbor. Here they remained waiting for calm weather to venture upon the broad gulf, when they were suddenly surrounded and taken prisoners by a number of hostile Indians, who carried them off a distance of three leagues, where they determined to kill them. Some dispute arose about the division of the spoils taken from the Spaniards, whereupon the savages agreed to settle it by a game of chance. While they were thus engaged, Diego Mendez escaped, found his way to his canoe, embarked in it, and returned alone to the harbor after fifteen days' absence.

What became of his companions he does not mention, being seldom apt to speak of any person but himself. This account is taken from the narrative inserted in his last will and testament.

Columbus, though grieved at the failure of his message, was rejoiced at the escape of the faithful Mendez. The latter, nothing daunted by the perils and hardships he had undergone, offered to depart immediately on a second attempt, provided he could have persons to accompany him to the end of the island, and protect him from the natives. This the adelantado offered to undertake, with a large party well armed. Bartholomew Fiesco, a Genoese, who had been captain of one of the caravels, was associated with Mendez in this second expedition. He was a man of great worth, strongly attached to the admiral, and much esteemed by him. Each had a large canoe under his command, in which were six Spaniards and ten Indians—the latter were to serve as oarsmen. The canoes were to keep in company. On reaching Hispaniola, Fiesco was to return immediately to Jamaica, to relieve the anxiety of the admiral and his crew, by tidings of the safe arrival of their messenger. In the meantime Diego Mendez was to proceed to San Domingo, deliver his letter to Ovando, procure and dispatch a ship, and then depart for Spain with a letter to the sovereigns.

All arrangements being made, the Indians placed in the canoes their frugal provision of cassava bread, and each his calabash of water. The Spaniards, besides their bread, had a supply of the flesh of utias, and each his sword and target. In this way they launched forth upon their long and perilous voyage, followed by the prayers of their countrymen.

The adelantado, with his armed band, kept pace with them along the coast. There was no attempt of the natives to molest them, and they arrived in safety at the end of the island. Here they remained three days before the sea was sufficiently calm for them to venture forth in their feeble barks. At length, the weather being quite serene, they bade farewell to their comrades, and committed themselves to the broad sea. The adelantado remained watching them, until they became mere specks on the ocean, and the evening hid them from his view. The next day he set out on his return to the harbor, stopping at various villages on the way, and endeavoring to confirm the good-will of the natives.*

CHAPTER TWO

MUTINY OF PORRAS

[1503]

IT might have been thought that the adverse fortune which had so long persecuted Columbus was now exhausted. The envy which had once sickened at his glory and prosperity could scarcely have devised for him a more forlorn heritage in the world he had discovered. The tenant of a wreck on a savage coast, in an untraversed ocean, at the mercy of barbarous hordes, who, in a moment, from precarious friends, might be transformed into ferocious enemies; afflicted, too, by excruciating maladies which confined him to his bed, and by the pains and infirmities which hardship and anxiety had heaped upon his advancing age. But he had not yet exhausted his cup of bitterness. He had yet to experience an evil worse than storm, or shipwreck, or bodily anguish, or the violence of savage hordes—the perfidy of those in whom he confided.

Mendez and Fiesco had not long departed when the Spaniards in the wreck began to grow sickly, partly from the toils and exposures of the recent voyage, partly from being crowded in narrow quarters in a moist and sultry climate and partly from want of their accustomed food, for they could not habituate themselves to the vegetable diet of the Indians. Their maladies were rendered more insupportable by mental suffering, by that suspense which frets the spirit, and that

---

* Hist. del Almirante, cap. 101.

hope deferred which corrodes the heart. Accustomed to a
life of bustle and variety, they had now nothing to do but
loiter about the dreary hulk, look out upon the sea, watch for
the canoe of Fiesco, wonder at its protracted absence, and
doubt its return. A long time elapsed, much more than
sufficient for the voyage, but nothing was seen or heard of
the canoe. Fears were entertained that their messenger had
perished. If so, how long were they to remain here, vainly
looking for relief which was never to arrive? Some sank
into deep despondency, others became peevish and impatient.
Murmurs broke forth, and, as usual with men in distress,
murmurs of the most unreasonable kind. Instead of sym-
pathizing with their aged and infirm commander, who was
involved in the same calamity, who in suffering transcended
them all, and yet who was incesssatly studious of their welfare, they began to rail against him as the cause of all their
misfortunes.

The factious feeling of an unreasonable multitude would
be of little importance if left to itself, and might end in idle
clamor; it is the industry of one or two evil spirits which
generally directs it to an object and makes it mischievous.
Among the officers of Columbus were two brothers, Francisco
and Diego de Porras. They were related to the royal treasurer Morales, who had married their sister, and had made
interest with the admiral to give them some employment in
the expedition.* To gratify the treasurer, he had appointed
Francisco de Porras captain of one of the caravels, and had
obtained for his brother Diego the situation of notary and
accountant-general of the squadron. He had treated them,
as he declares, with the kindness of relatives, though both
proved incompetent to their situations. They were vain and
insolent men, and, like many others whom Columbus had
benefited, requited his kindness with black ingratitude.†

These men, finding the common people in a highly impa-

---

* Hist. del Almirante, cap. 102.
† Letter of Columbus to his son Diego. Navarrete Colec.

tient and discontented state, wrought upon them with sedi-
tious insinuations, assuring them that all hope of relief
through the agency of Mendez was idle; it being a mere
delusion of the admiral to keep them quiet, and render them
subservient to his purposes. He had no desire nor intention
to return to Spain; and in fact was banished thence. Hispaniola was equally closed to him, as had been proved by the
exclusion of his ships from its harbor in a time of peril. To
him, at present, all places were alike, and he was content to
remain in Jamaica until his friends could make interest at
court, and procure his recall from banishment. As to Mendez and Fiesco, they had been sent to Spain by Columbus on
his own private affairs, not to procure a ship for the relief of
his followers. If this were not the case, why did not the
ships arrive, or why did not Fiesco return, as had been promised? Or if the canoes had really been sent for succor, the
long time that had elapsed without tidings of them gave
reason to believe they had perished by the way. In such
case, their only alternative would be to take the canoes of the
Indians and endeavor to reach Hispaniola. There was no
hope, however, of persuading the admiral to such an undertaking; he was too old, and too helpless from the gout, to
expose himself to the hardships of such a voyage. What
then? were they to be sacrificed to his interests or his infirmities?—to give up their only chance for escape, and linger and
perish with him in this desolate wreck? If they succeeded in
reaching Hispaniola, they would be the better received for
having left the admiral behind. Ovando was secretly hostile
to him, fearing that he would regain the government of the
island; on their arrival in Spain, the Bishop Fonseca, from
his enmity to Columbus, would be sure to take their part;
the brothers Porras had powerful friends and relatives at
court, to counteract any representations that might be made
by the admiral; and they cited the case of Roldan's rebellion,
to show that the prejudices of the public and of men in
power would always be against him. Nay, they insinuated
that the sovereigns, who, on that occasion, had deprived

him of part of his dignities and privileges, would rejoice at a pretext for stripping him of the remainder.*

Columbus was aware that the minds of his people were imbittered against him. He had repeatedly been treated with insolent impatience, and reproached with being the cause of their disasters. Accustomed, however, to the unreasonableness of men in adversity, and exercised, by many trials, in the mastery of his passions, he bore with their petulance, soothed their irritation, and endeavored to cheer their spirits by the hopes of speedy succor. A little while longer, and he trusted that Fiesco would arrive with good tidings, when the certainty of relief would put an end to all these clamors. The mischief, however, was deeper than he apprehended; a complete mutiny had been organized.

On the 2d of January, 1504, he was in his small cabin, on the stern of his vessel, being confined to his bed by the gout, which had now rendered him a complete cripple. While ruminating on his disastrous situation, Francisco de Porras suddenly entered. His abrupt and agitated manner betrayed the evil nature of his visit. He had the flurried impudence of a man about to perpetrate an open crime. Breaking forth into bitter complaints, at their being kept, week after week, and month after month, to perish piece-meal in that desolate place, he accused the admiral of having no intention to return to Spain. Columbus suspected something sinister from his unusual arrogance; he maintained, however, his calmness, and, raising himself in his bed, endeavored to reason with Porras. He pointed out the impossibility of departing until those who had gone to Hispaniola should send them vessels. He represented how much more urgent must be his desire to depart, since he had not merely his own safety to provide for, but was accountable to God and his sovereigns for the welfare of all who had been committed to his charge. He reminded Porras that he had always consulted with them all, as to the measures to be

---

* Hist. del Almirante, cap. 102.

taken for the common safety, and that what he had done had
been with the general approbation; still, if any other measure
appeared advisable, he recommended that they should assemble together and consult upon it, and adopt whatever course
appeared most judicious.

The measures of Porras and his comrades, however, were
already concerted, and when men are determined on mutiny
they are deaf to reason. He bluntly replied that there was
no time for further consultations. "Embark immediately or
remain in God's name, were the only alternatives." "For
my part," said he, turning his back upon the admiral, and
elevating his voice so that it resounded all over the vessel,
"I am for Castile! those who choose may follow me!"
Shouts arose immediately from all sides, "I will follow you!
and I! and I!" Numbers of the crew sprang upon the most
conspicuous parts of the ship, brandishing weapons, and
uttering mingled threats and cries of rebellion. Some called
upon Porras for orders what to do; others shouted "To Castile! to Castile!" while, amid the general uproar, the voices
of some desperadoes were heard menacing the life of the
admiral.

Columbus, hearing the tumult, leaped from his bed, ill
and infirm as he was, and tottered out of the cabin, stumbling
and falling in the exertion, hoping by his presence to pacify
the mutineers. Three or four of his faithful adherents, however, fearing some violence might be offered him, threw himself between him and the throng, and taking him in their
arms compelled him to return to his cabin.

The adelantado likewise sallied forth, but in a different
mood. He planted himself, with lance in hand, in a situation to take the whole brunt of the assault. It was with the
greatest difficulty that several of the loyal part of the crew
could appease his fury, and prevail upon him to relinquish
his weapon, and retire to the cabin of his brother. They
now entreated Porras and his companions to depart peaceably, since no one sought to oppose them. No advantage
could be gained by violence; but should they cause the death

of the admiral, they would draw upon themselves the severest punishment from the sovereigns.*

These representations moderated the turbulence of the mutineers, and they now proceeded to carry their plans into execution. Taking ten canoes, which the admiral had purchased of the Indians, they embarked in them with as much exultation as if certain of immediately landing on the shores of Spain. Others, who had not been concerned in the mutiny, seeing so large a force departing, and fearing to remain behind, when so reduced in number, hastily collected their effects and entered likewise into the canoes. In this way forty-eight abandoned the admiral. Many of those who remained were only detained by sickness, for had they been well most of them would have accompanied the deserters.†
The few who remained faithful to the admiral, and the sick, who crawled forth from their cabins, saw the departure of the mutineers with tears and lamentations, giving themselves up for lost. Notwithstanding his malady, Columbus left his bed, mingling among those who were loyal, and visiting those who were ill, endeavoring in every way to cheer and comfort them. He entreated them to put their trust in God, who would yet relieve them; and he promised, on his return to Spain, to throw himself at the feet of the queen, represent their loyalty and constancy, and obtain for them rewards that should compensate for all their sufferings.‡

In the meantime Francisco de Porras and his followers, in their squadron of canoes, coasted the island to the eastward, following the route taken by Mendez and Fiesco. Wherever they landed they committed outrages upon the Indians, robbing them of their provisions, and of whatever they coveted of their effects. They endeavored to make their own crimes redound to the prejudice of Columbus, pretending to act under his authority, and affirming that he would pay for everything

---

* Las Casas, Hist. Ind., lib. ii., cap. 32. Hist. del Almirante, cap. 102.

† Hist. del Almirante, cap. 102.   ‡ Las Casas, lib. ii., cap. 32.

they took. If he refused, they told the natives to kill him.
They represented him as an implacable foe to the Indians; as
one who had tyrannized over other islands, causing the misery
and death of the natives, and who only sought to gain a sway
here for the purpose of inflicting like calamities.

Having reached the eastern extremity of the island, they
waited until the weather should be perfectly calm before they
ventured to cross the gulf. Being unskilled in the management of canoes, they procured several Indians to accompany them. The sea being at length quite smooth, they set
forth upon their voyage. Scarcely had they proceeded
four leagues from land when a contrary wind arose and the
waves began to swell. They turned immediately for shore.
The canoes, from their light structure, and being nearly
round and without keels, were easily overturned, and required
to be carefully balanced. They were now deeply freighted
by men unaccustomed to them, and as the sea rose they frequently let in the water. The Spaniards were alarmed, and
endeavored to lighten them by throwing overboard everything
that could be spared; retaining only their arms and a part of
their provisions. The danger augmented with the wind.
They now compelled the Indians to leap into the sea, excepting such as were absolutely necessary to navigate the canoes.
If they hesitated, they drove them overboard with the edge
of the sword. The Indians were skillful swimmers, but the
distance to land was too great for their strength. They kept
about the canoes, therefore, taking hold of them occasionally
to rest themselves and recover breath. As their weight disturbed the balance of the canoes, and endangered their over-
turning, the Spaniards cut off their hands and stabbed them
with their swords. Some died by the weapons of these cruel
men, others were exhausted and sank beneath the waves;
thus eighteen perished miserably, and none survived but such
as had been retained to manage the canoes.

When the Spaniards got back to land, different opinions
arose as to what course they should next pursue. Some were
for crossing to Cuba, for which island the wind was favor-

able. It was thought they might easily cross thence to the end of Hispaniola. Others advised that they should return and make their peace with the admiral, or take from him what remained of arms and stores, having thrown almost everything overboard during their late danger. Others counseled another attempt to cross over to Hispaniola, as soon as the sea should become tranquil.

This last advice was adopted. They remained for a month at an Indian village near the eastern point of the island, living on the substance of the natives, and treating them in the most arbitrary and capricious manner. When at length the weather became serene, they made a second attempt, but were again driven back by adverse winds. Losing all patience, therefore, and despairing of the enterprise, they abandoned their canoes, and returned westward, wandering from village to village, a dissolute and lawless gang, supporting themselves by fair means or foul, according as they met with kindness or hostility, and passing like a pestilence through the island.*

CHAPTER THREE

SCARCITY OF PROVISIONS—STRATAGEM OF COLUMBUS TO OBTAIN SUPPLIES FROM THE NATIVES

[1504]

WHILE Porras and his crew were raging about with that desperate and joyless licentiousness which attends the abandonment of principle, Columbus presented the opposite picture of a man true to others and to himself, and supported, amid hardships and difficulties, by conscious rectitude. Deserted by the healthful and vigorous portion of his garrison, he exerted himself to soothe and encourage the infirm and desponding remnant which remained. Regardless of his own painful maladies, he was only attentive to relieve their suffer-

---

* Hist. del Almirante, cap. 102. Las Casas, lib. ii., cap. 32.

ings. The few who were fit for service were required to mount guard on the wreck or attend upon the sick; there were none to forage for provisions. The scrupulous good faith and amicable conduct maintained by Columbus toward the natives had now their effect. Considerable supplies of provisions were brought by them from time to time, which he purchased at a reasonable rate. The most palatable and nourishing of these, together with the small stock of European biscuit that remained, he ordered to be appropriated to the sustenance of the infirm. Knowing how much the body is affected by the operations of the mind, he endeavored to rouse the spirits and animate the hopes of the drooping sufferers. Concealing his own anxiety, he maintained a serene and even cheerful countenance, encouraging his men by kind words, and holding forth confident anticipations of speedy relief. By his friendly and careful treatment, he soon recruited both the health and spirits of his people, and brought them into a condition to contribute to the common safety. Judicious regulations, calmly but firmly enforced, maintained everything in order. The men became sensible of the advantages of wholesome discipline, and perceived that the restraints imposed upon them by their commander were for their own good, and ultimately productive of their own comfort.

Columbus had thus succeeded in guarding against internal ills, when alarming evils began to menace from without. The Indians, unused to lay up any stock of provisions, and unwilling to subject themselves to extra labor, found it difficult to furnish the quantity of food daily required for so many hungry men. The European trinkets, once so precious, lost their value in proportion as they became more common. The importance of the admiral had been greatly diminished by the desertion of so many of his followers, and the malignant instigations of the rebels had awakened jealousy and enmity in several of the villages which had been accustomed to furnish provisions.

By degrees, therefore, the supplies fell off. The arrangements for the daily delivery of certain quantities, made by
* * * 6—VOL. VII.

Diego Mendez, were irregularly attended to, and at length ceased entirely. The Indians no longer thronged to the harbor with provisions, and often refused them when applied for. The Spaniards were obliged to forage about the neighborhood for their daily food, but found more and more difficulty in procuring it; thus, in addition to their other causes for despondency, they began to entertain horrible apprehensions of famine.

The admiral heard their melancholy forebodings, and beheld the growing evil, but was at a loss for a remedy. To resort to force was an alternative full of danger, and of but temporary efficacy. It would require all those who were well enough to bear arms to sally forth, while he and the rest of the infirm would be left defenseless on board of the wreck, exposed to the vengeance of the natives.

In the meantime the scarcity daily increased. The Indians perceived the wants of the white men, and had learned from them the art of making bargains. They asked ten times the former quantity of European articles for any amount of provisions, and brought their supplies in scanty quantities, to enhance the eagerness of the hungry Spaniards. At length even this relief ceased, and there was an absolute distress for food. The jealousy of the natives had been univer·sally roused by Porras and his followers, and they withheld all provisions, in hopes either of starving the admiral and his people, or of driving them from the island.

In this extremity a fortunate idea presented itself to Co·lumbus. From his knowledge of astronomy, he ascertained that, within three days, there would be a total eclipse of the moon in the early part of the night. He sent, therefore, an Indian of Hispaniola, who served as his interpreter, to summon the principal caciques to a grand conference, appointing for it the day of the eclipse. When all were assembled he told them by his interpreter that he and his followers were worshipers of a Deity who dwelt in the skies; who favored such as did well, but punished all transgressors. That, as they must all have noticed, he had protected Diego Mendez and his companions in their voyage, because they went in obedience to the orders of their commanders, but had visited Porras and his companions with all kinds of afflictions, in consequence of their rebellion. This great Deity, he added, was incensed against the Indians who refused to furnish his faithful worshipers with provisions, and intended to chastise them with famine and pestilence. Lest they should disbelieve this warning, a signal would be given that night. They would behold the moon change its color and gradually lose its light; a token of the fearful punishment which awaited them.

Many of the Indians were alarmed at the prediction, others treated it with derision—all, however, awaited with solicitude the coming of the night. When they beheld a dark shadow stealing over the moon they began to tremble; with the progress of the eclipse their fears increased, and when they saw a mysterious darkness covering the whole face of nature, there were no bounds to their terror. Seizing upon whatever provisions were at hand, they hurried to the ships, threw themselves at the feet of Columbus, and implored him to intercede with his God to withhold the threatened calamities, assuring him they would thenceforth bring him whatever he required. Columbus shut himself up in his cabin, as if to commune with the Deity, and remained there during the increase of the eclipse, the forests and shores all the while resounding with the howlings and supplications of the savages. When the eclipse was about to diminish he came forth and informed the natives that his God had deigned to pardon them, on condition of their fulfilling their promises; in sign of which he would withdraw the darkness from the moon.

When the Indians saw that planet restored to its brightness, and rolling in all its beauty through the firmament, they overwhelmed the admiral with thanks for his intercession, and repaired to their homes, joyful at having escaped such great disasters. Regarding Columbus with awe and reverence, as a man in the peculiar favor and confidence of the Deity, since he knew upon earth what was passing in the heavens, they hastened to propitiate him with gifts; supplies again arrived daily at the harbor, and from that time forward there was no want of provisions.*

CHAPTER FOUR

MISSION OF DIEGO DE ESCOBAR TO THE ADMIRAL

[1504]

EIGHT months had now elapsed since the departure of Mendez and Fiesco without any tidings of their fate. For a long time the Spaniards had kept a wistful lookout upon the ocean, flattering themselves that every Indian canoe, gliding at a distance, might be the harbinger of deliverance. The hopes of the most sanguine were now fast sinking into despondency. What thousand perils awaited such frail barks, and so weak a party, on an expedition of the kind! Either the canoes had been swallowed up by boisterous waves and adverse currents, or their crews had perished among the rugged mountains and savage tribes of Hispaniola. To increase their despondency, they were informed that a vessel had been seen, bottom upward, drifting with the currents along the coasts of Jamaica. This might be the vessel sent to their relief; and if so, all their hopes were shipwrecked with it. This rumor, it is affirmed, was invented and circulated in the island by the rebels, that it might reach the ears of those who remained faithful to the admiral, and reduce them to despair.† It no doubt had its effect. Losing all hope of aid from a distance, and considering themselves abandoned and forgotten by the world, many grew wild and desperate in their plans. Another conspiracy was formed by one Bernardo, an apothecary of Valencia, with two confederates, Alonzo de Zamora and Pedro de Villatoro.

---

* Hist. del Almirante, cap. 103.   Las Casas, Hist. Ind., lib. ii., cap. 33.
† Hist. del Almirante, cap. 104.

They designed to seize upon the remaining canoes and seek their way to Hispaniola.*

The mutiny was on the very point of breaking out, when one evening, toward dusk, a sail was seen standing toward the harbor. The transports of the poor Spaniards may be more easily conceived than described. The vessel was of small size; it kept out to sea, but sent its boat to visit the ships. Every eye was eagerly bent to hail the countenances of Christians and deliverers. As the boat approached, they descried in it Diego de Escobar, a man who had been one of the most active confederates of Roldan in his rebellion, who had been condemned to death under the administration of Columbus, and pardoned by his successor Bobadilla. There was bad omen in such a messenger.

Coming alongside of the ships, Escobar put a letter on board from Ovando, governor of Hispaniola, together with a barrel of wine and a side of bacon, sent as presents to the admiral. He then drew off, and talked with Columbus from a distance. He told him that he was sent by the governor to express his great concern at his misfortunes, and his regret at not having in port a vessel of sufficient size to bring off himself and his people, but that he would send one as soon as possible. Escobar gave the admiral assurances likewise that his concerns in Hispaniola had been faithfully attended to. He requested him, if he had any letter to write to the governor in reply, to give it to him as soon as possible, as he wished to return immediately.

There was something extremely singular in this mission, but there was no time for comments, Escobar was urgent to depart. Columbus hastened, therefore, to write a reply to Ovando, depicting the dangers and distresses of his situation, increased as they were by the rebellion of Porras, but expressing his reliance on his promise to send him relief, confiding in which he should remain patiently on board of his wreck. He recommended Diego Mendez and Bartholomew Fiesco to

---

* Las Casas, Hist. Ind., lib. ii., cap. 33.

his favor, assuring him that they were not sent to San Domingo with any artful design, but simply to represent his perilous situation, and to apply for succor.* When Escobar received this letter, he returned immediately on board of his vessel, which made all sail, and soon disappeared in the gathering gloom of the night.

If the Spaniards had hailed the arrival of this vessel with transport, its sudden departure and the mysterious conduct of Escobar inspired no less wonder and consternation. He had kept aloof from all communication with them, as if he felt no interest in their welfare or sympathy in their misfortunes. Columbus saw the gloom that had gathered in their countenances, and feared the consequences. He eagerly sought, therefore, to dispel their suspicions, professing himself satisfied with the communications received from Ovando, and assuring them that vessels would soon arrive to take them all away. In confidence of this, he said, he had declined to depart with Escobar, because his vessel was too small to take the whole, preferring to remain with them and share their lot, and had dispatched the caravel in such haste that no time might be lost in expediting the necessary ships. These assurances, and the certainty that their situation was known in San Domingo, cheered the hearts of the people. Their hopes again revived, and the conspiracy, which had been on the point of breaking forth, was completely disconcerted.

In secret, however, Columbus was exceedingly indignant at the conduct of Ovando. He had left him for many months in a state of the utmost danger, and most distressing uncertainty, exposed to the hostilities of the natives, the seditions of his men, and the suggestions of his own despair. He had, at length, sent a mere tantalizing message, by a man known to be one of his bitterest enemies, with a present of food, which, from its scantiness, seemed intended to mock their necessities.

---

* Las Casas, Hist. Ind., lib. ii., cap. 34.

Columbus believed that Ovando had purposely neglected him, hoping that he might perish on the island, being apprehensive that, should he return in safety, he would be reinstated in the government of Hispaniola; and he considered Escobar merely as a spy sent to ascertain the state of himself and his crew, and whether they were yet in existence. Las Casas, who was then at San Domingo, expresses similar suspicions. He says that Escobar was chosen because Ovando was certain that, from ancient enmity, he would have no sympathy for the admiral. That he was ordered not to go on board of the vessels, nor to land, neither was he to hold conversation with any of the crew, nor to receive any letters, except those of the admiral. In a word, that he was a mere scout to collect information.*

Others have ascribed the long neglect of Ovando to extreme caution. There was a rumor prevalent that Columbus, irritated at the suspension of his dignities by the court of Spain, intended to transfer his newly-discovered countries into the hands of his native republic Genoa, or of some other power. Such rumors had long been current, and to their recent circulation Columbus himself alludes in his letter sent to the sovereigns by Diego Mendez. The most plausible apology given is that Ovando was absent for several months in the interior, occupied in wars with the natives, and that there were no ships at San Domingo of sufficient burden to take Columbus and his crew to Spain. He may have feared that, should they come to reside for any length of time on the island, either the admiral would interfere in public affairs, or endeavor to make a party in his favor; or that, in consequence of the number of his old enemies still resident there, former scenes of faction and turbulence might be revived.† In the meantime the situation of Columbus in Jamaica, while it disposed of him quietly until vessels should arrive from Spain,

---

* Las Casas, Hist. Ind., lib. ii., cap. 33. Hist. del Almirante, cap. 103.

† Las Casas, ubi sup. Hist. del Almirante, ubi sup.

could not, he may have thought, be hazardous. He had sufficient force and arms for defense, and he had made amicable arrangements with the natives for the supply of provisions, as Diego Mendez, who had made those arrangements, had no doubt informed him. Such may have been the reasoning by which Ovando, under the real influence of his interest, may have reconciled his conscience to a measure which excited the strong reprobation of his contemporaries and has continued to draw upon him the suspicions of mankind.

CHAPTER FIVE

VOYAGE OF DIEGO MENDEZ AND BARTHOLOMEW FIESCO
IN A CANOE TO HISPANIOLA

[1504]

IT is proper to give here some account of the mission of Diego Mendez and Bartholomew Fiesco, and of the circumstances which prevented the latter from returning to Jamaica. Having taken leave of the adelantado at the east end of the island, they continued all day in a direct course, animating the Indians who navigated their canoes, and who frequently paused at their labor. There was no wind, the sky was without a cloud, and the sea perfectly calm; the heat was intolerable, and the rays of the sun reflected from the surface of the ocean seemed to scorch their very eyes. The Indians, exhausted by heat and toil, would often leap into the water to cool and refresh themselves, and, after remaining there a short time, would return with new vigor to their labors. At the going down of the sun they lost sight of land. During the night the Indians took turns, one half to row while the others slept. The Spaniards, in like manner, divided their forces: while one half took repose the others kept guard with their weapons in hand, ready to defend themselves in case of any perfidy on the part of their savage companions.

Watching and toiling in this way through the night, they were exceedingly fatigued at the return of day. Nothing was to be seen but sea and sky. Their frail canoes, heaving up and down with the swelling and sinking of the ocean, seemed scarcely capable of sustaining the broad undulations of a calm; how would they be able to live amid waves and surges, should the wind arise? The commanders did all they could to keep up the flagging spirits of the men. Sometimes they permitted them a respite; at other times they took the paddles and shared their toils. But labor and fatigue were soon forgotten in a new source of suffering. During the preceding sultry day and night, the Indians, parched and fatigued, had drunk up all the water. They now began to experience the torments of thirst. In proportion as the day advanced their thirst increased; the calm, which favored the navigation of the canoes, rendered this misery the more intense. There was not a breeze to fan the air nor counteract the ardent rays of a tropical sun. Their sufferings were irritated by the prospect around them—nothing but water, while they were perishing with thirst. At midday their strength failed them, and they could work no longer. Fortunately, at this time the commanders of the canoes found, or pretended to find, two small kegs of water, which they had perhaps secretly reserved for such an extremity. Administering the precious contents from time to time, in sparing mouthfuls to their companions, and particularly to the laboring Indians, they enabled them to resume their toils. They cheered them with the hopes of soon arriving at a small island called Navasa, which lay directly in their way, and was only eight leagues from Hispaniola. Here they would be able to procure water, and might take repose.

For the rest of the day they continued faintly and wearily laboring forward, and keeping an anxious lookout for the island. The day passed away, the sun went down, yet there was no sign of land, not even a cloud on the horizon that might deceive them into a hope. According to their calculations, they had certainly come the distance from Jamaica at

which Navasa lay. They began to fear that they had devi-
ated from their course. If so, they should miss the island
entirely, and perish with thirst before they could reach Hispaniola.

The night closed upon them without any sight of the isl-
and. They now despaired of touching at it, for it was so
small and low that, even if they were to pass near, they
would scarcely be able to perceive it in the dark. One of
the Indians sank and died, under the accumulated sufferings
of labor, heat, and raging thirst. His body was thrown into
the sea. Others lay panting and gasping at the bottom of
the canoes. Their companions, troubled in spirit, and exhausted in strength, feebly continued their toils. Sometimes
they endeavored to cool their parched palates by taking sea-
water in their mouths, but its briny acrimony rather increased their thirst. Now and then, but very sparingly,
they were allowed a drop of water from the kegs; but this
was only in cases of the utmost extremity, and principally to
those who were employed in rowing. The night had far advanced, but those whose turn it was to take repose were unable to sleep from the intensity of their thirst; or if they slept,
it was but to be tantalized by dreams of cool fountains and
running brooks, and to awaken in redoubled torment. The
last drop of water had been dealt out to the Indian rowers,
but it only served to irritate their sufferings. They scarce
could move their paddles; one after another gave up, and
it seemed impossible they should live to reach Hispaniola.

The commanders, by admirable management, had hitherto
kept up this weary struggle with suffering and despair: they
now, too, began to despond. Diego Mendez sat watching the
horizon, which was gradually lighting up with those faint
rays which precede the rising of the moon. As that planet
rose, he perceived it to emerge from behind some dark mass
elevated above the level of the ocean. He immediately gave
the animating cry of "land!" His almost expiring companions were roused by it to new life. It proved to be the island
of Navasa, but so small, and low, and distant, that had it

not been thus revealed by the rising of the moon they would never have discovered it. The error in their reckoning with respect to the island had arisen from miscalculating the rate of sailing of the canoes, and from not making sufficient allowance for the fatigue of the rowers and the opposition of the current.

New vigor was now diffused throughout the crews. They exerted themselves with feverish impatience; by the dawn of day they reached the land, and, springing on shore, returned thanks to God for such signal deliverance. The island was a mere mass of rocks half a league in circuit. There was neither tree, nor shrub, nor herbage, nor stream, nor fountain. Hurrying about, however, with anxious search, they found to their joy abundance of rain-water in the hollows of the rocks. Eagerly scooping it up with their calabashes, they quenched their burning thirst by immoderate draughts. In vain the more prudent warned the others of their danger. The Spaniards were in some degree restrained; but the poor Indians, whose toils had increased the fever of their thirst, gave way to a kind of frantic indulgence. Several died upon the spot, and others fell dangerously ill.*

Having allayed their thirst, they now looked about in search of food. A few shellfish were found along the shore, and Diego Mendez, striking a light, and gathering driftwood, they were enabled to boil them, and to make a delicious banquet. All day they remained reposing in the shade of the rocks, refreshing themselves after their intolerable sufferings, and gazing upon Hispaniola, whose mountains rose above the horizon, at eight leagues' distance.

In the cool of the evening they once more embarked, invigorated by repose, and arrived safely at Cape Tiburon on the following day, the fourth since their departure from

---

* Not far from the island of Navasa there gushes up in the sea a pure fountain of fresh water that sweetens the surface for some distance; this circumstance was of course unknown to the Spaniards at the time. (Oviedo, Cronica, lib. vi., cap. 12.)

Jamaica. Here they landed on the banks of a beautiful river, where they were kindly received and treated by the natives. Such are the particulars, collected from different sources, of this adventurous and interesting voyage, on the precarious success of which depended the deliverance of Columbus and his crews.* The voyagers remained for two days among the hospitable natives on the banks of the river to refresh themselves. Fiesco would have returned to Jamaica, according to promise, to give assurance to the admiral and his companions of the safe arrival of their messenger; but both Spaniards and Indians had suffered so much during the voyage that nothing could induce them to encounter the perils of a return in the canoes.

Parting with his companions, Diego Mendez took six Indians of the island, and set off resolutely to coast in his canoe one hundred and thirty leagues to San Domingo. After proceeding for eighty leagues, with infinite toil, always against the currents, and subject to perils from the native tribes, he was informed that the governor had departed for Xaragua, fifty leagues distant. Still undaunted by fatigues and difficulties, he abandoned his canoe, and proceeded alone and on foot through forests and over mountains, until he arrived at Xaragua, achieving one of the most perilous expeditions ever undertaken by a devoted follower for the safety of his commander.

Ovando received him with great kindness, expressing the utmost concern at the unfortunate situation of Columbus. He made many promises of sending immediate relief, but suffered day after day, week after week, and even month after month to elapse, without carrying his promises into effect. He was at that time completely engrossed by wars with the natives, and had a ready plea that there were no ships of sufficient burden at San Domingo. Had he felt a proper zeal, however, for the safety of a man like Colum-

---

* Hist. del Almirante, cap. 105. Las Casas, lib. ii., cap. 81. Testament of Diego Mendez. Navarrete, tom. i.

bus, it would have been easy, within eight months, to have devised some means, if not of delivering him from his situation, at least of conveying to him ample re-enforcements and supplies.

The faithful Mendez remained for seven months in Xaragua, detained there under various pretexts by Ovando, who was unwilling that he should proceed to San Domingo; partly, as is intimated, from his having some jealousy of his being employed in secret agency for the admiral, and partly from a desire to throw impediments in the way of his obtaining the required relief. At length, by daily importunity, he obtained permission to go to San Domingo and await the arrival of certain ships which were expected, of which he proposed to purchase one on the account of the admiral. He immediately set out on foot a distance of seventy leagues, part of his toilsome journey lying through forests and among mountains infested by hostile and exasperated Indians. It was after his departure that Ovando dispatched the caravel commanded by the pardoned rebel Escobar, on that singular and equivocal visit, which, in the eyes of Columbus, had the air of a mere scouting expedition to spy into the camp of an enemy.

CHAPTER SIX

OVERTURES OF COLUMBUS TO THE MUTINEERS—BATTLE
OF THE ADELANTADO WITH PORRAS AND HIS
FOLLOWERS.

[1503]

WHEN Columbus had soothed the disappointment of his men at the brief and unsatisfactory visit and sudden departure of Escobar, he endeavored to turn the event to some advantage with the rebels: he knew them to be disheartened by the inevitable miseries attending a lawless and dissolute life; that many longed to return to the safe and quiet path of duty; and that the most malignant, seeing how he had foiled all their intrigues among the natives to produce a famine, began to fear his ultimate triumph and consequent vengeance. A favorable opportunity, he thought, now presented to take advantage of these feelings, and by gentle means to bring them back to their allegiance. He sent two of his people, therefore, who were most intimate with the rebels, to inform them of the recent arrival of Escobar with letters from the governor of Hispaniola, promising him a speedy deliverance from the island. He now offered a free pardon, kind treatment, and a passage with him in the expected ships, on condition of their immediate return to obedience. To convince them of the arrival of the vessel, he sent them a part of the bacon which had been brought by Escobar.

On the approach of these embassadors, Francisco de Porras came forth to meet them, accompanied solely by a few of the ringleaders of his party. He imagined that there might be some propositions from the admiral, and he was fearful of their being heard by the mass of his people, who, in their dissatisfied and repentant mood, would be likely to desert him on the least prospect of pardon. Having listened to the tidings and overtures brought by the messengers, he and his confidential confederates consulted for some time together. Perfidious in their own nature, they suspected the sincerity of the admiral; and conscious of the extent of their offenses, doubted his having the magnanimity to pardon them. Determined, therefore, not to confide in his proffered amnesty, they replied to the messengers that they had no wish to return to the ships, but preferred living at large about the island. They offered to engage, however, to conduct themselves peaceably and amicably, on receiving a solemn promise from the admiral that, should two vessels arrive, they should have one to depart in; should but one arrive, that half of it should be granted to them; and that, moreover, the admiral should share with them the stores and articles of Indian traffic remaining in the ships; having lost all that they had in the sea. These demands were pronounced extravagant and inadmissible, upon which they replied insolently that, if they were not peaceably conceded, they would take them **by force; and** with this menace they dismissed the embassadors. *

. This conference was not conducted so privately but that the rest of the rebels learned the purport of the mission; and the offer of pardon and deliverance occasioned great tumult and agitation. Porras, fearful of their desertion, assured them that these offers of the admiral were all deceitful; that he was naturally cruel and vindictive, and only sought to get them into his power to wreak on them his vengeance. He exhorted them to persist in their opposition to his tyranny; reminding them that those who had formerly done so in Hispaniola had eventually triumphed, and sent him home in irons; he assured them that they might do the same, and again made vaunting promises of protection in Spain, through the influence of his relatives. But the boldest of his assertions was with respect to the caravel of Escobar. It shows the ignorance of the age, and the superstitious awe which the common people entertained with respect to Columbus and his astronomical knowledge. Porras assured them that no real caravel had arrived, but a mere phantasm conjured up by the admiral, who was deeply versed in necromancy. In proof of this he adverted to its arriving in the dusk of the evening; its holding communication with no one but the admiral, and its sudden disappearance in the night. Had it been a real caravel, the crew would have sought to talk with their countrymen; the admiral, his son, and brother, would have eagerly embarked on board, and it would at any rate have remained a little while in port, and not have vanished so suddenly and mysteriously.†

By these and similar delusions Porras succeeded in working upon the feelings and credulity of his followers. Fearful, however, that they might yield to after reflection, and to further offers from the admiral, he determined to involve them **in** some act of violence which would commit them beyond all

---

* Las Casas, lib. ii., cap. 35. Hist. del Almirante, cap. 106.
† Hist. del Almirante, cap. 106. Las Casas, lib. ii., cap. 35.

hopes of forgiveness. He marched them, therefore, to an Indian village called Maima,* about a quarter of a league from the ships, intending to plunder the stores remaining on board the wreck, and to take the admiral prisoner.†

Columbus had notice of the designs of the rebels and of their approach. Being confined by his infirmities, he sent his brother to endeavor with mild words to persuade them from their purpose and win them to obedience; but with sufficient force to resist any violence. The adelantado, who was a man rather of deeds than of words, took with him fifty followers, men of tried resolution, and ready to fight in any cause. They were well armed and full of courage, though many were pale and debilitated from recent sickness, and from long confinement to the ships. Arriving on the side of a hill, within a bow-shot of the village, the adelantado discovered the rebels, and dispatched the same two messengers to treat with them, who had already carried them the offer of pardon. Porras and his fellow leaders, however, would not permit them to approach. They confided in the superiority of their numbers, and in their men being, for the most part, hardy sailors, rendered robust and vigorous by the roving life they had been leading in the forests and the open air. They knew that many of those who were with the adelantado were men brought up in a softer mode of life. They pointed to their pale countenances, and persuaded their followers that they were mere household men, fair-weather troops, who could never stand before them. They did not reflect that, with such men, pride and lofty spirit often more than supply the place of bodily force, and they forgot that their adversaries had the incalculable advantage of justice and law upon their side. Deluded by their words, their followers were excited to a transient glow of courage, and brandishing their weapons, refused to listen to the messengers.

Six of the stoutest rebels made a league to stand by one

---

* At present Mammee Bay.
† Hist. del Almirante, ubi sup.

another and attack the adelantado; for, he being killed, the
rest would be easily defeated. The main body formed themselves into a squadron, drawing their swords and shaking
their lances. They did not wait to be assailed, but, uttering
shouts and menaces, rushed upon the enemy. They were so
well received, however, that at the first shock four or five
were killed, most of them the confederates who had leagued
to attack the adelantado. The latter, with his own hand,
killed Juan Sanchez, the same powerful mariner who had
carried off the cacique Quibian; and Juan Barber also, who
had first drawn a sword against the admiral in this rebellion.
The adelantado with his usual vigor and courage was dealing
his blows about him in the thickest of the affray, where several lay killed and wounded, when he was assailed by Francisco de Porras. The rebel with a blow of his sword cleft the
buckler of Don Bartholomew, and wounded the hand which
grasped it. The sword remained wedged in the shield, and
before Porras could withdraw it the adelantado closed upon
him, grappled him, and, being assisted by others, after a
severe struggle took him prisoner.*

When the rebels beheld their leader a captive, their transient courage was at an end and they fled in confusion. The
adelantado would have pursued them, but was persuaded to
let them escape with the punishment they had received; especially as it was necessary to guard against the possibility of
an attack from the Indians.

The latter had taken arms and drawn up in battle array,
gazing with astonishment at this fight between white men,
but without taking part on either side. When the battle was
over, they approached the field, gazing upon the dead bodies
of the beings they had once fancied immortal. They were
curious in examining the wounds made by the Christian
weapons. Among the wounded insurgents was Pedro Ledesma, the same pilot who so bravely swam ashore at Veragua,

* Hist. del Almirante, cap. 107. Las Casas, Hist. Ind., lib. ii.,
Cap. 35.

to procure tidings of the colony. He was a man of prodigious muscular force and a hoarse, deep voice. As the
Indians, who thought him dead, were inspecting the wounds
with which he was literally covered, he suddenly uttered an
ejaculation in his tremendous voice, at the sound of which the
savages fled in dismay. This man, having fallen into a cleft
or ravine, was not discovered by the white men until the
dawning of the following day, having remained all that time
without a drop of water. The number and severity of the
wounds he is said to have received would seem incredible,
but they are mentioned by Fernando Columbus, who was an
eye-witness, and by Las Casas, who had the account from
Ledesma himself. For want of proper remedies his wounds
were treated in the roughest manner, yet, through the aid of
a vigorous constitution, he completely recovered. Las Casas
conversed with him several years afterward at Seville, when
he obtained from him various particulars concerning this
voyage of Columbus. Some few days after this conversation,
however, he heard that Ledesma had fallen under the knife
of an assassin.*

The adelantado returned in triumph to the ships, where he
was received by the admiral in the most affectionate manner;
thanking him as his deliverer. He brought Porras and several of his followers prisoners. Of his own party only two
had been wounded; himself in the hand, and the admiral's
steward, who had received an apparently slight wound with
a lance, equal to one of the most insignificant of those with
which Ledesma was covered; yet, in spite of careful treatment, he died.

On the next day, the 20th of May, the fugitives sent a
petition to the admiral, signed with all their names, in which,
says Las Casas, they confessed all their misdeeds and cruelties and evil intentions, supplicating the admiral to have pity
on them and pardon them for their rebellion, for which God
had already punished them. They offered to return to their

---

* Las Casas, Hist. Ind., lib. ii., cap. 35.

obedience, and to serve him faithfully in future, making an oath to that effect upon a cross and a missal, accompanied by an imprecation worthy of being recorded: "They hoped, should they break their oath, that no priest nor other Christian might ever confess them; that repentance might be of no avail; that they might be deprived of the holy sacraments of the church; that at their death they might receive no benefit from bulls nor indulgences; that their bodies might be cast out into the fields, like those of heretics and renegadoes, instead of being buried in holy ground; and that they might not receive absolution from the Pope, nor from cardinals, nor archbishops, nor bishops, nor any other Christian priests."* Such were the awful imprecations by which these men endeavored to add validity to an oath. The worthlessness of a man's word may always be known by the extravagant means he uses to enforce it.

The admiral saw, by the abject nature of this petition, how completely the spirit of these misguided men was broken; with his wonted magnanimity, he readily granted their prayer, and pardoned their offenses; but on one condition, that their ringleader, Francisco Porras, should remain a prisoner.

As it was difficult to maintain so many persons on board of the ships, and as quarrels might take place between per· sons who had so recently been at blows, Columbus put the late followers of Porras under the command of a discreet and faithful man; and giving in his charge a quantity of European articles for the purpose of purchasing food of the natives, directed him to forage about the island until the expected vessels should arrive.

At length, after a long year of alternate hope and despondency, the doubts of the Spaniards were joyfully dispelled by the sight of two vessels standing into the harbor. One proved to be a ship hired and well victualed, at the expense of the admiral, by the faithful and indefatigable Diego

---

* Las Casas, Hist. Ind., lib. ii., cap. 32.

Mendez; the other had been subsequently fitted out by Ovando, and put under the command of Diego de Salcedo, the admiral's agent employed to collect his rents in San Domingo.

The long neglect of Ovando to attend to the relief of Columbus had, it seems, roused the public indigation, insomuch that animadversions had been made upon his conduct even in the pulpits. This is affirmed by Las Casas, who was at San Domingo at the time. If the governor had really entertained hopes that, during the delay of relief, Columbus might perish in the island, the report brought back by Escobar must have completely disappointed him. No time was to be lost if he wished to claim any merit in his deliverance, or to avoid the disgrace of having totally neglected him. He exerted himself, therefore, at the eleventh hour, and dispatched a caravel at the same time with the ship sent by Diego Mendez. The latter having faithfully discharged this part of his mission, and seen the ships depart, proceeded to Spain on the further concerns of the admiral.*

---

* Some brief notice of the further fortunes of Diego Mendez may be interesting to the reader. When King Ferdinand heard of his faithful services, says Oviedo, he bestowed rewards upon Mendez, and permitted him to bear a canoe in his coat of arms, as a memento of his loyalty. He continued devotedly attached to the admiral, serving him zealously after his return to Spain, and during his last illness. Columbus retained the most grateful and affectionate sense of his fidelity. On his death-bed he promised Mendez that, in reward for his services, he should be appointed principal alguazil of the island of Hispaniola, an engagement which the admiral's son, Don Diego, who was present, cheerfully undertook to perform. A few years afterward, when the latter succeeded to the office of his father, Mendez reminded him of the promise, but Don Diego informed him that he had given the office to his uncle Don Bartholomew; he assured him, however, that he should receive something equivalent. Mendez shrewdly replied that the equivalent had better be given to Don Bartholomew, and the office to himself, according to agreement. The promise, however, remained unperformed, and Diego Mendez unrewarded. He was afterward engaged on voyages of discovery in vessels of his own, but met with many vicissitudes, and appears to have died in impoverished circum-

BOOK SEVENTEEN

CHAPTER ONE

ADMINISTRATION OF OVANDO IN HISPANIOLA—OPPRESSION
OF THE NATIVES

[1503]

BEFORE relating the return of Columbus to Hispaniola, it
is proper to notice some of the principal occurrences which
took place in that island under the government of Ovando.
A great crowd of adventurers of various ranks had thronged
his fleet—eager speculators, credulous dreamers, and broken-
down gentlemen of desperate fortunes; all expecting to enrich themselves suddenly in an island where gold was to be
picked up from the surface of the soil or gathered from the
mountain brooks.   They had scarcely landed, says Las Casas,
who accompanied the expedition, when they all hurried off

---

stances. His last will, from which these particulars are principally
gathered, was dated in Valladolid, the 19th of June, 1536, by which it
is evident he must have been in the prime of life at the time of his
voyage with the admiral. In this will he requested that the reward
which had been promised to him should be paid to his children, by
making his eldest son principal alguazil for life of the city of San
Domingo, and his other son lieutenant to the admiral for the same city.
It does not appear whether this request was complied with under the
successors of Don Diego.

In another clause of his will he desired that a large stone should be
placed upon his sepulcher, on which should be engraved, "Here lies the
honorable Cavalier Diego Mendez, who served greatly the royal crown
of Spain, in the conquest of the Indies, with the Admiral Don Christopher Columbus of glorious memory, who made the discovery; and
afterward by himself with ships at his own cost. He died, etc., etc.
Bestow in charity a Paternoster, and an Ave Maria."

He ordered that in the midst of this stone there should be carved an to the mines, about eight leagues' distance. The roads swarmed like ant-hills, with adventurers of all classes. Every one had his knapsack stored with biscuit or flour, and his mining implements on his shoulders. Those hidalgos, or gentlemen, who had no servants to carry their burdens, bore them on their own backs, and lucky was he who had a horse for the journey; he would be able to bring back the greater load of treasure. They all set out in high spirits, eager who should first reach the golden land; thinking they had but to arrive at the mines and collect riches: "For they fancied," says Las Casas, "that gold was to be gathered as easily and readily as fruit from the trees." When they arrived, however, they discovered, to their dismay, that it was necessary to dig painfully into the bowels of the earth—a labor to which most of them had never been accustomed; that it required experience and sagacity to detect the veins of ore; that, in fact, the whole process of mining was exceedingly toilsome, demanded vast patience and much experience, and, after all, was full of uncertainty. They dug eagerly for a time, but found no ore. They grew hungry, threw by their implements, sat down to eat, and then returned to work. It was all in vain. "Their labor," says Las Casas, "gave them a keen appetite and quick digestion, but no gold." They soon consumed their provisions, exhausted their patience, cursed their infatuation, and

---

Indian canoe, as given him by the king for armorial bearings in memorial of his voyage from Jamaica to Hispaniola, and above it should be engraved, in large letters, the word "CANOA." He enjoined upon his heirs to be loyal to the admiral (Don Diego Columbus) and his lady, and gave them much ghostly counsel, mingled with pious benedictions. As an heirloom in his family, he bequeathed his library, consisting of a few volumes, which accompanied him in his wanderings; viz., "The Art of Holy Dying, by Erasmus; A Sermon of the same author, in Spanish; The Lingua and the Colloquies of the same; The History of Josephus; The Moral Philosophy of Aristotle; The Book of the Holy Land; A Book called the Contemplation of the Passion of our Saviour; A Tract on the Vengeance of the Death of Agamemnon, and several other short treatises." This curious and characteristic testament is in the archives of the Duke of Veragua in Madrid.

in eight days set off drearily on their return along the roads they had lately trod so exultingly. They arrived at San Domingo without an ounce of gold, half-famished, downcast, and despairing.* Such is too often the case of those who ignorantly engage in mining—of all speculations the most brilliant, promising, and fallacious.

Poverty soon fell upon these misguided men. They exhausted the little property brought from Spain. Many suffered extremely from hunger, and were obliged to exchange even their apparel for bread. Some formed connections with the old settlers of the island; but the greater part were like men lost and bewildered, and just awakened from a dream. The miseries of the mind, as usual, heightened the sufferings of the body. Some wasted away and died broken-hearted; others were hurried off by raging fevers, so that there soon perished upward of a thousand men.

Ovando was reputed a man of great prudence and sagacity, and he certainly took several judicious measures for the regulation of the island and the relief of the colonists. He made arrangements for distributing the married persons and the families which had come out in his fleet, in four towns in the interior, granting them important privileges. He revived the drooping zeal for mining, by reducing the royal share of the product from one-half to a third, and shortly after to a fifth; but he empowered the Spaniards to avail themselves, in the most oppressive manner, of the labor of the unhappy natives in working the mines. The charge of treating the natives with severity had been one of those chiefly urged against Columbus. It is proper, therefore, to notice in this respect the conduct of his successor, a man chosen for his prudence and his supposed capacity to govern.

It will be recollected that when Columbus was in a manner compelled to assign lands to the rebellious followers of Francisco Roldan, in 1499, he had made an arrangement that the caciques in their vicinity should, in lieu of tribute, fur-

---

* Las Casas, Hist. Ind., lib. ii. cap. 6.

nish a number of their subjects to assist them in cultivating their estates. This, as has been observed, was the commencement of the disastrous system of repartimientos or distributions of Indians. When Bobadilla administered the government, he constrained the caciques to furnish a certain number of Indians to each Spaniard, for the purpose of working the mines, where they were employed like beasts of burden. He made an enumeration of the natives to prevent evasion; reduced them into classes, and distributed them among the Spanish inhabitants. The enormous oppressions which ensued have been noticed. They roused the indignation of Isabella; and when Ovando was sent out to supersede Bobadilla, in 1502, the natives were pronounced free; they immediately refused to labor in the mines.

Ovando represented to the Spanish sovereigns, in 1503, that ruinous consequences resulted to the colony from this entire liberty granted to the Indians. He stated that the tribute could not be collected, for the Indians were lazy and improvident; that they could only be kept from vices and irregularities by occupation; that they now kept aloof from the Spaniards, and from all instruction in the Christian faith.

The last representation had an influence with Isabella, and drew a letter from the sovereigns to Ovando, in 1503, in which he was ordered to spare no pains to attach the natives to the Spanish nation and the Catholic religion. To make them labor moderately, if absolutely essential to their own good; but to temper authority with persuasion and kindness. To pay them regularly and fairly for their labor, and to have them instructed in religion on certain days.

Ovando availed himself of the powers given him by this letter to their fullest extent. He assigned to each Castilian a certain number of Indians, according to the quality of the applicant, the nature of the application, or his own pleasure. It was arranged in the form of an order on a cacique for a certain number of Indians, who were to be paid by their employer, and instructed in the Catholic faith. The pay was so small as to be little better than nominal; the instruction was little more than the mere ceremony of baptism; and the term of labor was at first six months, and then eight months in the year. Under cover of this hired labor, intended for the good both of their bodies and their souls, more intolerable toil was exacted from them, and more horrible cruelties were inflicted, than in the worst days of Bobadilla. They were separated often the distance of several days' journey from their wives and children, and doomed to intolerable labor of all kinds, extorted by the cruel infliction of the lash. For food they had the cassava bread, an unsubstantial support for men obliged to labor; sometimes a scanty portion of pork was distributed among a great number of them, scarce a mouthful to each. When the Spaniards who superintended the mines were at their repast, says Las Casas, the famished Indians scrambled under the table, like dogs, for any bone thrown to them. After they had gnawed and sucked it, they pounded it between stones and mixed it with their cassava bread, that nothing of so precious a morsel might be lost. As to those who labored in the fields, they never tasted either flesh or fish; a little cassava bread and a few roots were their support. While the Spaniards thus withheld the nourishment necessary to sustain their health and strength, they exacted a degree of labor sufficient to break down the most vigorous man. If the Indians fled from this incessant toil and barbarous coercion, and took refuge in the mountains, they were hunted out like wild beasts, scourged in the most inhuman manner, and laden with chains to prevent a second escape. Many perished long before their term of labor had expired. Those who survived their term of six or eight months were permitted to return to their homes until the next term commenced. But their homes were often forty, sixty, and eighty leagues distant. They had nothing to sustain them through the journey but a few roots or agi peppers, or a little cassava bread. Worn down by long toil and cruel hardships, which their feeble constitutions were incapable of sustaining, many had not strength to perform the journey, but sank down and died by the way; some by the

* * * 7—VOL. VII.

side of a brook, others under the shade of a tree, where they had crawled for shelter from the sun. "I have found many dead in the road," says Las Casas, "others gasping under the trees, and others in the pangs of death, faintly crying Hunger! hunger!" * Those who reached their homes most commonly found them desolate. During the eight months they had been absent, their wives and children had either perished or wandered away; the fields on which they depended for food were overrun with weeds, and nothing was left them but to lie down, exhausted and despairing, and die at the threshold of their habitations.†

It is impossible to pursue any further the picture drawn by the venerable Las Casas, not of what he had heard, but of what he had seen; nature and humanity revolt at the details. Suffice it to say that, so intolerable were the toils and sufferings inflicted upon this weak and unoffending race, that they sank under them, dissolving, as it were, from the face of the earth. Many killed themselves in despair, and even mothers overcame the powerful instinct of nature, and destroyed the infants at their breasts, to spare them a life of wretchedness. Twelve years had not elapsed since the discovery of the island, and several hundred thousand of its native inhabitants had perished, miserable victims to the grasping avarice of the white men.

CHAPTER TWO

MASSACRE AT XARAGUA—FATE OF ANACAONA

[1503]

THE sufferings of the natives under the civil policy of Ovando have been briefly shown; it remains to give a concise view of the military operations of this commander, so lauded by certain of the early historians for his prudence.

---

* Las Casas, Hist. Ind., lib. ii., cap. 14, MS.   † Ibid., ubi sup.

By this notice a portion of the eventful history of this island
will be recounted which is connected with the fortunes of
Columbus, and which comprises the thorough subjugation,
and, it may almost be said, extermination of the native inhabitants. And first, we must treat of the disasters of the
beautiful province of Xaragua, the seat of hospitality, the
refuge of the suffering Spaniards; and of the fate of the female cacique, Anacaona, once the pride of the island, and
the generous friend of white men.

Behechio, the ancient cacique of this province, being dead,
Anacaona, his sister, had succeeded to the government. The
marked partiality which she once manifested for the Spaniards had been greatly weakened by the general misery they
had produced in her country, and by the brutal profligacy
exhibited in her immediate dominions by the followers of
Roldan. The unhappy story of the loves of her beautiful
daughter Higuamota, with the young Spaniard Hernando
de Guevara, had also caused her great affliction; and, finally,
the various and enduring hardships, inflicted on her once
happy subjects by the grinding systems of labor enforced by
Bobadilla and Ovando, had at length, it is said, converted
her friendship into absolute detestation.

This disgust was kept alive and aggravated by the Spaniards who lived in her immediate neighborhood, and had obtained grants of land there; a remnant of the rebel faction
of Roldan, who retained the gross licentiousness and open
profligacy in which they had been indulged under the loose
misrule of that commander, and who made themselves odious
to the inferior caciques, by exacting services tyrannically and
capriciously under the baneful system of repartimientos.

The Indians of this province were uniformly represented
as a more intelligent, polite, and generous-spirited race than
any others of the islands. They were the more prone to feel
and resent the overbearing treatment to which they were subjected. Quarrels sometimes took place between the caciques
and their oppressors. These were immediately reported to
the governor as dangerous mutinies, and a resistance to any

capricious and extortionate exaction was magnified into a rebellious resistance to the authority of government. Complaints of this kind were continually pouring in upon Ovando, until he was persuaded by some alarmist, or some designing mischief maker, that there was a deep-laid conspiracy among the Indians of this province to rise upon the Spaniards.

Ovando immediately set out for Xaragua at the head of three hundred foot-soldiers, armed with swords, arquebuses, and crossbows, and seventy horsemen, with cuirasses, bucklers, and lances. He pretended that he was going on a mere visit of friendship to Anacaona, and to make arrangements about the payment of tribute.

When Anacaona heard of the intended visit, she summoned all her tributary caciques and principal subjects to assemble at her chief town, that they might receive the commander of the Spaniards with becoming homage and distinction. As Ovando, at the head of his little army, approached, she went forth to meet him, according to the custom of her nation, attended by a great train of her most distinguished subjects, male and female; who, as has been before observed, were noted for superior grace and beauty. They received the Spaniards with their popular areytos, their national songs; the young women waving palm branches and dancing before them, in the way that had so much charmed the followers of the adelantado, on his first visit to the province.

Anacaona treated the governor with that natural graciousness and dignity for which she was celebrated. She gave him the largest house in the place for his residence, and his people were quartered in the houses adjoining. For several days the Spaniards were entertained with all the natural luxuries that the province afforded. National songs and dances and games were performed for their amusement, and there was every outward demonstration of the same hospitality, the same amity, that Anacaona had uniformly shown to white men.

Notwithstanding all this kindness, and notwithstanding her uniform integrity of conduct, and open generosity of character, Ovando was persuaded that Anacaona was secretly meditating a massacre of himself and his followers. Historians tell us nothing of the grounds for such a belief. It was too probably produced by the misrepresentations of the unprincipled adventurers who infested the province. Ovando should have paused and reflected before he acted upon it. He should have considered the improbability of such an attempt by naked Indians against so large a force of steel-clad troops, armed with European weapons; and he should have reflected upon the general character and conduct of Anacaona. At any rate, the example set repeatedly by Columbus and his brother the adelantado should have convinced him that it was a sufficient safeguard against the machinations of the natives to seize upon their caciques and detain them as hostages. The policy of Ovando, however, was of a more rash and sanguinary nature; he acted upon suspicion as upon conviction. He determined to anticipate the alleged plot by a counter artifice, and to overwhelm this defenseless people in an indiscriminate and bloody vengeance.

As the Indians had entertained their guests with various national games, Ovando invited them in return to witness certain games of his country. Among these was a tilting match or joust with reeds; a chivalrous game which the Spaniards had learned from the Moors of Granada. The Spanish cavalry, in those days, were as remarkable for the skillful management as for the ostentatious caparison of their horses. Among the troops brought out from Spain by Ovando, one horseman had disciplined his horse to prance and curvet in time to the music of a viol.* The joust was appointed to take place of a Sunday after dinner, in the public square, before the house where Ovando was quartered. The cavalry and foot-soldiers had their secret instructions. The former were to parade, not merely with reeds or blunted tilting lances, but with weapons of a more deadly character. The foot-soldiers were to come apparently as mere spectators, but likewise armed and ready for action at a concerted signal.

* Las Casas, Hist. Ind., lib. ii., cap. 9.

At the appointed time the square was crowded with the Indians, waiting to see this military spectacle. The caciques were assembled in the house of Ovando, which looked upon the square. None were armed; an unreserved confidence prevailed among them, totally incompatible with the dark treachery of which they were accused. To prevent all suspicion, and take off all appearance of sinister design, Ovando, after dinner, was playing at quoits with some of his principal officers, when the cavalry having arrived in the square, the caciques begged the governor to order the joust to commence.[*] Anacaona, and her beautiful daughter Higuamota, with several of her female attendants, were present and joined in the request.

Ovando left his game and came forward to a conspicuous place. When he saw that everything was disposed according to his orders, he gave the fatal signal. Some say it was by taking hold of a piece of gold which was suspended about his neck;[†] others by laying his hand on the cross of Alcantara, which was embroidered on his habit.[‡] A trumpet was immediately sounded. The house in which Anacaona and all the principal caciques were assembled was surrounded by soldiery, commanded by Diego Velasquez and Rodrigo Mexia-trillo, and no one was permitted to escape. They entered, and seizing upon the caciques, bound them to the posts which supported the roof. Anacaona was led forth a prisoner. The unhappy caciques were then put to horrible tortures, until some of them, in the extremity of anguish, were made to accuse their queen and themselves of the plot with which they were charged. When this cruel mockery of judicial form had been executed, instead of preserving them for after-examination, fire was set to the house, and all the caciques perished miserably in the flames.

While these barbarities were practiced upon the chieftains,

---

† Oviedo, Cronica de las Indias, lib. iii., cap. 12.
‡ Las Casas, Hist. Ind., lib. ii., cap. 9.
§ Charlevoix, Hist. San Domingo, lib. xxiv., p. 285.

a horrible massacre took place among the populace. At the
signal of Ovando, the horsemen rushed into the midst of the
naked and defenseless throng, trampling them under the hoofs
of their steeds, cutting them down with their swords, and
transfixing them with their spears. No mercy was shown
to age or sex; it was a savage and indiscriminate butchery.
Now and then a Spanish horseman, either through an emo-
tion of pity or an impulse of avarice, caught up a child to
bear it off in safety; but it was barbarously pierced by the
lances of his companions. Humanity turns with horror from
such atrocities, and would fain discredit them; but they are
circumstantially and still more minutely recorded by the venerable Bishop Las Casas, who was resident in the island at
the time, and conversant with the principal actors in this
tragedy. He may have colored the picture strongly, in his
usual indignation when the wrongs of the Indians are in
question; yet, from all concurring accounts, and from many
precise facts which speak for themselves, the scene must
have been most sanguinary and atrocious. Oviedo, who is
loud in extolling the justice, and devotion, and charity, and
meekness of Ovando, and his kind treatment of the Indians,
and who visited the province of Xaragua a few years afterward, records several of the preceding circumstances; especially the cold-blooded game of quoits played by the governor on the verge of such a horrible scene, and the burning
of the caciques, to the number, he says, of more than forty.
Diego Mendez, who was at Xaragua at the time, and doubtless present on such an important occasion, says incidentally,
in his last will and testament, that there were eighty-four caciques either burned or hanged.* Las Casas says that there
were eighty who entered the house with Anacaona. The
slaughter of the multitude must have been great; and this
was inflicted on an unarmed and unresisting throng. Several who escaped from the massacre fled in their canoes to

* Relacion hecha por Don Diego Mendez. Navarrete, Col., tom. i.,
p. 314.

an island about eight leagues distant called Guanabo. They were pursued and taken, and condemned to slavery.

As to the princess Anacaona, she was carried in chains to San Domingo. The mockery of a trial was given her, in which she was found guilty on the confessions wrung by tortures from her subjects, and on the testimony of their butchers; and she was ignominiously hanged in the presence of the people whom she had so long and so signally befriended.* Oviedo has sought to throw a stigma on the character of this unfortunate princess, accusing her of great licentiousness; but he was prone to criminate the character of the native princes, who fell victims to the ingratitude and injustice of his countrymen. Contemporary writers of great authority have concurred in representing Anacaona as remarkable for her native propriety and dignity. She was adored by her subjects, so as to hold a kind of dominion over them even during the lifetime of her brother; she is said to have been skilled in composing the areytos or legendary ballads of her nation, and may have conducted much toward producing that superior degree of refinement remarked among her people. Her grace and beauty had made her renowned throughout the island, and had excited the admiration both of the savage and the Spaniard. Her magnanimous spirit was evinced in her amicable treatment of the white men, although her husband, the brave Caonabo, had perished a prisoner in their hands; and defenseless parties of them had been repeatedly in her power, and lived at large in her dominions. After having for several years neglected all safe opportunities of vengeance, she fell a victim to the absurd charge of having conspired against an armed body of nearly four hundred men, seventy of them horsemen; a force sufficient to have subjugated large armies of naked Indians.

After the massacre of Xaragua the destruction of its inhabitants still continued. The favorite nephew of Anacaona,

---

* Oviedo, Cronica de las Indias, lib. iii., cap. 12. Las Casas, Hist. Ind., lib. ii., cap. 9.

the cacique Guaora, who had fled to the mountains, was hunted like a wild beast, until he was taken, and likewise hanged. For six months the Spaniards continued ravaging the country with horse and foot, under pretext of quelling insurrections; for, wherever the affrighted natives took refuge in their despair, herding in dismal caverns and in the fastnesses of the mountains, they were represented as assembling in arms to make a head of rebellion. Having at length hunted them out of their retreats, destroyed many, and reduced the survivors to the most deplorable misery and abject submission, the whole of that part of the island was considered as restored to good order; and in commemoration of this great triumph Ovando founded a town near to the lake, which he called Santa Maria de la Verdadera Paz (St. Mary of the True Peace).*

Such is the tragical history of the delightful region of Xaragua, and of its amiable and hospitable people. A place which the Europeans, by their own account, found a perfect paradise, but which, by their vile passions, they filled with horror and desolation.

CHAPTER THREE

WAR WITH THE NATIVES OF HIGUEY

[1504]

THE subjugation of four of the Indian sovereignties of Hispaniola, and the disastrous fate of their caciques, have been already related. Under the administration of Ovando was also accomplished the downfall of Higuey, the last of those independent districts; a fertile province which comprised the eastern extremity of the island.

The people of Higuey were of a more warlike spirit than

---

* Oviedo, Cronica de las Indias, lib. iii., cap. 12.

those of the other provinces, having learned the effectual use of their weapons from frequent contests with their Carib invaders. They were governed by a cacique named Cotabanama. Las Casas describes this chieftain from actual observation, and draws the picture of a native hero. He was, he says, the strongest of his tribe, and more perfectly formed than one man in a thousand, of any nation whatever. He was taller in stature than the tallest of his countrymen, a yard in breadth from shoulder to shoulder, and the rest of his body in admirable proportion. His aspect was not handsome, but grave and courageous. His bow was not easily bent by a common man; his arrows were three pronged, tipped with the bones of fishes, and his weapons appeared to be intended for a giant. In a word, he was so nobly proportioned as to be the admiration even of the Spaniards.

While Columbus was engaged in his fourth voyage, and shortly after the accession of Ovando to office, there was an insurrection of this cacique and his people. A shallop, with eight Spaniards, was surprised at the small island of Saona, adjacent to Higuey, and all the crew slaughtered. This was in revenge for the death of a cacique, torn to pieces by a dog wantonly set upon him by a Spaniard, and for which the natives had in vain sued for redress.

Ovando immediately dispatched Juan de Esquibel, a courageous officer, at the head of four hundred men, to quell the insurrection and punish the massacre. Cotabanama assembled his warriors, and prepared for vigorous resistance. Distrustful of the mercy of the Spaniards, the chieftain rejected all overtures of peace, and the war was prosecuted with some advantage to the natives. The Indians had now overcome their superstitious awe of the white men as supernatural beings, and though they could ill withstand the superiority of European arms, they manifested a courage and dexterity that rendered them enemies not to be despised. Las Casas and other historians relate a bold and romantic encounter between a single Indian and two mounted cavaliers named Valtenebro and Portevedra, in which the Indian, though pierced through the body by the lances and swords of both his assailants, retained his fierceness, and continued the combat until he fell dead in the possession of all their weapons.* This gallant action, says Las Casas, was public and notorious.

The Indians were soon defeated and driven to their mountain retreats. The Spaniards pursued them into their recesses, discovered their wives and children, wreaked on them the most indiscriminate slaughter, and committed their chieftains to the flames. An aged female cacique of great distinction, named Higuanama, being taken prisoner, was hanged.

A detachment was sent in a caravel to the island of Saona to take particular vengeance for the destruction of the shallop and its crew. The natives made a desperate defense and fled. The island was mountainous and full of caverns, in which the Indians vainly sought for refuge. Six or seven hundred were imprisoned in a dwelling, and all put to the sword or poniarded. Those of the inhabitants who were spared were carried off as slaves, and the island was left desolate and deserted.

The natives of Higuey were driven to despair, seeing that there was no escape for them even in the bowels of the earth;† they sued for peace, which was granted them, and protection promised on condition of their cultivating a large tract of land, and paying a great quantity of bread in tribute. The peace being concluded, Cotabanama visited the Spanish camp, where his gigantic proportions and martial demeanor made him an object of curiosity and admiration. He was received with great distinction by Esquibel, and they exchanged names, an Indian league of fraternity and perpetual friendship. The natives thenceforward called the cacique Juan de Esquibel, and the Spanish commander Cotabanama. Esquibel then built a wooden fortress in an Indian village near the sea, and left in it nine men, with a captain named Martin de Villaman. After this the troops dispersed, every man returning home, with his proportion of slaves gained in this expedition.

---

* Las Casas, Hist. Ind., lib. ii., cap. 8.   † Ibid., ubi sup.

The pacification was not of long continuance. About the time that succors were sent to Columbus, to rescue him from the wrecks of his vessels at Jamaica, a new revolt broke out in Higuey, in consequence of the oppressions of the Spaniards, and a violation of the treaty made by Esquibel. Martin de Villaman demanded that the natives should not only raise the grain stipulated for by the treaty, but convey it to San Domingo, and he treated them with the greatest severity on their refusal. He connived also at the licentious conduct of his men toward the Indian women; the Spaniards often taking from the natives their daughters and sisters, and even their wives.* The Indians, roused at last to fury, rose on their tyrants, slaughtered them, and burned their wooden fortress to the ground. Only one of the Spaniards escaped, and bore the tidings of this catastrophe to the city of San Domingo.

Ovando gave immediate orders to carry fire and sword into the province of Higuey. The Spanish troops mustered from various quarters on the confines of that province, when Juan de Esquibel took the command, and had a great number of Indians with him as allies. The towns of Higuey were generally built among the mountains. Those mountains rose in terraces from ten to fifteen leagues in length and breadth; rough and rocky, interspersed with glens of a red soil, remarkably fertile, where they raised their cassava bread. The ascent from terrace to terrace was about fifty feet; steep and precipitous, formed of the living rock, and resembling a wall wrought with tools into rough diamond points. Each village had four wide streets, a stone's throw in length, forming a cross, the trees being cleared away from them, and from a public square in the center.

When the Spanish troops arrived on the frontiers, alarm fires along the mountains and columns of smoke spread the intelligence by night and day. The old men, the women, and children, were sent off to the forests and caverns, and the

---

* Las Casas, ubi sup.

warriors prepared for battle. The Castilians paused in one of the plains clear of forests, where their horses could be of use. They made prisoners of several of the natives, and tried to learn from them the plans and forces of the enemy. They applied tortures for the purpose, but in vain, so devoted was the loyalty of these people to their caciques. The Spaniards penetrated into the interior. They found the warriors of several towns assembled in one, and drawn up in the streets with their bows and arrows, but perfectly naked, and without defensive armor. They uttered tremendous yells, and discharged a shower of arrows; but from such a distance that they fell short of their foe. The Spaniards replied with their crossbows, and with two or three arquebuses, for at this time they had but few firearms. When the Indians saw several of their comrades fall dead, they took to flight, rarely waiting for the attack with swords; some of the wounded, in whose bodies the arrows from the crossbows had penetrated to the very feather, drew them out with their hands, broke them with their teeth, and, hurling them at the Spaniards with impotent fury, fell dead upon the spot.

The whole force of the Indians was routed and dispersed; each family, or band of neighbors, fled in its own direction, and concealed itself in the fastnesses of the mountains. The Spaniards pursued them, but found the chase difficult amid the close forests, and the broken and stony heights. They took several prisoners as guides, and inflicted incredible torments on them, to compel them to betray their countrymen. They drove them before them, secured by cords fastened round their necks; and some of them, as they passed along the brinks of precipices, suddenly threw themselves headlong down, in hopes of dragging after them the Spaniards. When at length the pursuers came upon the unhappy Indians in their concealments, they spared neither age nor sex; even pregnant women, and mothers with infants in their arms, fell beneath their merciless swords. The cold-blooded acts of cruelty which followed this first slaughter would be shocking to relate.

Hence Esquibel marched to attack the town where Cotabanama resided, and where that cacique had collected a great
force to resist him. He proceeded direct for the place along
the seacoast, and came to where two roads led up the mountain to the town. One of the roads was open and inviting;
the branches of the trees being lopped, and all the underwood
cleared away. Here the Indians had stationed an ambuscade
to take the Spaniards in the rear. The other road was almost
closed up by trees and bushes cut down and thrown across
each other. Esquibel was wary and distrustful; he suspected the stratagem, and chose the encumbered road. The
town was about a league and a half from the sea. The Spaniards made their way with great difficulty for the first half
league. The rest of the road was free from all embarrass-
ment, which confirmed their suspicion of a stratagem. They
now advanced with great rapidity, and, having arrived near
the village, suddenly turned into the other road, took the
party in ambush by surprise, and made great havoc among
them with their crossbows.

The warriors now sallied from their concealment, others
rushed out of the houses into the streets, and discharged
flights of arrows, but from such a distance as generally to
fall harmless. They then approached nearer, and hurled
stones with their hands, being unacquainted with the use of
slings. Instead of being dismayed at seeing their companions fall, it rather increased their fury. An irregular battle,
probably little else than wild skirmishing and bush fighting,
was kept up from two o'clock in the afternoon until night.
Las Casas was present on the occasion, and, from his account,
the Indians must have shown instances of great personal
bravery, though the inferiority of their weapons, and the
want of all defensive armor, rendered their valor totally ineffectual. As the evening shut in, their hostilities gradually
ceased, and they disappeared in the profound gloom and close
thickets of the surrounding forest. A deep silence succeeded
to their yells and war-whoops, and throughout the night the
Spaniards remained in undisturbed possession of the village.

CHAPTER FOUR

CLOSE OF THE WAR WITH HIGUEY—FATE OF COTABANAMA

[1504]

ON the morning after the battle not an Indian was to be seen. Finding that even their great chief, Cotabanama, was incapable of vying with the prowess of the white men, they had given up the contest in despair, and fled to the mountains. The Spaniards, separating into small parties, hunted them with the utmost diligence; their object was to seize the caciques, and, above all, Cotabanama. They explored all the glens and concealed paths leading into the wild recesses where the fugitives had taken refuge. The Indians were cautious and stealthy in their mode of retreating, treading in each other's footprints, so that twenty would make no more track than one, and stepping so lightly as scarce to disturb the herbage; yet there were Spaniards so skilled in hunting Indians that they could trace them even by the turn of a withered leaf, and among the confused tracks of a thousand animals.

They could scent afar off also the smoke of the fires which the Indians made whenever they halted, and thus they would come upon them in their most secret haunts. Sometimes they would hunt down a straggling Indian, and compel him, by torments, to betray the hiding-place of his companions, binding him and driving him before them as a guide. Wherever they discovered one of these places of refuge, filled with the aged and the infirm, with feeble women and helpless children, they massacred them without mercy. They wished to inspire terror throughout the land, and to frighten the whole tribe into submission. They cut off the hands of those whom they took roving at large, and sent them, as they said, to deliver them as letters to their friends, demanding their surrender. Numberless were those, says Las Casas, whose hands were amputated in this manner, and many of them sank down and died by the way, through anguish and loss of blood.

The conquerors delighted in exercising strange and ingenious cruelties. They mingled horrible levity with their blood-thirstiness. They erected gibbets long and low, so that the feet of the sufferers might reach the ground and their death be lingering. They hanged thirteen together, in reverence, says the indignant Las Casas, of our blessed Saviour and the twelve apostles. While their victims were suspended, and still living, they hacked them with their swords, to prove the strength of their arms and the edge of their weapons. They wrapped them in dry straw, and setting fire to it, terminated their existence by the fiercest agony.

These are horrible details, yet a veil is drawn over others still more detestable. They are related circumstantially by Las Casas, who was an eye-witness. He was young at the time, but records them in his advanced years. "All these things," said the venerable bishop, "and others revolting to human nature, did my own eyes behold; and now I almost fear to repeat them, scarce believing myself, or whether I have not dreamed them."*

These details would have been withheld from the present work as disgraceful to human nature, and from an unwillingness to advance anything which might convey a stigma upon a brave and generous nation. But it would be a departure from historical veracity, having the documents before my eyes, to pass silently over transactions so atrocious, and vouched for by witnesses beyond all suspicion of falsehood. Such occurrences show the extremity to which human cruelty may extend, when stimulated by avidity of gain, by a thirst of vengeance, or even by a perverted zeal in the holy cause of religion. Every nation has in turn furnished proofs of this disgraceful truth. As in the present instance, they are com-

* Las Casas, lib. ii., cap. 17, MS.

monly the crimes of individuals rather than of the nation. Yet it behooves governments to keep a vigilant eye upon those to whom they delegate power in remote and helpless colonies. It is the imperious duty of the historian to place these matters upon record, that they may serve as warning beacons to future generations.

Juan de Esquibel found that, with all his severities, it would be impossible to subjugate the tribe of Higuey as long as the cacique Cotabanama was at large. That chieftain had retired to the little island of Saona, about two leagues from the coast of Higuey, in the center of which, amid a labyrinth of rocks and forests, he had taken shelter, with his wife and children, in a vast cavern.

A caravel, recently arrived from the city of San Domingo with supplies for the camp, was employed by Esquibel to entrap the cacique. He knew that the latter kept a vigilant lookout, stationing scouts upon the lofty rocks of his island to watch the movements of the caravel. Esquibel departed by night, therefore, in the vessel, with fifty followers, and keeping under the deep shadows cast by the land, arrived at Saona unperceived, at the dawn of morning. Here he anchored close in with the shore, hid by its cliffs and forests, and landed forty men, before the spies of Cotabanama had taken their station. Two of these were surprised and brought to Esquibel, who, having learned from them that the cacique was at hand, poniarded one of the spies, and bound the other, making him serve as guide.

A number of Spaniards ran in advance, each anxious to signalize himself by the capture of the cacique. They came to two roads, and the whole party pursued that to the right, excepting one Juan Lopez, a powerful man, skillful in Indian warfare. He proceeded in a footpath to the left, winding among little hills, so thickly wooded that it was impossible to see any one at the distance of half a bow shot. Suddenly, in a narrow pass, overshadowed by rocks and trees, he encountered twelve Indian warriors, armed with bows and arrows, and following each other in single file according to

their custom. The Indians were confounded at the sight of
Lopez, imagining that there must be a party of soldiers behind
him. They might readily have transfixed him with their
arrows, but they had lost all presence of mind. He demanded their chieftain. They replied that he was behind,
and, opening to let him pass, Lopez beheld the cacique in
the rear. At sight of the Spaniard Cotabanama bent his
gigantic bow, and was on the point of lanching one of his
three-pronged arrows, but Lopez rushed upon him and
wounded him with his sword. The other Indians, struck
with panic, had already fled. Cotabanama, dismayed at the
keenness of the sword, cried out that he was Juan de Esquibel, claiming respect as having exchanged names with the
Spanish commander. Lopez seized him with one hand by
the hair, and with the other aimed a thrust at his body;
but the cacique struck down the sword with his hand, and,
grappling with his antagonist, threw him with his back upon
the rocks. As they were both men of great power, the struggle was long and violent. The sword was beneath them, but
Cotabanama, seizing the Spaniard by the throat with his
mighty hand, attempted to strangle him. The sound of the
contest brought the other Spaniards to the spot. They found
their companion writhing and gasping, and almost dead in
the grip of the gigantic Indian. They seized the cacique,
bound him, and carried him captive to a deserted Indian village in the vicinity. They found the way to his secret cave,
but his wife and children having received notice of his capture by the fugitive Indians, had taken refuge in another
part of the island. In the cavern was found the chain with
which a number of Indian captives had been bound, who had
risen upon and slain three Spaniards who had them in charge,
and had made their escape to this island. There were also
the swords of the same Spaniards, which they had brought
off as trophies to their cacique. The chain was now employed to manacle Cotabanama.

The Spaniards prepared to execute the chieftain on the
spot, in the center of the deserted village. For this purpose

a pyre was built of logs of wood laid crosswise, in form of a
gridiron, on which he was to be slowly broiled to death. On
further consultation, however, they were induced to forego
the pleasure of this horrible sacrifice. Perhaps they thought
the cacique too important a personage to be executed thus
obscurely. Granting him, therefore, a transient reprieve, they
conveyed him to the caravel and sent him, bound with heavy
chains, to San Domingo. Ovando saw him in his power, and
incapable of doing further harm; but he had not the magnanimity to forgive a fallen enemy, whose only crime was
the defense of his native soil and lawful territory. He ordered him to be publicly hanged like a common culprit.* In
this ignominious manner was the cacique Cotabanama executed, the last of the five sovereign princes of Hayti. His
death was followed by the complete subjugation of his people, and sealed the last struggle of the natives against their
oppressors. The island was almost unpeopled of its original
inhabitants, and meek and mournful submission and mute
despair settled upon the scanty remnant that survived.

Such was the ruthless system which had been pursued,
during the absence of the admiral, by the commander Ovando; this man of boasted prudence and moderation, who was
sent to reform the abuses of the island, and above all, to redress the wrongs of the natives. The system of Columbus
may have borne hard upon the Indians, born and brought
up in untasked freedom, but it was never cruel nor sanguinary. He inflicted no wanton massacres nor vindictive punishments; his desire was to cherish and civilize the Indians,
and to render them useful subjects; not to oppress, and persecute, and destroy them. When he beheld the desolation
that had swept them from the land during his suspension
from authority, he could not restrain the strong expression
of his feelings. In a letter written to the king after his return to Spain, he thus expresses himself on the subject: "The
Indians of Hispaniola were and are the riches of the island;

---

* Las Casas, Hist. Ind., lib. ii., cap. 18.

for it is they who cultivate and make the bread and the provisions for the Christians; who dig the gold from the mines, and perform all the offices and labors both of men and beasts. I am informed that, since I left this island, six parts out of seven of the natives are dead; all through ill treatment and inhumanity; some by the sword, others by blows and cruel usage, others through hunger. The greater part have perished in the mountains and glens, whither they had fled, from not being able to support the labor imposed upon them." For his own part, he added, although he had sent many Indians to Spain to be sold, it was always with a view to their being instructed in the Christian faith, and in civilized arts and usages, and afterward sent back to their island to assist in civilizing their countrymen.[*]

The brief view that has been given of the policy of Ovando on certain points on which Columbus was censured, may enable the reader to judge more correctly of the conduct of the latter. It is not to be measured by the standard of right and wrong established in the present more enlightened age. We must consider him in connection with the era in which he lived. By comparing his measures with those men of his own times praised for their virtues and abilities, placed in precisely his own situation, and placed there expressly to correct his faults, we shall be the better able to judge how virtuously and wisely, under the peculiar circumstances of the case, he may be considered to have governed.

---

[*] Las Casas, Hist. Ind., lib. ii., cap. 36.

BOOK EIGHTEEN

CHAPTER ONE

DEPARTURE OF COLUMBUS FOR SAN DOMINGO—HIS RETURN
TO SPAIN

THE arrival at Jamaica of the two vessels under the command of Salcedo had caused a joyful reverse in the situation of Columbus. He hastened to leave the wreck in which he had been so long immured, and hoisting his flag on board of one of the ships, felt as if the career of enterprise and glory were once more open to him. The late partisans of Porras, when they heard of the arrival of the ships, came wistful and abject to the harbor, doubting how far they might trust to the magnanimity of a man whom they had so greatly injured, and who had now an opportunity of vengeance. The generous mind, however, never harbors revenge in the hour of returning prosperity; but feels noble satisfaction in sharing its happiness even with its enemies. Columbus forgot, in his present felicity, all that he had suffered from these men; he ceased to consider them enemies, now that they had lost the power to injure; and he not only fulfilled all that he had promised them, by taking them on board the ships, but relieved their necessities from his own purse, until their return to Spain; and afterward took unwearied pains to recommend them to the bounty of the sovereigns. Francisco Porras alone continued a prisoner, to be tried by the tribunals of his country.

Oviedo assures us that the Indians wept when they beheld the departure of the Spaniards; still considering them as beings from the skies. From the admiral, it is true, they had experienced nothing but just and gentle treatment, and continual benefits; and the idea of his immediate influence with the Deity, manifested on the memorable occasion of the eclipse, may have made them consider him as more than human, and his presence as propitious to their island; but it is not easy to believe that a lawless gang like that of Porras could have been ranging for months among their villages, without giving cause for the greatest joy at their departure.

On the 28th of June the vessels set sail for San Domingo. The adverse winds and currents which had opposed Columbus throughout this ill-starred expedition still continued to harass him. After a weary struggle of several weeks he reached, on the 3d of August, the little island of Beata, on the coast of Hispaniola. Between this place and San Domingo the currents are so violent that vessels are often detained months, waiting for sufficient wind to enable them to stem the stream. Hence Columbus dispatched a letter by land to Ovando, to inform him of his approach, and to remove certain absurd suspicions of his views, which he had learned from Salcedo were still entertained by the governor; who feared his arrival in the island might produce factions and disturbances. In this letter he expresses, with his usual warmth and simplicity, the joy he felt at his deliverance, which was so great, he says, that, since the arrival of Diego de Salcedo with succor, he had scarcely been able to sleep. The letter had barely time to precede the writer, for, a favorable wind springing up, the vessels again made sail, and, on the 13th of August, anchored in the harbor of San Domingo.

If it is the lot of prosperity to awaken envy and excite detraction, it is certainly the lot of misfortune to atone for a multitude of faults. San Domingo had been the very hot-bed of sedition against Columbus in the day of his power; he had been hurried from it in ignominious chains, amid the shouts and taunts of the triumphant rabble; he had been excluded from its harbor when, as commander of a squadron, he craved shelter from an impending tempest; but now that he arrived in its waters, a broken down and shipwrecked man, all past hostility was overpowered by the popular sense of his late disasters. There was a momentary burst of enthusiasm in his favor; what had been denied to his merit was granted to his misfortune; and even the envious, appeased by his present reverses, seemed to forgive him for having once been so triumphant.

The governor and principal inhabitants came forth to meet him, and received him with signal distinction. He was lodged as a guest in the house of Ovando, who treated him with the utmost courtesy and attention. The governor was a shrewd and discreet man, and much of a courtier; but there were causes of jealousy and distrust between him and Columbus too deep to permit of cordial intercourse. The admiral and his son Fernando always pronounced the civility of Ovando overstrained and hypocritical; intended to obliterate the remembrance of past neglect, and to conceal lurking enmity. While he professed the utmost friendship and sympathy for the admiral, he set at liberty the traitor Porras, who was still a prisoner, to be taken to Spain for trial. He also talked of punishing those of the admiral's people who had taken arms in his defense, and in the affray at Jamaica had killed several of the mutineers. These circumstances were loudly complained of by Columbus; but, in fact, they rose out of a question of jurisdiction between him and the governor. Their powers were so undefined as to clash with each other, and they were both disposed to be extremely punctilious. Ovando assumed a right to take cognizance of all transactions at Jamaica; as happening within the limits of his government, which included all the islands and Terra Firma. Columbus, on the other hand, asserted the absolute command, and the jurisdiction both civil and criminal given to him by the sovereigns, over all persons who sailed in his expedition, from the time of departure until their return to Spain. To prove this, he produced his letter of instructions. The governor heard him with great courtesy and a smiling countenance; but observed that the letter of instructions gave him no authority within the bounds of his government.* He relin-

---

* Letter of Columbus to his son Diego, Seville, Nov. 21, 1504. Navarrete, Colec., tom. i.

quished the idea, however, of investigating the conduct of the followers of Columbus, and sent Porras to Spain to be examined by the board which had charge of the affairs of the Indies.

The sojourn of Columbus at San Domingo was but little calculated to yield him satisfaction. He was grieved at the desolation of the island by the oppressive treatment of the natives, and the horrible massacre which had been perpetrated by Ovando and his agents. He had fondly hoped, at one time, to render the natives civilized, industrious, and tributary subjects to the crown, and to derive from their well-regulated labor a great and steady revenue. How different had been the event! The five great tribes which peopled the mountains and the valleys at the time of the discovery, and rendered, by their mingled towns and villages and tracts of cultivation, the rich levels of the vegas so many "painted gardens," had almost all passed away, and the native princes had perished chiefly by violent or ignominious deaths. Columbus regarded the affairs of the island with a different eye from Ovando. He had a paternal feeling for its prosperity, and his fortunes were implicated in its judicious management. He complained, in subsequent letters to the sovereigns, that all the public affairs were ill-conducted; that the ore collected lay unguarded in large quantities in houses slightly built and thatched, inviting depredation; that Ovando was unpopular, the people were dissolute, and the property of the crown and the security of the island in continual risk from mutiny and sedition.* While he saw all this, he had no power to interfere, and any observation or remonstrance on his part was ill received by the governor.

He found his own immediate concerns in great confusion. His rents and dues were either uncollected, or he could not obtain a clear account and a full liquidation of them. Whatever he could collect was appropriated to the fitting out of the

---

* Letter of Columbus to his son Diego, dated Seville, 3d Dec., 1504. Navarrete, tom. i., p. 341.

vessels which were to convey himself and his crews to Spain. He accuses Ovando, in his subsequent letters, of having neglected, if not sacrificed, his interests during his long absence, and of having impeded those who were appointed to attend to his concerns. That he had some grounds for these complaints would appear from two letters still extant,* written by Queen Isabella to Ovando, on the 27th of November, 1503, in which she informs him of the complaint of Alonzo Sanchez de Carvajal that he was impeded in collecting the rents of the admiral; and expressly commands Ovando to observe the capitulations granted to Columbus; to respect his agents, and to facilitate, instead of obstructing, his concerns. These letters, while they imply ungenerous conduct on the part of the governor toward his illustrious predecessor, evince likewise the personal interest taken by Isabella in the affairs of Columbus during his absence. She had, in fact, signified her displeasure at his being excluded from the port of San Domingo, when he applied there for succor for his squadron, and for shelter from a storm, and had censured Ovando for not taking his advice and detaining the fleet of Bobadilla, by which it would have escaped its disastrous fate.† And here it may be observed that the sanguinary acts of Ovando toward the natives, in particular the massacre at Xaragua and the execution of the unfortunate Anacaona, awakened equal horror and indignation in Isabella; she was languishing on her deathbed when she received the intelligence, and with her dying breath she exacted a promise from King Ferdinand that Ovando should immediately be recalled from his government. The promise was tardily and reluctantly fulfilled, after an interval of about four years, and not until induced by other circumstances; for Ovando contrived to propitiate the monarch by forcing a revenue from the island.

The continual misunderstandings between the admiral and the governor, though always qualified on the part of the latter with great complaisance, induced Columbus to

---

* Navarrete, Colec., tom. ii., decad. 151, 152.

† Herrera, Hist. Ind., decad. i., lib. v., cap. 12.

hasten as much as possible his departure from the island. The ship in which he had returned from Jamaica was repaired and fitted out, and put under the command of the adelantado; another vessel was freighted, in which Columbus embarked with his son and his domestics. The greater part of his late crews remained at San Domingo; as they were in great poverty, he relieved their necessities from his own purse, and advanced the funds necessary for the voyage home of those who chose to return. Many thus relieved by his generosity had been among the most violent of the rebels.

On the 12th of September he set sail; but had scarcely left the harbor, when, in a sudden squall, the mast of his ship was carried away. He immediately went with his family on board of the vessel commanded by the adelantado, and, sending back the damaged ship to port, continued on his course. Throughout the voyage he experienced the most tempestuous weather. In one storm the mainmast was sprung in four places. He was confined to his bed at the time by the gout; by his advice, however, and the activity of the adelantado, the damage was skillfully repaired; the mast was shortened; the weak parts were fortified by wood taken from the castles or cabins, which the vessels in those days carried on the prow and stern; and the whole was well secured by cords. They were still more damaged in a succeeding tempest, in which the ship sprung her foremast. In this crippled state they had to traverse seven hundred leagues of a stormy ocean. Fortune continued to persecute Columbus to the end of this, his last and most disastrous expedition. For several weeks he was tempest-tossed—suffering at the same time the most excruciating pains from his malady —until, on the seventh day of November, his crazy and shattered bark anchored in the harbor of San Lucar. Hence he had himself conveyed to Seville, where he hoped to enjoy repose of mind and body, and to recruit his health after such a long series of fatigues, anxieties, and hardships.*

---

* Hist. del Almirante, cap. 108. Las Casas, Hist. Ind., lib. ii., cap. 36.

CHAPTER TWO

ILLNESS OF COLUMBUS AT SEVILLE—APPLICATION TO THE CROWN FOR A RESTITUTION OF HIS HONORS— DEATH OF ISABELLA

[1504]

BROKEN by age and infirmities, and worn down by the toils and hardships of his recent expedition, Columbus had looked forward to Seville as to a haven of rest, where he might repose a while from his troubles. Care and sorrow, however, followed him by sea and land. In varying the scene he but varied the nature of his distress. "Wearisome days and nights" were appointed to him for the remainder of his life; and the very margin of his grave was destined to be strewed with thorns.

On arriving at Seville, he found all his affairs in confusion. Ever since he had been sent home in chains from San Domingo, when his house and effects had been taken possession of by Bobadilla, his rents and dues had never been properly collected; and such as had been gathered had been retained in the hands of the governor Ovando. "I have much vexation from the governor," says he in a letter to his son Diego.* "All tell me that I have there eleven or twelve thousand castellanos; and I have not received a quarto. . . . I know well that since my departure he must have received upward of five thousand castellanos." He entreated that a letter might be written by the king, commanding the payment of these arrears without delay; for his agents would not venture even to speak to Ovando on the subject, unless empowered by a letter from the sovereign.

Columbus was not of a mercenary spirit; but his rank

---

* Let. Seville, 13 Dec., 1504. Navarrete, v. i., p. 343.

and situation required large expenditure. The world thought
him in the possession of sources of inexhaustible wealth; but
as yet those sources had furnished him but precarious and
scanty streams. His last voyage had exhausted his finances
and involved him in perplexities. All that he had been able
to collect of the money due to him in Hispaniola, to the
amount of twelve hundred castellanos, had been expended in
bringing home many of his late crew, who were in distress;
and for the greater part of the sum the crown remained his
debtor. While struggling to obtain his mere pecuniary dues,
he was absolutely suffering a degree of penury. He repeatedly urges the necessity of economy to his son Diego,
until he can obtain a restitution of his property and the payment of his arrears. "I receive nothing of the revenue due
to me," says he in one letter; "I live by borrowing." "Little have I profited," he adds, in another, "by twenty years
of service, with such toils and perils; since, at present, I do
not own a roof in Spain. If I desire to eat or sleep, I have
no resort but an inn; and, for the most times, have not
wherewithal to pay my bill."

Yet in the midst of these personal distresses he was more
solicitous for the payment of his seamen than of himself. He
wrote strongly and repeatedly to the sovereigns, entreating
the discharge of their arrears, and urged his son Diego, who
was at court, to exert himself in their behalf. "They are
poor," said he, "and it is now nearly three years since they
left their homes. They have endured infinite toils and perils,
and they bring invaluable tidings, for which their majesties
ought to give thanks to God and rejoice." Notwithstanding
his generous solicitude for these men, he knew several of
them to have been his enemies; nay, that some of them were
at this very time disposed to do him harm rather than good;
such was the magnanimity of his spirit and his forgiving
disposition.

The same zeal, also, for the interests of his sovereigns,
which had ever actuated his loyal mind, mingled with his
other causes of solicitude. He represented, in his letter to

the king, the mismanagement of the royal rents in Hispaniola, under the administration of Ovando. Immense quantities of ore lay unprotected in slightly built houses, and liable to depredations. It required a person of vigor, and one who had an individual interest in the property of the island, to restore its affairs to order, and draw from it the immense revenues which it was capable of yielding; and Columbus plainly intimated that he was the proper person.

In fact, as to himself, it was not so much pecuniary indemnification that he sought as the restoration of his offices and dignities. He regarded them as the trophies of his illustrious achievements; he had received the royal promise that he should be reinstated in them; and he felt that as long as they were withheld, a tacit censure rested upon his name. Had he not been proudly impatient on this subject he would have belied the loftiest part of his character; for he who can be indifferent to the wreath of triumph is deficient in the noble ambition which incites to glorious deeds.

The unsatisfactory replies received to his letters disquieted his mind. He knew that he had active enemies at court ready to turn all things to his disadvantage, and felt the importance of being there in person to defeat their machinations; but his infirmities detained him at Seville. He made an attempt to set forth on the journey, but the severity of the winter and the virulence of his malady obliged him to relinquish it in despair. All that he could do was to reiterate his letters to the sovereigns, and to entreat the intervention of his few but faithful friends. He feared the disastrous occurrences of the last voyage might be represented to his prejudice. The great object of the expedition, the discovery of a strait opening from the Caribbean to a southern sea, had failed. The secondary object, the acquisition of gold, had not been completed. He had discovered the gold mines of Veragua, it is true; but he had brought home no treasure; because, as he said, in one of his letters, "I would not rob nor outrage the country; since reason requires that it should be settled, and then the gold may be procured without violence."

He was especially apprehensive that the violent scenes in the island of Jamaica might, by the perversity of his enemies and the effrontery of the delinquents, be wrested into matters of accusation against him, as had been the case with the rebellion of Roldan. Porras, the ringleader of the late faction, had been sent home by Ovando, to appear before the board of the Indies, but without any written process, setting forth the offenses charged against him. While at Jamaica Columbus had ordered an inquest of the affair to be taken; but the notary of the squadron who took it, and the papers which he drew up, were on board of the ship in which the admiral had sailed from Hispaniola, but which had put back dismasted. No cognizance of the case, therefore, was taken by the Council of the Indies; and Porras went at large, armed with the power and the disposition to do mischief. Being related to Morales, the royal treasurer, he had access to people in place, and an opportunity of enlisting their opinions and prejudices on his side. Columbus wrote to Morales, inclosing a copy of the petition which the rebels had sent to him when in Jamaica, in which they acknowledged their culpability, and implored his forgiveness; and he entreated the treasurer not to be swayed by the representations of his relative, nor to pronounce an opinion unfavorable to him, until he had an opportunity of being heard.

The faithful and indefatigable Diego Mendez was at this time at the court, as well as Alonzo Sanchez de Carvajal, and an active friend of Columbus named Geronimo. They could bear the most important testimony as to his conduct, and he wrote to his son Diego to call upon them for their good offices. "I trust," said he, "that the truth and diligence of Diego Mendez will be of as much avail as the lies of Porras." Nothing can surpass the affecting earnestness and simplicity of the general declaration of loyalty contained in one of his letters. "I have served their majesties," says he, "with as much zeal and diligence as if it had been to gain Paradise; and if I have failed in anything, it has been because my knowledge and powers went no further."

While reading these touching appeals we can scarcely realize the fact that the dejected individual thus wearily and vainly applying for unquestionable rights, and pleading almost like a culprit, in cases wherein he had been flagrantly injured, was the same who but a few years previously had been received at this very court with almost regal honors, and idolized as a national benefactor; that this, in a word, was Columbus, the discoverer of the New World; broken in health, and impoverished in his old days by his very discoveries.

At length the caravel bringing the official proceedings relative to the brothers Porras arrived at the Algarves, in Portugal, and Columbus looked forward with hope that all matters would soon be placed in a proper light. His anxiety to get to court became every day more intense. A litter was provided to convey him thither, and was actually at the door, but the inclemency of the weather and his increasing infirmities obliged him again to abandon the journey. His resource of letter-writing began to fail him: he could only write at night, for in the daytime the severity of his malady deprived him of the use of his hands. The tidings from the court were every day more and more adverse to his hopes; the intrigues of his enemies were prevailing; the cold-hearted Ferdinand treated all his applications with indifference; the generous Isabella lay dangerously ill. On her justice and magnanimity he still relied for the full restoration of his rights, and the redress of all his grievances. "May it please the Holy Trinity," says he, "to restore our sovereign queen to health; for by her will everything be adjusted which is now in confusion." Alas! while writing that letter, his noble benefactress was a corpse!

The health of Isabella had long been undermined by the shocks of repeated domestic calamities. The death of her only son, the Prince Juan; of her beloved daughter and bosom friend, the Princess Isabella; and of her grandson and prospective heir, the Prince Miguel, had been three cruel wounds to a heart full of the tenderest sensibility. To these was added the constant grief caused by the evident infirmity of intellect of her daughter Juana, and the domestic unhappiness of that princess with her husband, the archduke Philip. The desolation which walks through palaces admits not the familiar sympathies and sweet consolations which alleviate the sorrows of common life. Isabella pined in state, amid the obsequious homages of a court, surrounded by the trophies of a glorious and successful reign, and placed at the summit of earthly grandeur. A deep and incurable melancholy settled upon her, which undermined her constitution, and gave a fatal acuteness to her bodily maladies. After four months of illness she died, on the 26th of November, 1504, at Medina del Campo, in the fifty-fourth year of her age; but long before her eyes closed upon the world her heart had closed on all its pomps and vanities. "Let my body," said she in her will, "be interred in the monastery of San Francisco, which is in the Alhambra of the city of Granada, in a low sepulcher, without any monument except a plain stone, with the inscription cut on it. But I desire and command that if the king, my lord, should choose a sepulcher in any church or monastery in any other part or place of these my kingdoms, my body be transported thither and buried beside the body of his highness; so that the union we have enjoyed while living, and which, through the mercy of God, we hope our souls will experience in heaven, may be represented by our bodies in the earth."*

Such was one of several passages in the will of this admirable woman, which bespoke the chastened humility of her heart; and in which, as has been well observed, the affections of conjugal love were delicately entwined with piety,

---

* The dying command of Isabella has been obeyed. The author of this work has seen her tomb in the royal chapel of the Cathedral of Granada, in which her remains are interred with those of Ferdinand. Their effigies, sculptured in white marble, lie side by side on a magnificent sepulcher. The altar of the chapel is adorned with bass-reliefs representing the conquest and surrender of Granada.

and with the most tender melancholy.* She was one of the purest spirits that ever ruled over the destinies of a nation. Had she been spared, her benignant vigilance would have prevented many a scene of horror in the colonization of the New World, and might have softened the lot of its native inhabitants. As it is, her fair name will ever shine with celestial radiance in the dawning of its history.

The news of the death of Isabella reached Columbus when he was writing a letter to his son Diego. He notices it in a postscript or memorandum, written in the haste and brevity of the moment, but in beautifully touching and mournful terms. "A memorial," he writes, "for thee, my dear son Diego, of what is at present to be done. The principal thing is to commend affectionately, and with great devotion, the soul of the queen our sovereign to God. Her life was always catholic and holy, and prompt to all things in His holy service; for this reason we may rest assured that she is received into His glory, and beyond the cares of this rough and weary world. The next thing is to watch and labor in all matters for the service of our sovereign the king, and to endeavor to alleviate his grief. His majesty is the head of Christendom. Remember the proverb which says, when the head suffers all the members suffer. Therefore, all good Christians should pray for his health and long life; and we who are in his employ ought more than others to do this with all study and diligence." †

It is impossible to read this mournful letter without being moved by the simply eloquent yet artless language in which Columbus expresses his tenderness for the memory of his benefactress, his weariness under the gathering cares and ills of life, and his persevering and enduring loyalty toward the sovereign who was so ungratefully neglecting him. It is in these unstudied and confidential letters that we read the heart of Columbus.

---

* Elogio de la Reina Catolica por D. Diego Clemencin. Illustration 19.

† Letter to his son Diego, Dec. 3, 1504.

CHAPTER THREE

COLUMBUS ARRIVES AT COURT—FRUITLESS APPLICATION
TO THE KING FOR REDRESS

[1505]

THE death of Isabella was a fatal blow to the fortunes of Columbus. While she lived he had everything to anticipate from her high sense of justice, her regard for her royal word, her gratitude for his services and her admiration of his character. With her illness, however, his interests had languished, and when she died he was left to the justice and generosity of Ferdinand!

During the remainder of the winter and a part of the spring he continued at Seville, detained by painful illness, and endeavoring to obtain redress from the government by ineffectual letters. His brother the adelantado, who supported him with his accustomed fondness and devotion through all his trials, proceeded to court to attend to his interests, taking with him the admiral's younger son Fernando, then aged about seventeen. The latter, the affec-tionate father repeatedly represents to his son Diego as a man in understanding and conduct, though but a stripling in years; and inculcates the strongest fraternal attachment, alluding to his own brethren with one of those simply eloquent and affecting expressions which stamp his heart upon his letters. "To thy brother conduct thyself as the elder brother should unto the younger. Thou hast no other, and I praise God that this is such a one as thou dost need. Ten brothers would not be too many for thee. Never have I found a better friend to right or left than my brothers."

Among the persons whom Columbus employed at this time in his missions to the court was Amerigo Vespucci. He describes him as a worthy but unfortunate man, who had not profited as much as he deserved by his undertakings, and who had always been disposed to render him service. His object in employing him appears to have been to prove the value of his last voyage, and that he had been in the most opulent parts of the New World; Vespucci having since touched upon the same coast, in a voyage with Alonzo de Ojeda.

One circumstance occurred at this time which shed a gleam of hope and consolation over his gloomy prospects. Diego de Deza, who had been for some time Bishop of Palencia, was expected at court. This was the same worthy friar who had aided him to advocate his theory before the board of learned men at Salamanca, and had assisted him with his purse when making his proposals to the Spanish court. He had just been promoted and made Archbishop of Seville, but had not yet been installed in office. Columbus directs his son Diego to intrust his interests to this worthy prelate. "Two things," says he, "require particular attention. Ascertain whether the queen, who is now with God, has said anything concerning me in her testament, and stimulate the Bishop of Palencia, he who was the cause that their highnesses obtained possession of the Indies, who induced me to remain in Castile when I was on the road to leave it." * In another letter he says: "If the Bishop of Palencia has arrived, or should arrive, tell him how much I have been gratified by his prosperity, and that if I come, I shall lodge with his grace, even though he should not invite me, for we must return to our ancient fraternal affection."

The incessant applications of Columbus, both by letter and by the intervention of friends, appear to have been listened to with cool indifference. No compliance was yielded to his requests, and no deference was paid to his opinions, on various points, concerning which he interested himself. New instructions were sent out to Ovando, but not a word of their purport was mentioned to the admiral. It was proposed to

---

* Letter of December 21, 1504. Navarrete, tom. i., p. 346.

send out three bishops, and he entreated in vain to be heard previous to their election. In short, he was not in any way consulted in the affairs of the New World. He felt deeply this neglect, and became every day more impatient of his absence from court. To enable himself to perform the journey with more ease, he applied for permission to use a mule, a royal ordinance having prohibited the employment of those animals under the saddle, in consequence of their universal use having occasioned a decline in the breed of horses. A royal permission was accordingly granted to Columbus, in consideration that his age and infirmities incapacitated him from riding on horseback; but it was a considerable time before the state of his health would permit him to avail himself of that privilege.

The foregoing particulars, gleaned from letters of Columbus recently discovered, show the real state of his affairs, and the mental and bodily affliction sustained by him during his winter's residence at Seville, on his return from his last disastrous voyage. He has generally been represented as reposing there from his toils and troubles. Never was honorable repose more merited, more desired, and less enjoyed.

It was not until the month of May that he was able, in company with his brother the adelantado, to accomplish his journey to court, at that time held at Segovia. He who but a few years before had entered the city of Barcelona in triumph, attended by the nobility and chivalry of Spain, and hailed with rapture by the multitude, now arrived within the gates of Segovia, a wayworn, melancholy, and neglected man; oppressed more by sorrow than even by his years and infirmities. When he presented himself at court he met with none of that distinguished attention, that cordial kindness, that cherishing sympathy, which his unparalleled services and his recent sufferings had merited.[*]

The selfish Ferdinand had lost sight of his past services,

---

[*] Las Casas, Hist. Ind., lib. ii., cap. 37. Herrera, Hist. Ind., decad. i., lib. vi., cap. 13.

in what appeared to him the inconvenience of his present demands. He received him with many professions of kindness; but with those cold, ineffectual smiles which pass like wintry sunshine over the countenance, and convey no warmth to the heart.

The admiral now gave a particular account of his late voyage, describing the great tract of Terra Firma, which he had explored, and the riches of the province of Veragua. He related also the disaster sustained in the island of Jamaica; the insurrection of the Porras and their band; and all the other griefs and troubles of this unfortunate expedition. He had but a cold-hearted auditor in the king; and the benignant Isabella was no more at hand to soothe him with a smile of kindness or a tear of sympathy. "I know not," says the venerable Las Casas, "what could cause this dislike and this want of princely countenance in the king toward one who had rendered him such pre-eminent benefits; unless it was that his mind was swayed by the false testimonies which had been brought against the admiral; of which I have been enabled to learn something from persons much in favor with the sovereigns." *

After a few days had elapsed Columbus urged his suit in form, reminding the king of all that he had done, and all that had been promised him under the royal word and seal, and supplicating that the restitutions and indemnifications which had been so frequently solicited might be awarded to him; offering in return to serve his majesty devotedly for the short time he had yet to live; and trusting, from what he felt within him, and from what he thought he knew with certainty, to render services which should surpass all that he had yet performed a hundred-fold. The king, in reply, acknowledged the greatness of his merits, and the importance of his services, but observed that, for the more satisfactory adjustment of his claims, it would be advisable to refer all points in dispute to the decision of some discreet and able

---

* Las Casas, Hist. Ind., lib. ii., cap. 37, MS.

person. The admiral immediately proposed as arbiter his friend the archbishop of Seville, Don Diego de Deza, one of the most able and upright men about the court, devotedly loyal, high in the confidence of the king, and one who had always taken great interest in the affairs of the New World. The king consented to the arbitration, but artfully extended it to questions which he knew would never be put at issue by Columbus; among these was his claim to the restoration of his office of viceroy. To this Columbus objected with becoming spirit, as compromising a right which was too clearly defined and solemnly established, to be put for a moment in dispute. It was the question of rents and revenues alone, he observed, which he was willing to submit to the decision of a learned man, not that of the government of the Indies. As the monarch persisted, however, in embracing both questions in the arbitration, the proposed measure was never carried into effect.

It was, in fact, on the subject of his dignities alone that Columbus was tenacious; all other matters he considered of minor importance. In a conversation with the king he abso·lutely disavowed all wish of entering into any suit or pleading as to his pecuniary dues; on the contrary, he offered to put all his privileges and writings into the hands of his sovereign, and to receive out of the dues arising from them whatever his majesty might think proper to award. All that he claimed without qualification or reserve were his official dignities, assured to him under the royal seal with all the solemnity of a treaty. He entreated, at all events, that these matters might speedily be decided, so that he might be released from a state of miserable suspense, and enabled to retire to some quiet corner, in search of that tranquillity and repose necessary to his fatigues and his infirmities.

To this frank appeal to his justice and generosity, Ferdinand replied with many courteous expressions, and with those general evasive promises which beguile the ear of the court applicant, but convey no comfort to his heart. "As far as actions went," observes Las Casas, "the king not merely showed him no signs of favor, but, on the contrary, discountenanced him as much as possible; yet he was never wanting in complimentary expressions."

Many months were passed by Columbus in unavailing solicitation, during which he continued to receive outward demonstrations of respect from the king, and due attention from Cardinal Ximenes, Archbishop of Toledo, and other principal personages; but he had learned to appreciate and distrust the hollow civilities of a court. His claims were referred to a tribunal called "The council of the discharges of the conscience of the deceased queen and of the king." This is a kind of tribunal commonly known by the name of the Junta de Descargos, composed of persons nominated by the sovereign to superintend the accomplishment of the last will of his predecessor and the discharge of his debts. Two consultations were held by this body, but nothing was determined. The wishes of the king were too well known to be thwarted. "It was believed," says Las Casas, "that if the king could have done so with a safe conscience, and without detriment to his fame, he would have respected few or none of the privileges which he and the queen had conceded to the admiral, and which had been so justly merited." *

Columbus still flattered himself that, his claims being of such importance, and touching a question of sovereignty, the adjustment of them might be only postponed by the king until he could consult with his daughter Juana, who had succeeded to her mother as Queen of Castile, and who was daily expected from Flanders with her husband, King Philip. He endeavored, therefore, to bear his delays with patience; but he had no longer the physical strength and glorious anticipations which once sustained him through his long application at this court. Life itself was drawing to a close.

He was once more confined to his bed by a tormenting attack of the gout, aggravated by the sorrows and disappointments which preyed upon his heart. From this couch

_____

* Las Casas, Hist. Ind., lib. ii., cap. 37.

of anguish he addressed one more appeal to the justice of the king. He no longer petitioned for himself; it was for his son Diego. Nor did he dwell upon his pecuniary dues; it was the honorable trophies of his services which he wished to secure and perpetuate in his family. He entreated that his son Diego might be appointed, in his place, to the government of which he had been so wrongfully deprived. "This," he said, "is a matter which concerns my honor; as to all the rest, do as your majesty may think proper; give or withhold, as may be most for your interest, and I shall be content. I believe the anxiety caused by the delay of this affair is the principal cause of my ill health." A petition to the same purpose was presented at the same time by his son Diego, offering to take with him such persons for counselors as the king should appoint, and to be guided by their advice.

These petitions were treated by Ferdinand with his usual professions and evasions. "The more applications were made to him," observes Las Casas, "the more favorably did he reply; but still he delayed, hoping, by exhausting their patience, to induce them to waive their privileges and accept in place thereof titles and estates in Castile." Columbus rejected all propositions of the kind with indignation, as calculated to compromise those titles which were the trophies of his achievements. He saw, however, that all further hope of redress from Ferdinand was vain. From the bed to which he was confined he addressed a letter to his constant friend Diego de Deza, expressive of his despair. "It appears that his majesty does not think fit to fulfill that which he, with the queen, who is now in glory, promised me by word and seal. For me to contend for the contrary would be to contend with the wind. I have done all that I could do. I leave the rest to God, whom I have ever found propitious to me in my necessities."*

The cold and calculating Ferdinand beheld this illustrious man sinking under infirmity of body, heightened by that

---

* Navarrete, Colec., tom. i.

deferred hope which "maketh the heart sick." A little more delay, a little more disappointment, and a little longer infliction of ingratitude, and this loyal and generous heart would cease to beat: he should then be delivered from the just claims of a well-tried servant, who, in ceasing to be useful, was considered by him to have become importunate.

CHAPTER FOUR

DEATH OF COLUMBUS

In the midst of illness and despondency, when both life and hope were expiring in the bosom of Columbus, a new gleam was awakened and blazed up for the moment with characteristic fervor. He heard with joy of the landing of King Philip and Queen Juana, who had just arrived from Flanders to take possession of their throne of Castile. In the daughter of Isabella he trusted once more to find a patroness and a friend. King Ferdinand and all the court repaired to Laredo to receive the youthful sovereigns. Columbus would gladly have done the same, but he was confined to his bed by a severe return of his malady; neither in his painful and helpless situation could he dispense with the aid and ministry of his son Diego. His brother, the adelantado, therefore, his main dependence in all emergencies, was sent to represent him, and to present his homage and congratulations. Columbus wrote by him to the new king and queen, expressing his grief at being prevented by illness from coming in person to manifest his devotion, but begging to be considered among the most faithful of their subjects. He expressed a hope that he should receive at their hands the restitution of his honors and estates, and assured them that, though cruelly tortured at present by disease, he would yet be able to render them services, the like of which had never been witnessed.

Such was the last sally of his sanguine and unconquerable spirit; which, disregarding age and infirmities, and all past sorrows and disappointments, spoke from his dying bed with all the confidence of youthful hope; and talked of still greater enterprises, as if he had a long and vigorous life before him. The adelantado took leave of his brother, whom he was never to behold again, and set out on his mission to the new sovereigns. He experienced the most gracious reception. The claims of the admiral were treated with great attention by the young king and queen, and flattering hopes were given of a speedy and prosperous termination to his suit.

In the meantime the cares and troubles of Columbus were drawing to a close. The momentary fire which had reanimated him was soon quenched by accumulating infirmities. Immediately after the departure of the adelantado, his illness increased in violence. His last voyage had shattered beyond repair a frame already worn and wasted by a life of hardship; and continual anxieties robbed him of that sweet repose so necessary to recruit the weariness and debility of age. The cold ingratitude of his sovereign chilled his heart. The continued suspension of his honors, and the enmity and defamation experienced at every turn, seemed to throw a shadow over that glory which had been the great object of his ambition. This shadow, it is true, could be but of transient duration; but it is difficult for the most illustrious man to look beyond the present cloud which may obscure his fame, and anticipate its permanent luster in the admiration of posterity.

Being admonished by failing strength and increasing sufferings that his end was approaching, he prepared to leave his affairs in order for the benefit of his successors.

It is said that on the 4th of May he wrote an informal testamentary codicil on the blank page of a little breviary, given him by Pope Alexander VI. In this he bequeathed that book to the Republic of Genoa, which he also appointed successor to his privileges and dignities, on the extinction of his male line. He directed likewise the erection of a hospital in that city with the produce of his possessions in Italy   The au·

thenticity of this document is questioned, and has become a point of warm contest among commentators. It is not, however, of much importance. The paper is such as might readily have been written by a person like Columbus in the paroxysm of disease, when he imagined his end suddenly approaching, and shows the affection with which his thoughts were bent on his native city. It is termed among commentators a military codicil, because testamentary dispositions of this kind are executed by the soldier at the point of death, without the usual formalities required by the civil law. About two weeks afterward, on the eve of his death, he executed a final and regularly authenticated codicil, in which he bequeathed his dignities and estates with better judgment.

In these last and awful moments, when the soul has but a brief space in which to make up its accounts between heaven and earth, all dissimulation is at an end, and we read unequivocal evidences of character. The last codicil of Columbus, made at the very verge of the grave, is stamped with his ruling passion and his benignant virtues. He repeats and enforces several clauses of his original testament, constituting his son Diego his universal heir. The entailed inheritance, or mayorazgo, in case he died without male issue, was to go to his brother Don Fernando, and from him, in like case, to pass to his uncle Don Bartholomew, descending always to the nearest male heir; in failure of which it was to pass to the female nearest in lineage to the admiral. He enjoined upon whoever should inherit his estate never to alienate or diminish it, but to endeavor by all means to augment its prosperity and importance. He likewise enjoined upon his heirs to be prompt and devoted at all times, with person and estate, to serve their sovereign and promote the Christian faith. He ordered that Don Diego should devote one-tenth of the revenues which might arise from his estate, when it came to be productive, to the relief of indigent relatives, and of other persons in necessity; that, out of the remainder he should yield certain yearly proportions to his brother Don Fernando, and his uncles Don Bartholomew and

Don Diego; and that the part allotted to Don Fernando
should be settled upon him and his male heirs in an entailed
and inalienable inheritance. Having thus provided for the
maintenance and perpetuity of his family and dignities, he
ordered that Don Diego, when his estates should be sufficiently productive, should erect a chapel in the island of
Hispaniola, which God had given to him so marvelously, at
the town of Conception, in the Vega, where masses should
be daily performed for the repose of the souls of himself, his
father, his mother, his wife, and of all who died in the faith.
Another clause recommends to the care of Don Diego, Beatrix
Enriquez, the mother of his natural son Fernando. His connection with her had never been sanctioned by matrimony,
and either this circumstance, or some neglect of her, seems
to have awakened deep compunction in his dying moments.
He orders Don Diego to provide for her respectable maintenance; "and let this be done," he adds, "for the discharge
of my conscience, for it weighs heavy on my soul."* Finally
he noted with his own hand several minute sums, to be paid
to persons at different and distant places, without their being
told whence they received them. These appear to have been
trivial debts of conscience, or rewards for petty services received in times long past. Among them is one of half a
mark of silver to a poor Jew, who lived at the gate of the
Jewry, in the city of Lisbon. These minute provisions
evince the scrupulous attention to justice in all his dealings,
and that love of punctuality in the fulfillment of duties, for
which he was remarked. In the same spirit he gave much
advice to his son Diego, as to the conduct of his affairs, en-

---

* Diego, the son of the admiral, notes in his own testament this
bequest of his father, and says that he was charged by him to pay
Beatrix Enriquez ten thousand maravedis a year, which for some time
he had faithfully performed; but as he believes that for three or four
years previous to her death he had neglected to do so, he orders that
the deficiency shall be ascertained and paid to her heirs. Memorial
ajustado sobre la propriedad del mayorazgo que fondo D. Christ.
Colon, § 245.

joining upon him to take every month an account with his own hand of the expenses of his household, and to sign it with his name; for a want of regularity in this, he observed, lost both property and servants, and turned the last into enemies.* His dying bequests were made in presence of a few faithful followers and servants, and among them we find the name of Bartholomew Fiesco, who had accompanied Diego Mendez in the perilous voyage in a canoe from Jamaica to Hispaniola.

Having thus scrupulously attended to all the claims of affection, loyalty, and justice upon earth, Columbus turned his thoughts to heaven; and having received the holy sacrament, and performed all the pious offices of a devout Christian, he expired with great resignation, on the day of Ascension, the 20th of May, 1506, being about seventy years of age.† His last words were, "*In manus tuas Domine, commendo spiritum meum:*" Into thy hands, O Lord, I commend my spirit.‡

His body was deposited in the convent of St. Francisco, and his obsequies were celebrated with funereal pomp at Valladolid, in the parochial church of Santa Maria de la Antigua. His remains were transported afterward, in 1513, to the Carthusian monastery of Las Cuevas of Seville, to the chapel of St. Ann or of Santo Christo, in which chapel were likewise deposited those of his son Don Diego, who died in the village of Montalban, on the 23d of February, 1526. In the year 1536 the bodies of Columbus and his son Diego were removed to Hispaniola, and interred in the principal chapel of the cathedral of the city of San Domingo; but even here they did not rest in quiet, having since been again disinterred and conveyed to the Havana, in the island of Cuba.

We are told that Ferdinand, after the death of Columbus, showed a sense of his merits by ordering a monument to be

---

* Memorial ajustado, § 248.　　† Cura de los Palacios, cap. 121.
‡ Las Casas, Hist. Ind., lib. ii., cap. 38. Hist. del Almirante, cap. 108.

erected to his memory, on which was inscribed the motto already cited, which had formerly been granted to him by the sovereigns: A CASTILLA Y A LEON NUEVO MUNDO DIO COLON (*To Castile and Leon Columbus gave a new world*). However great an honor a monument may be for a subject to receive, it is certainly but a cheap reward for a sovereign to bestow. As to the motto inscribed upon it, it remains engraved in the memory of mankind more indelibly than in brass or marble; a record of the great debt of gratitude due to the discoverer, which the monarch had so faithlessly neglected to discharge.

Attempts have been made in recent days, by loyal Spanish writers, to vindicate the conduct of Ferdinand toward Columbus. They were doubtless well intended, but they have been futile, nor is their failure to be regretted. To screen such injustice in so eminent a character from the reprobation of mankind is to deprive history of one of its most important uses. Let the ingratitude of Ferdinand stand recorded in its full extent, and endure throughout all time. The dark shadow which it casts upon his brilliant renown will be a lesson to all rulers, teaching them what is important to their own fame in their treatment of illustrious men.

CHAPTER FIVE

OBSERVATIONS ON THE CHARACTER OF COLUMBUS

IN narrating the story of Columbus, it has been the endeavor of the author to place him in a clear and familiar point of view; for this purpose he has rejected no circumstance, however trivial, which appeared to evolve some point of character; and he has sought all kinds of collateral facts which might throw light upon his views and motives. With this view also he has detailed many facts hitherto passed over in silence, or vaguely noticed by historians, probably because they might be deemed instances of error or misconduct on the part of Columbus; but he who paints a great man merely in great and heroic traits, though he may produce a fine picture, will never present a faithful portrait. Great men are compounds of great and little qualities. Indeed, much of their greatness arises from their mastery over the imperfections of their nature, and their noblest actions are sometimes struck forth by the collision of their merits and their defects.

In Columbus were singularly combined the practical and the poetical. His mind had grasped all kinds of knowledge, whether procured by study or observation, which bore upon his theories; impatient of the scanty aliment of the day, "his impetuous ardor," as has well been observed, "threw him into the study of the fathers of the church; the Arabian Jews, and the ancient geographers"; while his daring but irregular genius, bursting from the limits of imperfect science, bore him to conclusions far beyond the intellectual vision of his contemporaries. If some of his conclusions were erroneous, they were at least ingenious and splendid; and their error resulted from the clouds which still hung over his peculiar path of enterprise. His own discoveries enlightened the ignorance of the age; guided conjecture to certainty, and dispelled that very darkness with which he had been obliged to struggle.

In the progress of his discoveries he has been remarked for the extreme sagacity and the admirable justness with which he seized upon the phenomena of the exterior world. The variations, for instance, of terrestrial magnetism, the direction of currents, the groupings of marine plants, fixing one of the grand climacteric divisions of the ocean, the temperatures changing not solely with the distance to the equator, but also with the difference of meridians: these and similar phenomena, as they broke upon him, were discerned with wonderful quickness of perception, and made to contribute important principles to the stock of general knowledge. This lucidity of spirit, this quick convertibility of facts to principles, distinguish him from the dawn to the

close of his sublime enterprise, insomuch that, with all the
sallying ardor of his imagination, his ultimate success has
been admirably characterized as a "conquest of reflection."*

It has been said that mercenary views mingled with the
ambition of Columbus, and that his stipulations with the
Spanish court were selfish and avaricious. The charge is
inconsiderate and unjust. He aimed at dignity and wealth
in the same lofty spirit in which he sought renown; they
were to be part and parcel of his achievement, and palpable
evidence of its success; they were to arise from the territories
he should discover, and be commensurate in importance. No
condition could be more just. He asked nothing of the
sovereigns but a command of the countries he hoped to give
them, and a share of the profits to support the dignity of his
command. If there should be no country discovered, his
stipulated viceroyalty would be of no avail; and if no revenues should be produced, his labor and peril would produce
no gain. If his command and revenues ultimately proved
magnificent, it was from the magnificence of the regions he
had attached to the Castilian crown. What monarch would
not rejoice to gain empire on such conditions? But he did
not risk merely a loss of labor, and a disappointment of ambition, in the enterprise. On his motives being questioned,
he voluntarily undertook, and, with the assistance of his
coadjutors, actually defrayed one-eighth of the whole charge
of the first expedition.

It was, in fact, this rare union already noticed, of the
practical man of business with the poetical projector, which
enabled him to carry his grand enterprises into effect through
so many difficulties; but the pecuniary calculations and cares,
which gave feasibility to his schemes, were never suffered to
chill the glowing aspirations of his soul. The gains that
promised to arise from his discoveries he intended to appro-
priate in the same princely and pious spirit in which they
were demanded. He contemplated works and achievements

* D. Humboldt. Examen Critique.

of benevolence and religion; vast contributions for the relief
of the poor of his native city; the foundations of churches,
where masses should be said for the souls of the departed;
and armies for the recovery of the holy sepulcher in Palestine. Thus his ambition was truly noble and lofty; instinct
with high thought and prone to generous deed.

In the discharge of his office he maintained the state and
ceremonial of a viceroy, and was tenacious of his rank and
privileges; not from a mere vulgar love of titles, but because
he prized them as testimonials and trophies of his achievements: these he jealously cherished as his great rewards.
In his repeated applications to the king, he insisted merely
on the restitution of his dignities. As to his pecuniary dues
and all questions relative to mere revenue, he offered to leave
them to arbitration or even to the absolute disposition of the
monarch; but not so his official dignities: "these things,"
said he nobly, "affect my honor." In his testament, he enjoined on his son Diego, and whoever after him should
inherit his estates, whatever dignities and titles might afterward be granted by the king, always to sign himself simply
"the admiral," by way of perpetuating in the family its real
source of greatness.

His conduct was characterized by the grandeur of his
views and the magnanimity of his spirit. Instead of scouring the newly-found countries, like a grasping adventurer
eager only for immediate gain, as was too generally the case
with contemporary discoverers, he sought to ascertain their
soil and productions, their rivers and harbors: he was desirous of colonizing and cultivating them; of conciliating and
civilizing the natives; of building cities; introducing the
useful arts; subjecting everything to the control of law,
order, and religion; and thus of founding regular and prosperous empires. In this glorious plan he was constantly defeated by the dissolute rabble which it was his misfortune to
command; with whom all law was tyranny, and all order
restraint. They interrupted all useful works by their seditions; provoked the peaceful Indians to hostility; and after

they had thus drawn down misery and warfare upon their
own heads, and overwhelmed Columbus with the ruins of the
edifice he was building, they charged him with being the
cause of the confusion.

Well would it have been for Spain had those who followed
in the track of Columbus possessed his sound policy and
liberal views. The New World, in such cases, would have
been settled by pacific colonists, and civilized by enlightened
legislators; instead of being overrun by desperate adventurers, and desolated by avaricious conquerors.

Columbus was a man of quick sensibility, liable to great
excitement, to sudden and strong impressions, and powerful
impulses. He was naturally irritable and impetuous, and
keenly sensible to injury and injustice; yet the quickness of
his temper was counteracted by the benevolence and generosity of his heart. The magnanimity of his nature shone
forth through all the troubles of his stormy career. Though
continually outraged in his dignity, and braved in the exercise of his command; though foiled in his plans, and endangered in his person by the seditions of turbulent and worthless
men, and that too at times when suffering under anxiety of
mind and anguish of body sufficient to exasperate the most
patient, yet he restrained his valiant and indignant spirit, by
the strong powers of his mind, and brought himself to forbear, and reason, and even to supplicate; nor should we fail
to notice how free he was from all feeling of revenge, how
ready to forgive and forget, on the least signs of repentance
and atonement. He has been extolled for his skill in con-
trolling others; but far greater praise is due to him for his
firmness in governing himself.

His natural benignity made him accessible to all kinds of
pleasurable sensations from external objects. In his letters
and journals, instead of detailing circumstances with the
technical precision of a mere navigator, he notices the beauties of nature with the enthusiasm of a poet or a painter. As
he coasts the shores of the New World, the reader partici-
pates in the enjoyment with which he describes, in his imper-

fect but picturesque Spanish, the varied objects around him; the blandness of the temperature, the purity of the atmosphere, the fragrance of the air, "full of dew and sweetness," the verdure of the forests, the magnificence of the trees, the grandeur of the mountains, and the limpidity and freshness of the running streams. New delight springs up for him in every scene. He extols each new discovery as more beautiful than the last, and each as the most beautiful in the world; until, with his simple earnestness, he tells the sovereigns that, having spoken so highly of the preceding islands, he fears that they will not credit him, when he declares that the one he is actually describing surpasses them all in excellence.

In the same ardent and unstudied way he expresses his emotions on various occasions, readily affected by impulses of joy or grief, of pleasure or indignation. When surrounded and overwhelmed by the ingratitude and violence of worthless men, he often, in the retirement of his cabin, gave way to bursts of sorrow, and relieved his overladen heart by sighs and groans. When he returned in chains to Spain, and came into the presence of Isabella, instead of continuing the lofty pride with which he had hitherto sustained his injuries, he was touched with grief and tenderness at her sympathy, and burst forth into sobs and tears.

He was devoutly pious: religion mingled with the whole course of his thoughts and actions, and shone forth in his most private and unstudied writings. Whenever he made any great discovery, he celebrated it by solemn thanks to God. The voice of prayer and melody of praise rose from his ships when they first beheld the New World, and his first action on landing was to prostrate himself upon the earth and return thanksgivings. Every evening the "Salve Regina" and other vesper hymns were chanted by his crew, and masses were performed in the beautiful groves bordering the wild shores of this heathen land. All his great enterprises were undertaken in the name of the Holy Trinity, and he partook of the communion previous to embarkation. He was a firm believer in the efficacy of vows and penances and pilgrimages, and resorted to them in times of difficulty and danger. The religion thus deeply seated in his soul diffused a sober dignity and benign composure over his whole demeanor. His language was pure and guarded, and free from all imprecations, oaths, and other irreverent expressions.

It cannot be denied, however, that his piety was mingled with superstition, and darkened by the bigotry of the age. He evidently concurred in the opinion, that all nations which did not acknowledge the Christian faith were destitute of natural rights; that the sternest measures might be used for their conversion, and the severest punishments inflicted upon their obstinacy in unbelief. In this spirit of bigotry he considered himself justified in making captives of the Indians, and transporting them to Spain to have them taught the doctrines of Christianity, and in selling them for slaves if they pretended to resist his invasions. In so doing he sinned against the natural goodness of his character, and against the feelings which he had originally entertained and expressed toward this gentle and hospitable people; but he was goaded on by the mercenary impatience of the crown, and by the sneers of his enemies at the unprofitable result of his enterprises. It is but justice to his character to observe, that the enslavement of the Indians thus taken in battle was at first openly countenanced by the crown, and that, when the question of right came to be discussed at the entreaty of the queen, several of the most distinguished jurists and theologians advocated the practice; so that the question was finally settled in favor of the Indians solely by the humanity of Isabella. As the venerable Bishop Las Casas observes, where the most learned men have doubted it is not surprising that an unlearned mariner should err.

These remarks, in palliation of the conduct of Columbus, are required by candor. It is proper to show him in connection with the age in which he lived, lest the errors of the times should be considered as his individual faults. It is not the intention of the author, however, to justify Columbus on a point where it is inexcusable to err.   Let it remain a blot on his illustrious name, and let others derive a lesson from it.

We have already hinted at a peculiar trait in his rich and varied character; that ardent and enthusiastic imagination which threw a magnificence over his whole course of thought. Herrera intimates that he had a talent for poetry, and some slight traces of it are on record in the book of prophecies which he presented to the Catholic sovereigns.   But his poetical temperament is discernible throughout all his writings and in all his actions.   It spread a golden and glorious world around him, and tinged everything with its own gorgeous colors.   It betrayed him into visionary speculations, which subjected him to the sneers and cavilings of men of cooler and safer, but more groveling minds.   Such were the conjectures formed on the coast of Paria about the form of the earth, and the situation of the terrestrial paradise; about the mines of Ophir in Hispaniola, and the Aurea Chersonesus in Veragua; and such was the heroic scheme of a crusade for the recovery of the holy sepulcher.   It mingled with his religion, and filled his mind with solemn and visionary meditations on mystic passages of the Scriptures, and the shadowy portents of the prophecies.   It exalted his office in his eyes, and made him conceive himself an agent sent forth upon a sublime and awful mission, subject to impulses and supernatural intimations from the Deity; such as the voice which he imagined spoke to him in comfort amid the troubles of Hispaniola and in the silence of the night on the disastrous coast of Veragua.

He was decidedly a visionary, but a visionary of an uncommon and successful kind.   The manner in which his ardent, imaginative, and mercurial nature was controlled by a powerful judgment, and directed by an acute sagacity, is the most extraordinary feature in his character.   Thus governed, his imagination, instead of exhausting itself in idle flights, lent aid to his judgment, and enabled him to form conclusions at which common minds could never have arrived, nay, which they could not perceive when pointed out.

To his intellectual vision it was given to read the signs of the times, and to trace, in the conjectures and reveries of past ages, the indications of an unknown world; as soothsayers were said to read predictions in the stars, and to foretell events from the visions of the night. "His soul," observes a Spanish writer, "was superior to the age in which he lived. For him was reserved the great enterprise of traversing that sea which had given rise to so many fables, and of deciphering the mystery of his time." *

With all the visionary fervor of his imagination, its fondest dreams fell short of the reality. He died in ignorance of the real grandeur of his discovery. Until his last breath he entertained the idea that he had merely opened a new way to the old resorts of opulent commerce, and had discovered some of the wild regions of the East. He supposed Hispaniola to be the ancient Ophir which had been visited by the ships of Solomon, and that Cuba and Terra Firma were but remote parts of Asia. What visions of glory would have broken upon his mind could he have known that he had indeed discovered a new continent, equal to the whole of the Old World in magnitude, and separated by two vast oceans from all the earth hitherto known by civilized man! And how would his magnanimous spirit have been consoled, amid the afflictions of age and the cares of penury, the neglect of a fickle public and the injustice of an ungrateful king, could he have anticipated the splendid empires which were to spread over the beautiful world he had discovered; and the nations, and tongues, and languages which were to fill its lands with his renown, and revere and bless his name to the latest posterity!

---

* Cladera. Investigaciones historias, p. 43.

APPENDIX

CONTAINING ILLUSTRATIONS AND DOCUMENTS

No. I

TRANSPORTATION OF THE REMAINS OF COLUMBUS FROM SAN DOMINGO TO THE HAVANA

At the termination of a war between France and Spain, in 1795, all the Spanish possessions in the island of Hispaniola were ceded to France, by the 9th article of the treaty of peace. To assist in the accomplishment of this cession, a Spanish squadron was dispatched to the island at the appointed time, commanded by Don Gabriel de Aristizabal, lieutenant-general of the royal armada. On the 11th of December, 1795, that commander wrote to the field-marshal and governor, Don Joaquin Garcia, resident at San Domingo, that, being informed that the remains of the celebrated Admiral Don Christopher Columbus lay in the cathedral of that city, he felt it incumbent on him as a Spaniard, and as commander-in-chief of his majesty's squadron of operations, to solicit the translation of the ashes of that hero to the island of Cuba, which had likewise been discovered by him, and where he had first planted the standard of the cross. He expressed a desire that this should be done officially, and with great care and formality, that it might not remain in the power of any one, by a careless transportation of these honored remains, to lose a relic connected with an event which formed the most glorious epoch of Spanish history, and that it might be manifested to all nations that Spaniards, notwithstanding the lapse of ages, never ceased to pay all honors to the remains of that "worthy and adventurous general of the seas"; nor abandoned them when the various public bodies, representing the Spanish dominion, emigrated from the island.

As he had not time, without great inconvenience, to consult the sovereign on this subject, he had recourse to the governor, as royal vice-patron of the island, hoping that his solicitation might be granted, and the remains of the admiral exhumed and conveyed to the island of Cuba, in the ship "San Lorenzo."

The generous wishes of this high-minded Spaniard met with warm concurrence on the part of the governor. He informed him, in reply, that the Duke of Veraguas, lineal successor of Columbus, had manifested the same solicitude, and had sent directions that the necessary measures should be taken at his expense; and had at the same time expressed a wish that the bones of the adelantado, Don Bartholomew Columbus, should likewise be exhumed; transmitting inscriptions to be put upon the sepulchers of both. He added, that although the king had given no orders on the subject, yet the proposition being so accordant with the grateful feelings of the Spanish nation, and meeting with the concurrence of all the authorities of the island, he was ready on his part to carry it into execution.

The commandant-general Aristizabal then made a similar communication to the archbishop of Cuba, Don Fernando Portillo y Torres, whose metropolis was then the city of San Domingo, hoping to receive his countenance and aid in this pious undertaking.

The reply of the archbishop was couched in terms of high courtesy toward the gallant commander, and deep reverence for the memory of Columbus, and expressed a zeal in rendering this tribute of gratitude and respect to the remains of one who had done so much for the glory of the nation.

The persons empowered to act for the Duke of Veraguas, the venerable dean and chapter of the cathedral, and all the other persons and authorities to whom Don Gabriel de Aristizabal made similar communications, manifested the same eagerness to assist in the performance of this solemn and affecting rite.

The worthy commander Aristizabal, having taken all these preparatory steps with great form and punctilio, so as that the ceremony should be performed in a public and striking manner, suitable to the fame of Columbus, the whole was carried into effect with becoming pomp and solemnity.

On the 20th of December, 1795, the most distinguished persons of the place, the dignitaries of the church, and civil and military officers, assembled in the metropolitan cathedral. In the presence of this august assemblage, a small vault was opened above the chancel, in the principal wall on the right side of the high altar. Within were found the fragments of a leaden coffin, a number of bones, and a quantity of mould, evidently the remains of a human body. These were carefully collected and put into a case of gilded lead, about half an ell in length and breadth, and a third in height, secured by an iron lock, the key of which was delivered to the archbishop. The case was inclosed in a coffin covered with black velvet, and ornamented with lace and fringe of gold. The whole was then placed in a temporary tomb or mausoleum.

On the following day there was another grand convocation at the cathedral, when the vigils and masses for the dead were solemnly chanted by the archbishop, accompanied by the commandant-general of the armada, the Dominican and Franciscan friars, and the friars of the Order of Mercy, together with the rest of the distinguished assemblage. After this a funeral sermon was preached by the archbishop.

On the same day, at four o'clock in the afternoon, the coffin was transported to the ship with the utmost state and ceremony, with a civil, religious, and military procession, banners wrapped in mourning, chants and responses and discharges of artillery. The most distinguished persons of the several orders took turn to support the coffin. The key was taken with great formality from the hands of the archbishop by the governor, and given into the hands of the commander of the armada, to be delivered by him to the governor of the Havana, to be held in deposit until the pleasure of the king should be known. The coffin was received on board of a brigantine called the "Discoverer," which, with all the other shipping, displayed mourning signals, and saluted the remains with the honors paid to an admiral.

From the port of San Domingo the coffin was conveyed to the bay of Ocoa and there transferred to the ship "San Lorenzo." It was accompanied by a portrait of Columbus, sent from Spain by the Duke of Veraguas, to be suspended close by the place where the remains of his illustrious ancestor should be deposited.

The ship immediately made sail, and arrived at Havana, in Cuba, on the 15th of January, 1796. Here the same deep feeling of reverence to the memory of the discoverer was evinced. The principal authorities repaired on board of the ship, accompanied by the superior naval and military officers.

Everything was conducted with the same circumstantial and solemn ceremonial. The remains were removed with great reverence, and placed in a felucca, in which they were conveyed to land in the midst of a procession of three columns of feluccas and boats in the royal service, all properly decorated, containing distinguished military and ministerial officers. Two feluccas followed, in one of which was a marine guard of honor, with mourning banners and muffled drums; and in the other were the commandant-general, the principal minister of marine, and the military staff. In passing the vessels of war in the harbor, they all paid the honors due to an admiral and captain-general of the navy. On arriving at the mole the remains were met by the governor of the island, accompanied by the generals and the military staff. The coffin was then conveyed, between files of soldiery which lined the streets, to the obelisk, in the place of arms, where it was received in a hearse prepared for the purpose. Here the remains were formally delivered to the governor and captain-general of the island, the key given up to him, the coffin opened and examined, and the safe transportation of its contents authenticated. This ceremony being concluded, it was conveyed in grand procession and with the utmost pomp to the cathedral. Masses and the solemn ceremonies of the dead were performed by the bishop, and the mortal remains of Columbus deposited with great reverence in the wall on the right side of the grand altar. "All these honors and ceremonies," says the document, from whence this notice is digested,* "were attended by the ecclesiastical and secular dignitaries, the public bodies and all the nobility and gentry of Havana, in proof of the high estimation and respectful remembrance in which they held the hero who had discovered the New World, and had been the first to plant the standard of the cross on that island."

This is the last occasion that the Spanish nation has had to testify its feelings toward the memory of Columbus, and it is with deep satisfaction that the author of this work has been able to cite at large a ceremonial so solemn, affecting, and noble in its details, and so honorable to the national character.

When we read of the remains of Columbus, thus conveyed from the port of San Domingo, after an interval of nearly three hundred years, as sacred national relics, with civic and

---

* Navarrete, Colec., tom. ii., p. 365.

military pomp, and high religious ceremonial; the most dignified and illustrious men striving who most should pay them reverence; we cannot but reflect that it was from this very port he was carried off loaded with ignominious chains, blasted apparently in fame and fortune, and followed by the revilings of the rabble. Such honors, it is true, are nothing to the dead, nor can they atone to the heart, now dust and ashes, for all the wrongs and sorrows it may have suffered; but they speak volumes of comfort to the illustrious, yet slandered and persecuted living, encouraging them bravely to bear with present injuries, by showing them how true merit outlives all calumny, and receives its glorious reward in the admiration of after ages.

No. II

NOTICE OF THE DESCENDANTS OF COLUMBUS

On the death of Columbus his son Diego succeeded to his rights as viceroy and governor of the New World, according to the express capitulations between the sovereigns and his father. He appears by the general consent of historians to have been a man of great integrity, of respectable talents, and of a frank and generous nature. Herrera speaks repeatedly of the gentleness and urbanity of his manners, and pronounces him of a noble disposition, and without deceit. This absence of all guile frequently laid him open to the stratagems of crafty men, grown old in deception, who rendered his life a continued series of embarrassments; but the probity of his character, with the irresistible power of truth, bore him through difficulties in which more politic and subtle men would have been entangled and completely lost.

Immediately after the death of the admiral, Don Diego came forward as lineal successor, and urged the restitution of the family offices and privileges, which had been suspended during the latter years of his father's life. If the cold and wary Ferdinand, however, could forget his obligations of gratitude and justice to Columbus, he had less difficulty in turning a deaf ear to the solicitations of his son. For two years Don Diego pressed his suit with fruitless diligence. He felt the apparent distrust of the monarch the more sensibly from having been brought up under his eye as a page in the royal household, where his character ought to be well known and appreciated. At length, on the return of Ferdinand from Naples in 1508, he put to him a direct question, with the frankness attributed to his character. He demanded "why his majesty would not grant to him as a favor that which was his right, and why he hesitated to confide in the fidelity of one who had been reared in his house." Ferdinand replied that he could fully confide in him, but could not repose so great a trust at a venture in his children and successors. To this Don Diego rejoined that it was contrary to all justice and reason to make him suffer for the sins of his children, who might never be born.*

Still, though he had reason and justice on his side, the young admiral found it impossible to bring the wary monarch to a compliance. Finding all appeal to all his ideas of equity or sentiments of generosity in vain, he solicited permission to pursue his claim in the ordinary course of law. The king could not refuse so reasonable a request, and Don Diego commenced a process against King Ferdinand before the Council of the Indies, founded on the repeated capitulations between the crown and his father, and embracing all the dignities and immunities ceded by them.

One ground of opposition to these claims was that if the capitulation, made by the sovereigns in 1492, had granted a perpetual viceroyalty to the admiral and his heirs, such grant could not stand; being contrary to the interest of the state, and to an express law promulgated in Toledo in 1480; wherein it was ordained that no office, involving the administration of justice, should be given in perpetuity; that, therefore, the viceroyalty granted to the admiral could only have been for his life; and that, even during that term, it had justly been taken from him for his misconduct. That such concessions were contrary to the inherent prerogatives of the crown, of which the government could not divest itself. To this Don Diego replied that as to the validity of the capitulation, it was a binding contract, and none of its privileges ought to be restricted. That as by royal schedules dated in Villa Franca, June 2, 1506, and Almazan, August 28, 1507, it had been ordered that he, Don Diego, should receive the tenths, so equally ought the other privileges to be accorded to him. As to the allegation that his father had been deprived of his viceroyalty for his demerits, it was contrary to

* Herrera, Hist. Ind., decad. ii., lib vii., cap. 4.

all truth. It had been audacity on the part of Bobadilla to send him a prisoner to Spain in 1500, and contrary to the will and command of the sovereigns, as was proved by their letter, dated from Valencia de la Torre in 1502, in which they expressed grief at his arrest, and assured him that it should be redressed, and his privileges guarded entire to himself and his children.*

This memorable suit was commenced in 1508, and continued for several years. In the course of it the claims of Don Diego were disputed, likewise, on the plea that his father was not the original discoverer of Terra Firma, but only subsequently of certain portions of it. This, however, was completely controverted by overwhelming testimony. The claims of Don Diego were minutely discussed and rigidly examined, and the unanimous decision of the Council of the Indies in his favor, while it reflected honor on the justice and independence of that body, silenced many petty cavilers at the fair fame of Columbus.† Notwithstanding this decision, the wily monarch wanted neither means nor pretexts to delay the ceding of such vast powers, so repugnant to his cautious policy. The young admiral was finally indebted for his success in this suit to previous success attained in a suit of a different nature. He had become enamored of Dona Maria de Toledo, daughter of Fernando de Toledo, grand commander of Leon, and niece to Don Fadrique Toledo, the celebrated Duke of Alva, chief favorite of the king. This was aspiring to a high connection. The father and uncle of the lady were the most powerful grandees of the proud kingdom of Spain, and cousins-german to Ferdinand. The glory, however, which Columbus had left behind rested upon his children, and the claims of Don Diego, recently confirmed by the council, involved dignities and wealth sufficient to raise him to a level with the loftiest alliance. He found no difficulty in obtaining the hand of the lady, and thus was the foreign family of Columbus ingrafted on one of the proudest races of Spain. The natural consequences followed. Diego had secured that magical power called "connections"; and the favor of Ferdinand, which had been so long withheld from him, as the son of Columbus, shone upon him, though

---

* Extracts from the minutes of the process taken by the historian Muñoz, MS.

† Further mention will be found of this lawsuit in the article relative to Amerigo Vespucci.

coldly, as the nephew of the Duke of Alva. The father and uncle of his bride succeeded, though with great difficulty, in conquering the repugnance of the monarch, and after all he but granted in part the justice they required. He ceded to Don Diego merely the dignities and powers enjoyed by Nicholas de Ovando, who was recalled, and he cautiously withheld the title of viceroy.

The recall of Ovando was not merely a measure to make room for Don Diego: it was the tardy performance of a promise made to Isabella on her deathbed. The expiring queen had demanded it as a punishment for the massacre of her poor Indian subjects at Xaragua, and the cruel and ignominious execution of the female cacique Anacaona. Thus retribution was continually going its rounds in the checkered destinies of this island, which has ever presented a little epitome of human history; its errors and crimes, and consequent disasters.

In complying with the request of the queen, however, Ferdinand was favorable toward Ovando. He did not feel the same generous sympathies with his late consort, and, however Ovando had sinned against humanity in his treatment of the Indians, he had been a vigilant officer, and his very oppressions had in general proved profitable to the crown. Ferdinand directed that the fleet which took out the new governor should return under the command of Ovando, and that he should retain undisturbed enjoyment of any property or Indian slaves that might be found in his possession. Some have represented Ovando as a man far from mercenary; that the wealth wrung from the miseries of the natives was for his sovereign, not for himself; and it is intimated that one secret cause of his disgrace was his having made an enemy of the all powerful and unforgiving Fonseca.*

The new admiral embarked at St. Lucar, June 9, 1509, with his wife, his brother Don Fernando, who was now grown to man's estate, and had been well educated, and his two uncles, Don Bartholomew and Don Diego. They were accompanied by a numerous retinue of cavaliers, with their wives, and of young ladies of rank and family, more distinguished, it is hinted, for high blood than large fortune, and who were sent out to find wealthy husbands in the New World.†

---

* Charlevoix, ut supra, v. i., p. 272, id. 274.
† Las Casas, lib. ii., cap. 49, MS.

Though the king had not granted Don Diego the dignity
of viceroy, the title was generally given to him by courtesy,
and his wife was universally addressed by that of vice queen.
Don Diego commenced his rule with a degree of splendor
hitherto unknown in the colony. The vice-queen, who was
a lady of great desert, surrounded by the noble cavaliers and
the young ladies of family who had come in her retinue, established a sort of court, which threw a degree of luster over the
half-savage island. The young ladies were soon married to
the wealthiest colonists, and contributed greatly to soften
those rude manners which had grown up in a state of society
hitherto destitute of the salutary restraint and pleasing decorum produced by female influence.

Don Diego had considered his appointment in the light of
a viceroyalty, but the king soon took measures which showed
that he admitted of no such pretensio . Without any reference to Don Diego, he divided the coast of Darien into two
great provinces, separated by an imaginary line running
through the Gulf of Uraba, appointing Alonzo de Ojeda
governor of the eastern province, which he called New Andalusia, and Diego de Nicuesa, governor of the western
province, which included the rich coast of Veragua, and
which he called Castilla del Oro, or Golden Castile. Had
the monarch been swayed by principles of justice and gratitude, the settlement of this coast would have been given to
the adelantado, Don Bartholomew Columbus, who had assisted in the discovery of the country, and, together with his
brother the admiral, had suffered so greatly in the enterprise.
Even his superior abilities for the task should have pointed
him out to the policy of the monarch; but the cautious and
calculating Ferdinand knew the lofty spirit of the adelantado,
and that he would be disposed to demand high and dignified
terms. He passed him by, therefore, and preferred more
eager and accommodating adventurers.

Don Diego was greatly aggrieved at this measure, thus
adopted without his participation or knowledge. He justly
considered it an infringement of the capitulations granted
and repeatedly confirmed to his father and his heirs. He
had further vexations and difficulties with respect to the government of the island of St. Juan, or Porto Rico, which was
conquered and settled about this time; but after a variety of
cross purposes, the officers whom he appointed were ultimately
recognized by the crown.

Like his father, he had to contend with malignant factions

in his government; for the enemies of the father transferred their enmity to the son. There was one Miguel Pasamonte, the king's treasurer, who became his avowed enemy, under the support and chiefly at the instigation of the Bishop Fonseca, who continued to the son the implacable hostility which he had manifested to the father. A variety of trivial circumstances contributed to embroil him with some of the petty officers of the colony, and there was a remnant of the followers of Roldan who arrayed themselves against him.*

Two factions soon arose in the island; one of the admiral, the other of the treasurer Pasamonte. The latter affected to call themselves the party of the king. They gave all possible molestation to Don Diego, and sent home the most virulent and absurd misrepresentations of his conduct. Among others, they represented a large house with many windows which he was building, as intended for a fortress, and asserted that he had a design to make himself sovereign of the island. King Ferdinand, who was now advancing in years, had devolved the affairs of the Indies in a great measure on Fonseca,† who had superintended them from the first, and he was greatly guided by the advice of that prelate, which was not likely to be favorable to the descendants of Columbus. The complaints from the colonies were so artfully enforced, therefore, that he established in 1510 a sovereign court at San Domingo, called the royal audience, to which an appeal might be made from all sentences of the admiral, even in cases reserved hitherto exclusively for the crown. Don Diego considered this a suspicious and injurious measure intended to demolish his authority.

Frank, open, and unsuspicious, the young admiral was not formed for a contest with the crafty politicians arrayed against him, who were ready and adroit in seizing upon his slightest errors, and magnifying them into crimes. Difficulties were multiplied in his path which it was out of his power to overcome. He had entered upon office full of magnanimous intentions, determined to put an end to oppression and correct all abuses; all good men therefore had rejoiced at his appointment; but he soon found that he had overrated his strength, and undervalued the difficulties awaiting him. He calculated from his own good heart, but he had no idea of the wicked hearts of others. He was opposed to the repartimientos of Indians, that source of all kinds of inhumanity;

---

* Herrera, decad. i., lib. vii., cap. 12.   † Ibid.

but he found all the men of wealth in the colony, and most of the important persons of the court, interested in maintaining them. He perceived that the attempt to abolish them would be dangerous, and the result questionable; at the same time this abuse was a source of immense profit to himself. Self-interest, therefore, combined with other considerations, and what at first appeared difficult seemed presently impracticable. The repartimientos continued in the state in which he found them, excepting that he removed such of the superintendents as had been cruel and oppressive, and substituted men of his own appointment, who probably proved equally worthless. His friends were disappointed, his enemies encouraged; a hue and cry was raised against him by the friends of those he had displaced; and it was even said that if Ovando had not died about this time he would have been sent out to supplant Don Diego.

The subjugation and settlement of the island of Cuba, in 1510, was a fortunate event in the administration of the present admiral. He congratulated King Ferdinand on having acquired the largest and most beautiful island in the world without losing a single man. The intelligence was highly acceptable to the king; but it was accompanied by a great number of complaints against the admiral. Little affection as Ferdinand felt for Don Diego, he was still aware that most of these representations were false, and had their origin in the jealousy and envy of his enemies. He judged it expedient, however, in 1512, to send out Don Bartholomew Columbus with minute instructions to his nephew the admiral.

Don Bartholomew still retained the office of adelantado of the Indies; although Ferdinand, through selfish motives, detained him in Spain, while he employed inferior men in voyages of discovery. He now added to his appointments the property and government of the little island of Mona during life, and assigned him a repartimiento of two hundred Indians, with the superintendence of the mines which might be discovered in Cuba; an office which proved very lucrative.*

Among the instructions given by the king to Don Diego, he directed that, in consequence of the representations of the Dominican friars, the labor of the natives should be reduced to one-third; that negro slaves should be procured from Guinea as a relief to the Indians,† and that Carib slaves should be

---

* Charlevoix, Hist. S. Domingo, p. 321.
† Herrera, Hist. Ind., decad. i., lib. ix., cap. 5.

branded on the leg to prevent other Indians from being confounded with them and subjected to harsh treatment.*

The two governors, Ojeda and Nicuesa, whom the king had appointed to colonize and command at the Isthmus of Darien, in Terra Firma, having failed in their undertaking, the sovereign, in 1514, wrote to Hispaniola, permitting the adelantado, Don Bartholomew, if so inclined, to take charge of settling the coast of Veragua, and to govern that country under the admiral Don Diego conformably to his privileges. Had the king consulted his own interest, and the deference due to the talents and services of the adelantado, this measure would have been taken at an earlier date. It was now too late: illness prevented Don Bartholomew from executing the enterprise, and his active and toilsome life was drawing to a close.

Many calumnies having been sent home to Spain by Pasamonte and other enemies of Don Diego, and various measures being taken by government which he conceived derogatory to his dignity and injurious to his privileges, he requested and obtained permission to repair to court, that he might explain and vindicate his conduct. He departed, accordingly, on April 9, 1515, leaving the adelantado with the vice-queen Dona Maria. He was received with great honor by the king, and he merited such a reception. He had succeeded in every enterprise he had undertaken or directed. The pearl fishery had been successfully established on the coast of Cubagua; the islands of Cuba and of Jamaica had been subjected and brought under cultivation without bloodshed; his conduct as governor had been upright; and he had only excited the representations made against him by endeavoring to lessen the oppression of the natives. The king ordered that all processes against him in the court of appeal and elsewhere, for damages done to individuals in regulating the repartimientos, should be discontinued, and the cases sent to himself for consideration. But with all these favors, as the admiral claimed a share of the profits of the provinces of Castilla del Oro, saying that it was discovered by his father, as the names of its places, such as Nombre de Dios, Porto Bello, and El Retrete, plainly proved, the king ordered that interrogatories should be made among the mariners who had sailed with Christopher Columbus, in the hope of proving that he had not discovered the coast of Darien nor the Gulf of Uraba. "Thus,"

---

* Herrera, Hist. Ind., decad. i., lib. ix., cap. 5.

adds Herrera, "Don Diego was always involved in litigations with the fiscal, so that he might truly say that he was heir to the troubles of his father." *

Not long after the departure of Don Diego from San Domingo, his uncle, Don Bartholomew, ended his active and laborious life. No particulars are given of his death, nor is there mention made of his age, which must have been advanced. King Ferdinand is said to have expressed great concern at the event, for he had a high opinion of the character and talents of the adelantado: "A man," says Herrera, "of not less worth than his brother the admiral, and who, if he had been employed, would have given great proofs of it; for he was an excellent seaman, valiant and of great heart." †
Charlevoix attributes the inaction in which Don Bartholomew had been suffered to remain for several years to the jealousy and parsimony of the king. He found the house already too powerful; and the adelantado, had he discovered Mexico, was a man to make as good conditions as had been made by the admiral his brother.‡ It was said, observed Herrera, that the king rather preferred to employ him in his European affairs, though it could only have been to divert him from other objects. On his death the king resumed to himself the island of Mona, which he had given to him for life, and transferred his repartimiento of two hundred Indians to the vice-queen Dona Maria.

While the admiral Don Diego was pressing for an audience in his vindication at court, King Ferdinand died, on the 23d of January, 1516. His grandson and successor, Prince Charles, afterward the Emperor Charles V., was in Flanders. The government rested for a time with Cardinal Ximenes, who would not undertake to decide on the representations and claims of the admiral. It was not until 1520 that he obtained from the Emperor Charles V. a recognition of his innocence of all the charges against him. The emperor finding that what Pasamonte and his party had written were notorious calumnies, ordered Don Diego to resume his charge, although the process with the fiscal was still pending, and that Pasamonte should be written to, requesting him to forget all past passions and differences, and to enter into amicable relations with Don Diego. Among other acts of indemnification

---

* Herrera, Hist. Ind., decad. ii., lib. ii., cap. 7.
† Ibid., decad. i., lib. x., cap. 16.
‡ Charlevoix, Hist. S. Domingo, lib. 5.

he acknowledged his right to exercise his office of viceroy and governor in the island of Hispaniola, and in all parts discovery by his father.* His authority was, however, much diminished by new regulations, and a supervisor appointed over him with the right to give information to the council against him, but with no other powers. Don Diego sailed in the beginning of September, 1520, and on his arrival at San Domingo, finding that several of the governors, presuming on his long absence, had arrogated to themselves independence, and had abused their powers, he immediately sent persons to supersede them, and demanded an account of their administration. This made him a host of active and powerful enemies both in the colonies and in Spain.

Considerable changes had taken place in the island of Hispaniola during the absence of the admiral. The mines had fallen into neglect, the cultivation of the sugar cane having been found a more certain source of wealth. It became a by-word in Spain that the magnificent palaces erected by Charles V. at Madrid and Toledo were built of the sugar of Hispaniola. Slaves had been imported in great numbers from Africa, being found more serviceable in the culture of the cane than the feeble Indians. The treatment of the poor negroes was cruel in the extreme; and they seem to have had no advocates even among the humane. The slavery of the Indians had been founded on the right of the strong; but it was thought that the negroes, from their color, were born to slavery; and that from being bought and sold in their own country, it was their natural condition. Though a patient and enduring race, the barbarities inflicted on them at length roused them to revenge, and on the 27th of December, 1522, there was the first African revolt in Hispaniola. It began in a sugar plantation of the admiral Don Diego, where about twenty slaves, joined by an equal number from a neighboring plantation, got possession of arms, rose on their superintendents, massacred them, and sallied forth upon the country. It was their intention to pillage certain plantations, to kill the whites, re-enforce themselves by freeing their countrymen, and either to possess themselves of the town of Agua or to escape to the mountains.

Don Diego set out from San Domingo in search of the rebels, followed by several of the principal inhabitants. On the second day he stopped on the banks of the River Nizao to

---

* Herrera, Hist. Ind., decad. ii., lib. ix., cap. 7.

rest his party and suffer re-enforcements to overtake him. Here one Melchor de Castro, who accompanied the admiral, learned that the negroes had ravaged his plantation, sacked his house, killed one of his men, and carried off his Indian slaves. Without asking leave of the admiral, he departed in the night with two companions, visited his plantation, found all in confusion, and pursuing the negroes, sent to the admiral for aid. Eight horsemen were hastily dispatched to his assistance, armed with bucklers and lances, and having six of the infantry mounted behind them. De Castro had three horsemen besides this re-enforcement, and at the head of this little band overtook the negroes at break of day. The insurgents put themselves in battle array, armed with stones and Indian spears, and uttering loud shouts and outcries. The Spanish horsemen braced their bucklers, couched their lances, and charged them at full speed. The negroes were soon routed, and fled to the rocks, leaving six dead and several wounded. De Castro also was wounded in the arm. The admiral coming up, assisted in the pursuit of the fugitives. As fast as they were taken they were hanged on the nearest trees, and remained suspended as spectacles of terror to their countrymen. This prompt severity checked all further attempts at revolt among the African slaves.[*]

In the meantime the various enemies whom Don Diego had created, both in the colonies and in Spain, were actively and successfully employed. His old antagonist, the treasurer Pasamonte, had charged him with usurping almost all the powers of the royal audience, and with having given to the royal declaration, re-establishing him in his office of viceroy, an extent never intended by the sovereign. These representations had weight at court, and in 1523 Don Diego received a most severe letter from the Council of the Indies, charging him with the various abuses and excesses alleged against him, and commanding him, on pain of forfeiting all his privileges and titles, to revoke the innovations he had made, and restore things to their former state. To prevent any plea of ignorance of this mandate, the royal audience was enjoined to promulgate it and to call upon all persons to conform to it, and to see that it was properly obeyed. The admiral received also a letter from the council, informing him that his presence was necessary in Spain, to give information of the foregoing matters, and advice relative to

---

[*] Herrera, Hist. Ind., decad. iii., lib. iv., cap. 9.

the reformation of various abuses, and to the treatment and preservation of the Indians; he was requested, therefore, to repair to court without waiting for further orders.[*]

Don Diego understood this to be a peremptory recall, and obeyed accordingly. On his arrival in Spain, he immediately presented himself before the court at Victoria, with the frank and fearless spirit of an upright man, and pleaded his cause so well that the sovereign and council acknowledged his innocence on all the points of accusation. He convinced them, moreover, of the exactitude with which he had discharged his duties; of his zeal for the public good, and the glory of the crown; and that all the representations against him rose from the jealousy and enmity of Pasamonte and other royal officers in the colonies, who were impatient of any superior authority in the island to restrain them.

Having completely established his innocence, and exposed the calumnies of his enemies, Don Diego trusted that he would soon obtain justice as to all his claims. As these, however, involved a participation in the profits of vast and richly productive provinces, he experienced the delays and difficulties usual with such demands, for it is only when justice costs nothing that it is readily rendered. His earnest solicitations at length obtained an order from the emperor that a commission should be formed, composed of the grand chancellor, the Friar Loyasa, confessor to the emperor, and president of the royal Council of the Indies, and a number of other distinguished personages. They were to inquire into the various points in dispute between the admiral and the fiscal, and into the proceedings which had taken place in the Council of the Indies, with the power of determining what justice required in the case.

The affair, however, was protracted to such a length, and accompanied by so many toils, vexations, and disappointments, that the unfortunate Diego, like his father, died in the pursuit. For two years he had followed the court from city to city, during its migrations from Victoria to Burgos, Valladolid, Madrid, and Toledo. In the winter of 1525, the emperor set out from Toledo for Seville. The admiral undertook to follow him, though his constitution was broken by fatigue and vexation, and he was wasting under the attack of a slow fever. Oviedo, the historian, saw him at Toledo two days before his departure, and joined with his

---

[*] Herrera., Hist. Ind., decad. iii., lib. v., cap. 4.

friends in endeavoring to dissuade him from a journey in such a state of health and at such a season. Their persuasions were in vain. Don Diego was not aware of the extent of his malady: he told them that he should repair to Seville by the church of our Lady of Guadaloupe, to offer up his devotions at that shrine; and he trusted, through the intercession of the mother of God, soon to be restored to health.*

He accordingly left Toledo in a litter on the 21st of February, 1526, having previously confessed and taken the communion, and arrived the same day at Montalvan, distant about six leagues. There his illness increased to such a degree that he saw his end approaching. He employed the following day in arranging the affairs of his conscience, and expired on February 23d, being little more than fifty years of age, his premature death having been hastened by the griefs and troubles he had experienced. "He was worn out," says Herrera, "by following up his claims, and defending himself from the calumnies of his competitors, who, with many stratagems and devices, sought to obscure the glory of the father and the virtue of the son." †

We have seen how the discovery of the New World rendered the residue of the life of Columbus a tissue of wrongs, hardships and afflictions, and how the jealousy and enmity he had awakened were inherited by his son. It remains to show briefly in what degree the anticipations of perpetuity, wealth, and honor to his family were fulfilled.

When Don Diego Columbus died, his wife and family were at San Domingo. He left two sons, Luis and Christopher, and three daughters—Maria, who afterward married Don Sancho de Cardona; Juana, who married Don Luis de Cueva; and Isabella, who married Don George of Portugal, Count of Gelves. He had also a natural son named Christopher.‡

After the death of Don Diego, his noble-spirited vice-

---

* Charlevoix, Hist. S. Domingo, lib. vi.
† Herrera, decad. iii., lib. viii., cap. 15.
‡ Memorial adjustado sobre el estado de Veragua.

Charlevoix mentions another son called Diego, and calls one of the daughters Phillipine. Spotorno says that the daughter Maria took the veil; confounding her with a niece. These are trivial errors, merely noticed to avoid the imputation of inaccuracy. The account of the descendants of Columbus here given, accords with a genealogical tree of the family, produced before the Council of the Indies, in a great lawsuit for the estates.

queen, left with a number of young children, endeavored to assert and maintain the rights of the family. Understanding that, according to the privileges accorded to Christopher Columbus, they had a just claim to the viceroyalty of the province of Veragua, as having been discovered by him, she demanded a license from the royal audience of Hispaniola, to recruit men and fit out an armada to colonize that country. This the audience refused, and sent information of the demand to the emperor. He replied that the vice-queen should be kept in suspense until the justice of her claim could be ascertained; as, although he had at various times given commissions to different persons to examine the doubts and objections which had been opposed by the fiscal, no decision had ever been made.* The enterprise thus contemplated by the vice-queen was never carried into effect.

Shortly afterward she sailed for Spain to protect the claim of her eldest son, Don Luis, then six years of age. Charles V. was absent, but she was most graciously received by the empress. The title of admiral of the Indies was immediately conferred on her son, Don Luis, and the emperor augmented his revenues, and conferred other favors on the family. Charles V., however, could never be prevailed on to give Don Luis the title of viceroy, although that dignity had been decreed to his father, a few years previous to his death, as a hereditary right.†

In 1538 the young admiral, Don Luis, then about eighteen years of age, was at court, having instituted proceedings before the proper tribunals for the recovery of the viceroyalty. Two years afterward the suit was settled by arbitration, his uncle Don Fernando and Cardinal Loyasa, president of the Council of the Indies, being umpires. By a compromise Don Luis was declared captain-general of Hispaniola, but with such limitations that it was little better than a bare title. Don Luis sailed for Hispaniola, but did not remain there long. He found his dignities and privileges mere sources of vexation, and finally entered into a compromise, which relieved himself and gratified the emperor. He gave up all pretensions to the viceroyalty of the New World, receiving in its stead the titles of Duke of Veragua and Marquis of Jamaica.‡ He commuted also the claim

---

* Herrera, decad. iv., lib. ii., cap. 6.
† Charlevoix, Hist. S. Domingo, lib. vi., p. 443.
‡ Ibid, tom. i., lib. vi., p. 446.

to the tenth of the produce of the Indies for a pension of one thousand doubloons of gold.[*]

Don Luis did not long enjoy the substitution of a certain, though moderate, revenue for a magnificent but unproductive claim. He died shortly afterward, leaving no other male issue than an illegitimate son, named Christopher. He left two daughters by his wife, Dona Maria de Mosquera, one named Phillippa, and the other Maria, which last became a nun in the convent of St. Quirce, at Valladolid.

Don Luis having no legitimate son, was succeeded by his nephew Diego, son to his brother Christopher. A litigation took place between this young heir and his cousin Phillippa, daughter of the late Don Luis. The convent of St. Quirce also put in a claim, on behalf of its inmate, Dona Maria, who had taken the veil. Christopher, natural son to Don Luis, likewise became a prosecutor in the suit, but was set aside on account of his illegitimacy. Don Diego and his cousin Phillippa soon thought it better to join claims and persons in wedlock, than to pursue a tedious contest. They were married, and their union was happy, though not fruitful. Diego died without issue in 1578, and with him the legitimate male line of Columbus became extinct.

One of the most important lawsuits that the world has ever witnessed now arose for the estates and dignities descended from the great discoverer. Don Diego had two sisters, Francisca and Maria, the former of whom, and the children of the latter, advanced their several claims. To these parties was added Bernard Colombo of Cogoleto, who claimed as lineal descendant from Bartholomew Columbus, the adelantado, brother to the discoverer. He was, however, pronounced ineligible, as the adelantado had no acknowledged, and certainly no legitimate offspring.

Baldassar, or Balthazar Colombo, of the house of Cuccaro and Conzano, in the dukedom of Montferrat, in Piedmont, was an active and persevering claimant. He came from Italy into Spain, where he devoted himself for many years to the prosecution of this suit. He produced a genealogical tree of his family, in which was contained one Domenico Colombo, Lord of Cuccaro, whom he maintained to be the identical father of Christopher Columbus, the admiral. He proved that this Domenico was living at the requisite era, and produced many witnesses who had heard that the navi-

---

[*] Spotorno, Hist. Colomb., p. 123.

gator was born in the castle of Cuccaro; whence, it was
added, he and his two brothers had eloped at an early age,
and had never returned.* A monk is also mentioned among
the witnesses, who made oath that Christopher and his
brothers were born in that castle of Cuccaro. This testimony was afterward withdrawn by the prosecutor, as it was
found that the monk's recollection must have extended back
considerably upward of a century.† The claim of Balthazar
was negatived. His proofs that Christopher Columbus was
a native of Cuccaro were rejected, as only hearsay, or traditionary evidence. His ancestor Domenico, it appeared from
his own showing, died in 1456; whereas it was established
that Domenico, the father of the admiral, was living upward
of thirty years after that date.

The cause was finally decided by the Council of the
Indies, on the 2d of December, 1608. The male line was
declared to be extinct. Don Nuno or Nugno Gelves de Portugallo was put in possession, and became Duke of Veragua.
He was grandson to Isabella, third daughter of Don Diego
(son of the discoverer) by his vice-queen, Dona Maria de
Toledo. The descendants of the two elder sisters of Isabella
had a prior claim, but their lines became extinct previous to
this decision of the suit. The Isabella just named had married Don George of Portugal, Count of Gelves. "Thus,"
says Charlevoix, "the dignities and wealth of Columbus
passed into a branch of the Portuguese house of Braganza,
established in Spain, of which the heirs are entitled De
Portugallo, Colon, Duke de Veragua, Marques de la Jamaica, y Almirante de las Indias."‡

The suit of Balthazar Colombo of Cuccaro was rejected
under three different forms, by the Council of the Indies;
and his application for an allowance of support, under the
legacy of Columbus, in favor of poor relations, was also refused; although the other parties had assented to the demand.§ He died in Spain, where he had resided many years
in prosecution of this suit. His son returned to Italy persisting in the validity of his claim: he said that it was in vain to
seek justice in Spain; they were too much interested to keep
those dignities and estates among themselves; but he gave

---

* Bossi, Hist. Colomb., Dissert., p. 67.
† Ibid., Dissert. on the Country of Columbus, p. 63.
‡ Charlevoix, Hist. S. Domingo, tom. i., lib. vi., p. 447.
§ Bossi, Dissertation on the Country of Columbus.

out that he had received twelve thousand doubloons of gold in compromise from the other parties. Spotorno, under sanction of Ignazio de Giovanni, a learned canon, treats this assertion as a bravado, to cover his defeat, being contradicted by his evident poverty.* The family of Cuccaro, however, still maintain their right, and express great veneration for the memory of their illustrious ancestor, the admiral; and travelers occasionally visit their old castle in Piedmont with great reverence, as the birthplace of the discoverer of the New World.

No. III

FERNANDO COLUMBUS

FERNANDO COLUMBUS (or Colon, as he is called in Spain), the natural son and historian of the admiral, was born in Cordova. There is an uncertainty about the exact time of his birth. According to his epitaph, it must have been on the 28th September, 1488; but according to his original papers preserved in the library of the cathedral of Seville, and which were examined by Don Diego Ortiz de Zuniga, historian of that city, it would appear to have been on the 29th of August, 1487. His mother, Dona Beatrix Enriquez, was of a respectable family, but was never married to the admiral, as has been stated by some of his biographers.

Early in 1494 Fernando was carried to court, together with his elder brother Diego, by his uncle Don Bartholomew, to enter the royal household in quality of page to the Prince Don Juan, son and heir to Ferdinand and Isabella. He and his brother remained in this situation until the death of the prince, when they were taken by Queen Isabella as pages into her own service. Their education, of course, was well attended to, and Fernando in after-life gave proofs of being a learned man.

In the year 1502, at the tender age of thirteen or fourteen years, Fernando accompanied his father in his fourth voyage of discovery, and encountered all its singular and varied hardships with a fortitude that is mentioned with praise and admiration by the admiral.

After the death of his father it would appear that Fer-

* Spotorno, p. 127.

nando made two voyages to the New World. He accompanied the Emperor Charles V. also, to Italy, Flanders, and Germany; and according to Zuniga (Anales de Seville de 1539, No. 3) traveled over all Europe and a part of Africa and Asia. Possessing talents, judgment, and industry, these opportunities were not lost upon him, and he acquired much information in geography, navigation, and natural history. Being of a studious habit, and fond of books, he formed a select, yet copious library, of more than twenty thousand volumes, in print and in manuscript. With the sanction of the Emperor Charles V. he undertook to establish an academy and college of mathematics at Seville; and for this purpose commenced the construction of a sumptuous edifice, without the walls of the city, facing the Guadalquivir, in the place where the monastery of San Laureano is now situated. His constitution, however, had been broken by the sufferings he had experienced in his travels and voyages, and a premature death prevented the completion of his plan of the academy, and broke off other useful labors. He died in Seville on the 12th of July, 1539, at the age, according to his epitaph, of fifty years, nine months and fourteen days. He left no issue, and was never married. His body was interred, according to his request, in the cathedral of Seville. He bequeathed his valuable library to the same establishment.

Don Fernando devoted himself much to letters. According to the inscription on his tomb, he composed a work in four books, or volumes, the title of which is defaced on the monument, and the work itself is lost. This is much to be regretted, as, according to Zuniga, the fragments of the inscription specify it to have contained, among a variety of matter, historical, moral, and geographical notices of the countries he had visited, but especially of the New World, and of the voyages and discoveries of his father.

His most important and permanent work, however, was a history of the admiral, composed in Spanish. It was translated into Italian by Alonzo de Ulloa, and from this Italian translation have proceeded the editions which have since appeared in various languages. It is singular that the work only exists in Spanish in the form of a re-translation from that of Ulloa, and full of errors in the orthography of proper names, and in dates and distances.

Don Fernando was an eye-witness of some of the facts which he relates, particularly of the fourth voyage wherein he accompanied his father. He had also the papers and

charts of his father, and recent documents of all kinds to
extract from, as well as familiar acquaintance with the principal personages who were concerned in the events which he
records. He was a man of probity and discernment, and
writes more dispassionately than could be expected, when
treating of matters which affected the honor, the interests, and
happiness of his father. It is to be regretted, however, that
he should have suffered the whole of his father's life, previous to his discoveries (a period of about fifty-six years), to
remain in obscurity. He appears to have wished to cast a
cloud over it, and only to have presented his father to the
reader after he had rendered himself illustrious by his actions, and his history had become in a manner identified with
the history of the world. His work, however, is an invaluable document, entitled to great faith, and is the corner-stone
of the history of the American Continent.

Galley, from the tomb of Fernando Columbus, at Seville.

No. IV

AGE OF COLUMBUS

As the date I have assigned for the birth of Columbus
makes him about ten years older than he is generally represented, at the time of his discoveries, it is proper to state
precisely my authority. In the valuable manuscript chronicle
of the reign of the Catholic sovereigns, written by Andres
Bernaldes, the curate of Los Palacios, there is a long tract
on the subject of the discoveries of Columbus; it concludes
with these words: *Murió en Valladolid, el año de 1506,
en el mes de Mayo, in senectute bona, de edad 70 años,*

poco mas ó menos. (He died in Valladolid in the year 1506,
in the month of May, in a good old age, being seventy years
old, a little more or less.) The curate of Los Palacios was a
contemporary, and an intimate friend of Columbus, who was
occasionally a guest in his house; no one was more competent, therefore, to form a correct idea of his age. It is
singular that, while the biographers of Columbus have been
seeking to establish the epoch of his birth by various calculations and conjectures, this direct testimony of honest
Andres Bernaldes has entirely escaped their notice, though
some of them had his manuscript in their hands. It was
first observed by my accurate friend Don Antonio Uguina
in the course of his exact investigations, and has been pointed
out and ably supported by Don Martin Fernandez de Navarrete, in the introduction to his valuable collection of voyages.

Various circumstances in the life of Columbus will be
found to corroborate the statement of the curate; such, for
example, as the increasing infirmities with which he struggled during his voyages, and which at last rendered him a
cripple and confined him to his bed. The allusion to his
advanced age in one of his letters to the sovereigns, wherein
he relates the consolation he had received from a secret voice
in the night season: *Tu vejez no impedira a toda cosa
grande. Abrahan pasaba cien años cuando engendro a
Isaac, etc.* (Thy old age shall be no impediment to any great
undertaking. Abraham was above a hundred years old,
when he begat Isaac, etc.) The permission granted him by
the king the year previous to his death to travel on a mule,
instead of a horse, on account of his *age* and infirmities; and
the assertion of Oviedo, that at the time of his death he was
quite old (*era ya viejo*).

This fact of the advanced age of Columbus throws quite
a new coloring over his character and history. How much
more extraordinary is the ardent enthusiasm which sustained
him through his long career of solicitation, and the noble
pride with which he refused to descend from his dignified demands, and to bargain about his proposition, though life was
rapidly wasting in delays. How much more extraordinary
is the hardihood with which he undertook repeated voyages
into unknown seas, amid all kinds of perils and hardships;
the fortitude with which he bore up against an accumulation
of mental and bodily afflictions, enough to have disheartened
and destroyed the most youthful and robust, and the irrepressible buoyancy of spirit with which to the last he still

rose from under the ruined concerns and disappointed hopes and blasted projects of one enterprise, to launch into another, still more difficult and perilous.

We have been accustomed to admire all these things in Columbus when we considered him in the full vigor of his life; how much more are they entitled to our wonder as the achievements of a man whom the weight of years and infirmities was pressing into the grave.

No. V

LINEAGE OF COLUMBUS

THE ancestry of Christopher Columbus has formed a point of zealous controversy which is not yet satisfactorily settled. Several honorable families, possessing domains in Placentia, Montferrat, and the different parts of the Genoese territories, claim him as belonging to their houses; and to these has recently been added the noble family of Colombo in Modena.* The natural desire to prove consanguinity with a man of distinguished renown has excited this rivalry; but it has been heightened, in particular instances, by the hope of succeeding to titles and situations of wealth and honor, when his male line of descendants became extinct. The investigation is involved in particular obscurity, as even his immediate relatives appear to have been in ignorance on the subject.

Fernando Columbus, in his biography of the admiral, after a pompous prelude, in which he attempts to throw a vague and cloudy magnificence about the origin of his father, notices slightly the attempts of some to obscure his fame, by making him a native of various small and insignificant villages; and dwells with more complacency upon others who make him a native of places in which there were persons of much honor of the name, and many sepulchral monuments with arms and epitaphs of the Colombos. He relates his having himself gone to the castle of Cucureo, to visit his two brothers of the family of Colombo, who were rich and noble, the youngest of whom was above one hundred years of age, and who he had heard were relatives of his father; but they could give him no information upon the subject; whereupon he breaks forth into his professed contempt for these adven-

* Spotorno, Hist. Mem., p. 5.

titious claims, declaring that he thinks it better to content himself with dating from the glory of the admiral than to go about inquiring whether his father "were a merchant or one who kept his hawks"; * since, adds he, of persons of similar pursuits, there are thousands who die every day, whose memory, even among their own neighbors and relatives, perishes immediately, without its being possible afterward to ascertain even whether they existed.

After this, and a few more expressions of similar disdain for these empty distinctions, he indulges in vehement abuse of Agostino Giustiniani, whom he calls a false historian, an inconsiderate, partial, or malignant compatriot, for having, in his psalter, traduced his father, by saying that in his youth he had been employed in mechanical occupations.

As, after all this discussion, Fernando leaves the question of his father's parentage in all its original obscurity, yet appears irritably sensitive to any derogatory suggestions of others, his whole evidence tends to the conviction that he really knew nothing to boast of in his ancestry.

Of the nobility and antiquity of the Colombo family, of which the admiral probably was a remote descendant, we have some account in Herrera. "We learn," he says, "that the Emperor Otto the Second, in 940, confirmed to the Counts Pietro, Giovanni, and Alexandro Colombo, brothers, the feudatory possessions which they held within the jurisdiction of the cities of Ayqui, Savona, Aste, Montferrato, Turin, Viceli, Parma, Cremona, and Bergamo, and all others which they held in Italy. It appears that the Colombos of Cuccaro, Cucureo, and Placentia were the same, and that the emperor in the same year, 940, made donation to the said three brothers of the castles of Cuccaro, Conzano, Rosignano, and others, and of the fourth part of Bistanio, which appertained to the empire."†

One of the boldest attempts of those biographers bent on ennobling Columbus has been to make him son of the Lord of Cuccaro, a burgh of Montferrat, in Piedmont, and to prove that he was born in his father's castle at that place; whence he and his brothers eloped at an early age, and never returned. This was asserted in the course of a process brought by a certain Baldassar or Balthazar Colombo, resident in

* Literally, in the original, *Cazador de Volateria*, a Falconer. Hawking was in those days an amusement of the highest classes; and to keep hawks was almost a sign of nobility.

† Herrera, decad. i., lib. i., cap. 7.

Genoa, but originally of Cuccaro, claiming the title and estates, on the death of Diego Colon, Duke of Veragua, in 1578, the great-grandson and last legitimate male descendant of the admiral. The Council of the Indies decided against this claim to relationship. Some account of the lawsuit will be found in another part of the work.

This romantic story, like all others of the nobility of his parentage, is at utter variance with the subsequent events of his life, his long struggles with indigence and obscurity, and the difficulties he endured from the want of family connections. How can it be believed, says Bossi, that this same man, who, in his most cruel adversities, was incessantly taunted by his enemies with the obscurity of his birth, should not reply to this reproach, by declaring his origin, if he were really descended from the Lords of Cuccaro, Conzano, and Rosignano? a circumstance which would have obtained him the highest credit with the Spanish nobility.*

The different families of Colombo which lay claim to the great navigator seem to be various branches of one tree, and there is little doubt of his appertaining remotely to the same respectable stock.

It appears evident, however, that Columbus sprang immediately from a line of humble but industrious citizens, which had existed in Genoa, even from the time of Giacomo Colombo the wool-carder, in 1311, mentioned by Spotorno; nor is this in any wise incompatible with the intimation of Fernando Columbus, that the family had been reduced from high estate to great poverty by the wars of Lombardy. The feuds of Italy, in those ages, had broken down and scattered many of the noblest families; and while some branches remained in the lordly heritage of castles and domains, others were confounded with the humblest population of the cities.

No. VI

BIRTHPLACE OF COLUMBUS

THERE has been much controversy about the birthplace of Columbus. The greatness of his renown has induced various places to lay claim to him as a native, and from motives of laudable pride; for nothing reflects greater luster upon a

* Dissertation, etc.

city than to have given birth to distinguished men. The original and long-established opinion was in favor of Genoa; but such strenuous claims were asserted by the states of Placentia, and in particular of Piedmont, that the Academy of Sciences and Letters of Genoa was induced, in 1812, to nominate three of its members, Signors Serra, Carrega, and Piaggio, commissioners to examine into these pretensions.

The claims of Placentia had been first advanced in 1662, by Pietro Maria Campi, in the ecclesiastical history of that place, who maintained that Columbus was a native of the village of Pradello, in that vicinity. It appeared probable, on investigation, that Bertolino Colombo, great-grandfather to the admiral, had owned a small property in Pradello, the rent of which had been received by Domenico Colombo of Genoa, and after his death by his sons Christopher and Bartholomew. Admitting this assertion to be correct, there was no proof that either the admiral, his father, or grandfather had ever resided on that estate. The very circumstances of the case indicated, on the contrary, that their home was in Genoa.

The claim of Piedmont was maintained with more plausibility. It was shown that a Domenico Colombo was lord of the castle of Cuccaro in Montferrat at the time of the birth of Christopher Columbus, who, it was asserted, was his son, and born in his castle. Balthazar Colombo, a descendant of this person, instituted a lawsuit before the Council of the Indies for the inheritance of the admiral, when his male line became extinct. The Council of the Indies decided against him, as is shown in an account of that process given among the illustrations of this history. It was proved that Domenico Colombo, father of the admiral, was resident in Genoa both before and many years after the death of this lord of Cuccaro, who bore the same name.

The three commissioners appointed by the Academy of Sciences and Letters of Genoa to examine into these pretensions, after a long and diligent investigation, gave a voluminous and circumstantial report in favor of Genoa. An ample digest of their inquest may be found in the "History of Columbus" by Signor Bossi, who, in an able dissertation on the question, confirms their opinion. It may be added, in further corroboration, that Peter Martyr and Bartholomew Las Casas, who were contemporaries and acquaintances of Columbus, and Juan de Barros, the Portuguese historian, all make Columbus a native of the Genoese territories.

There has been a question fruitful of discussion among the Genoese themselves whether Columbus was born in the city of Genoa or in some other part of the territory. Finale, and Oneglia, and Savona, towns on the Ligurian coast to the west, Boggiasco, Cogoleto, and several other towns and villages, claim him as their own. His family possessed a small property at a village or hamlet between Quinto and Nervi, called Terra Rossa; in Latin, Terra Rubra; which has induced some writers to assign his birth to one of those places. Bossi says that there is still a tower between Quinto and Nervi which bears the title of Torre dei Colombi.* Bartholomew Columbus, brother to the admiral, styled himself of Terra Rubra, in a Latin inscription on a map which he presented to Henry VII. of England, and Fernando Columbus states, in his history of the admiral, that he was accustomed to subscribe himself in the same manner before he attained to his dignities.

Cogoleto at one time bore away the palm. The families there claim the discoverer, and preserve a portrait of him. One or both of the two admirals named Colombo, with whom he sailed, are stated to have come from that place, and to have been confounded with him so as to have given support to this idea.†

Savona, a city in the Genoese territories, has claimed the same honor, and this claim has recently been very strongly brought forward. Signor Giovanni Battista Belloro, an advocate of Savona, has strenuously maintained this claim in an ingenious disputation, dated May 12, 1826, in form of a letter to the Baron du Zach, editor of a valuable astronomical and geographical journal, published monthly at Genoa.‡

Signor Belloro claims it as an admitted fact that Domenico Colombo was for many years a resident and citizen of Savona, in which place one Christopher Columbus is shown to have signed a document in 1472.

He states that a public square in that city bore the name of Platea Columbi, toward the end of the fourteenth century; that the Ligurian government gave the name of Jurisdizione di Colombi to that district of the republic, under the persuasion that the great navigator was a native of Savona, and that Columbus gave the name of Saona to a little island adjacent to Hispaniola, among his earliest discoveries.

---

* Bossi. French translation, Paris, 1824, p. 69. † Ibid.
‡ Correspondence Astronom. Geograph., etc., de Baron du Zach, Vol. 14, cahier 6, lettera 29. 1826.

He quotes many Savonese writers, principally poets, and various historians and poets of other countries, and thus establishes the point that Columbus was held to be a native of Savona by persons of respectable authority. He lays particular stress on the testimony of the Magnifico Francisco Spinola, as related by the learned prelate Felippo Alberto Pollero, stating that he had seen the sepulcher of Christopher Columbus in the cathedral at Seville, and that the epitaph states him expressly to be a native of Savona: "Hic jacet Christophorus Columbus Savonensis." *

The proofs advanced by Signor Belloro show his zeal for the honor of his native city, but do not authenticate the fact he undertakes to establish. He shows clearly that many respectable writers believed Columbus to be a native of Savona; but a far greater number can be adduced, and many of them contemporary with the admiral, some of them his intimate friends, others his fellow citizens, who state him to have been born in the city of Genoa. Among the Savonese writers, Giulio Salinorio, who investigated the subject, comes expressly to the same conclusion: "*Genova, cittá nobilissima, era la patria de Colombo.*"

Signor Belloro appears to be correct in stating that Domenico, the father of the admiral, was several years resident in Savona. But it appears from his own dissertation that the Christopher who witnessed the testament in 1472 styled himself of Genoa: "*Christophorus Columbus lanerius de Janua.*" This incident is stated by other writers, who presume this Christopher to have been the navigator on a visit to his father, in the interval of his early voyages. In as far as the circumstance bears on the point, it supports the idea that he was born at Genoa.

The epitaph, on which Signor Belloro places his principal reliance, entirely fails. Christopher Columbus was not interred in the cathedral of Seville, nor was any monument erected to him in that edifice. The tomb to which the learned prelate Felippo Alberto Pollero alludes may have been that of Fernando Columbus, son to the admiral, who, as has been already observed, was buried in the cathedral of Seville, to which he bequeathed his noble library. The place of his sepulture is designated by a broad slab of white marble, inserted in the pavement, with an inscription, partly in Span-

---

* Felippo Alberto Pollero, Epicherema, cioé breve discorso per difesa di sua persona e carrattere. Torino, per Gio Battista Zappata. MCDXCVI. (read 1696) in 4°, pag. 47.

ish, partly in Latin, recording the merits of Fernando and the achievements of his father. On either side of the epitaph is engraved an ancient Spanish Galley. The inscription quoted by Signor Belloro may have been erroneously written from memory by the Magnifico Francisco Spinola, under the mistaken idea that he had beheld the sepulcher of the great discoverer. As Fernando was born at Cordova, the term Savonensis must have been another error of memory in the Magnifico; no such word is to be found in the inscription.

This question of birthplace has also been investigated with considerable minuteness, and a decision given in favor of Genoa, by D. Gio Battista Spotorno, of the royal university in that city, in his historical memoir of Columbus. He shows that the family of the Columbi had long been resident in Genoa. By an extract from the notarial register, it appeared that one Giacomo Colombo, a wool-carder, resided without the gate of St. Andria, in the year 1311. An agreement, also, published by the academy of Genoa, proved that in 1489 Domenico Colombo possessed a house and shop, and a garden with a well, in the street of St. Andrew's Gate, anciently without the walls, presumed to have been the same residence with that of Giacomo Colombo. He rented also another house from the monks of St. Stephen, in the Via Mulcento, leading from the street of St. Andrew to the Strada Giulia. *

Signor Bossi states that documents lately found in the archives of the monastery of St. Stephen present the name of Domenico Colombo several times, from 1456 to 1459, and designate him as son of Giovanni Colombo, husband of Susanna Fontanarossa, and father of Christopher, Bartholomew and Giacomo † (or Diego). He states also that the receipts of the canons show that the last payment of rent was made by Domenico Colombo for his dwelling in 1489. He surmises that the admiral was born in the before-mentioned house belonging to those monks, in Via Mulcento, and that he was baptized in the church of St. Stephen. He adds that an ancient manuscript was submitted to the commissioners of the Genoese academy, in the margin of which the notary had stated that the name of Christopher was on the register of the parish as having been baptized in that church.‡

Andres Bernaldes, the curate of Los Palacios, who was an

---

* Spotorno, English trans., p. xi., xii.
† Bossi, French trans., p. 76.   ‡ Ibid., p. 88.

intimates friend of Columbus, says that he was of Genoa.* Agostino Giustiniani, a contemporary of Columbus, likewise asserts it in his Polyglot Psalter, published in Genoa in 1516. Antonio de Herrera, an author of great accuracy, who, though not a contemporary, had access to the best documents, asserts decidedly that he was born in the city of Genoa.

To these names may be added that of Alexander Geraldini, brother to the nuncio, and instructor to the children of Ferdinand and Isabella, a most intimate friend of Columbus.† Also Antonio Gallo,‡ Bartolomeo Senarega,§ and Uberto Foglieta,‖ all contemporaries with the admiral, and natives of Genoa, together with an anonymous writer, who published an account of his voyage of discovery at Venice in 1509.¶ It is unnecessary to mention historians of later date agreeing in the same fact, as they must have derived their information from some of these authorities.

The question in regard to the birthplace of Columbus has been treated thus minutely, because it has been, and still continues to be, a point of warm controversy. It may be considered, however, as conclusively decided by the highest authority, the evidence of Columbus himself. In a testament executed in 1498, which has been admitted in evidence before the Spanish tribunals in certain lawsuits among his descendants, he twice declares that he was a native of the city of Genoa: "*Siendo yo navido en Genova.*" "I being born in Genoa." And again, he repeats the assertion, as a reason for enjoining certain conditions on his heirs, which manifest the interest he takes in his native place. "I command the said Diego, my son, or the person who inherits the said mayorazgo (or entailed estate), that he maintain always in the city of Genoa a person of our lineage, who shall have a house and a wife there, and to furnish him with an income on which he can live decently, as a person connected with our family, and hold footing and root in that city as a native of it, so that he may have aid and favor in that city in case of need, *for from thence I came and there was born.*" **

---

* Cura de los Palacios, MS., cap. 118.
† Alex. Geraldini, Itin. ad. Reg. sub. Aquinor.
‡ Antonio Gallo, Anales of Genoa, Muratori, tom. 23.
§ Senarega, Muratori, tom. 24.
‖ Foglieta, Elog. Clar. Ligur.   ¶ Grineus, Nov. Orb.
** "Item. Mando el dicho Don Diego mi hijo, á la persona que heredare el dicho mayorazgo, que tenga y sostenga siempre en la ciudad de Genova una persona de nuestro linage que tenga alli casa é muger, é le

In another part of his testament he expresses himself with a filial fondness in respect to Genoa. "I command the said Don Diego, or whoever shall possess the said mayorazgo, that he labor and strive always for the honor, and welfare, and increase of the city of Genoa, and employ all his abilities and means in defending and augmenting the welfare and honor of her republic, in all matters which are not contrary to the service of the church of God, and the state of the king and queen our sovereigns, and their successors."

An informal codicil, executed by Columbus at Valladolid, May 4, 1506, sixteen days before his death, was discovered about 1785, in the Corsini library at Rome. It is termed a military codicil, from being made in the manner which the civil law allows to the soldier who executes such an instrument on the eve of battle, or in expectation of death. It was written on the blank page of a little breviary presented to Columbus by Pope Alexander VII. Columbus leaves the book "to his beloved country, the Republic of Genoa."

He directs the erection of a hospital in that city for the poor, with provision for its support; and he declares that republic his successor in the admiralty of the Indies, in the event of his male line becoming extinct.

The authenticity of this paper has been questioned. It has been said that there was no probability of Columbus having resort to a usage with which he was most likely unacquainted. The objections are not cogent. Columbus was accustomed to the peculiarities of a military life, and he repeatedly wrote letters in critical moments as a precaution against some fatal occurrence that seemed to impend. The present codicil, from its date, must have been written a few days previous to his death, perhaps at a moment when he imagined himself at extremity. This may account for any difference in the handwriting, especially as he was, at times, so affected by the gout in his hands as not to be able to write except at night. Particular stress has been laid on the signature; but it does not appear that he was uniform in regard to that, and it is a point to which any one who attempted a forgery would be attentive. It does not appear, likewise,

---

ordene renta con que pueda vivir honestamente, como persona tan llegada á nuestro linage, y haga pie y raiz en la dicha ciudad como natural della, porque podrá haber de la dicha ciudad ayuda e favor en las cosas del menester suyo, *pues que della sali y en ella naci.*"

that any advantage could have been obtained by forging the paper, or that any such was attempted.

In 1502, when Columbus was about to depart on his fourth and last voyage, he wrote to his friend, Dr. Nicolo Oderigo, formerly embassador from Genoa to Spain, and forwarded to him copies of all his grants and commissions from the Spanish sovereigns, authenticated before the alcaldes of Seville. He, at the same time, wrote to the bank of San Giorgio, at Genoa, assigning a tenth of his revenues to be paid to that city, in diminution of the duties on corn, wine, and other provisions.

Why should Columbus feel this strong interest in Genoa had he been born in any of the other Italian states which have laid claim to him? He was under no obligation to Genoa. He had resided there but a brief portion of his early life; and his proposition for discovery, according to some writers, had been scornfully rejected by that republic. There is nothing to warrant so strong an interest in Genoa but the filial tie which links the heart of a man to his native place, however he may be separated from it by time or distance, and however little he may be indebted to it for favors.

Again, had Columbus been born in any of the towns and villages of the Genoese coast which have claimed him for a native, why should he have made these bequests in favor of the *city* of Genoa, and not of his native town or village?

These bequests were evidently dictated by a mingled sentiment of pride and affection, which would be without all object if not directed to his native place. He was at this time elevated above all petty pride on the subject. His renown was so brilliant that it would have shed a luster on any hamlet, however obscure; and the strong love of country here manifested would never have felt satisfied until it had singled out the spot and nestled down in the very cradle of his infancy. These appear to be powerful reasons, drawn from natural feeling, for deciding in favor of Genoa.

No. VII

THE COLOMBOS

DURING the early part of the life of Columbus there were two other navigators, bearing the same name, of some rank and celebrity, with whom he occasionally sailed; their names occurring vaguely from time to time, during the obscure part of his career, have caused much perplexity to some of his bi ographers, who have supposed that they designated the discoverer. Fernando Columbus affirms them to have been family connections,* and his father says, in one of his letters, "I am not the first admiral of our family."

These two were uncle and nephew: the latter being termed by historians Colombo the younger (by the Spanish historians Colombo el mozo). They were in the Genoese service, but are mentioned, occasionally, in old chronicles as French commanders, because Genoa, during a great part of their time, was under the protection, or rather the sovereignty of France, and her ships and captains, being engaged in the expeditions of that power, were identified with the French marine.

Mention is made of the elder Colombo in Zurita's Annals of Aragon (L. xix., p. 261), in the war between Spain and Portugal, on the subject of the claim of the Princess Juana to the crown of Castile. In 1476, the king of Portugal determined to go to the Mediterranean coast of France, to incite his ally, Louis XI., to prosecute the war in the province of Guipuzcoa.

The king left Toro, says Zurita, on the 13th June, and went by the river to the city of Porto, in order to await the armada of the king of France, the captain of which was Colon (Colombo), who was to navigate by the straits of Gibraltar to pass to Marseilles.

After some delays Colombo arrived in the latter part of July with the French armada at Bermeo, on the coast of Biscay, where he encountered a violent storm, lost his principal ship, and ran to the coast of Galicia, with an intention of attacking Ribaldo, and lost a great many of his men. Thence he went to Lisbon to receive the king of Portugal, who em-

---

* Hist. del Almirante, cap. 1.

barked in the fleet in August, with a number of his noblemen, and took two thousand two hundred foot soldiers, and
four hundred and seventy horse, to strengthen the Portuguese
garrisons along the Barbary coast. There were in the squadron twelve ships and five caravels. After touching at Ceuta
the fleet proceeded to Colibre, where the king disembarked
in the middle of September, the weather not permitting them
to proceed to Marseilles. (Zurita, L. xix., Ch. 51.)

This Colombo is evidently the naval commander of whom
the following mention is made by Jaques George de Chaufepie, in his supplement to Bayle (vol. 2, p. 126 of letter C).

"I do not know what dependence," says Chaufepie, "is
to be placed on a fact reported in the 'Ducatiana' (Part 1, p.
143), that Columbus was in 1474 captain of several ships for
Louis XI., and that, as the Spaniards had made at that time
an irruption into Roussillon, he thought that, for reprisal, and
without contravening the peace between the two crowns, he
could run down Spanish vessels. He attacked, therefore, and
took two galleys of that nation, freighted on the account of
various individuals. On complaints of this action being made
to King Ferdinand, he wrote on the subject to Louis XI.; his
letter is dated the 9th December, 1474. Ferdinand terms
Christopher Columbus a subject of Louis; it was because, as
is known, Columbus was a Genoese, and Louis was sovereign
of Genoa; although that city and Savona were held of him
in fief by the Duke of Milan."

It is highly probable that it was the squadron of this same
Colombo of whom the circumstance is related by Bossi, and
after him by Spotorno on the authority of a letter found in
the archives of Milan, and written in 1476 by two illustrious
Milanese gentlemen, on their return from Jerusalem. The
letter states that in the previous year, 1475, as the Venetian
fleet was stationed off Cyprus to guard the island, a Genoese
squadron, commanded by one Colombo, sailed by them with
an air of defiance, shouting "Viva San Giorgia!" As the
republics were then at peace they were permitted to pass
unmolested.

Bossi supposes that the Colombo here mentioned was
Christopher Columbus the discoverer; but it appears rather
to have been the old Genoese admiral of that name, who, according to Zurita, was about that time cruising in the Mediterranean; and who, in all probability, was the hero of both
the preceding occurrences.

The nephew of this Colombo, called by the Spanish Colombo el mozo, commanded a few years afterward a squadron in the French service, as will appear in a subsequent illustration, and Columbus may at various times have held an inferior command under both uncle and nephew, and been present on the above cited occasions.

No. VIII

EXPEDITION OF JOHN OF ANJOU

ABOUT the time that Columbus attained his twenty-fourth year, his native city was in a state of great alarm and peril from the threatened invasion of Alphonso V. of Aragon, king of Naples. Finding itself too weak to contend singly with such a foe, and having in vain looked for assistance from Italy, it placed itself under the protection of Charles the VIIth of France. That monarch sent to its assistance John of Anjou, son of René or Renato, king of Naples, who had been dispossessed of his crown by Alphonso. John of Anjou, otherwise called the Duke of Calabria,* immediately took upon himself the command of the place, repaired its fortifications, and defended the entrance of the harbor with strong chains. In the meantime, Alphonso had prepared a large land force, and assembled an armament of twenty ships and ten galleys at Ancona, on the frontiers of Genoa. The situation of the latter was considered eminently perilous, when Alphonso suddenly fell ill of a calenture and died, leaving the kingdoms of Anjou and Sicily to his brother John, and the kingdom of Naples to his son Ferdinand.

The death of Alphonso, and the subsequent division of his dominions, while they relieved the fears of the Genoese, gave rise to new hopes on the part of the house of Anjou; and the Duke John, encouraged by emissaries from various powerful partisans among the Neapolitan nobility, determined to make a bold attempt upon Naples for the recovery of the crown. The Genoese entered into his cause with spirit, furnishing him with ships, galleys, and money. His father, Rene or Renato, fitted out twelve galleys for the expedition in the harbor of Marseilles, and sent him assurance of an

---

* Duke of Calabria was a title of the heir apparent to the crown of Naples.

abundant supply of money, and of the assistance of the king of France. The brilliant nature of the enterprise attracted the attention of the daring and restless spirits of the times. The chivalrous nobleman, the soldier of fortune, the hardy corsair, the bold adventurer or the military partisan, enlisted under the banners of the Duke of Calabria. It is stated by historians that Columbus served in the armament from Genoa, in a squadron commanded by one of the Colombos, his relations.

The expedition sailed in October, 1459, and arrived at Sessa between the mouths of the Garigliano and the Volturno. The news of its arrival was the signal of universal revolt; the factious barons and their vassals hastened to join the standard of Anjou, and the duke soon saw the finest provinces of the Neapolitan dominions at his command, and with his army and squadron menaced the city of Naples itself.

In the history of this expedition we meet with one hazardous action of the fleet in which Columbus had embarked.

The army of John of Anjou, being closely invested by a superior force, was in a perilous predicament at the mouth of the Sarno. In this conjuncture, the captain of the armada landed with his men, and scoured the neighborhood, hoping to awaken in the populace their former enthusiasm for the banner of Anjou, and perhaps to take Naples by surprise. A chosen company of Neapolitan infantry was sent against them. The troops from the fleet, having little of the discipline of regular soldiery, and much of the freebooting disposition of maritime rovers, had scattered themselves about the country, intent chiefly upon spoil. They were attacked by the infantry and put to rout, with the loss of many killed and wounded. Endeavoring to make their way back to the ships, they found the passes seized and blocked up by the people of Sorento, who assailed them with dreadful havoc. Their flight now became desperate and headlong, many threw themselves from rocks and precipices into the sea, and but a small portion regained the ships.

The contest of John of Anjou for the crown of Naples lasted four years. For a time fortune favored him, and the prize seemed almost within his grasp, but reverses succeeded; he was defeated at various points; the factious nobles, one by one, deserted him, and returned to their allegiance to Alphonso, and the duke was finally compelled to retire to the island of Ischia. Here he remained for some time, guarded

by eight galleys, which likewise harassed the Bay of Naples.*
In this squadron, which loyally adhered to him, until he ultimately abandoned this unfortunate enterprise, Columbus is
stated to have served.

No. IX

CAPTURE OF THE VENETIAN GALLEYS BY COLOMBO THE YOUNGER

As the account of the sea-fight by which Fernando Columbus asserts that his father was first thrown upon the
shores of Portugal has been adopted by various respectable
historians, it is proper to give particular reasons for discredit-
ing it.

Fernando expressly says that it was in an action mentioned by Marco Antonio Sabelico, in the eighth book of his
tenth Decade; that the squadron in which Columbus served
was commanded by a famous corsair called Columbus the
younger (Colombo el mozo), and that an embassy was sent
from Venice to thank the king of Portugal for the succor he
afforded to the Venetian captains and crews. All this is
certainly recorded in Sabellicus, but the battle took place in
1485, after Columbus had *left* Portugal. Zurita, in his annals of Aragon, under the date of 1485, mentions this same
action. He says, "At this time four Venetian galleys sailed
from the island of Cadiz, and took the route for Flanders;
they were laden with merchandise from the Levant, especially
from the island of Sicily, and passing by Cape St. Vincent,
they were attacked by a French corsair, son of Captain Colon
(Colombo), who had seven vessels in his armada; and the
galleys were captured the twenty-first of August."†

A much fuller account is given in the life of King John
II. of Portugal, by Garcia de Resende, who likewise records
it as happening in 1485. He says the Venetian galleys were
taken and robbed by the French and the captains and crews,
wounded, plundered, and maltreated, were turned on shore
at Cascoes. Here they were succored by Dona Maria de
Meneses, Countess of Monsanto.

When King John II. heard of the circumstance, being

---

* Golenuccio, Hist. Nap., lib. vii., cap 17.
† Zurita, Anales de Aragon, lib. xx., cap. 64.

much grieved that such an event should have happened on his coast, and being disposed to show his friendship for the republic of Venice, he ordered that the Venetian captains should be furnished with rich raiment of silks and costly cloths, and provided with horses and mules, that they might make their appearance before him in a style befitting themselves and their country. He received them with great kindness and distinction, expressing himself with princely courtesy, both as to themselves and the republic of Venice; and having heard their account of the battle, and of their destitute situation, he assisted them with a large sum of money to ransom their galleys from the French cruisers. The latter took all the merchandise on board of their ships, but King John prohibited any of the spoil from being purchased within his dominions. Having thus generously relieved and assisted the captains, and administered to the necessities of their crews, he enabled them all to return in their own galleys to Venice.

The dignitaries of the republic were so highly sensible of this munificence on the part of King John that they sent a stately embassy to that monarch, with rich presents and warm expressions of gratitude. Geronimo Donate was charged with this mission, a man eminent for learning and eloquence; he was honorably received and entertained by King John and dismissed with royal presents, among which were genets, and mules with sumptuous trappings and caparisons, and many negro slaves richly clad.*

The following is the account of this action as given by Sabellicus, in his history of Venice: †

Erano andate quattro Galee delle quali Bartolommeo Minio era capitano. Queste navigando per l'Iberico mare, Colombo il più giovane, nipote di quel Colombo famoso corsale, fecesi incontro a' Veniziani di notte, appresso il sacro Promontorio, che chiamasi ora capo di san Vincenzo, con sette navi guernite da combattere. Egli quantunque nel primo incontro avesse seco disposto d' opprimere le navi Veniziane, si ritenne però

---

* Obras de Garcia de Resende, cap. 58, Avora, 1554.

† Marco Antonio Coccio, better known under the name of Sabellicus, a cognomen which he adopted on being crowned poet in the pedantic academy of Pomponius Lætus. He was a contemporary of Columbus, and makes brief mention of his discoveries in the eighth book of the tenth Ennead of his universal history. By some writers he is called the Livy of his time; others accuse him of being full of misrepresentations in favor of Venice. The older Scaliger charges him with venality, and with being swayed by Venetian gold.

dal combattere sin al giorno: tuttavia per esser alla battaglia più acconcio così le seguia, che le prode del corsale toccavano le poppe de Veniziani. Venuto il giorno incontanente i Barbari diedero l'assalto. Sostennero i Veniziani allora l'empito del nemico, per numero di navi e di combattenti superiore, e durò il conflitto atroce per molte ore. Rare fiate fu combattuto contro simili nemici con tanta uccisione, perchè a pena si costuma d'attaccarsi contro di loro, se non per occasione. Affermano alcuni, che vi furono presenti, esser morte delle ciurme Veniziane da trecento uomini. Altri dicono che fu meno: morì in quella zuffa Lorenzo Michele capitano d'una galera e Giovanni Delfino, d'altro capitano fratello. Era durata lat zuffa dal fare del giorno fin' ad ore venti, e erano le genti Veneziane mal trattate. Era gia la nave Delfina in potere de' nemici quando le altre ad una ad una si renderono. Narrano alcuni, che furono di quel aspro conflitto partecipi, aver numerato nelle loro navi da prode a poppe ottanta valorosi uomini estinti, i quali dal nemico veduti lo mossero a gemere e dire con sdegno, che cosi avevano voluto, i Veniziani. I corpi morti furono gettati nel mare, e i feriti posti nel lido. Quei che rimasero vivi seguirono con e navi il capitano vittorioso sin' a Lisbona e ivi furono tutti licenziati. . . . Quivi furono i Veniziani benignamente ricevuti dal Re, gli infermi furono medicati, gli altri ebbero abiti e denari secondo la loro condizione. . . . Oltre ciò vietò in tutto il Regno, che alcuno non comprasse della preda Veniziana, portata dai corsali. La nuova dell' avuta rovina non poco afflisse la città, erano perduti in quella mercatanzia da ducento mila ducati; ma il danno particolare degli uomini uccisi diede maggior afflizione.—*Marc. Ant. Sabelico, Hist. Venet.*, decad. iv., lib. iii.

No. X

AMERIGO VESPUCCI

AMONG the earliest and most intelligent of the voyagers who followed the track of Columbus was Amerigo Vespucci. He has been considered by many as the first discoverer of the southern continent, and by a singular caprice of fortune his name has been given to the whole of the New World. It has been strenuously insisted, however, that he had no claim to the title of a discoverer; that he merely sailed in a subor-

dinate capacity in a squadron commanded by others; that
the account of his first voyage is a fabrication; and that he
did not visit the mainland until after it had been discovered
and coasted by Columbus. As this question has been made
a matter of warm and voluminous controversy, it is proper
to take a summary view of it in the present work.

Amerigo Vespucci was born in Florence, March 9, 1451,
of a noble, but not at that time a wealthy family; his father's
name was Anastatio; his mother's was Elizabetta Mini. He
was the third of their sons, and received an excellent education under his uncle, Georgio Antonio Vespucci, a learned
friar of the fraternity of San Marco, who was instructor to
several illustrious personages of that period.

Amerigo Vespucci visited Spain, and took up his residence
in Seville, to attend to some commercial transactions on account of the family of the Medici of Florence, and to repair,
by his ingenuity, the losses and misfortunes of an unskillful
brother.*

The date of his arrival in Spain is uncertain, but from
comparing dates and circumstances mentioned in his letters,
he must have been at Seville when Columbus returned from
his first voyage.

Padre Stanislaus Canovai, Professor of Mathematics at
Florence, who has published the life and voyages of Amerigo
Vespucci, says that he was commissioned by King Ferdinand,
and sent with Columbus in his second voyage in 1493. He
states this on the authority of a passage in the Cosmography
of Sebastian Munster, published at Basle in 1550;† but Munster mentions Vespucci as having accompanied Columbus in
his first voyage; the reference of Canovai is therefore incorrect; and the suggestion of Munster is disproved by the letters of Vespucci, in which he states his having been stimulated by the accounts brought of the newly discovered regions.
He never mentions such a voyage in any of his letters; which
he most probably would have done, or rather would have
made it the subject of a copious letter, had he actually performed it.

The first notice of a positive form which we have of Vespucci, as resident in Spain, is early in 1496. He appears,
from documents in the royal archives at Seville, to have
acted as agent or factor for the house of Juanoto Berardi,

---

* Bandini vita d'Amerigo Vespucci.
† Cosm. Munst., p. 1108.

a rich Florentine merchant, resident in Seville, who had contracted to furnish the Spanish sovereigns with three several armaments, of four vessels each, for the service of the newly discovered countries. He may have been one of the principals in this affair, which was transacted in the name of this established house. Berardi died in December, 1495, and in the following January we find Amerigo Vespucci attending to the concerns of the expeditions and settling with the masters of the ships for their pay and maintenance, according to the agreements made between them and the late Juanoto Berardi. On the 12th January, 1496, he received on this account ten thousand maravedis from Bernardo Pinelo the royal treasurer. He went on preparing all things for the dispatch of four caravels to sail under the same contract between the sovereigns and the house of Berardi and sent them to sea on the 3d February, 1496; but on the 8th they met with a storm and were wrecked; the crews were saved with the loss of only three men.* While thus employed, Amerigo Vespucci, of course, had occasional opportunity of conversing with Columbus, with whom, according to the expression of the admiral himself, in one of his letters to his son Diego, he appears to have been always on friendly terms. From these conversations, and from his agency in these expeditions, he soon became excited to visit the newly discovered countries, and to participate in enterprises which were the theme of every tongue. Having made himself well acquainted with geographical and nautical science, he prepared to launch into the career of discovery. It was not very long before he carried this design into execution.

In 1498 Columbus, in his third voyage, discovered the coast of Paria on Terra Firma; which he at that time imagined to be a great island, but that a vast continent lay immediately adjacent. He sent to Spain specimens of pearls found on this coast, and gave the most sanguine accounts of the supposed riches of the country.

In 1499 an expedition of four vessels, under command of Alonzo de Ojeda, was fitted out from Spain, and sailed for Paria, guided by charts and letters sent to the government by Columbus. These were communicated to Ojeda by his patron, the Bishop Fonseca, who had the superintendence of

---

* These particulars are from manuscript memoranda, extracted from the royal archives by the late accurate historian Muñoz.

* * * 11—VOL. VII.

India affairs, and who furnished him also with a warrant to undertake the voyage.

It is presumed that Vespucci aided in fitting out the armament, and sailed in a vessel belonging to the house of Berardi, and in this way was enabled to take a share in the gains and losses of the expedition; for Isabella, as Queen of Castile, had rigorously forbidden all strangers to trade with her transatlantic possessions, not even excepting the natives of the kingdom of Aragon.

This squadron visited Paria and several hundred miles of the coast, which they ascertained to be Terra Firma. They returned in June, 1500; and on the 18th of July, in that year, Amerigo Vespucci wrote an account of his voyage to Lorenzo de Pier Francisco de' Medici of Florence, which remained concealed in manuscript until brought to light and published by Bandini in 1745.

In his account of this voyage, and in every other narrative of his different expeditions, Vespucci never mentions any other person concerned in the enterprise. He gives the time of his sailing, and states that he went with two caravels, which were probably his share of the expedition, or rather vessels sent by the house of Berardi. He gives an interesting narrative of the voyage, and of the various transactions with the natives, which corresponds, in many substantial points, with the accounts furnished by Ojeda and his mariners of their voyage, in a lawsuit hereafter mentioned.

In May, 1501, Vespucci, having suddenly left Spain, sailed in the service of Emanuel, king of Portugal; in the course of which expedition he visited the coast of Brazil. He gives an account of this voyage in a second letter to Lorenzo de Pier Francisco de' Medici, which also remained in manuscript until published by Bartolozzi in 1789.[*]

No record nor notice of any such voyage undertaken by Amerigo Vespucci, at the command of Emanuel, is to be found in the archives of the Torre do Tombo, the general archives of Portugal, which have been repeatedly and diligently searched for the purpose. It is singular also that his name is not to be found in any of the Portuguese historians, who in general were very particular in naming all navigators who held any important station among them, or rendered any distinguished services. That Vespucci did sail along the coasts, however, is not questioned. His nephew, after his

---

* Bartolozzi, Recherche Historico.   Firenze, 1789.

death, in the course of evidence on some points in dispute, gave the correct latitude of Cape St. Augustine, which he said he had extracted from his uncle's journal.

In 1504 Vespucci wrote a third letter to the same Lorenzo de' Medici, containing a more extended account of the voyage just alluded to in the service of Portugal. This was the first of his narratives that appeared in print. It appears to have been published in Latin, at Strasburgh, as early as 1505, under the title "Americus Vesputius de Orbe Antarctica per Regem Portugalliæ pridem inventa." *

An edition of this letter was printed in Vicenza in 1507, in an anonymous collection of voyages edited by Francanzio di Monte Alboddo, an inhabitant of Vicenza. It was reprinted in Italian in 1508, at Milan, and also in Latin, in a book entitled "Itinerarium Portugalensium." In making the present illustration, the Milan edition in Italian † has been consulted, and also a Latin translation of it by Simon Grimæus, in his "Novus Orbis," published at Basle in 1532. It relates entirely the first voyage of Vespucci from Lisbon to the Brazils in 1501.

It is from this voyage to the Brazils that Amerigo Vespucci was first considered the discoverer of Terra Firma; and his name was at first applied to these southern regions, though afterward extended to the whole continent. The merits of his voyage were, however, greatly exaggerated. The Brazils had been previously discovered, and formally taken possession of for Spain in 1500, by Vicente Yanez Pinzon; and also in the same year by Pedro Alvarez Cabral, on the part of

---

* Panzer, tom. vi., p. 33, apud Esame Critico, p. 88, Anotazione 1.

† This rare book, in the possession of O. Rich, Esq., is believed to be the oldest printed collection of voyages extant. It has not the pages numbered, the sheets are merely marked with a letter of the alphabet at the foot of each eighth page. It contains the earliest account of the voyages of Columbus, from his first departure until his arrival at Cadiz in chains. The letter of Vespucci to Lorenzo de' Medici occupies the fifth book of this little volume. It is stated to have been originally written in Spanish, and translated into Italian by a person of the name of Jocondo. An earlier edition is stated to have been printed in Venice by Alberto Vercellese in 1504. The author is said to have been Angelo Trivigiani, secretary to the Venetian embassador in Spain. This Trivigiani appears to have collected many of the particulars of the voyages of Columbus from the manuscript decades of Peter Martyr, who erroneously lays the charge of the plagiarism to Aloysius Cadamosto, whose voyages are inserted in the same collection. The book was entitled "Libretto di tutta la navigazione del Re de Espagna, della Isole e terreni nuovamente trovati."

Portugal; circumstances unknown, however, to Vespucci and his associates. The country remained in possession of Portugal, in conformity to the line of demarcation agreed on between the two nations.

Vespucci made a second voyage in the service of Portugal. He says that he commanded a caravel in a squadron of six vessels destined for the discovery of Malacca, which they had heard to be the great depot and magazine of all the trade between the Ganges and the Indian sea. Such an expedition did sail about this time, under the command of Gonzalo Coelho. The squadron sailed, according to Vespucci, on the 10th of May, 1503. It stopped at the Cape de Verde Islands for refreshments, and afterward sailed by the coast of Sierra Leone, but was prevented from landing by contrary winds and a turbulent sea. Standing to the southwest, they ran three hundred leagues until they were three degrees to the southward of the equinoctial line, where they discovered an uninhabited island, about two leagues in length and one in breadth. Here, on the 10th of August, by mismanagement, the commander of the squadron ran his vessel on a rock and lost her. While the other vessels were assisting to save the crew and property from the wreck, Amerigo Vespucci was dispatched in his caravel to search for a safe harbor in the island. He departed in his vessel without his long boat, and with less than half of his crew, the rest having gone in the boat to the assistance of the wreck. Vespucci found a harbor, but waited in vain for several days for the arrival of the ships. Standing out to sea he met with a solitary vessel, and learned that the ship of the commander had sunk, and the rest had proceeded onward. In company with this vessel he stood for the Brazils, according to a command of the king, in case that any vessel should be parted from the fleet. Arriving on the coast he discovered the famous bay of All Saints, where he remained upward of two months, in hopes of being joined by the rest of the fleet. He at length ran two hundred and sixty leagues further south, where he remained five months building a fort and taking in a cargo of Brazil wood. Then, leaving in the fortress a garrison of twenty-four men with arms and ammunition, he set sail for Lisbon, where he arrived in June, 1504.* The commander of the squadron and the other four ships were never heard of afterward.

---

* Letter of Vespucci to Soderini or Renato—Edit. of Canovai.

Vespucci does not appear to have received the reward from the king of Portugal that his services merited, for we find him at Seville early in 1505, on his way to the Spanish court, in quest of employment; and he was bearer of a letter from Columbus to his son Diego, dated February 5th, which, while it speaks warmly of him as a friend, intimates his having been unfortunate. The following is the letter:

"MY DEAR SON—Diego Mendez departed hence on Monday, the third of this month. After his departure I conversed with Amerigo Vespucci, the bearer of this, who goes there (to court) summoned on affairs of navigation. Fortune has been adverse to him as to many others. His labors have not profited him as much as they reasonably should have done. He goes on my account, and with much desire to do something that may result to my advantage, if within his power. I cannot ascertain here in what I can employ him that will be serviceable to me, for I do not know what may be there required. He goes with the determination to do all that is possible for me; see in what he may be of advantage and co-operate with him, that he may say and do everything, and put his plans in operation; and let all be done secretly, that he may not be suspected. I have said everything to him that I can say touching the business, and have informed him of the pay I have received, and what is due," etc.*

About this time Amerigo Vespucci received letters of naturalization from King Ferdinand, and shortly afterward he and Vicente Yanez Pinzon were named captains of an armada about to be sent out in the spice trade and to make discoveries. There is a royal order, dated Toro, 11th of April, 1507, for twelve thousand maravedis for an outfit for "Americo de Vespuche, resident of Seville." Preparations were made for this voyage, and vessels procured and fitted out, but it was eventually abandoned. There are memoranda existing concerning it, dated in 1506, 1507, and 1508, from which it appears that Amerigo Vespucci remained at Seville, attending to the fluctuating concerns of this squadron, until the destination of the vessels was changed, their equipments were sold, and the accounts settled. During this time he had a salary of thirty thousand maravedis. On the 22d of March, 1508, he received the appointment of principal pilot, with a

---

* Navarrete, Collec. Viag., tom. i., p. 351.

salary of seventy thousand maravedis. His chief duties were to prepare charts, examine pilots, superintend the fitting out of expeditions, and prescribe the route that vessels were to pursue in their voyages to the New World. He appears to have remained at Seville, and to have retained this office until his death, on the 22d of February, 1512. His widow, Maria Corezo, enjoyed a pension of ten thousand maravedis. After his death, his nephew, Juan Vespucci, was nominated pilot with a salary of twenty thousand maravedis, commencing on the 22d of May, 1512. Peter Martyr speaks with high commendation of this young man. "Young Vesputius is one to whom Americus Vesputius his uncle left the exact knowledge of the mariner's faculties, as it were, by inheritance, after his death; for he was a very expert master in the knowledge of his carde, his compasse, and the elevation of the pole starre by the quadrant. . . . Vesputius is my very familiar friend, and a wittie young man, in whose company I take great pleasure, and therefore use him oftentymes for my guest. He hath also made many voyages into these coasts, and diligently noted such things as he hath seen." *

Vespucci, the nephew, continued in this situation during the lifetime of Fonseca, who had been the patron of his uncle and his family. He was divested of his pay and his employ by a letter of the council, dated the 18th of March, 1525, shortly after the death of the bishop. No further notice of Vespucci is to be found in the archives of the Indies.

Such is a brief view of the career of Amerigo Vespucci; it remains to notice the points of controversy. Shortly after his return from his last expedition to the Brazils, he wrote a letter dated Lisbon, 4th September, 1504, containing a summary account of all his voyages. This letter is of special importance to the matters under investigation, as it is the only one known that relates to the disputed voyage which would establish him as the discoverer of Terra Firma. It is presumed to have been written in Latin, and was addressed to Rene, Duke of Lorraine, who assumed the title of King of Sicily and Jerusalem.

The earliest known edition of this letter was published in Latin, in 1507, at St. Diez in Lorraine. A copy of it has been found in the library of the Vatican (No. 9688) by the Abbe Cancellieri. In preparing the present illustration, a

---

* Peter Martyr, decad. iii., lib. v., Eden's English trans.

reprint of this letter in Latin has been consulted, inserted in the Novus Orbis of Grinæus, published at Bath in 1532. The letter contains a spirited narrative of four voyages which he asserts to have made to the New World. In the prologue he excuses the liberty of addressing King Rene by calling to his recollection the ancient intimacy of their youth, when studying the rudiments of science together, under the paternal uncle of the voyager; and adds that if the present narrative should not altogether please his majesty, he must plead to him as Pliny said to Mecænas, that he used formerly to be amused with his triflings.

In the prologue to this letter, he informs King Rene that affairs of commerce had brought him to Spain, where he had experienced the various changes of fortune attendant on such transactions, and was induced to abandon that pursuit and direct his labors to objects of a more elevated and stable nature. He therefore purposed to contemplate various parts of the world, and to behold the marvels which it contains. To this object both time and place were favorable; for King Ferdinand was then preparing four vessels for the discovery of new lands in the west, and appointed him among the number of those who went in the expedition. "We departed," he adds, "from the port of Cadiz, May 20, 1497, taking our course on the great gulf of ocean; in which voyage we employed eighteen months, discovering many lands and innumerable islands, chiefly inhabited, of which our ancestors make no mention."

A duplicate of this letter appears to have been sent at the same time (written, it is said, in Italian) to Piere Soderini, afterward Gonfalonier of Florence, which was some years subsequently published in Italy, not earlier than 1510, and entitled "Lettera de Amerigo Vespucci delle Isole nuovamente trovate in quatro suoi viaggi." We have consulted the edition of this letter in Italian, inserted in the publication of Padre Stanislaus Canovai, already referred to.

It has been suggested by an Italian writer that this letter was written by Vespucci to Soderini only, and the address altered to King Rene through the flattery or mistake of the Lorraine editor, without perceiving how unsuitable the reference to former intimacy, intended for Soderini, was, when applied to a sovereign. The person making this remark can hardly have read the prologue to the Latin edition, in which the title of "your majesty" is frequently repeated, and the term "illustrious king" employed. It was first published also in Lorraine, the domains of Rene, and the publisher would not probably have presumed to take such a liberty with his sovereign's name. It becomes a question, whether Vespucci addressed the same letter to King Rene and to Piere Soderini, both of them having been educated with him, or whether he sent a copy of this letter to Soderini, which subsequently found its way into print. The address to Soderini may have been substituted, through mistake, by the Italian publisher. Neither of the publications could have been made under the supervision of Vespucci.

The voyage specified in this letter as having taken place in 1497 is the great point in controversy. It is strenuously asserted that no such voyage took place; and that the first expedition of Vespucci to the coast of Paria was in the enterprise commanded by Ojeda, in 1499. The books of the armadas existing in the archives of the Indies at Seville have been diligently examined, but no record of such voyage has been found, nor any official documents relating to it. Those most experienced in Spanish colonial regulations insist that no command like that pretended by Vespucci could have been given to a stranger, till he had first received letters of naturalization from the sovereigns for the kingdom of Castile, and he did not obtain such till 1505, when they were granted to him as preparatory to giving him the command in conjunction with Pinzon.

His account of a voyage made by him in 1497, therefore, is alleged to be a fabrication for the purpose of claiming the discovery of Paria; or rather it is affirmed that he has divided the voyage which he actually made with Ojeda, in 1499, into two; taking a number of incidents from his real voyage, altering them a little, and enlarging them with descriptions of the countries and people, so as to make a plausible narrative, which he gives as a distinct voyage; and antedating his departure to 1497, so as to make himself appear the first discoverer of Paria.

In support of this charge various coincidences have been pointed out between his voyage said to have taken place in 1497, and that described in his first letter to Lorenzo de' Medici in 1499. These coincidences are with respect to places visited, transactions and battles with the natives, and the number of Indians carried to Spain and sold as slaves.

But the credibility of this voyage has been put to a stronger test. About 1508 a suit was instituted against the crown of Spain by Don Diego, son and heir of Columbus, for the government of certain parts of Terra Firma, and for a share in the revenue arising from them, conformably to the capitulations made between the sovereigns and his father. It was the object of the crown to disprove the discovery of the coast of Paria and the pearl islands by Columbus, as it was maintained that, unless he had discovered them, the claim of his heir with respect to them would be of no validity.

In the course of this suit, a particular examination of witnesses took place in 1512–13 in the fiscal court. Alonzo de Ojeda, and nearly a hundred other persons, were interrogated on oath; that voyager having been the first to visit the coast of Paria after Columbus had left it, and that within a very few months. The interrogatories of these witnesses, and their replies, are still extant, in the archives of the Indies at Seville, in a packet of papers entitled "Papers belonging to the Admiral Don Luis Colon, about the conservation of his privileges, from ann. 1515 to 1564." The author of the present work has two several copies of these interrogatories lying before him. One made by the late historian Munoz, and the other made in 1826, and signed by Don Jose de la Higuera y Lara, keeper of the general archives of the Indies in Seville. In the course of this testimony, the fact that Amerigo Vespucci accompanied Ojeda in this voyage of 1499 appears manifest, first from the deposition of Ojeda himself. The following are the words of the record: "In this voyage which this said witness made, he took with him Juan de la Cosa and Morego Vespuche [Amerigo Vespucci] and other pilots."* Secondly, from the coincidence of many parts of the narrative of Vespucci with events in this voyage of Ojeda. Among these coincidences, one is particularly striking. Vespucci, in his letter to Lorenzo de' Medici, and also in that to Rene or Soderini, says that his ships, after leaving the coast of Terra Firma, stopped at Hispaniola, where they remained about two months and a half, procuring provisions, during which time, he adds, "we had many perils and troubles with the very Christians who were in that island with Columbus, and I believe through envy." †

---

* En este viage que este dicho testigo hizo trujo consigo a Juan de la Cosa, piloto, e Morego Vespuche, e otros pilotos.

† Per la necessitá del mantenimento fummo all' Isola d'Antiglia (Hispaniola) che é questa che descoperse Cristoval Colombo piú anni fa, dove facemmo molto mantenimento, e stemmo due mesi e 17 giorni; dove passammo moti pericoli e travagli con li medesimi christiani que in questa isola stavanno col Colombo (credo per invidia). Letter of Vespucci—Edit. of Canovai.

Now it is well known that Ojeda passed some time on the western end of the island victualing his ships; and that serious dissensions took place between him and the Spaniards in those parts, and the party sent by Columbus under Roldan to keep a watch upon his movements. If then Vespucci, as is stated upon oath, really accompanied Ojeda in this voyage, the inference appears almost irresistible that he had not made the previous voyage of 1497, for the fact would have been well known to Ojeda; he would have considered Vespucci as the original discoverer and would have had no motive for depriving him of the merit of it, to give it to Columbus, with whom Ojeda was not upon friendly terms.

Ojeda, however, expressly declares that the coast had been discovered by Columbus. On being asked how he knew the fact, he replied, because he saw the chart of the country discovered, which Columbus sent at the time to the king and queen, and that he came off immediately on a voyage of discovery, and found what was therein set down as discovered by the admiral was correct.*

Another witness, Bernaldo de Haro, states that he had been with the admiral, and had written (or rather copied) a letter for the admiral to the king and queen, designating, in an accompanying sea-chart, the courses and steerings and winds by which he had arrived at Paria; and that this witness had heard that from this chart others had been made, and that Pedro Alonzo Nino and Ojeda, and others, who had since visited these countries, had been guided by the same.†

Francisco de Morales, one of the best and credible of all the pilots, testified that he saw a sea-chart which Columbus had made of the coast of Paria, *and he believed that all governed themselves by it.*‡

Numerous witnesses in this process testify to the fact that

---

* Preguntado como lo sabe; dijo—que lo sabe porque vió estetestigo la figura que el dicho Almirante al dicho tiempo embió á Castilla al Rey e Reyna, nuestros Señores, de lo que habia descubierto, y porque este testigo luego vino á descubrir y halló que era verdad lo que dicho tiene que el dicho Almirante descubrió. MS. Process of D. Diego Colon, pregunta 2.

† Este testigo escrivió úna carta que el Almirante escriviera al Rey a Reyna N. N. S. S. haciendo les saber las perlas e cosas que habia hallado, y le embió señalado con la dicha carta, en una carta de marear, los rumbos y vientos por donde habia llegado á la Paria, e que este testigo oyó decir como pr. aquella carte se habian hecho otras e por ellas habian venido Pedro Alonzo Merino [Niño] e Ojeda e otros que despues han ido á aquellas partes. Idem, pregunta 9.

‡ Process of D. Diego Colon, pregunta 10.

Paria was first discovered by Columbus. Las Casas, who has been at the pains of counting them, says that the fact was established by twenty-five eye-witnesses and sixty ear-witnesses. Many of them testify also that the coast south of Paria, and that extending west of the island of Margarita, away to Venezuela, which Vespucci states to have been discovered by himself in 1497, was now first discovered by Ojeda, and had never before been visited either by the admiral "or any other Christian whatever."

Alonzo Sanchez de Carvajal says that all the voyages of discovery which were made to the Terra Firma were made by persons who had sailed with the admiral, or been benefited by his instructions and directions, following the course he had laid down;* and the same is testified by many other pilots and mariners of reputation and experience.

It would be a singular circumstance if none of these witnesses, many of whom must have sailed in the same squadron with Vespucci along this coast in 1499, should have known that he had discovered and explored it two years previously. If that had really been the case, what motive could he have for concealing the fact? and why, if they knew it, should they not proclaim it? Vespucci states his voyage in 1497 to have been made with four caravels; that they returned in October, 1498, and that he sailed again with two caravels in May, 1499 (the date of Ojeda's departure). Many of the mariners would therefore have been present in both voyages. Why, too, should Ojeda and the other pilots guide themselves by the charts of Columbus, when they had a man on board so learned in nautical science, and who, from his own recent observations, was practically acquainted with the coast? Not a word, however, is mentioned of the voyage and discovery of Vespucci by any of the pilots, though every other voyage and discovery is cited; nor does there even a seaman appear who has accompanied him in his asserted voyage.

Another strong circumstance against the reality of this voyage is that it was not brought forward in this trial to defeat the claims of the heirs of Columbus. Vespucci states the voyage to have been undertaken with the knowledge and

---

* Que en todos los viages que algunos hicieron descubriendo en la dicha tierra, ivan personas que ovieron navegado con el dicho Almirante, y a ellos mostró muchas cosas de marear, y ellos por imitacion ó industria del dicho Almirante las aprendian y aprendieron, e seguendo ag°. que el dicho Almirante les habia mostrado, hicieron los viages que descubrieron en la Tierra Firma. Process, pregunta 10.

countenance of King Ferdinand; it must, therefore, have been avowed and notorious. Vespucci was living at Seville in 1508, at the time of the commencement of this suit, and for four years afterward, a salaried servant of the crown. Many of the pilots and mariners must have been at hand who sailed with him in his pretended enterprise. If this voyage had once been proved, it would completely have settled the question, as far as concerned the coast of Paria, in favor of the crown. Yet no testimony appears ever to have been taken from Vespucci while living; and when the interrogatories were made in the fiscal court in 1512–13, not one of his seamen is brought up to give evidence. A voyage so important in its nature, and so essential to the question in dispute, is not even alluded to, while useless pains are taken to wrest evidence from the voyage of Ojeda, undertaken at a subsequent period.

It is a circumstance worthy of notice that Vespucci commences his first letters to Lorenzo de' Medici in 1500, within a month after his return from the voyage he had actually made to Paria, and apologizes for his long silence, by saying that nothing had occurred worthy of mention ("e gran tempo che non ho scritto á vostra magnifizensa, e non lo ha causato altra cosa ne nessuna salvo non mi essere occorso cosa degna di memoria"), and proceeds eagerly to tell him the wonders he had witnessed in the expedition from which he had but just returned. It would be a singular forgetfulness to say that nothing had occurred of importance, if he had made a previous voyage of eighteen months in 1497–8 to this newly-discovered world; and it would be almost equally strange that he should not make the slightest allusion to it in this letter.

It has been the endeavor of the author to examine this question dispassionately; and after considering the statements and arguments advanced on either side, he cannot resist a conviction that the voyage stated to have been made in 1497 did not take place, and that Vespucci has no title to the first discovery of the coast of Paria.

The question is extremely perplexing from the difficulty of assigning sufficient motives for so gross a deception. When Vespucci wrote his letters there was no doubt entertained but that Columbus had discovered the mainland in his first voyage; Cuba being always considered the extremity of Asia, until circumnavigated in 1508. Vespucci may have supposed Brazil, Paria, and the rest of that coast, part of a distinct continent, and have been anxious to arrogate to himself the fame of its discovery. It has been asserted that, on his return from his voyage to the Brazils, he prepared a maritime chart, in which he gave his name to that part of the mainland; but this assertion does not appear to be well substantiated. It would rather seem that his name was given to that part of the continent by others, as a tribute paid to his supposed merit, in consequence of having read his own account of his voyages.*

It is singular that Fernando, the son of Columbus, in his biography of his father, should bring no charge against Vespucci of endeavoring to supplant the admiral in this discovery. Herrera has been cited as the first to bring the accusation, in his history of the Indies, first published in 1601, and has been much criticised in consequence by the advocates of Vespucci, as making the charge on his mere assertion. But, in fact, Herrera did but copy what he found written by Las Casas, who had the proceedings of the fiscal court lying before him, and was moved to indignation against Vespucci, by what he considered proofs of great imposture.

It has been suggested that Vespucci was instigated to this deception at the time when he was seeking employment in the colonial service of Spain; and that he did it to conciliate the Bishop Fonseca, who was desirous of anything that might injure the interests of Columbus. In corroboration of this opinion, the patronage is cited, which was ever shown by

---

* The first suggestion of the name appears to have been in the Latin work already cited, published in St. Diez, in Lorraine, in 1507, in which was inserted the letter of Vespucci to King René. The author, after speaking of the other three parts of the world, Asia, Africa and Europe, recommends that the fourth shall be called Amerigo, or America, after Vespucci, whom he imagined its discoverer.

Note to the Revised Edition, 1848.—Humboldt, in his "Examen Critique," published in Paris in 1837, says: "I have been so happy as to discover, very recently, the name and the literary relations of the mysterious personage who (in 1507) was the first to propose the name of America to designate the new continent, and who concealed himself under the Grecianized name of Hylacomylas." He then, by a long and ingenious investigation, shows that the real name of this personage was Martin Waldseemüller, of Fribourg, an eminent cosmographer patronized by René, Duke of Lorraine, who, no doubt, put in his hands the letter received by him from Amerigo Vespucci. The geographical works of Waldseemüller, under the assumed name of Hylacomylas, had a wide circulation, went through repeated editions, and propagated the use of the name America throughout the world. There is no reason to suppose that this application of the name was in anywise suggested by Amerigo Vespucci. It appears to have been entirely gratuitous on the part of Waldseemüller.

Fonseca to Vespucci and his family. This is not, however, a satisfactory reason, since it does not appear that the bishop ever made any use of the fabrication. Perhaps some other means might be found of accounting for this spurious narration, without implicating the veracity of Vespucci. It may have been the blunder of some editor, or the interpolation of some book-maker, eager, as in the case of Trivigiani with the manuscripts of Peter Martyr, to gather together disjointed materials, and fabricate a work to gratify the prevalent passion of the day.

In the various editions of the letters of Vespucci, the grossest variations and inconsistencies in dates will be found, evidently the errors of hasty and careless publishers. Several of these have been corrected by the modern authors who have inserted these letters in their works.* The same disregard to exactness which led to these blunders may have produced the interpolation of this voyage, garbled out of the letters of Vespucci and the accounts of other voyagers. This is merely suggested as a possible mode of accounting for what appears so decidedly to be a fabrication, yet which we are loth to attribute to a man of the good sense, the character, and the reputed merit of Vespucci.

After all, this is a question more of curiosity than of real moment, although it is one of those perplexing points about which grave men will continue to write weary volumes, until the subject acquires a factitious importance from the mountain of controversy heaped upon it. It has become a question of local pride with the literati of Florence; and they emulate each other with patriotic zeal to vindicate the fame of their distinguished countryman. This zeal is laudable when kept within proper limits; but it is to be regretted that some of them have so far been heated by controversy as to become irascible against the very memory of Columbus, and to seek

---

* An instance of these errors may be cited in the edition of the letter of Amerigo Vespucci to King René, inserted by Grinæus in his Novus Orbis in 1532. In this Vespucci is made to state that he sailed from Cadiz May 20, MCCCCXCVII. (1497), that he was eighteen months absent, and returned to Cadiz Oct. 15, MCCCCXCIX. (1499), which would constitute an absence of twenty-nine months. He states his departure from Cadiz, on his second voyage, Sunday, May 11, MCCCCLXXXIX. (1489), which would have made his second voyage precede his first by eight years. If we substitute 1499 for 1489, the departure on his second voyage would still precede his return from his first by five months. Canovai, in his edition, has altered the date of the first return to 1498, to limit the voyage to eighteen months.

to disparage his general fame, as if the ruin of it would add anything to the reputation of Vespucci. This is discreditable to their discernment and their liberality; it injures their cause, and shocks the feelings of mankind, who will not willingly see a name like that of Columbus lightly or petulantly assailed in the course of these literary contests. It is a name consecrated in history, and is no longer the property of a city, or a state, or a nation, but of the whole world.

Neither should those who have a proper sense of the merit of Columbus put any part of his great renown at issue upon this minor dispute. Whether or not he was the discoverer of Paria was a question of interest to his heirs, as a share of the government and revenues of that country depended upon it; but it is of no importance to his fame. In fact, the European who first reached the mainland of the New World was most probably Sebastian Cabot, a native of Venice, sailing in the employ of England. In 1497 he coasted its shores from Labrador to Florida; yet the English have never set up any pretensions on his account.

The glory of Columbus does not depend upon the parts of the country he visited or the extent of coast along which he sailed; it embraces the discovery of the whole western world. With respect to him, Vespucci is as Yanez Pinzon, Bastides, Ojeda, Cabot, and the crowd of secondary discoverers who followed in his track, and explored the realms to which he had led the way. When Columbus first touched a shore of the New World, even though a frontier island, he had achieved his enterprises; he had accomplished all that was necessary to his fame: the great problem of the ocean was solved, the world which lay beyond its western waters was discovered.

No. XI

MARTIN ALONZO PINZON

In the course of the trial in the fiscal court, between Don Diego and the crown, an attempt was made to depreciate the merit of Columbus, and to ascribe the success of the great enterprise of discovery to the intelligence and spirit of Martin Alonzo Pinzon. It was the interest of the crown to do so, to justify itself in withholding from the heirs of Columbus the extent of his stipulated reward. The examinations of witnesses in this trial were made at various times and places, and upon a set of interrogatories formally drawn up by order of the fiscal. They took place upward of twenty years after the first voyage of Columbus, and the witnesses testified from recollection.

In reply to one of the interrogatories, Arias Perez Pinzon, son of Martin Alonzo, declared that, being once in Rome with his father on commercial affairs, before the time of the discovery, they had frequent conversations with a person learned in cosmography who was in the service of Pope Innocent VIII., and that, being in the library of the Pope, this person showed them many manuscripts, from one of which his father gathered intimation of these new lands; for there was a passage by a historian as old as the time of Solomon, which said, "Navigate the Meditreranean Sea to the end of Spain and thence toward the setting sun, in a direction between north and south, until ninety-five degrees of longitude, and you will find the land of Cipango, fertile and abundant, and equal in greatness to Africa and Europe." A copy of this writing, he added, his father brought from Rome with an intention of going in search of that land, and frequently expressed such determination; and that, when Columbus came to Palos with his project of discovery, Martin Alonzo Pinzon showed him the manuscript, and ultimately gave it to him just before they sailed.

It is extremely probable that this manuscript, of which Arias Perez gives so vague an account from recollection, but which he appears to think the main thing that prompted Columbus to his undertaking, was no other than the work of Marco Polo, which, at that time, existed in manuscript in most of the Italian libraries. Martin Alonzo was evidently acquainted with the work of the Venetian, and it would appear, from various circumstances, that Columbus had a copy of it with him in his voyages, which may have been the manuscript above mentioned. Columbus had long before, however, had a knowledge of the work, if not by actual inspection, at least through his correspondence with Toscanelli in 1474, and had derived from it all the light it was capable of furnishing, before he ever came to Palos. It is questionable, also, whether the visit of Martin Alonzo to Rome was not after his mind had been heated by conversations with Columbus in the convent of La Rabida. The testimony of Arias Perez is so worded as to leave it in doubt whether the visit was not in the very year prior to the discovery: "Fue el dicho su padre á Roma aquel dicho año antes que fuese a descubrir." Arias Perez always mentions the manuscript as having been imparted to Columbus, after he had come to Palos with an intention of proceeding on the discovery.

Certain witnesses who were examined on behalf of the crown, and to whom specific interrogatories were put, asserted, as has already been mentioned in a note to this work, that had it not been for Martin Alonzo Pinzon and his brothers, Columbus would have turned back for Spain, after having run seven or eight hundred leagues; being disheartened at not finding land, and dismayed by the mutiny and menaces of his crew. This is stated by two or three as from personal knowledge, and by others from hearsay. It is said especially to have occurred on the 6th of October. On this day, according to the journal of Columbus, he had some conversation with Martin Alonzo, who was anxious that they should stand more to the southwest. The admiral refused to do so, and it is very probable that some angry words may have passed between them. Various disputes appear to have taken place between Columbus and his colleagues respecting their route, previous to the discovery of land; in one or two instances he acceded to their wishes and altered his course, but in general he was inflexible in standing to the west. The Pinzons also, in all probability, exerted their influence in quelling the murmurs of their townsmen and encouraging them to proceed, when ready to rebel against Columbus. These circumstances may have become mixed up in the vague recollections of the seamen who gave the foregoing extravagant testimony, and who were evidently disposed to exalt the merits of the Pinzons at the expense of Columbus. They were in some measure prompted also in their replies by the written interrogatories put by order of the fiscal, which specified the conversations said to have passed between Columbus and the Pinzons, and notwithstanding these guides they differed widely in their statements, and ran into many absurdities. In a manuscript record in possession of the Pinzon family, I have even read the assertion of an old seaman that Columbus, in his eagerness to compel the Pinzons to turn back to Spain, *fired upon their ships*, but, they continuing on, he was obliged to follow, and within two days afterward discovered the island of Hispaniola.

It is evident the old sailor, if he really spoke conscientiously, mingled in his cloudy remembrance the disputes in the early part of the voyage, about altering their course to the southwest, and the desertion of Martin Alonzo, subsequent to the discovery of the Lucayos and Cuba, when, after parting company with the admiral, he made the island of Hispaniola.

The witness most to be depended upon as to these points of inquiry is the physician of Palos, Garcia Fernandez, a man of education, who sailed with Martin Alonzo Pinzon as steward of his ship, and of course was present at all the conversations which passed between the commanders. He testifies that Martin Alonzo urged Columbus to stand more to the southwest, and that the admiral at length complied, but, finding no land in that direction, they turned again to the west; a statement which completely coincides with the journal of Columbus. He adds that the admiral continually comforted and animated Martin Alonzo, and all others in his company. (Siempre los consolaba el dicho Almirante esforzandolos al dicho Martin Alonzo e â todos los que en su compania iban.) When the physician was specifically questioned as to the conversations pretended to have passed between the commanders, in which Columbus expressed a desire to turn back to Spain, he referred to the preceding statement as the only answer he had to make to these interrogatories.

The extravagant testimony before mentioned appears never to have had any weight with the fiscal; and the accurate historian Munoz, who extracted all these points of evidence from the papers of the lawsuit, has not deemed them worthy of mention in his work. As these matters, however, remain on record in the archives of the Indies, and in the archives of the Pinzon family, in both of which I have had a full opportunity of inspecting them, I have thought it advisable to make these few observations on the subject; lest, in the rage for research, they might hereafter be drawn forth as a new discovery, on the strength of which to impugn the merits of Columbus.

No. XII

RUMOR OF THE PILOT SAID TO HAVE DIED IN THE HOUSE OF COLUMBUS

AMONG the various attempts to injure Columbus by those who were envious of his fame was one intended to destroy all his merit as an original discoverer. It was said that he had received information of the existence of land in the western parts of the ocean from a tempest-tossed pilot, who had been driven there by violent easterly winds, and who, on his return to Europe, had died in the house of Columbus, leaving in his possession the chart and journal of his voyage, by which he was guided to his discovery.

This story was first noticed by Oviedo, a contemporary of Columbus, in his history of the Indies, published in 1535. He mentions it as a rumor circulating among the vulgar, without foundation in truth.

Fernando Lopez de Gomara first brought it forward against Columbus. In his history of the Indies, published in 1552, he repeats the rumor in the vaguest terms, manifestly from Oviedo, but without the contradiction given to it by that author. He says that the name and country of the pilot were unknown, some terming him an Andalusian, sailing between the Canaries and Madeira; others a Biscayan, trading to England and France; and others a Portuguese, voyaging between Lisbon and Mina, on the coast of Guinea. He expresses equal uncertainty whether the pilot brought the caravel to Portugal, to Madeira, or to one of the Azores. The only point on which the circulators of the rumor are agreed was that he died in the house of Columbus. Gomara adds that by this event Columbus was led to undertake his voyage to the new countries.*

The other early historians who mention Columbus and his voyages, and were his contemporaries; viz., Sabellicus, Peter Martyr, Giustiniani, Bernaldes, commonly called the curate of Los Palacios, Las Casas, Fernando, the son of the admiral, and the anonymous author of a voyage of Columbus, translated from the Italian into Latin by Madrignano,† are all silent in regard to this report.

Benzoni, whose history of the New World was published in 1565, repeats the story from Gomara, with whom he was contemporary; but decidedly expresses his opinion that Gomara had mingled up much falsehood with some truth, for the purpose of detracting from the fame of Columbus, through

---

* Gomara, Hist. Ind., cap. 14.

† Navigatio Christophori Columbi, Madrignano Interprete. It is contained in a collection of voyages called Novus Orbis Regionum, edition of 1555, but was originally published in Italian as written by Montalbodo Francanzano (or Francapano de Montaldo), in a collection of voyages entitled Nuovo Mundo, in Vicenza, 1507.

jealousy that any one but a Spaniard should enjoy the honor of the discovery.*

Acosta notices the circumstance slightly in his Natural and Moral History of the Indies, published in 1591, and takes it evidently from Gomara.†

Mariana, in his history of Spain, published in 1592, also mentions it, but expresses a doubt of its truth, and derives his information manifestly from Gomara.‡

Herrera, who published his history of the Indies in 1601, takes no notice of the story. In not noticing it, he may be considered as rejecting it; for he is distinguished for his minuteness, and was well acquainted with Gomara's history, which he expressly contradicts on a point of considerable interest.‖

Garcilaso de la Vega, a native of Cusco in Peru, revived the tale with very minute particulars, in his Commentaries of the Incas, published in 1609. He tells it smoothly and circumstantially; fixes the date of the occurrence 1484, "one year more or less"; states the name of the unfortunate pilot, Alonzo Sanchez de Huelva; the destination of his vessel, from the Canaries to Madeira; and the unknown land to which they were driven, the island of Hispaniola. The pilot, he says, landed, took an altitude, and wrote an account of all he saw, and all that had occurred in the voyage. He then took in wood and water, and set out to seek his way home. He succeeded in returning, but the voyage was long and tempestuous, and twelve died of hunger and fatigue, out of seventeen, the original number of the crew. The five survivors arrived at Tercera, where they were hospitably entertained by Columbus, but all died in his house in consequence of the hardships they had sustained; the pilot was the last that died, leaving his host heir to his papers. Columbus kept them profoundly secret, and by pursuing the route therein prescribed, obtained the credit of discovering the New World.¶

Such are the material points of the circumstantial relation furnished by Garcilaso de la Vega, one hundred and twenty years after the event. In regard to authority, he recollects

---

* Girolamo Benzoni, Hist. del Nuevo Mundo, lib. i., fo. 12. In Venetia, 1572.

† Padre Joseph de Acosta, Hist. Ind., lib. i., cap. 19.

‡ Juan de Mariana, Hist. España, lib. xxvi., cap. 8.

‖ Herrera, Hist. Ind., decad. ii., lib. iii., cap. 1.

¶ Commentarios de los Incas, lib. i., cap. 8.

to have heard the story when he was a child, as a subject of conversation between his father and the neighbors, and he refers to the histories of the Indies, by Acosta and Gomara, for confirmation. As the conversations to which he listened must have taken place sixty or seventy years after the date of the report, there had been sufficient time for the vague rumors to become arranged into a regular narrative, and thus we have not only the name, country, and destination of the pilot, but also the name of the unknown land to which his vessel was driven.

This account given by Garcilaso de la Vega has been adopted by many old historians, who have felt a confidence in the peremptory manner in which he relates it, and in the authorities to whom he refers.* These have been echoed by others of more recent date; and thus a weighty charge of fraud and imposture has been accumulated against Columbus, apparently supported by a crowd of respectable accusers. The whole charge is to be traced to Gomara, who loosely repeated a vague rumor, without noticing the pointed contradiction given to it seventeen years before by Oviedo, an ear-witness, from whose book he appears to have actually gathered the report.

It is to be remarked that Gomara bears the character, among historians, of inaccuracy, and of great credulity in adopting unfounded stories.†

---

* Names of historians who either adopted this story in detail or the charge against Columbus, drawn from it.

Bernardo Aldrete, Antiguedad de España, lib. iv., cap. 17, p. 567.
Roderigo Caro, Antiguedad, lib. iii., cap. 76.
Juan de Solorzano, Ind. Jure, tom. i., lib. i., cap. 5.
Fernando Pizarro, Varones Illust. del Nuevo Mundo, cap. 2.
Agostino Torniel, Annal. Sacr., tom. i., ann. Mund., 1931, No. 48.
Pet. Damarez or De Mariz, Dial. iv., de Var. Hist., cap. 4.
Gregoria Garcia, Orig. de los Indios, lib. i., cap. 4, § 1.
Juan de Torquemanda, Monarch. Ind., lib. xviii., cap. 1.
John Baptiste Riccioli, Geograf. Reform., lib. iii.
To this list of old authors may be added many others of more recent date.

† "Francisco Lopez de Gomara, Presbitero, Sevillano, escribio con elegante estilo acerca de la cosas de las Indies, pero dexandose llevar de falsas narraciones." Hijos de Sevilla, Numero ii., p. 42, Let. F. The same is stated in Bibliotheca Hispaña Nova, lib. i., p. 437.

"El Francisco Lopez de Gomara escrivio tantos borrones é cosas que no son verdaderas, de que ha hecho mucho daño a muchos escritores e coronistas, que despues del Gomara han escrito en las cosas de la Nueva España . . . es porque les ha hecho errar el Gomara."

It is unnecessary to give further refutation to this charge, especially as it is clear that Colum·us communicated his idea of discovery to Paulo Toscanelli of Florence, in 1474, ten years previous to the date assigned by Garcilaso de la Vega for this occurrence.

No. XIII

MARTIN BEHEM

THIS able geographer was born in Nuremberg, in Germany, about the commencement of the year 1430. His ancestors were from the circle of Pilsner, in Bohemia, hence he is called by some writers Martin of Bohemia, and the resemblance of his own name to that of the country of his ancestors frequently occasions a confusion in the appellation.

It has been said by some that he studied under Philip Bervalde the elder, and by others under John Muller, otherwise called Regiomontanus, though De Murr, who has made diligent inquiry into his history, discredits both assertions. According to a correspondence between Behem and his uncle, discovered of late years by De Murr, it appears that the early part of his life was devoted to commerce. Some have given him the credit of discovering the island of Fayal, but this is an error, arising probably from the circumstance that Job de Huertar, father-in-law of Behem, colonized that island in 1466.

He is supposed to have arrived at Portugal in 1841, while Alphonso V. was still on the throne; it is certain that shortly afterward he was in high repute for his science in the court of Lisbon, insomuch that he was one of the council appointed by King John II. to improve the art of navigation, and by some he has received the whole credit of the memorable service rendered to commerce by that council, in the introduction of the astrolabe into nautical use.

In 1484 King John sent an expedition under Diego Cam, as Barros calls him, Cano according to others, to prosecute discoveries along the coast of Africa. In this expedition Be-

---

Bernal Diaz del Castillo, Hist. de la Conquest de la Nueva España, Fin de cap. 18.

"Tenia Gomara doctrina y estilo . . . pero empleose en ordinar sin discernimiento lo que halló escrito por sus antecesores, y dió credito á petrañas no solo falsas sino inverisimiles." Juan Bautista Muñoz, Hist. N. Mundo, Prologo, p. 18.

hem sailed as cosmographer. They crossed the equinoctial line, discovered the coast of Congo, advanced to twenty-two degrees forty-five minutes of south latitude,* and erected two columns, on which were engraved the arms of Portugal, in the mouth of the River Zagra, in Africa, which thence, for some time, took the name of the River of Columns.†

For the services rendered on this and on previous occasions, it is said that Behem was knighted by King John in 1485, though no mention is made of such a circumstance in any of the contemporary historians. The principal proof of his having received this mark of distinction is his having given himself the title on his own globe of "Eques Lusitanus."

In 1486 he married at Fayal the daughter of Job de Huertar, and is supposed to have remained there for some years, where he had a son named Martin, born in 1489. During his residence at Lisbon and Fayal, it is probable the acquaintance took place between him and Columbus, to which Herrera and others allude; and the admiral may have heard from him some of the rumors circulating in the islands of indications of western lands floating to their shores.

In 1491 he returned to Nuremberg to see his family, and while there, in 1492, he finished a terrestrial globe, considered a masterpiece in those days, which he had undertaken at the request of the principal magistrates of his native city.

In 1493 he returned to Portugal, and from thence proceeded to Fayal.

In 1494 King John II., who had a high opinion of him, sent him to Flanders to his natural son Prince George, the intended heir of his crown. In the course of his voyage Behem was captured and carried to England, where he remained for three months detained by illness. Having recovered, he again put to sea, but was captured by a corsair and carried to France. Having ransomed himself, he proceeded to Antwerp and Bruges, but returned almost immediately to Portugal. Nothing more is known of him for several years, during which time it is supposed he remained with his family in Fayal, too old to make further voyages. In 1506 he went forth from Fayal to Lisbon, where he died.

The assertion that Behem had discovered the western world previous to Columbus, in the course of the voyage with Cam, was founded on a misinterpretation of a passage interpolated in the chronicle of Hartmann Schedel, a contem-

---

* Vasconcelos, lib. 4.   † Murr, Notice sur M. Behaim.

porary writer. This passage mentions that when the voyagers were in the Southern Ocean not far from the coast, and had passed the line, they came into another hemisphere, where, when they looked toward the east, their shadows fell toward the south, on their right hand; that here they discovered a new world, unknown until then, and which for many years had never been sought except by the Genoese, and by them unsuccessfully.

"Hii duo, bono deorum auspicio, mare meridionale sulcantes, a littore non longe evagantes, superato circulo equinoctiali, in alterum orbem excepti sunt. Ubi ipsis stantibus orientem versus, umbra ad meridiem et dextram projiciebatur. Aperuêre igitur sua industria, alium orbem hactenus nobis incognitum et multis annis, a nullis quam Januensibus, licet frustra temptatum."

These lines are part of a passage which it is said is interpolated by a different hand, in the original manuscript of the chronicle of Schedel. De Murr assures us that they are not to be found in the German translation of the book by George Alt, which was finished the 5th October, 1493. But even if they were, they relate merely to the discovery which Diego Cam made of the southern hemisphere, previously unknown, and of the coast of Africa beyond the equator, all which appeared like a new world, and as such was talked of at the time.

The Genoese alluded to who had made an unsuccessful attempt were Antonio de Nolle with Bartholomeo his brother, and Raphael de Nolle his nephew. Antonio was of a noble family, and, for some disgust, left his country and went to Lisbon with his before-mentioned relatives in two caravels; sailing whence, in the employ of Portugal, they discovered the island of St. Jago.*

This interpolated passage of Schedel was likewise inserted into the work De Europâ sub Frederico III. of Æneas Silvius, afterward Pope Pius II., who died in 1464, long before the voyage in question. The misinterpretation of the passage first gave rise to the incorrect assertion that Behem had discovered the New World prior to Columbus; as if it were possible such a circumstance could have happened without Behem's laying claim to the glory of the discovery, and without the world immediately resounding with so important an event. This error had been adopted by various authors with-

* Barros, decad. i., lib. ii., cap. 1. Lisbon, 1552.

out due examination; some of whom had likewise taken from Magellan the credit of having discovered the strait which goes by his name, and had given it to Behem. The error was too palpable to be generally prevalent, but was suddenly revived in the year 1786 by a French gentleman of highly respectable character of the name of Otto, then resident in New York, who addressed a letter to Dr. Franklin to be submitted to the Philosophical Society of Philadelphia, in which he undertook to establish the title of Behem to the discovery of the New World. His memoir was published in the Transactions of the American Philosophical Society, vol. ii., for 1786, article No. 35, and has been copied into the journals of most of the nations of Europe.

The authorities cited by M. Otto in support of his assertion are generally fallacious, and for the most part given without particular specification. His assertion has been diligently and satisfactorily refuted by Don Christoval Cladera.[*]

The grand proof of M. Otto is a globe which Behem made during his residence in Nuremberg, in 1492, the very year that Columbus set out on his first voyage of discovery. This globe, according to M. Otto, is still preserved in the library of Nuremberg, and on it are painted all the discoveries of Behem, which are so situated that they can be no other than the coast of Brazil and the straits of Magellan. This authority staggered many, and, if supported, would demolish the claims of Columbus.

Unluckily for M. Otto, in his description of the globe, he depended on the inspection of a correspondent. The globe in the library of Nuremberg was made in 1520, by John Schoener, professor of mathematics,[†] long after the discoveries and death of Columbus and Behem. The real globe of Behem, made in 1492, does not contain any of the islands or shores of the New World, and thus proves that he was totally unacquainted with them. A copy, or planisphere, of Behem's globe is given by Cladera in his Investigations.

---

[*] Investigaciones Historicas. Madrid 1794.
[†] Cladera, Investig. Hist., p. 115.

No. XIV

VOYAGES OF THE SCANDINAVIANS

MANY elaborate dissertations have been written to prove that discoveries were made by the Scandinavians on the northern coast of America long before the era of Columbus; but the subject appears still to be wrapped in much doubt and obscurity.

It has been asserted that the Norwegians, as early as the ninth century, discovered a great tract of land to the west of Iceland, which they called Grand Iceland; but this has been pronounced a fabulous tradition. The most plausible account is one given by Snorro Sturleson, in his Saga or Chronicle of King Olaus. According to this writer, one Biorn of Iceland, sailing to Greenland in search of his father, from whom he had been separated by a storm, was driven by tempestuous weather far to the southwest, until he came in sight of a low country, covered with wood, with an island in its vicinity. The weather becoming favorable, he turned to the northeast without landing, and arrived safe at Greenland. His account of the country he had beheld, it is said, excited the enterprise of Leif, son of Eric Rauda (or Redhead), the first settler of Greenland. A vessel was fitted out, and Leif and Biorn departed alone in quest of this unknown land. They found a rocky and sterile island, to which they gave the name of Helleland; also a low sandy country covered with wood, to which they gave the name of Markland; and, two days afterward, they observed a continuance of the coast, with an island to the north of it. This last they described as fertile, well wooded, producing agreeable fruits, and particularly grapes, a fruit with which they were unacquainted. On being informed by one of their companions, a German, of its qualities and name, they called the country, from it, Vinland. They ascended a river, well stored with fish, particularly salmon, and came to a lake from which the river took its origin, where they passed the winter. The climate appeared to them mild and pleasant; being accustomed to the rigorous climates of the north. On the shortest day, the sun was eight hours above the horizon. Hence it has been concluded that the country was about the 49th degree of north latitude, and was either Newfoundland, or some part of the coast of North America about the Gulf of St. Lawrence.* It is added that the relatives of Leif made several voyages to Vinland; that they traded with the natives for furs; and that, in 1121, a bishop named Eric went from Greenland to Vinland to convert the inhabitants to Christianity. From this time, says Forster, we know nothing of Vinland, and there is every appearance that the tribe which still exists in the interior of Newfoundland, and which is so different from the other savages of North America, both in their appearance and mode of living, and always in a state of warfare with the Esquimaux of the northern coast, are descendants of the ancient Normans.

The author of the present work has not had the means of tracing this story to its original sources. He gives it on the authority of M. Malte-Brun and Mr. Forster. The latter extracts it from the Saga or Chronicle of Snorro, who was born in 1179, and wrote in 1215; so that his account was formed long after the event is said to have taken place. Forster says: "The facts which we report have been collected from a great number of Icelandic manuscripts, and transmitted to us by Torfæus in his two works entitled Veteris Grœnlandiæ Descriptio, Hafnia, 1706, and Historia Winlandiæ Antiquæ, Hafnia, 1705." Forster appears to have no doubt of the authenticity of the facts. As far as the author of the present work has had experience in tracing these stories of early discoveries of portions of the New World, he has generally found them very confident deductions drawn from very vague and questionable facts. Learned men are too prone to give substance to mere shadows, when they assist some preconceived theory. Most of these accounts, when divested of the erudite comments of their editors, have proved little better than the traditionary fables, noticed in another part of this work, respecting the imaginary islands of St. Brandan, and of the Seven Cities.

There is no great improbability, however, that such enterprising and roving voyagers as the Scandinavians may have wandered to the northern shores of America, about the coast of Labrador, or the shores of Newfoundland; and if the Icelandic manuscripts said to be of the thirteenth century can be relied upon as genuine, free from modern interpolation, and correctly quoted, they would appear to prove the fact. But granting the truth of the alleged discoveries, they led to

---

* Forster's Northern Voyages, book ii., chap. 2.

no more result than would the interchange of communication
between the natives of Greenland and the Esquimaux. The
knowledge of them appears not to have extended beyond
their own nation, and to have been soon neglected and forgotten by themselves.

Another pretension to an early discovery of the American
continent has been set up, founded on an alleged map and
narrative of two brothers of the name of Zeno, of Venice;
but it seems more invalid than those just mentioned. The
following is the substance of this claim.

Nicolo Zeno, a noble Venetian, is said to have made a
voyage to the north in 1380, in a vessel fitted out at his own
cost, intending to visit England and Flanders; but meeting
with a terrible tempest, was driven for many days he knew
not whither, until he was cast away upon Friseland, an isl-
and much in dispute among geographers, but supposed to be
the archipelago of the Ferroe islands. The shipwrecked voyagers were assailed by the natives; but rescued by Zichmni,
a prince of the islands lying on the south side of Friseland,
and duke of another district lying over against Scotland.
Zeno entered into the service of this prince, and aided him
in conquering Friseland and other northern islands. He was
soon joined by his brother Antonio Zeno, who remained fourteen years in those countries.

During his residence in Friseland, Antonio Zeno wrote to
his brother Carlo, in Venice, giving an account of a report
brought by a certain fisherman, about a land to the westward. According to the tale of this mariner, he had been
one of a party who sailed from Friseland about twenty-six
years before, in four fishing-boats. Being overtaken by a
mighty tempest, they were driven about the sea for many
days, until the boat containing himself and six companions
was cast upon an island called Estotiland, about one thousand miles from Friseland. They were taken by the inhabitants, and carried to a fair and populous city, where the
king sent for many interpreters to converse with them, but
none that they could understand, until a man was found who
had likewise been cast away upon the coast, and who spoke
Latin. They remained several days upon the island, which
was rich and fruitful, abounding with all kinds of metals,
and especially gold.* There was a high mountain in the

* This account is taken from Hackluyt, Vol. III., p. 123. The passage about gold and other metals is not to be found in the original Italian of Ramusio (tom. ii., p. 23), and is probably an interpolation.

center, from which flowed four rivers which watered the whole country. The inhabitants were intelligent and acquainted with the mechanical arts of Europe. They cultivated grain, made beer, and lived in houses built of stone. There were Latin books in the king's library, though the inhabitants had no knowledge of that language. They had many cities and castles, and carried on a trade with Greenland for pitch, sulphur, and peltry. Though much given to navigation, they were ignorant of the use of the compass, and finding the Frieslanders acquainted with it, held them in great esteem; and the king sent them with twelve barks to visit a country to the south called Drogeo. They had nearly perished in a storm, but were cast away upon the coast of Drogeo. They found the people to be cannibals, and were on the point of being killed and devoured, but were spared on account of their great skill in fishing.

The fisherman described this Drogeo as being a country of vast extent, or rather a new world; that the inhabitants were naked and barbarous; but that far to the southwest there was a more civilized region, and temperate climate, where the inhabitants had a knowledge of gold and silver, lived in cities, erected splendid temples to idols, and sacrificed human victims to them, which they afterward devoured.

After the fisherman had resided many years on this continent, during which time he had passed from the service of one chieftain to another, and traversed various parts of it, certain boats of Estotiland arrived on the coast of Drogeo. The fisherman went on board of them, acted as interpreter, and followed the trade between the mainland and Estotiland for some time, until he became very rich: then he fitted out a bark of his own, and with the assistance of some of the people of the island made his way back, across the thousand intervening miles of ocean, and arrived safe at Friseland. The account he gave of these countries determined Zichmni, the prince of Friseland, to send an expedition thither, and Antonio Zeno was to command it. Just before sailing, the fisherman, who was to have acted as guide, died; but certain mariners, who had accompanied him from Estotiland, were taken in his place. The expedition sailed under command of Zichmni; the Venetian, Zeno, merely accompanied it. It was unsuccessful. After having discovered an island called Icaria, where they met with a rough reception from the inhabitants, and were obliged to withdraw, the ships were

driven by a storm to Greenland. No record remains of any
further prosecution of the enterprise.

The countries mentioned in the account of Zeno were laid
down on a map originally engraved on wood. The island of
Estotiland has been supposed by M. Malte-Brun to be Newfoundland; its partially civilized inhabitants the descendants
of the Scandinavian colonists of Vinland; and the Latin
books in the king's library to be the remains of the library
of the Greenland bishop, who emigrated thither in 1121.
Drogeo, according to the same conjecture, was Nova Scotia
and New England. The civilized people to the southwest,
who sacrificed human victims in rich temples, he surmises to
have been the Mexicans, or some ancient nation of Florida
or Louisiana.

The premises do not appear to warrant this deduction.
The whole story abounds with improbabilities; not the least
of which is the civilization prevalent among the inhabitants;
their houses of stone, their European arts, the library of their
king, no traces of which were to be found on their subsequent
discovery. Not to mention the information about Mexico
penetrating through the numerous savage tribes of a vast
continent. It is proper to observe that this account was not
published until 1558, long after the discovery of Mexico. It
was given to the world by Francisco Marcolini, a descendant
of the Zeni, from the fragments of letters said to have been
written by Antonio Zeno to Carlo his brother. "It grieves
me," says the editor, "that the book, and divers other writings concerning these matters, are miserably lost; for being
but a child when they came to my hands, and not knowing
what they were, I tore them and rent them to pieces, which
now I cannot call to remembrance but to my exceeding great
grief."*

This garbled statement by Marcolini derived considerable
authority by being introduced by Abraham Ortelius, an able
geographer, in his Theatrum Orbis; but the whole story has
been condemned by able commentators as a gross fabrication.
Mr. Forster resents this, as an instance of obstinate incredulity, saying that it is impossible to doubt the existence of the
country of which Carlo, Nicolo, and Antonio Zeno talk; as
original acts in the archives of Venice prove that the chevalier undertook a voyage to the north; that his brother Antonio followed him; that Antonio traced a map, which he

---

* Hackluyt, Collect., Vol. III., p. 127.

brought back and hung up in his house, where it remained subject to public examination, until the time of Marcolini, as an incontestable proof of the truth of what he advanced. Granting all this, it merely proves that Antonio and his brotł **r** were at Friseland and Greenland. Their letters neve. assert that Zeno made the voyage to Estotiland. The fleet was carried by a tempest to Greenland, after which we hear no more of him; and his account of Estotiland and Drogeo rests simply on the tale of the fisherman, after whose descriptions his map must have been conjecturally projected. The whole story resembles much the fables circulated shortly after the discovery of Columbus, to arrogate to other nations and individuals the credit of the achievement.

M. Malte-Brun intimates that the alleged discovery of Vinland may have been known to Columbus when he made a voyage in the North Sea in 1477,* and that the map of Zeno, being in the national library at London, in a Danish work, at the time when Bartholomew Columbus was in that city, employed in making maps, he may have known something of it, and have communicated it to his brother.† Had M. Malte-Brun examined the history of Columbus with his usual accuracy, he would have perceived that, in his correspondence with Paulo Toscanelli in 1474, he had expressed his intention of seeking India by a route directly to the west. His voyage to the north did not take place until three years afterward. As to the residence of Bartholomew in London, it was not until after Columbus had made his propositions of discovery to Portugal, if not to the courts of other powers. Granting, therefore, that he had subsequently heard the dubious stories of Vinland, and of the fisherman's adventures, as related by Zeno, or at least by Marcolini, they evidently could not have influenced him in his great enterprise. His route had no reference to them, but was a direct western course, not toward Vinland, and Estotiland, and Drogeo, but in search of Cipango, and Cathay, and the other countries described by Marco Polo as lying at the extremity of India.

---

* Malte-Brun, Hist. de Geog., tom. i., lib. xvii.

† Idem, Geog. Universelle, tom. xiv. Note sur la decouverte de l'Amerique.

No. XV

CIRCUMNAVIGATION OF AFRICA BY THE ANCIENTS

THE knowledge of the ancients with respect to the Atlantic coast of Africa is considered by modern investigators much less extensive than had been imagined; and it is doubted whether they had any practical authority for the belief that Africa was circumnavigable. The alleged voyage of Eudoxus of Cyzicus, from the Red Sea to Gibraltar, though recorded by Pliny, Pomponius Mela, and others, is given entirely on the assertion of Cornelius Nepos, who does not tell from whence he derived his information. Posidonius (cited by Strabo) gives an entirely different account of this voyage, and rejects it with contempt.*

The famous voyage of Hanno, the Carthaginian, is supposed to have taken place about a thousand years before the Christian era. The Periplus Hannonis remains, a brief and obscure record of this expedition, and a subject of great comment and controversy. By some it has been pronounced a fictitious work, fabricated among the Greeks, but its authenticity has been ably vindicated. It appears to be satisfactorily proved, however, that the voyage of this navigator has been greatly exaggerated, and that he never circumnavigated the extreme end of Africa. Mons. de Bougainville† traces his route to a promontory which he named the West Horn, supposed to be Cape Palmas, about five or six degrees north of the equinoctial line, whence he proceeded to another promontory, under the same parallel, which he called the South Horn, supposed to be Cape de Tres Puntas. Mons. Gosselin, however, in his Researches into the Geography of the Ancients (tome 1, p. 162, etc.), after a rigid examination of the Periplus of Hanno, determines that he had not sailed further south than Cape Non. Pliny, who makes Hanno range the whole coast of Africa, from the straits to the confines of Arabia, had never seen his Periplus, but took his idea from the works of Xenophon of Lampsaco. The Greeks sur-

---

* Gosselin, Recherches sur la Geographie des Anciens, tom. i., p. 162, etc.
 † Memoirs de l'Acad. des Inscript., tom. xxvi.

charged the narration of the voyage with all kinds of fables, and on their unfaithful copies, Strabo founded many of his assertions. According to M. Gosselin, the itineraries of Hanno, of Scylax, Polybius, Statius, Sebosus and Juba; the recitals of Plato, of Aristotle, of Pliny, of Plutarch, and the tables of Ptolemy, all bring us to the same results, and, notwithstanding their apparent contradictions, fix the limit of southern navigation about the neighborhood of Cape Non, or Cape Bojador.

The opinion that Africa was a peninsula, which existed among the Persians, the Egyptians, and perhaps the Greeks, several centuries prior to the Christian era, was not, in his opinion, founded upon any known facts; but merely on conjecture, from considering the immensity and unity of the ocean; or perhaps on more ancient traditions; or on ideas produced by the Carthaginian discoveries, beyond the Straits of Gibraltar, and those of the Egyptians beyond the Gulf of Arabia. He thinks that there was a very remote period, when geography was much more perfect than in the time of the Phenicians and the Greeks, whose knowledge was but confused traces of what had previously been better known.

The opinion that the Indian Sea joined the ocean was admitted among the Greeks, and in the school of Alexandria, until the time of Hipparchus. It seemed authorized by the direction which the coast of Africa took after Cape Aromata, always tending westward, as far as it had been explored by navigators.

It was supposed that the western coast of Africa rounded off to meet the eastern, and that the whole was bounded by the ocean, much to the northward of the equator. Such was the opinion of Crates, who lived in the time of Alexander; of Aratus, of Cleanthes, of Cleomedes, of Strabo, of Pomponius Mela, of Macrobius, and many others.

Hipparchus proposed a different system, and led the world into an error, which for a long time retarded the maritime communication of Europe and India. He supposed that the seas were separated into distinct basins, and that the eastern shores of Africa made a circuit round the Indian Sea, so as to join those of Asia beyond the mouth of the Ganges. Subsequent discoveries, instead of refuting this error, only placed the junction of the continents at a greater distance. Marinus of Tyre, and Ptolemy, adopted this opinion in their works, and illustrated it in their maps, which for centuries controlled the general belief of mankind, and perpetuated the idea that

Africa extended onward to the south pole, and that it was impossible to arrive by sea at the coasts of India. Still there were geographers who leaned to the more ancient idea of a communication between the Indian Sea and the Atlantic Ocean. It had its advocates in Spain, and was maintained by Pomponius Mela and by Isidore of Seville. It was believed also by some of the learned in Italy in the thirteenth, fourteenth, and fifteenth centuries; and thus was kept alive until it was acted upon so vigorously by Prince Henry of Portugal, and at length triumphantly demonstrated by Vasco de Gama, in his circumnavigation of the Cape of Good Hope.

No. XVI

OF THE SHIPS OF COLUMBUS

In remarking on the smallness of the vessels with which Columbus made his first voyage, Dr. Robertson observes that, "in the fifteenth century, the bulk and construction of vessels were accommodated to the short and easy voyages along the coast which they were accustomed to perform." We have many proofs, however, that even anterior to the fifteenth century there were large ships employed by the Spaniards as well as by other nations. In an edict published in Barcelona, in 1354, by Pedro IV., enforcing various regulations for the security of commerce, mention is made of Catalonian merchant ships of two and three decks and from eight thousand to twelve thousand quintals burden.

In 1419, Alonzo of Aragon hired several merchant ships to transport artillery, horses, etc., from Barcelona to Italy, among which were two, each carrying one hundred and twenty horses, which it is computed would require a vessel of at least six hundred tons.

In 1463, mention is made of a Venetian ship of seven hundred tons which arrived at Barcelona from England, laden with wheat.

In 1497, a Castilian vessel arrived there being of twelve thousand quintals burden. These arrivals incidentally mentioned among others of similar size, as happening at one port, show that large ships were in use in those days.[*] Indeed,

---

* Capmany, Questiones Criticas. Quest. 6.

at the time of fitting out the second expedition of Columbus, there were prepared in the port of Bermeo, a caracca of twelve hundred and fifty tons, and four ships of from one hundred and fifty to four hundred and fifty tons burden. Their destination, however, was altered, and they were sent to convoy Muley Boabdil, the last Moorish king of Granada, from the coast of his conquered territory to Africa.*

It was not for want of large vessels in the Spanish ports, therefore, that those of Columbus were of so small a size. He considered them best adapted to voyages of discovery, as they required but little depth of water, and therefore could more easily and safely coast unknown shores, and explore bays and rivers. He had some purposely constructed of a very small size for this service; such was the caravel which in his third voyage he dispatched to look out for an opening to the sea at the upper part of the Gulf of Paria, when the water grew too shallow for his vessel of one hundred tons burden.

The most singular circumstance with respect to the ships of Columbus is that they should be open vessels: for it seems difficult to believe that a voyage of such extent and peril should be attempted in barks of so frail a construction. This, however, is expressly mentioned by Peter Martyr, in his Decades written at the time; and mention is made occasionally, in the memoirs relative to the voyages written by Columbus and his son, of certain of his vessels being without decks. He sometimes speaks of the same vessel as a ship and a caravel. There has been some discussion of late as to the precise meaning of the term caravel. The Chevalier Bossi, in his dissertations on Columbus, observes that in the Mediterranean caravel designates the largest class of ships of war among the Mussulmans, and that in Portugal it means a small vessel of from one hundred and twenty to one hundred and forty tons burden; but Columbus sometimes applies it to a vessel of forty tons.

Du Cange, in his glossary, considers it a word of Italian origin. Bossi thinks it either Turkish or Arabic, and probably introduced into the European languages by the Moors. Mr. Edward Everett, in a note to his Plymouth oration, considers that the true origin of the word is given in "Ferrarii Origines Linguæ Italicæ," as follows: "Caravela, navigii minoris genus. Lat. Carabus: Græce Karabron."

---

* Archives de Ind. en Sevilla.

That the word caravel was intended to signify a vessel of a small size is evident from a naval classification made by King Alonzo in the middle of the thirteenth century. In the first class he enumerates *Naos*, or large ships which go only with sails, some of which have two masts, and others but one. In the second class smaller vessels as Carracas, Fustas, Ballenares, Pinazas, *Carabelas*, etc. In the third class vessels with sails and oars, as Galleys, Galeots, Tardantes, and Saetias.[*]

Bossi gives a copy of a letter written by Columbus to Don Raphael Xansis, treasurer of the king of Spain, an edition of which exists in the public library at Milan. With this letter he gives several woodcuts of sketches made with a pen, which accompanied this letter, and which he supposes to have been from the hand of Columbus. In these are represented vessels which are probably caravels. They have high bows and sterns, with castles on the latter. They have short masts with large square sails. One of them, besides sails, has benches of oars, and is probably intended to represent a galley. They are all evidently vessels of small size and light construction.

In a work called "Recherches sur le Commerce," published in Amsterdam, 1799, is a plate representing a vessel of the latter part of the fifteenth century. It is taken from a picture in the church of St. Giovanni e Paolo in Venice. The vessel bears much resemblance to those said to have been sketched by Columbus; it has two masts, one of which is extremely small with a lateen sail. The mainmast has a large square sail. The vessel has a high poop and prow, is decked at each end, and is open in the center.

It appears to be the fact, therefore, that most of the vessels with which Columbus undertook his long and perilous voyages were of this light and frail construction, and little superior to the small craft which ply on rivers and along coasts in modern days.

---

[*] Capmany, Quest. Crit.

No. XVII

ROUTE OF COLUMBUS IN HIS FIRST VOYAGE *

IT has hitherto been supposed that one of the Bahama Islands, at present bearing the name of San Salvador, and which is also known as Cat Island, was the first point where Columbus came in contact with the New World. Navarrete, however, in his introduction to the "Collection of Spanish Voyages and Discoveries," recently published at Madrid, has endeavored to show that it must have been Turk's Island, one of the same group, situated about one hundred leagues (of twenty to the degree) S.E. of San Salvador. Great care has been taken to examine candidly the opinion of Navarrete, comparing it with the journal of Columbus, as published in the above-mentioned work, and with the personal observations of the writer of this article, who has been much among these islands.

Columbus describes Guanahani, on which he landed, and to which he gave the name of San Salvador, as being a beautiful island, and very large; as being level, and covered with forests, many of the trees of which bore fruit; as having abundance of fresh water, and a large lake in the center; that it was inhabited by a numerous population; that he proceeded for a considerable distance in his boats along the shore, which trended to the N.N.E., and as he passed, was visited by the inhabitants of several villages. Turk's Island does not answer to this description.

Turk's Island is a low key composed of sand and rocks, and lying north and south, less than two leagues in extent. It is utterly destitute of wood, and has not a single tree of native growth. It has no fresh water, the inhabitants depending entirely on cisterns and casks in which they preserve the rain; neither has it any lake, but several salt ponds, which furnish the sole production of the island.

---

* The author of this work is indebted for this able examination of the route of Columbus to an officer of the navy of the United States, whose name he regrets the not being at liberty to mention. He has been greatly benefited, in various parts of this history, by nautical information from the same intelligent source.

Turk's Island cannot be approached on the east or north-east side, in consequence of the reef that surrounds it. It has no harbor, but has an open road on the west side, which vessels at anchor there have to leave and put to sea whenever the wind comes from any other quarter than that of the usual trade breeze of N.E. which blows over the island; for the shore is so bold that there is no anchorage except close to it; and when the wind ceases to blow from the land, vessels remaining at their anchors would be swung against the rocks, or forced high upon the shore, by the terrible surf that then prevails. The unfrequented road of the Hawk's Nest, at the south end of the island, is even more dangerous. This island, which is not susceptible of the slightest cultivation, furnishes a scanty subsistence to a few sheep and horses. The inhabitants draw all their consumption from abroad, with the exception of fish and turtle, which are taken in abundance, and supply the principal food of the slaves employed in the salt-works. The whole wealth of the island consists in the produce of the salt-ponds, and in the salvage and plunder of the many wrecks which take place in the neighborhood. Turk's Island, therefore, would never be inhabited in a savage state of society, where commerce does not exist, and where men are obliged to draw their subsistence from the spot which they people.

Again: when about to leave Guanahani, Columbus was at a loss to choose which to visit of a great number of islands in sight. Now there is no land visible from Turk's Island, excepting the two salt keys which lie south of it, and with it form the group known as Turk's Islands. The journal of Columbus does not tell us what course he steered in going from Guanahani to Concepcion, but he states that it was five leagues distant from the former, and that the current was against him in sailing to it: whereas the distance from Turk's Island to the Gran Caico, supposed by Navarrete to be the Concepcion of Columbus, is nearly double, and the current sets constantly to the W.N.W. among these islands, which would be favorable in going from Turk's Island to the Caicos.

From Concepcion Columbus went next to an island which he saw nine leagues off in a westerly direction, to which he gave the name of Fernandina. This Navarrete takes to be Little Inagua, distant no less than twenty-two leagues from Gran Caico. Besides, in going to Little Inagua, it would be necessary to pass quite close to three islands, each larger than Turk's Island, none of which are mentioned in the journal.

Columbus describes Fernandina as stretching twenty-eight leagues S.E. and N.W., whereas Little Inagua has its greatest length of four leagues in a S.W. direction. In a word, the description of Fernandina has nothing in common with Little Inagua. From Fernandina Columbus sailed S.E. to Isabella, which Navarrete takes to be Great Inagua; whereas this latter bears S.W. from Little Inagua, a course differing 90° from the one followed by Columbus. Again: Columbus, on the 20th of November, takes occasion to say that Guanahani was distant eight leagues from Isabella; whereas Turk's Island is thirty-five leagues from Great Inagua.

Leaving Isabella, Columbus stood W.S.W. for the island of Cuba, and fell in with the Islas Arenas. This course drawn from Great Inagua would meet the coast of Cuba about Port Nipe: whereas Navarrete supposes that Columbus next fell in with the keys south of the Jumentos, and which bear W.N.W. from Inagua; a course differing 45° from the one steered by the ships. After sailing for some time in the neighborhood of Cuba, Columbus finds himself, on the 14th of November, in the sea of Nuestra Señora, surrounded by so many islands that it was impossible to count them: whereas, on the same day, Navarrete places him off Cape Moa, where there is but one small island, and more than fifty leagues distant from any group that can possibly answer the description.

Columbus informs us that San Salvador was distant from Port Principe forty-five leagues: whereas Turk's Island is distant from the point, supposed by Navarrete to be the same, eighty leagues.

On taking leave of Cuba, Columbus remarks that he had followed its coast for an extent of one hundred and twenty leagues. Deducting twenty leagues for his having followed its windings, there still remain one hundred. Now, Navarrete only supposes him to have coasted this island an extent of seventy leagues.

Such are the most important difficulties which the theory of Navarrete offers, and which appear insurmountable. Let us now take up the route of Columbus as recorded in his journal, and, with the best charts before us, examine how it agrees with the popular and traditional opinion, that he first landed on the island of San Salvador.

We learn from the journal of Columbus that, on the 11th of October, 1492, he continued steering W.S.W. until sunset, when he returned to his old course of west, the vessels running at the rate of three leagues an hour. At ten o'clock he and several of his crew saw a light, which seemed like a torch carried about on land. He continued running on four hours longer, and had made a distance of twelve leagues further west, when at two in the morning land was discovered ahead, distant two leagues. The twelve leagues which they ran since ten o'clock, with the two leagues' distance from the land, form a total corresponding essentially with the distance and situation of Watling's Island from San Salvador; and it is thence presumed that the light seen at that hour was on Watling's Island, which they were then passing. Had the light been seen on land ahead, and they had kept running on four hours at the rate of three leagues an hour, they must have run high and dry on shore. As the admiral himself received the royal reward for having seen this light, as the first discovery of land, Watling's Island is believed to be the point for which this premium was granted.

On making land, the vessels were hove to until daylight of the same 12th of October; they then anchored off an island of great beauty, covered with forests, and extremely populous.

It was called Guanahani by the natives, but Columbus gave it the name of San Salvador. Exploring its coast, where it ran to the N.N.E., he found a harbor capable of sheltering any number of ships. This description corresponds minutely with the S.E. part of the island known as San Salvador, or Cat Island, which lies east and west, bending at its eastern extremity to the N.N.E., and has the same verdant and fertile appearance. The vessels had probably drifted into this bay at the S.E. side of San Salvador, on the morning of the 12th, while lying to for daylight; nor did Columbus, while remaining at the island, or when sailing from it, open the land so as to discover that what he had taken for its whole length was but a bend at one end of it, and that the main body of the island lay behind, stretching far to the N.W. From Guanahani, Columbus saw so many other islands that he was at a loss which next to visit. The Indians signified that they were innumerable, and mentioned the names of above a hundred. He determined to go to the largest in sight, which appeared to be about five leagues distant; some of the others were nearer, and some further off. The island thus selected, it is presumed, was the present island of Concepcion; and that the others were that singular belt of small islands known as La Cadena (or the chain), stretching past the island of San Salvador in a S.E. and

N.W. direction; the nearest of the group being nearer than Concepcion, while the rest are more distant.

Leaving San Salvador in the afternoon of the 14th for the island thus selected, the ships lay by during the night, and did not reach it until late in the following day, being retarded by adverse currents. Columbus gave this island the name of Santa Maria de la Concepcion; he does not mention either its bearings from San Salvador or the course which he steered in going to it. We know that in all this neighborhood the current sets strongly and constantly to the W.N.W.; and since Columbus had the current against him, he must have been sailing in an opposite direction, or to the E.S.E. Besides, when near Concepcion, Columbus sees another island to the westward, the largest he had yet seen; but he tells us that he anchored off Concepcion, and did not stand for this larger island, because he could not have sailed to the west. Hence it is rendered certain that Columbus did not sail westward in going from San Salvador to Concepcion; for, from the opposition of the wind, as there could be no other cause, he could not sail toward that quarter. Now, on reference to the chart, we find the island at present known as Concepcion situated E.S.E. from San Salvador, and at a corresponding distance of five leagues.

Leaving Concepcion on the 16th October, Columbus steered for a very large island seen to the westward nine leagues off, and which extended itself twenty-eight leagues in a S.E. and N.W. direction. He was becalmed the whole day, and did not reach the island until the following morning, 17th October. He named it Fernandina. At noon he made sail again, with a view to run round it, and reach another island called Samoet; but the wind being at S.E. by S., the course he wished to steer, the natives signified that it would be easier to sail round this island by running to the N.W. with a fair wind. He therefore bore up to the N.W., and having run two leagues found a marvelous port, with a narrow entrance, or rather with two entrances, for there was an island which shut it in completely, forming a noble basin within. Sailing out of this harbor by the opposite entrance at the N.W., he discovered that part of the island which runs east and west. The natives signified to him that this island was smaller than Samoet, and that it would be better to return toward the latter. It had now become calm, but shortly after there sprung up a breeze from W.N.W., which was ahead for the course they had been steering; so they bore up and stood to the E.S.E. in order to get an offing, for the weather threatened a storm, which, however, dissipated itself in rain. The next day, being the 18th October, they anchored opposite the extremity of Fernandina.

The whole of this description answers most accurately to the island of Exuma, which lies south from San Salvador, and S.W. by S. from Concepcion. The only inconsistency is that Columbus states that Fernandina bore nearly west from Concepcion, and was twenty-eight leagues in extent. This mistake must have proceeded from his having taken the long chain of keys called La Cadena for part of the same Exuma; which continuous appearance they naturally assume when seen from Concepcion, for they run in the same S.E. and N.W. direction. Their bearings, when seen from the same point, are likewise westerly as well as southwesterly. As a proof that such was the case, it may be observed that, after having approached these islands, instead of the extent of Fernandina being increased to his eye, he now remarks that it was twenty leagues long, whereas before it was estimated by him at twenty-eight; he now discovers that instead of one island there were many, and alters his course southerly to reach the one that was most conspicuous.

The identity of the island here described with Exuma is irresistibly forced upon the mind. The distance from Concepcion, the remarkable port with an island in front of it, and further on its coast turning off to the westward, are all so accurately delineated that it would seem as though the chart had been drawn from the description of Columbus.

On the 19th October, the ships left Fernandina, steering S.E. with the wind at north. Sailing three hours on this course, they discovered Samoet to the east, and steered for it, arriving at its north point before noon. Here they found a little island surrounded by rocks, with another reef of rocks lying between it and Samoet. To Samoet Columbus gave the name of Isabella, and to the point of it opposite the little island, that of Cabo del Isleo; the cape at the S.W. point of Samoet Columbus called Cabo de Laguna, and off this last his ships were brought to anchor. The little island lay in the direction from Fernandina to Isabella, east and west. The coast from the small island lay westerly twelve leagues to a cape, which Columbus called Fermosa from its beauty; this he believed to be an island apart from Samoet or Isabella, with another one between them. Leaving Cape Laguna, where he remained until the 20th October, Columbus steered to the N.E. toward Cabo del Isleo, but meeting with shoals inside the small island, he did not come to anchor until the day following. Near this extremity of Isabella they found a lake, from which the ships were supplied with water.

This island of Isabella, or Samoet, agrees so accurately in its description with Isla Larga, which lies east of Exuma, that it is only necessary to read it with the chart unfolded to become convinced of the identity.

Having resolved to visit the island which the natives called Cuba, and described as bearing W.S.W. from Isabella, Columbus left Cabo del Isleo at midnight, the commencement of the 24th October, and shaped his course accordingly to the W.S.W. The wind continued light, with rain, until noon, when it freshened up, and in the evening Cape Verde, the S.W. point of Fernandina, bore N.W. distant seven leagues. As the night became tempestuous, he lay to until morning, drifting according to the reckoning two leagues.

On the morning of the 25th he made sail again to W.S.W., until nine o'clock, when he had run five leagues; he then steered west until three, when he had run eleven leagues, at which hour land was discovered, consisting of seven or eight keys lying north and south, and distant five leagues from the ships. Here he anchored the next day, south of these islands, which he called Islas de Arena; they were low, and five or six leagues in extent.

The distances run by Columbus, added to the departure taken from Fernandina and the distance from these islands of Arena at the time of discovering, give a sum of thirty leagues. This sum of thirty leagues is about three less than the distance from the S.W. point of Fernandina or Exuma, whence Columbus took his departure, to the group of Mucaras, which lie east of Cayo Lobo on the grand bank of Bahama, and which correspond to the description of Columbus. If it were necessary to account for the difference of three leagues in a reckoning, where so much is given on conjecture, it would readily occur to a seaman that an allowance of two leagues for drift, during a long night of blowy weather, is but a small one. The course from Exuma to the Mucaras is about S.W. by W. The course followed by Columbus differs a little from this, but as it was his intention, on setting sail from Isabella, to steer W.S.W., and since he afterward altered it to west, we may conclude that he did so in consequence of having been run out of his course to the southward, while lying to the night previous.

Oct. 27.—At sunrise Columbus set sail from the isles Arenas or Mucaras, for an island called Cuba, steering S.S.W. At dark, having made seventeen leagues on that course, he saw the land, and hove his ships to until morning. On the 28th he made sail again at S.S.W., and entered a beautiful river with a fine harbor, which he named San Salvador. The journal in this part does not describe the localities with the minuteness with which everything has hitherto been noted; the text also is in several places obscure.

This port of San Salvador we take to be the one now known as Caravelas Grandes, situated eight leagues west of Nuevitas del Principe. Its bearings and distance from the Mucaras coincide exactly with those run by Columbus; and its description agrees, as far as can be ascertained by charts, with the port which he visited.

Oct. 29.—Leaving this port, Columbus stood to the west, and having sailed six leagues, he came to a point of the island running N.W., which we take to be the Punta Gorda; and, ten leagues further, another stretching easterly, which will be Punta Curiana. One league further he discovered a small river, and beyond this another very large one, to which he gave the name of Rio de Mares. This river emptied into a fine basin resembling a lake, and having a bold entrance: it had for landmarks two round mountains at the S.W., and to the W.N.W. a bold promontory, suitable for a fortification, which projected far into the sea. This we take to be the fine harbor and river situated west of Point Curiana; its distance corresponds with that run by Columbus from Caravelas Grandes, which we have supposed identical with Port San Salvador. Leaving Rio de Mares the 30th of October, Columbus stood to the N.W. for fifteen leagues, when he saw a cape, to which he gave the name of Cabo de Palmas. This, we believe, is the one which forms the eastern entrance to Laguna de Moron. Beyond this cape was a river, distant, according to the natives, four days' journey from the town of Cuba; Columbus determined therefore to make for it.

Having lain to all night, he reached the river on the 31st of October, but found that it was too shallow to admit his ships. This is supposed to be what is now known as Laguna de Moron. Beyond this was a cape surrounded by shoals, and another projected still further out. Between these two capes was a bay capable of receiving small vessels. The identity here of the description with the coast near Laguna de Moron seems very clear. The cape east of Laguna de Moron coincides with Cape Palmas, the Laguna de Moron with the shoal river described by Columbus; and in the western point of entrance, with the island of Cabrion opposite it, we recognize the two projecting capes he speaks of, with what appeared to be a bay between them. This all is a remarkable combination, difficult to be found anywhere but in the same spot which Columbus visited and described. Further, the coast from the port of San Salvador had run west to Rio de Mares, a distance of seventeen leagues, and from Rio de Mares it had extended N.W. fifteen leagues to Cabo de Palmas; all of which agrees fully with what has been here supposed. The wind having shifted to north, which was contrary to the course they had been steering, the vessels bore up and returned to Rio de Mares.

On the 12th of November the ships sailed out of Rio de Mares to go in quest of Babeque, an island believed to abound in gold, and to lie E. by S. from that port. Having sailed eight leagues with a fair wind, they came to a river, in which may be recognized the one which lies just west of Punta Gorda. Four leagues further they saw another, which they called Rio del Sol. It appeared very large, but they did not stop to examine it, as the wind was fair to advance. This we take to be the river now known as Sabana. Columbus was now retracing his steps, and had made twelve leagues from Rio de Mares, but in going west from Port San Salvador to Rio de Mares he had run seventeen leagues. San Salvador, therefore, remains five leagues east of Rio del Sol; and, accordingly, on reference to the chart, we find Caravelas Grandes situated a corresponding distance from Sabana.

Having run six leagues from Rio del Sol, which makes in all eighteen leagues from Rio de Mares, Columbus came to a cape which he called Cabo de Cuba, probably from supposing it to be the extremity of that island. This corresponds precisely in distance from Punta Curiana with the lesser island of Guajava, situated near Cuba, and between which and the greater Guajava Columbus must have passed in running in for Port San Salvador. Either he did not notice it, from his attention being engrossed by the magnificent island before him, or, as is also possible, his vessels may have been drifted through the passage, which is two leagues wide, while lying to the night previous to their arrival at Port San Salvador.

On the 13th of November, having hove to all night, in the morning the ships passed a point two leagues in extent, and then entered into a gulf that made into the S.S.W., and which

Columbus thought separated Cuba from Bohio. At the bottom of the gulf was a large basin between two mountains. He could not determine whether or not this was an arm of the sea; for not finding shelter from the north wind, he put to sea again. Hence it would appear that Columbus must have partly sailed round the smaller Guajava, which he took to be the extremity of Cuba, without being aware that a few hours' sail would have taken him, by this channel, to Port San Salvador, his first discovery in Cuba, and so back to the same Rio del Sol which he had passed the day previous. Of the two mountains seen on both sides of this entrance, the principal one corresponds with the peak called Alto de Juan Daune, which lies seven leagues west of Punta de Maternillos. The wind continuing north, he stood east fourteen leagues from Cape Cuba, which we have supposed the lesser island of Guajava. It is here rendered sure that the point of little Guajava was believed by him to be the extremity of Cuba; for he speaks of the land mentioned as lying to leeward of the above-mentioned gulf as being the island of Bohio, and says that he discovered twenty leagues of it running E.S.E. and W.N.W.

On the 14th November, having lain to all night with a N.E. wind, he determined to seek a port, and if he found none to return to those which he had left in the island of Cuba; for it will be remembered that all east of little Guajava he supposed to be Bohio. He steered E. by S. therefore six leagues, and then stood in for the land. Here he saw many ports and islands; but as it blew fresh, with a heavy sea, he dared not enter, but ran the coast down N.W. by W. for a distance of eighteen leagues, where he saw a clear entrance and a port, in which he stood S.S.W. and afterward S.E., the navigation being all clear and open. Here Columbus beheld so many islands that it was impossible to count them. They were very lofty, and covered with trees. Columbus called the neighboring sea Mar de Nuestra Señora, and to the harbor near the entrance to these islands he gave the name of Puerto del Principe. This harbor he says he did not enter until the Sunday following, which was four days after. This part of the text of Columbus's journal is confused, and there are also anticipations as if it had been written subsequently, or mixed together in copying. It appears evident that while lying to the night previous, with the wind at N.E., the ships had drifted to the N.W., and been carried by the powerful current of the Bahama channel far in the same direction. When they bore up, therefore, to return to the ports which they had left in the island of Cuba, they fell in to leeward of them, and now first discovered the numerous group of islands of which Cayo Romano is the principal. The current of this channel is of itself sufficient to have carried the vessels to the westward a distance of twenty leagues, which is what they had run easterly since leaving Cape Cuba, or Guajava, for it had acted upon them during a period of thirty hours. There can be no doubt as to the identity of these keys with those about Cayo Romano; for they are the only ones in the neighborhood of Cuba that are not of a low and swampy nature, but large and lofty. They inclose a free, open navigation, and abundance of fine harbors, in late years the resort of pirates, who found security and concealment for themselves and their prizes in the recesses of these lofty keys. From the description of Columbus, the vessels must have entered between the islands of Baril and Pacedon, and sailing along Cayo Romano on a S.E. course, have reached in another day their old cruising ground in the neighborhood of lesser Guajava. Not only Columbus does not tell us here of his having changed his anchorage among these keys, but his journal does not even mention his having anchored at all, until the return from the ineffectual search after Babeque. It is clear, from what has been said, that it was not in Port Principe that the vessels anchored on this occasion; but it could not have been very distant, since Columbus went from the ships in his boats on the 18th November, to place a cross at its entrance. He had probably seen the entrance from without, when sailing east from Guajava on the 13th of November. The identity of this port with the one now known as Nuevitas el Principe seems certain, from the description of its entrance. Columbus, it appears, did not visit its interior.

On the 19th November the ships sailed again, in quest of Babeque. At sunset Port Principe bore S.S.W. distant seven leagues, and having sailed all night at N.E. by N. and until ten o'clock of the next day (20th November), they had run a distance of fifteen leagues on that course. The wind blowing from E.S.E., which was the direction in which Babeque was supposed to lie, and the weather being foul, Columbus determined to return to Port Principe, which was then distant twenty-five leagues. He did not wish to go to Isabella, distant only twelve leagues, lest the Indians whom he had brought from San Salvador, which lay eight leagues from

Isabella, should make their escape. Thus, in sailing N.E. by N. from near Port Principe, Columbus had approached within a short distance of Isabella. That island was then, according to his calculations, thirty-seven leagues from Port Principe; and San Salvador was forty-five leagues from the same point. The first differs but eight leagues from the truth, the latter nine; or from the actual distance of Nuevitas el Principe from Isla Larga and San Salvador. Again, let us now call to mind the course made by Columbus in going from Isabella to Cuba; it was first W.S.W., then W., and afterward S.S.W. Having consideration for the different distances run on each, these yield a medium course not materially different from S.W. Sailing then S.W. from Isabella, Columbus had reached Port San Salvador, on the coast of Cuba. Making afterward a course of N.E. by N. from off Port Principe, he was going in the direction of Isabella. Hence we deduce that Port San Salvador, on the coast of Cuba, lay west of Port Principe, and the whole combination is thus bound together and established. The two islands seen by Columbus at ten o'clock of the same 20th November must have been some of the keys which lie west of the Jumentos. Running back toward Port Principe, Columbus made it at dark, but found that he had been carried to the westward by the currents. This furnishes a sufficient proof of the strength of the current in the Bahama channel; for it will be remembered that he ran over to Cuba with a fair wind. After contending for four days, until the 24th November, with light winds against the force of these currents, he arrived at length opposite the level island whence he had set out the week before when going to Babeque.

We are thus accidentally informed that the point from which Columbus started in search of Babeque was the same island of Guajava the lesser, which lies west of Nuevitas el Principe. Further: at first he dared not enter into the opening between the two mountains, for it seemed as though the sea broke upon them; but having sent the boat ahead, the vessels followed in at S.W. and then W. into a fine harbor. The level island lay north of it, and with another island formed a secure basin capable of sheltering all the navy of Spain. This level island resolves itself then into our late Cape Cuba, which we have supposed to be little Guajava, and the entrance east of it becomes identical with the gulf above mentioned which lay between two mountains, one of which we have supposed the Alto de Juan Daune, and which gulf appeared to divide Cuba from Bohio. Our course now becomes a plain one. On the 26th of November, Columbus sailed from Santa Catalina (the name given by him to the port last described) at sunrise, and stood for the cape at the S.E. which he called Cabo del Pico. In this it is easy to recognize the high peak already spoken of as the Alto de Juan Daune. Arrived off this he saw another cape, distant fifteen leagues, and still further another five leagues beyond it, which he called Cabo de Campana. The first must be that now known as Point Padre, the second Point Mulas: their distances from Alto de Juan Daune are underrated; but it requires no little experience to estimate correctly the distances of the bold headlands of Cuba, as seen through the pure atmosphere that surrounds the island.

Having passed Point Mulas in the night, on the 27th Columbus looked into the deep bay that lies S.E. of it, and see-ing the bold projecting headland that makes out between Port Nipe and Port Banes, with those deep bays on each side of it, he supposed it to be an arm of the sea dividing one land from another with an island between them.

Having landed at Taco for a short time, Columbus arrived in the evening of the 27th at Baracoa, to which he gave the name of Puerto Santo. From Cabo del Pico to Puerto Santo, a distance of sixty leagues, he had passed no fewer than nine good ports and five rivers to Cape Campana, and thence to Puerto Santo eight more rivers, each with a good port; all of which may be found on the chart between Alto de Juan Daune and Baracoa. By keeping near the coast he had been assisted to the S.E. by the eddy current of the Bahama chan-nel. Sailing from Puerto Santo or Baracoa on the 4th of December, he reached the extremity of Cuba the following day, and striking off upon a wind to the S.E. in search of Babeque, which lay to the N.E., he came in sight of Bohio, to which he gave the name of Hispaniola.

On taking leave of Cuba, Columbus tells us that he had coasted it a distance of one hundred and twenty leagues. Allowing twenty leagues of this distance for his having followed the undulations of the coast, the remaining one hundred measured from Point Maysi fall exactly upon Cabrion Key, which we have supposed the western boundary of his discoveries.

The astronomical observations of Columbus form no objection to what has been here advanced; for he tells us that the instrument which he made use of to measure the meridian altitudes of the heavenly bodies was out of order and not to

* * * 13—Vol. VII.

be depended upon. He places his first discovery, Guanahani, in the latitude of Ferro, which is about 27° 30' north. San Salvador we find in 24° 30', and Turk's Island in 21° 30': both are very wide of the truth, but it is certainly easier to conceive an error of three than one of six degrees.

Laying aside geographical demonstration, let us now examine how historical records agree with the opinion here supported, that the island of San Salvador was the first point where Columbus came in contact with the New World. Herrera, who is considered the most faithful and authentic of Spanish historians, wrote his History of the Indies toward the year 1600. In describing the voyage of Juan Ponce de Leon, made to Florida in 1512, he makes the following remarks:* "Leaving Aguada in Porto Rico, they steered to the N.W. by N., and in five days arrived at an island called El Viejo, in latitude 22° 30' north. The next day they ar· rived at a small island of the Lucayos called Caycos. On the eighth day they anchored at another island called Yaguna in 24°, on the eighth day out from Porto Rico. Thence they passed to the island of Manuega, in 24° 30', and on the eleventh day they reached Guanahani, which is in 25° 40' north. This island of Guanahani was the first discovered by Columbus on his first voyage, and which he called San Salvador." This is the substance of the remarks of Herrera, and is entirely conclusive as to the location of San Salvador. The latitudes, it is true, are all placed higher than we now know them to be; that of San Salvador being such as to correspond with no other land than that now known as the Berry Islands, which are seventy leagues distant from the nearest coast of Cuba: whereas Columbus tells us that San Salvador was only forty-five leagues from Port Principe. But in those infant days of navigation, the instruments for measuring the altitudes of the heavenly bodies, and the tables of declinations for deducing the latitude, must have been so imperfect as to place the most scientific navigator of the time below the most mechanical one of the present.

The second island arrived at by Ponce de Leon, in his northwestern course, was one of the Caycos; the first one, then, called El Viejo, must have been Turk's Island, which lies S.E. of the Caycos. The third island they came to was probably Mariguana; the fourth, Crooked Island; and the fifth, Isla Larga. Lastly they came to Guanahani, the San

---

* Herrera, Hist. Ind., decad. i., lib. ix., cap. 10.

Salvador of Columbus. If this be supposed identical with Turk's Island, where do we find the succession of islands touched at by Ponce de Leon on his way from Porto Rico to San Salvador? * No stress has been laid, in these remarks, on the identity of name which has been preserved to San Salvador, Concepcion, and Port Principe, with those given by Columbus, though traditional usage is of vast weight in such matters. Geographical proof of a conclusive kind, it is thought, has been advanced, to enable the world to remain in its old hereditary belief that the present island of San Salvador is the spot where Columbus first set foot upon the New World. Established opinions of the kind should not be lightly molested. It is a good old rule, that ought to be kept in mind in curious research as well as territorial dealings, "Do not disturb the ancient landmarks."

Note to the Revised Edition of 1848.—The Baron de Humboldt, in his "Examen Critique de l'histoire de la geographie du nouveau continent," published in 1837, speaks repeatedly in high terms of the ability displayed in the above examination of the route of Columbus, and argues at great length and quite conclusively in support of the opinion contained in it. Above all, he produces a document hitherto unknown, and the great importance of which had been discovered by M. Valeknaer and himself in 1832. This is a map made in 1500 by that able mariner Juan de la Cosa, who accompanied Columbus in his second voyage and sailed with other of the discoverers. In this map, of which the Baron de Humboldt gives an engraving, the islands as laid down agree completely with the bearings and distances given in the journal of Columbus, and establishes the identity of San Salvador, or Cat Island, and Guanahani.

"I feel happy," says M. de Humboldt, "to be enabled to destroy the incertitudes (which rested on this subject) by a document as ancient as it is unknown; a document which confirms irrevocably the arguments which Mr. Washington Irving has given in his work against the hypotheses of the Turk's Island."

In the present revised edition the author feels at liberty

---

* In the first chapter of Herrera's description of the Indes, appended to his history, is another scale of the Bahama Islands, which corroborates the above. It begins at the opposite end, at the N.W., and runs down to the S. E. It is thought unnecessary to cite it particularly.

to give the merit of the very masterly paper on the route of Columbus where it is justly due. It was furnished him at Madrid by the late commander Alexander Slidel Mackenzie, of the United States navy, whose modesty shrunk from affixing his name to an article so calculated to do him credit, and which has since challenged the high eulogiums of men of nautical science.

No. XVIII

PRINCIPLES UPON WHICH THE SUMS MENTIONED IN THIS WORK HAVE BEEN REDUCED INTO MODERN CURRENCY

IN the reign of Ferdinand and Isabella the mark of silver, which was equal to 8 ounces or to 50 castellanos was divided into 65 reals, and each real into 34 maravedis; so that there were 2,210 maravedis in the mark of silver. Among other silver coins there was the real of 8, which, consisting of 8 reals, was, within a small fraction, the eighth part of a mark of silver, or one ounce. Of the gold coins then in circulation the castellano or *dobla de la vanda* was worth 490 maravedis, and the ducado 383 maravedis.

If the value of the maravedi had remained unchanged in Spain down to the present day, it would be easy to reduce a sum of the time of Ferdinand and Isabella into a corresponding sum of current money; but by the successive depreciations of the coin of Vellon, or mixed metals, issued since that period, the *real* and maravedi of Vellon, which had replaced the ancient currency, were reduced toward the year 1700 to about a third of the old *real* and maravedi, now known as the *real* and maravedi of silver. As, however, the ancient piece of 8 reals was equal approximately to the ounce of silver, and the duro, or dollar of the present day, is likewise equal to an ounce, they may be considered identical. Indeed, in Spanish America, the dollar, instead of being divided into 20 reals, as in Spain, is divided into only 8 parts called reals, which evidently represent the real of the time of Ferdinand and Isabella, as the dollar does the real of 8. But the ounce of silver was anciently worth $276\frac{1}{4}$ maravedis; the dollar, therefore, is likewise equal to $276\frac{1}{4}$ maravedis. By converting then the sums mentioned in this work into maravedis they have been afterward reduced into dollars by dividing by $276\frac{1}{4}$.

There is still, however, another calculation to be made, before we can arrive at the actual value of any sum of gold and silver mentioned in former times. It is necessary to notice the variation which has taken place in the value of the metals themselves. In Europe, previous to the discovery of the New World, an ounce of gold commanded an amount of food or labor which would cost three ounces at the present day; hence an ounce of gold was then estimated at three times its present value. At the same time an ounce of silver commanded an amount which at present costs 4 ounces of silver. It appears from this that the value of gold and silver varied with respect to each other, as well as with respect to all other commodities. This is owing to there having been much more silver brought from the New World, with respect to the quantity previously in circulation, than there has been of gold. In the fifteenth century one ounce of gold was equal to about 12 of silver; and now, in the year 1827, it is exchanged against 16.

Hence giving an idea of the relative value of the sums mentioned in this work, it has been found necessary to multiply them by three when in gold, and by four when expressed in silver.*

It is expedient to add that the dollar is reckoned in this work at 100 cents of the United States of North America, and four shillings and sixpence of England.

No. XIX

PRESTER JOHN

SAID to be derived from the Persian *Prestegani* or *Perestigani*, which signifies apostolique; or *Preschtak Geham*, angel of the world. It is the name of a potent Christian monarch of shadowy renown, whose dominions were placed by writers of the middle ages sometimes in the remote parts of Asia and sometimes in Africa, and of whom such contradictory accounts were given by the travelers of those days that the very existence either of him or his kingdom came to be considered doubtful. It now appears to be admitted that there really was such a potentate in a remote part of Asia.

* See Caballero Pesos y Medidas. J. B. Say, "Economie Politique."

He was of the Nestorian Christians, a sect spread throughout Asia, and taking its name and origin from Nestorius, a
Christian patriarch of Constantinople.

The first vague reports of a Christian potentate in the interior of Asia, or, as it was then called, India, were brought
to Europe by the Crusaders, who, it is supposed, gathered
them from the Syrian merchants who traded to the very confines of China.

In subsequent ages, when the Portuguese in their travels
and voyages discovered a Christian king among the Abys-
sinians called Baleel-Gian, they confounded him with the
potentate already spoken of.   Nor was the blunder extraordinary, since the original Prester John was said to reign over
a remote part of India; and the ancients included in that
name Ethiopia and all the regions of Africa and Asia bordering on the Red Sea and on the commercial route from
Egypt to India.

Of the Prester John of India we have reports furnished
by William Ruysbrook, commonly called Rubruquis, a Franciscan friar sent by Louis IX., about the middle of the thirteenth century, to convert the Grand Khan.   According to
him, Prester John was originally a Nestorian priest, who on
the death of the sovereign made himself king of the Nay-
mans, all Nestorian Christians.   Carpini, a Franciscan friar,
sent by Pope Innocent in 1245 to convert the Mongols of
Persia, says that Ocoday, one of the sons of Genghis Khan
of Tartary, marched with an army against the Christians of
Grand India.   The king of that country, who was called
Prester John, came to their succor.   Having had figures of
men made of bronze, he had them fastened on the saddles
of horses, and put fire within, with a man behind with a bellows.   When they came to battle these horses were put in
the advance, and the men who were seated behind the figures threw something into the fire, and blowing with their
bellows, made such a smoke that the Tartars were quite covered with it.   They then fell on them, dispatched many with
their arrows, and put the rest to flight.

Marco Polo (1271) places Prester John near the great wall
of China, to the north of Chan-si, in Teudich, a populous region full of cities and castles.

Mandeville (1332) makes Prester sovereign of Upper India
(Asia), with four thousand islands tributary to him.

When John II., of Portugal, was pushing his discoveries
along the African coast, he was informed that three hundred

and fifty leagues to the east of the kingdom of Benin in the profound depths of Africa, there was a puissant monarch called Ogave who had spiritual and temporal jurisdiction over all the surrounding kings.

An African prince assured him, also, that to the east of Timbuctoo there was a sovereign who professed a religion similar to that of the Christians, and was king of a Mosaic people.

King John now supposed he had found traces of the real Prester John, with whom he was eager to form an alliance, religious as well as commercial. In 1487 he sent envoys by land in quest of him. One was a gentleman of his household, Pedro de Covilham; the other, Alphonso de Paiva. They went by Naples to Rhodes, thence to Cairo, thence to Aden on the Arabian Gulf above the mouth of the Red Sea.

Here they separated with an agreement to rendezvous at Cairo. Alphonso de Paiva sailed direct for Ethiopia; Pedro de Covilham for the Indies. The latter passed to Calicut and Goa, where he embarked for Sofala on the eastern coast of Africa, thence returned to Aden, and made his way back to Cairo. Here he learned that his coadjutor, Alphonso de Paiva, had died in that city. He found two Portuguese Jews waiting for him with fresh orders from King John not to give up his researches after Prester John until he found him. One of the Jews he sent back with a journal and verbal accounts of his travels. With the other he set off again for Aden; thence to Ormuz, at the entrance of the Gulf of Persia, where all the rich merchandise of the East was brought to be transported thence by Syria and Egypt into Europe.

Having taken note of everything here, he embarked on the Red Sea, and arrived at the court of an Abyssinian prince named Escander (the Arabic version of Alexander), whom he considered the real Prester John. The prince received him graciously, and manifested a disposition to favor the object of his embassy, but died suddenly, and his successor Naut refused to let Covilham depart, but kept him for many years about his person, as his prime councilor, lavishing on him wealth and honors. After all, this was not the real Prester John, who, as has been observed, was an Asiatic potentate.

No. XX

MARCO POLO *

THE travels of Marco Polo, or Paolo, furnish a key to many parts of the voyages and speculations of Columbus, which without it would hardly be comprehensible.

Marco Polo was a native of Venice, who, in the thirteenth century, made a journey into the remote, and, at that time, unknown regions of the East, and filled all Christendom with curiosity by his account of the countries he had visited. He was preceded in his travels by his father Nicholas and his uncle Maffeo Polo. These two brothers were of an illustrious family in Venice, and embarked about the year 1255 on a commercial voyage to the East. Having traversed the Mediterranean and through the Bosphorus, they stopped for a short time at Constantinople, which city had recently been wrested from the Greeks by the joint arms of France and Venice. Here they disposed of their Italian merchandise, and, having purchased a stock of jewelry, departed on an adventurous expedition to trade with the western Tartars, who, having overrun many parts of Asia and Europe, were settling and forming cities in the vicinity of the Wolga. After traversing the Euxine to Soldaia (at present Sudak), a port in the Crimea, they continued on, by land and water, until they reached the military court or rather camp of a Tartar prince named Barkah, a descendant of Genghis Khan, into whose hands they confided all their merchandise. The barbaric chieftain, while he was dazzled by their precious commodities, was flattered by the entire confidence in his justice manifested by these strangers. He repaid them with princely munificence, and loaded them with favors during a year that they remained at his court. A war breaking out between their

---

* In preparing the first edition of this work for the press the author had not the benefit of the English translation of Marco Polo, published a few years since, with admirable commentaries, by William Marsden, F.R.S. He availed himself, principally, of an Italian version in the Venetian edition of Ramusio (1606), the French translation by Bergeron, and an old and very incorrect Spanish translation. Having since procured the work of Mr. Marsden, he has made considerable alterations in these notices of Marco Polo

patron and his cousin Hulagu, chief of the eastern Tartars, and Barkah being defeated, the Polos were embarrassed how to extricate themselves from the country and return home in safety. The road to Constantinople being cut off by the enemy, they took a circuitous route, round the head of the Caspian Sea, and through the deserts of Transoxiana, until they arrived in the city of Bokhara, where they resided for three years.

While here there arrived a Tartar nobleman who was on an embassy from the victorious Hulagu to his brother the Grand Khan. The embassador became acquainted with the Venetians, and finding them to be versed in the Tartar tongue and possessed of curious and valuable knowledge, he prevailed upon them to accompany him to the court of the emperor, situated, as they supposed, at the very extremity of the East.

After a march of several months, being delayed by snowstorms and inundations, they arrived at the court of Cublai, otherwise called the Great Khan, which signifies King of Kings, being the sovereign potentate of the Tartars. This magnificent prince received them with great distinction; he made inquiries about the countries and princes of the West, their civil and military government, and the manners and customs of the Latin nation. Above all, he was curious on the subject of the Christian religion. He was so much struck by their replies that, after holding a council with the chief persons of his kingdom, he entreated the two brothers to go on his part as embassadors to the Pope, to entreat him to send a hundred learned men well instructed in the Christian faith, to impart a knowledge of it to the sages of his empire. He also entreated them to bring him a little oil from the lamp of our Saviour, in Jerusalem, which he concluded must have marvelous virtues. It has been supposed, and with great reason, that under this covert of religion the shrewd Tartar sovereign veiled motives of a political nature. The influence of the Pope in promoting the Crusades had caused his power to be known and respected throughout the East; it was of some moment, therefore, to conciliate his good-will. Cublai Khan had no bigotry nor devotion to any particular faith, and probably hoped, by adopting Christianity, to make it a common cause between himself and the warlike princes of Christendom, against his and their inveterate enemies, the soldan of Egypt and the Saracens.

Having written letters to the Pope in the Tartar language, he delivered them to the Polos, and appointed one of the principal noblemen of his court to accompany them in their mission. On their taking leave he furnished them with a tablet of gold on which was engraved the royal arms; this was to serve as a passport, at sight of which the governors of the various provinces were to entertain them, to furnish them with escorts through dangerous places, and render them all other necessary services at the expense of the Great Khan.

They had scarce proceeded twenty miles, when the nobleman who accompanied them fell ill, and they were obliged to leave him and continue on their route. Their golden passport procured them every attention and facility throughout the dominions of the Great Khan. They arrived safely at Acre, in April, 1269. Here they received news of the recent death of Pope Clement IV., at which they were much grieved, fearing it would cause delay in their mission. There was at that time in Acre a legate of the holy chair, Tebaldo di Vesconti, of Placentia, to whom they gave an account of their embassy. He heard them with great attention and interest, and advised them to await the election of a new Pope, which must soon take place, before they proceeded to Rome on their mission. They determined in the interim to make a visit to their families, and accordingly departed for Negropont, and thence to Venice, where great changes had taken place in their domestic concerns during their long absence. The wife of Nicholas, whom he had left pregnant, had died, in giving birth to a son, who had been named Marco.

As the contested election for the new pontiff remained pending for two years, they were uneasy, lest the Emperor of Tartary should grow impatient at so long a postponement of the conversion of himself and his people; they determined, therefore, not to wait the election of a Pope, but to proceed to Acre, and get such dispatches and such ghostly ministry for the Grand Khan as the legate could furnish. On the second journey, Nicholas Polo took with him his son Marco, who afterward wrote an account of these travels.

They were again received with great favor by the legate Tebaldo, who, anxious for the success of their mission, furnished them with letters to the Grand Khan, in which the doctrines of the Christian faith were fully expounded. With these, and with a supply of the holy oil from the sepulcher, they once more set out, in September, 1271, for the remote parts of Tartary. They had not long departed, when missives arrived from Rome, informing the legate of his own election to the holy chair. He took the name of Gregory X..

and decreed that in future, on the death of a Pope, the cardinals should be shut up in conclave until they elected a successor; a wise regulation, which has since continued, enforcing a prompt decision and preventing intrigue.

Immediately on receiving intelligence of his election, he dispatched a courier to the king of Armenia, requesting that the two Venetians might be sent back to him, if they had not departed. They joyfully returned, and were furnished with new letters to the Khan. Two eloquent friars, also, Nicholas Vincent and Gilbert de Tripoli, were sent with them, with powers to ordain priests and bishops and to grant absolution. They had presents of crystal vases and other costly articles to deliver to the Grand Khan; and thus well provided, they once more set forth on their journey.*

Arriving in Armenia, they ran great risk of their lives from the war which was raging, the soldan of Babylon having invaded the country. They took refuge for some time with the superior of a monastery. Here the two reverend fathers, losing all courage to prosecute so perilous an enterprise, determined to remain, and the Venetians continued their journey. They were a long time on the way, and exposed to great hardships and sufferings from floods and snowstorms, it being the winter season. At length they reached a town in the dominions of the Khan. That potentate sent officers to meet them at forty days' distance from the court, and to provide quarters for them during their journey.† He received them with great kindness, was highly gratified with the result of their mission and with the letters of the Pope, and having received from them some oil from the lamp of the holy sepulcher, he had it locked up, and guarded it as a precious treasure.

The three Venetians, father, brother, and son, were treated with such distinction by the Khan that the courtiers were filled with jealousy. Marco soon, however, made himself popular, and was particularly esteemed by the emperor. He acquired the four principal languages of the country, and was of such remarkable capacity that, notwithstanding his youth, the Khan employed him in missions and services of importance, in various parts of his dominions, some to the distance

---

* Ramusio, tom. iii.

† Bergeron, by blunder in the translation from the original Latin, has stated that the Khan sent 40,000 men to escort them. This has drawn the ire of the critics upon Marco Polo, who have cited it as one of his monstrous exaggerations.

of even six months' journey. On these expeditions he was industrious in gathering all kinds of information respecting that vast empire; and from notes and minutes made for the satisfaction of the Grand Khan he afterward composed the history of his travels.

After about seventeen years' residence in the Tartar court the Venetians felt a longing to return to their native country. Their patron was advanced in age and could not survive much longer, and after his death their return might be difficult if not impossible. They applied to the Grand Khan for permission to depart, but for a time met with a refusal, accompanied by friendly upbraidings. At length a singular train of events operated in their favor; an embassy arrived from a Mogul Tartar prince, who ruled in Persia, and who was grand-nephew to the emperor. The object was to entreat, as a spouse, a princess of the imperial lineage. A granddaughter of Cublai Khan, seventeen years of age, and of great beauty and accomplishments, was granted to the prayer of the prince, and departed for Persia with the embassadors, and with a splendid retinue, but after traveling for some months was obliged to return on account of the distracted state of the country.

The embassadors despaired of conveying the beautiful bride to the arms of her expecting bridegroom, when Marco Polo returned from a voyage to certain of the Indian islands. His representations of the safety of a voyage in those seas, and his private instigations, induced the embassadors to urge the Grand Khan for permission to convey the princess by sea to the Gulf of Persia, and that the Christians might accompany them, as being best experienced in maritime affairs. Cublai Khan consented with great reluctance, and a splendid fleet was fitted out and victualed for two years, consisting of fourteen ships of four masts, some of which had crews of two hundred and fifty men.

On parting with the Venetians the munificent Khan gave them rich presents of jewels, and made them promise to return to him after they had visited their families. He authorized them to act as his embassadors to the principal courts of Europe, and, as on a former occasion, furnished them with tablets of gold, to serve, not merely as passports, but as orders upon all commanders in his territories for accommodations and supplies.

They set sail therefore in the fleet with the Oriental princess and her attendants and the Persian embassadors. The ships swept along the coast of Cochin China, stopped for three months at a port of the island of Sumatra near the western entrance of the Straits of Malacca, waiting for the change of the monsoon to pass the Bay of Bengal. Traversing this vast expanse, they touched at the island of Ceylon and then crossed the strait to the southern part of the great peninsula of India. Thence sailing up the Pirate coast, as it is called, the fleet entered the Persian Gulf and arrived at the famous port of Olmuz, where it is presumed the voyage terminated, after eighteen months spent in traversing the Indian seas.

Unfortunately for the royal bride who was the object of this splendid naval expedition, her bridegroom, the Mogul king, had died some time before her arrival, leaving a son named Ghazan, during whose minority the government was administered by his uncle Kai-Khatu. According to the directions of the regent, the princess was delivered to the youthful prince, son of her intended spouse. He was at that time at the head of an army on the borders of Persia. He was of a diminutive stature but of a great soul, and, on afterward ascending the throne, acquired renown for his talents and virtues. What became of the Eastern bride, who had traveled so far in quest of a husband, is not known; but everything favorable is to be inferred from the character of Ghazan.

The Polos remained some time in the court of the regent, and then departed, with fresh tablets of gold given by that prince, to carry them in safety and honor through his dominions. As they had to traverse many countries where the traveler is exposed to extreme peril, they appeared on their journeys as Tartars of low condition, having converted all their wealth into precious stones and sewn them up in the folds and linings of their coarse garments. They had a long, difficult, and perilous journey to Trebizond, whence they proceeded to Constantinople, thence to Negropont, and finally to Venice, where they arrived in 1295, in good health, and literally laden with riches. Having heard during their journey of the death of their old benefactor, Cublai Khan, they considered their diplomatic functions at an end, and also that they were absolved from their promise to return to his dominions.

Ramusio, in his preface to the narrative of Marco Polo, gives a variety of particulars concerning their arrival, which he compares to that of Ulysses. When they arrived at Venice, they were known by nobody. So many years had elapsed since their departure without any tidings of them that they were either forgotten or considered dead. Besides, their foreign garb, the influence of southern suns, and the similitude which men acquire to those among whom they reside for any length of time, had given them the look of Tartars rather than Italians.

They repaired to their own house, which was a noble palace, situated in the street of St. Giovanne Chrisostomo, and was afterward known by the name of la Corte de la Milione. They found several of their relatives still inhabiting it; but they were slow in recollecting the travelers, not knowing of their wealth, and probably considering them, from their coarse and foreign attire, poor adventurers returned to be a charge upon their families. The Polos, however, took an effectual mode of quickening the memories of their friends, and insuring themselves a loving reception. They invited them all to a grand banquet. When their guests arrived, they received them richly dressed in garments of crimson satin of Oriental fashion. When water had been served for the washing of hands, and the company were summoned to table, the travelers, who had retired, appeared again in still richer robes of crimson damask. The first dresses were cut up and distributed among the servants, being of such length that they swept the ground, which, says Ramusio, was the mode in those days with dresses worn within doors. After the first course, they again retired and came in dressed in crimson velvet; the damask dresses being likewise given to the domestics, and the same was done at the end of the feast with their velvet robes, when they appeared in the Venetian dress of the day. The guests were lost in astonishment, and could not comprehend the meaning of this masquerade. Having dismissed all the attendants, Marco Polo brought forth the coarse Tartar dresses in which they had arrived. Slashing them in several places with a knife, and ripping open the seams and lining, there tumbled forth rubies, sapphires, emeralds, diamonds, and other precious stones, until the whole table glittered with inestimable wealth, acquired from the munificence of the Grand Khan, and conveyed in this portable form through the perils of their long journey.

The company, observes Ramusio, were out of their wits with amazement, and now clearly perceived what they had at first doubted, that these in very truth were those honored and valiant gentlemen the Polos, and, accordingly, paid them great respect and reverence.

The account of this curious feast is given by Ramusio, on traditional authority, having heard it many times related by the illustrious Gasparo Malipiero, a very ancient gentleman, and a senator, of unquestionable veracity, who had it from his father, who had it from his grandfather, and so on up to the fountain-head.

When the fame of this banquet and of the wealth of the travelers came to be divulged throughout Venice, all the city, noble and simple, crowded to do honor to the extraordinary merit of the Polos. Maffeo, who was the eldest, was admitted to the dignity of the magistracy. The youth of the city came every day to visit and converse with Marco Polo, who was extremely amiable and communicative. They were insatiable in their inquiries about Cathay and the Grand Khan, which he answered with great courtesy, giving details with which they were vastly delighted, and, as he always spoke of the wealth of the Grand Khan in round numbers, they gave him the name of Messer Marco Milioni.

Some months after their return, Lampa Doria, commander of the Genoese navy, appeared in the vicinity of the island of Curzola with seventy galleys. Andrea Dandolo, the Venetian admiral, was sent against him. Marco Polo commanded a galley of the fleet. His usual good fortune deserted him. Advancing the first in the line with his galley, and not being properly seconded, he was taken prisoner, thrown in irons, and carried to Genoa. Here he was detained for a long time in prison, and all offers of ransom rejected. His imprisonment gave great uneasiness to his father and uncle, fearing that he might never return. Seeing themselves in this unhappy state, with so much treasure and no heirs, they consulted together. They were both very old men; but Nicolo, observes Ramusio, was of a galliard complexion: it was determined he should take a wife. He did so; and, to the wonder of his friends, in four years had three children.

In the meanwhile the fame of Marco Polo's travels had circulated in Genoa. His prison was daily crowded with nobility, and he was supplied with everything that could cheer him in his confinement. A Genoese gentleman, who visited him every day, at length prevailed upon him to write an account of what he had seen. He had his papers and journals sent to him from Venice, and with the assistance of his friend, or, as some will have it, his fellow prisoner, produced the work which afterward made such noise throughout the world.

The merit of Marco Polo at length procured him his lib-

erty. He returned to Venice, where he found his father with
a house full of children. He took it in good part, followed
the old man's example, married, and had two daughters,
Moretta and Fantina. The date of the death of Marco Polo
is unknown; he is supposed to have been, at the time, about
seventy years of age. On his deathbed he is said to have
been exhorted by his friends to retract what he had published, or at least to disavow those parts commonly regarded
as fictions. He replied indignantly that, so far from having
exaggerated, he had not told one-half of the extraordinary
things of which he had been an eye-witness.

Marco Polo died without male issue. Of the three sons
of his father by the second marriage, one only had children;
viz., five sons and one daughter. The sons died without leaving issue; the daughter inherited all her father's wealth and
married into the noble and distinguished house of Trevesino.
Thus the male line of the Polos ceased in 1417, and the family name was extinguished.

Such are the principal particulars known of Marco Polo,
a man whose travels for a long time made a great noise in
Europe, and will be found to have had a great effect on modern discovery. His splendid account of the extent, wealth,
and population of the Tartar territories filled every one with
admiration. The possibility of bringing all those regions under the dominion of the Church, and rendering the Grand
Khan an obedient vassal to the holy chair, was for a long
time a favorite topic among the enthusiastic missionaries of
Christendom, and there were many saints-errant who undertook to effect the conversion of this magnificent infidel.

Even at the distance of two centuries, when the enterprises
for the discovery of the new route to India had set all the
warm heads of Europe madding about these remote regions
of the East, the conversion of the Grand Khan became again
a popular theme; and it was too speculative and romantic an
enterprise not to catch the vivid imagination of Columbus.
In all his voyages, he will be found continually to be seeking
after the territories of the Grand Khan, and even after his
last expedition, when nearly worn out by age, hardships, and
infirmities, he offered, in a letter to the Spanish monarchs,
written from a bed of sickness, to conduct any missionary to
the territories of the Tartar emperor who would undertake
his conversion.

No. XXI

THE WORK OF MARCO POLO

THE work of Marco Polo is stated by some to have been originally written in Latin,* though the most probable opinion is that it was written in the Venetian dialect of the Italian. Copies of it in manuscript were multiplied and rapidly circulated; translations were made into various languages, until the invention of printing enabled it to be widely diffused throughout Europe. In the course of these translations and successive editions, the original text, according to Purchas, has been much vitiated, and it is probable many extravagances in numbers and measurements with which Marco Polo is charged may be the errors of translators and printers. When the work first appeared, it was considered by some as made up of fictions and extravagances, and Vossius assures us that even after the death of Marco Polo he continued to be a subject of ridicule among the light and unthinking, insomuch that he was frequently personated at masquerades by some wit or droll, who, in his feigned character, related all kinds of extravagant fables and adventures. His work, however, excited great attention among thinking men, containing evidently a fund of information concerning vast and splendid countries, before unknown to the European world. Vossius assures us that it was at one time highly esteemed by the learned. Francis Pepin, author of the Brandenburgh version, styles Polo a man commendable for his piety, prudence, and fidelity. Athanasius Kircher, in his account of China, says that none of the ancients have described the kingdoms of the remote East with more exactness. Various other learned men of past times have borne testimony to his character, and most of the substantial parts of his work have been authenticated by subsequent travelers. The most able and ample vindication of Marco Polo, however, is to be found in the English translation of his work, with copious notes and commentaries, by William Marsden, F.R.S. He has diligently discriminated between what Marco Polo relates from his own observation and what he relates as gathered from

---

* Hist. des Voyages, tom. xxvii., lib. iv., cap. 8. Paris, 1549.

others; he points out the errors that have arisen from misin-
terpretations, omissions, or interpretations of translators, and
he claims all proper allowance for the superstitious coloring
of parts of the narrative from the belief, prevalent among the
most wise and learned of his day, in miracles and magic.
After perusing the work of Mr. Marsden, the ·character of
Marco Polo rises in the estimation of the reader.   It is evident that his narration, as far as related form his own observations, is correct, and that he had really traversed a
great part of Tartary and China, and navigated in the Indian seas.   Some of the countries and many of the islands,
however, are evidently described from accounts given by
others, and in these accounts are generally found the fables
which have excited incredulity and ridicule.   As he composed his work after his return home, partly from memory
and partly from memorandums, he was liable to confuse
what he had heard with what he had seen, and thus to give
undue weight to many fables and exaggerations which he
had received from others.

Much has been said of a map brought from Cathay by
Marco Polo, which was conserved in the convent of San
Michale de Murano in the vicinity of Venice, and in which
the Cape of Good Hope and the island of Madagascar were
indicated, countries which the Portuguese claim the merit of
having discovered two centuries afterward.   It has been suggested also that Columbus had visited the convent and examined this map, whence he derived some of his ideas concerning the coast of India.   According to Ramusio, however, who
had been at the convent, and was well acquainted with the
prior, the map preserved there was one copied by a friar from
the original one of Marco Polo, and many alterations and additions had since been made by other hands, so that for a
long time it lost all credit with judicious people, until on
comparing it with the work of Marco Polo it was found in
the main to agree with his descriptions.*   The Cape of Good
Hope was doubtless among the additions made subsequent
to the discoveries of the Portuguese.†   Columbus makes no

---

* Ramusio, Vol. II., p. 17.

† Mr. Marsden, who has inspected a splendid fac-simile of this map
preserved in the British Museum, objects even to the fundamental part
of it: "Where," he observes, "situations are given to places that seem
quite inconsistent with the descriptions in the travels, and cannot be
attributed to their author, although inserted on the supposed authority
of his writings."   Marsden's Marco Polo, Introd., p. 42.

mention of this map, which he most probably would have done had he seen it. He seems to have been entirely guided by the one furnished by Paulo Toscanelli, and which was apparently projected after the original map, or after the descriptions of Marco Polo and the maps of Ptolemy.

When the attention of the world was turned toward the remote parts of Asia in the fifteenth century, and the Portuguese were making their attempts to circumnavigate Africa, the narration of Marco Polo again rose to notice. This, with the travels of Nicolo de Comte, the Venetian, and of Hieronimo da San Stefano, a Genoese, are said to have been the principal lights by which the Portuguese guided themselves in their voyages.*

Above all, the influence which the work of Marco Polo had over the mind of Columbus gives it particular interest and importance. It was evidently an oracular work with him. He frequently quotes it, and on his voyages, supposing himself to be on the Asiatic coast, he is continually endeavoring to discover the islands and mainlands described in it, and to find the famous Cipango.

It is proper, therefore, to specify some of those places, and the manner in which they are described by a Venetian traveler, that the reader may more fully understand the anticipations which were haunting the mind of Columbus in his voyages among the West Indian islands, and along the coast of Terra Firma.

The winter residence of the Great Khan, according to Marco Polo, was in the city of Cambalu, or Kanbalu (since ascertained to be Pekin), in the province of Cathay. This city, he says, was twenty-four miles square, and admirably built. It was impossible, according to Marco Polo, to describe the vast amount and variety of merchandise and manufactures brought there; it would seem they were enough to furnish the universe. "Here are to be seen in wonderful abundance the precious stones, the pearls, the silks, and the diverse perfumes of the East; scarce a day passes that there does not arrive nearly a thousand cars laden with silk, of which they make admirable stuffs in this city."

The palace of the Great Khan is magnificently built, and four miles in circuit. It is rather a group of palaces. In the interior it is resplendent with gold and silver; and in it are guarded the precious vases and jewels of the sovereign.

---

* Hist. des Voyages, tom. xl., lib. xi., chap. 4.

All the appointments of the Khan for war, for the chase, for various festivities, are described in gorgeous terms. But though Marco Polo is magnificent in his description of the provinces of Cathay, and its imperial city of Cambalu, he outdoes himself when he comes to describe the province of Mangi. This province is supposed to be the southern part of China. It contains, he says, twelve hundred cities. The capital Quinsai (supposed to be the city of Hang-cheu) was twenty-five miles from the sea, but communicated by a river with a port situated on the seacoast, and had great trade with India.

The name Quinsai, according to Marco Polo, signifies the city of heaven; he says he has been in it and examined it diligently, and affirms it to be the largest in the world; and so undoubtedly it is if the measurement of the traveler is to be taken literally, for he declares that it is one hundred miles in circuit. This seeming exaggeration has been explained by supposing him to mean Chinese miles or *li*, which are to the Italian miles in the proportion of three to eight; and Mr. Marsden observes that the walls even of the modern city, the limits of which have been considerably contracted, are estimated by travelers at sixty *li*. The ancient city has evidently been of immense extent, and as Marco Polo could not be supposed to have measured the walls himself, he has probably taken the loose and incorrect estimates of the inhabitants. He describes it also as built upon little islands like Venice, and has twelve thousand stone bridges,* the arches of which are so high that the largest vessels can pass under them without lowering their masts. It has, he affirms, three thousand baths, and six hundred thousand families, including domestics. It abounds with magnificent houses, and has a lake thirty miles in circuit within its walls, on the banks of which are superb palaces of people of rank.† The inhabitants of

---

* Another blunder in translation has drawn upon Marco Polo the indignation of George Hornius, who (in his Origin of America, iv., 3), exclaims, "Who can believe all that he says of the city of Quinsai? as, for example, that it has stone bridges twelve thousand miles high!" etc. It is probable that many of the exaggerations in the accounts of Marco Polo are in fact the errors of his translators.

Mandeville, speaking of this same city, which he calls Causai, says it is built on the sea, like Venice, and has twelve hundred bridges.

† Sir George Staunton mentions this lake as being a beautiful sheet of water, about three or four miles in diameter, its margin ornamented with houses and gardens of mandarins, together with temples, monasteries for the priests of Fo, and an imperial palace.

Quinsai are very voluptuous, and indulge in all kinds of luxuries and delights, particularly the women, who are extremely beautiful. There are many merchants and artisans, but the masters do not work, they employ servants to do all their labor. The province of Mangi was conquered by the Great Khan, who divided it into nine kingdoms, appointing to each a tributary king. He drew from it an immense revenue, for the country abounded in gold, silver, silks, sugar, spices, and perfumes.

ZIPANGU, ZIPANGRI, OR CIPANGO

Fifteen hundred miles from the shores of Mangi, according to Marco Polo, lay the great island of Zipangu, by some written Zipangri, and by Columbus Cipango.* Marco Polo describes it as abounding in gold, which, however, the king seldom permits to be transported out of the island. The king has a magnificent palace covered with plates of gold, as in other countries the palaces are covered with sheets of lead or copper. The halls and chambers are likewise covered with gold, the windows adorned with it, sometimes in plates of the thickness of two fingers. The island also produces vast quantities of the largest and finest pearls, together with a variety of precious stones; so that, in fact, it abounds in riches. The Great Khan made several attempts to conquer this island, but in vain; which is not to be wondered at, if it be true what Marco Polo relates, that the inhabitants had certain stones of a charmed virtue inserted between the skin and the flesh of their right arms, which, through the power of diabolical enchantments, rendered them invulnerable. This island was an object of diligent search to Columbus.

About the island of Zipangu or Cipango, and between it and the coast of Mangi, the sea, according to Marco Polo, is studded with small islands to the number of seven thousand four hundred and forty, of which the greater part are inhabited. There is not one which does not produce odoriferous

---

* Supposed to be those islands collectively called Japan. They are named by the Chinese Ge-pen, the terminating syllable *gu*, added by Marco Polo, is supposed to be the Chinese word *kue*, signifying kingdom, which is commonly annexed to the names of foreign countries. As the distance of the nearest part of the southern island from the coast of China, near Ning-po, is not more than five hundred Italian miles, Mr. Marsden supposes Marco Polo, in stating it to be 1500, means Chinese miles, or li, which are in the proportion of somewhat more than one-third of the former.

trees and perfumes in abundance. Columbus thought himself at one time in the midst of these islands.

These are the principal places described by Marco Polo, which occur in the letters and journals of Columbus. The island of Cipango was the first land he expected to make, and he intended to visit afterward the province of Mangi, and to seek the Great Khan in his city of Cambalu, in the province of Cathay. Unless the reader can bear in mind these sumptuous descriptions of Marco Polo, of countries teeming with wealth, and cities where the very domes and palaces flamed with gold, he will have but a faint idea of the splendid anticipations which filled the imagination of Columbus when he discovered, as he supposed, the extremity of Asia. It was his confident expectation of soon arriving at these countries, and realizing the accounts of the Venetian, that induced him to hold forth those promises of immediate wealth to the sovereigns, which caused so much disappointment, and brought upon him the frequent reproach of exciting false hopes and indulging in willful exaggeration.

No. XXII

SIR JOHN MANDEVILLE

NEXT to Marco Polo the travels of Sir John Mandeville, and his account of the territories of the Great Khan along the coast of Asia, seem to have been treasured up in the mind of Columbus.

Mandeville was born in the city of St. Albans. He was devoted to study from his earliest childhood, and after finishing his general education applied himself to medicine. Having a great desire to see the remotest parts of the earth, then known, that is to say, Asia and Africa, and, above all, to visit the Holy Land, he left England in 1332, and passing through France embarked at Marseilles. According to his own account he visited Turkey, Armenia, Egypt, Upper and Lower Libya, Syria, Persia, Chaldea, Ethiopia, Tartary, Amazonia and the Indies, residing in their principal cities. But most he says he delighted in the Holy Land, where he remained for a long time, examining it with the greatest minuteness, and endeavoring to follow all the traces of our Saviour. After an absence of thirty-four years he returned to England, but found himself forgotten and unknown by the greater part of his countrymen, and a stranger in his native place. He wrote a history of his travels in three languages—English, French, and Latin—for he was master of many tongues. He addressed his work to Edward III. His wanderings do not seem to have made him either pleased with the world at large or contented with his home. He railed at the age, saying that there was no more virtue extant; that the Church was ruined; error prevalent among the clergy; simony upon the throne; and, in a word, that the devil reigned triumphant. He soon returned to the continent, and died at Liege in 1372. He was buried in the abbey of the Gulielmites, in the suburbs of that city, where Ortelius, in his Itinerarium Belgiæ, says that he saw his monument, on which was the effigy, in stone, of a man with a forked beard and his hands raised toward his head (probably folded as in prayer, according to the manner of old tombs) and a lion at his feet. There was an inscription stating his name, quality, and calling (viz., professor of medicine), that he was very pious, very learned, and very charitable to the poor, and that after having traveled over the whole world he had died at Liege. The people of the convent showed also his spurs, and the housings of the horses which he had ridden in his travels.

The descriptions given by Mandeville of the Grand Khan, of the province of Cathay, and the city of Cambalu, are no less splendid than those of Marco Polo. The royal palace was more than two leagues in circumference. The grand hall had twenty-four columns of copper and gold. There were more than three hundred thousand men occupied and living in and about the palace, of which more than one hundred thousand were employed in taking care of ten thousand elephants and of a vast variety of other animals, birds of prey, falcons, parrots, and paroquets. On days of festival there were even twice the number of men employed. The title of this potentate in his letters was "Khan, the son of God, exalted possessor of all the earth, master of those who are masters of others." On his seal was engraved, "God reigns in heaven, Khan upon earth."

Mandeville has become proverbial for indulging in a traveler's exaggerations; yet his accounts of the countries which he visited have been found far more veracious than had been imagined. His descriptions of Cathay and the wealthy province of Mangi, agreeing with those of Marco Polo, had great authority with Columbus.

No. XXIII

THE ZONES

THE zones were imaginary bands or circles in the heavens producing an effect of climate on corresponding belts on the globe of the earth. The polar circles and the tropics mark these divisions.

The central region, lying beneath the track of the sun, was termed the torrid zone; the two regions between the tropics and the polar circles were termed the temperate zones, and the remaining parts, between the polar circles and the poles, the frigid zones.

The frozen regions near the poles were considered uninhabitable and unnavigable on account of the extreme cold. The burning zone, or rather the central part of it, immediately about the equator, was considered uninhabitable, unproductive, and impassable in consequence of the excessive heat. The temperate zones, lying between them, were supposed to be fertile and salubrious, and suited to the purposes of life.

The globe was divided into two hemispheres by the equator, an imaginary line encircling it at equal distance from the poles. The whole of the world known to the ancients was contained in the temperate zone of the northern hemisphere.

It was imagined that if there should be inhabitants in the temperate zone of the southern hemisphere, there could still be no communication with them on account of the burning zone which intervened.

Parmenides, according to Strabo, was the inventor of this theory of the five zones, but he made the torrid zone extend on each side of the equator beyond the tropics. Aristotle supported this doctrine of the zones. In his time nothing was known of the extreme northern parts of Europe and Asia, nor of interior Ethiopia and the southern part of Africa, extending beyond the tropic of Capricorn to the Cape of Good Hope. Aristotle believed that there was habitable earth in the southern hemisphere, but that it was forever divided from the part of the world already known by the impassable zone of scorching heat at the equator.*

---

* Aristot., 2 Met., cap. 5.

Pliny supported the opinion of Aristotle concerning the burning zone. "The temperature of the central region of the earth," he observes, "where the sun runs his course, is burned up as with fire. The temperate zones which lie on either side can have no communication with each other in consequence of the fervent heat of this region."*

Strabo (lib. xi.), in mentioning this theory, gives it likewise his support; and others of the ancient philosophers, as well as the poets, might be cited to show the general prevalence of the belief.

It must be observed that, at the time when Columbus defended his proposition before the learned board at Salamanca, the ancient theory of the burning zone had not yet been totally disproved by modern discovery. The Portuguese, it is true, had penetrated within the tropics; but, though the whole of the space between the tropic of Cancer and that of Capricorn, in common parlance, was termed the torrid zone, the uninhabitable and impassable part, strictly speaking, according to the doctrine of the ancients, only extended a limited number of degrees on each side of the equator, forming about a third, or at most, the half of the zone. The proofs which Columbus endeavored to draw therefore from the voyages made to St. George la Mina were not conclusive with those who were bigoted to the ancient theory, and who placed this scorching region still further southward, and immediately about the equator.

No. XXIV

OF THE ATLANTIS OF PLATO

THE island Atlantis is mentioned by Plato in his dialogue of Timæus. Solon, the Athenian lawgiver, is supposed to have traveled into Egypt. He is in an ancient city on the Delta, the fertile island formed by the Nile, and is holding converse with certain learned priests on the antiquities of remote ages, when one of them gives him a description of the island of Atlantis, and of its destruction, which he describes as having taken place before the conflagration of the world by Phaeton.

This island, he was told, had been situated in the West-

---

* Pliny, lib. i., cap. 61.

ern Ocean, opposite to the Straits of Gibraltar. There was
an easy passage from it to other islands, which lay adjacent
to a large continent, exceeding in size all Europe and Asia.
Neptune settled in this island, from whose son Atlas its name
was derived, and he divided it among his ten sons. His descendants reigned here in regular succession for many ages.
They made irruptions into Europe and Africa, subduing all
Libya as far as Egypt, and Europe to Asia Minor. They
were resisted, however, by the Athenians, and driven back
to their Atlantic territories. Shortly after this there was a
tremendous earthquake and an overflowing of the sea, which
continued for a day and a night. In the course of this the
vast island of Atlantis, and all its splendid cities and warlike nations, were swallowed up, and sunk to the bottom of
the sea, which, spreading its waters over the chasm, formed
the Atlantic Ocean. For a long time, however, the sea was
not navigable, on account of rocks and shelves, of mud and
slime, and of the ruins of that drowned country.

Many, in modern times, have considered this a mere fable;
others suppose that Plato, while in Egypt, had received some
vague accounts of the Canary Islands, and, on his return to
Greece, finding those islands so entirely unknown to his countrymen, had made them the seat of his political and moral
speculations. Some, however, have been disposed to give
greater weight to this story of Plato. They imagine that
such an island may really have existed, filling up a great
part of the Atlantic, and that the continent beyond it was
America, which, in such case, was not unknown to the ancients. Kircher supposes it to have been an island extending
from the Canaries to the Azores; that it was really engulfed
in one of the convulsions of the globe, and that those small
islands are mere shattered fragments of it.

As a further proof that the New World was not unknown
to the ancients, many have cited the singular passage in the
Medea of Seneca, which is wonderfully apposite, and shows,
at least, how nearly the warm imagination of a poet may approach to prophecy. The predictions of the ancient oracles
were rarely so unequivocal.

> Venient annis
> Sæcula seris, quibus Oceanus
> Vincula rerum laxet, et ingens
> Pateat tellus, Typhisque novos
> Detegat orbes, nec sit terris
> Ultima Thule.

Gosselin, in his able research into the voyages of the ancients, supposes the Atlantis of Plato to have been nothing
more nor less than one of the nearest of the Canaries, viz.,
Fortaventura or Lancerote.

No. XXV

THE IMAGINARY ISLAND OF ST. BRANDAN

ONE of the most singular geographical illusions on record
is that which for a long while haunted the imaginations of
the inhabitants of the Canaries. They fancied they beheld
a mountainous island, about ninety leagues in length, lying
far to the westward. It was only seen at intervals, but in
perfectly clear and serene weather. To some it seemed one
hundred leagues distant, to others forty, to others only fifteen or eighteen.* On attempting to reach it, however, it
somehow or other eluded the search, and was nowhere to be
found. Still there were so many eye-witnesses of credibility
who concurred in testifying to their having seen it, and the
testimony of the inhabitants of different islands agreed so
well as to its form and position, that its existence was generally believed, and geographers inserted it in their maps. It
is laid down on the globe of Martin Behem, projected in 1492,
as delineated by M. de Murr, and it will be found in most of
the maps of the time of Columbus, placed commonly about
two hundred leagues west of the Canaries. During the time
that Columbus was making his proposition to the court of
Portugal, an inhabitant of the Canaries applied to King John
II. for a vessel to go in search of this island. In the archives
of the Torre do Tombo,† also, there is a record of a contract
made by the crown of Portugal with Fernando de Ulmo,
cavalier of the royal household, and captain of the island of
Tercera, wherein he undertakes to go at his own expense, in
quest of an island or islands, or Terra Firma, supposed to be
the island of the Seven Cities, on condition of having jurisdiction over the same for himself and his heirs, allowing one-
tenth of the revenues to the king. This Ulmo, finding the
expedition above his capacity, associated one Juan Alfonso

---

* Feyjoo, Theatro Critico, tom. iv., d. 10, § 29.
† Lib. iv., de la Chancelaria del Rey Don Juan II., fol. 101.

del Estreito in the enterprise. They were bound to be ready
to sail with two caravels in the month of March, 1487.*
The fate of their enterprise is unknown.

The name of St. Brandan, or Borondon, given to this
imaginary island from time immemorial, is said to be derived
from a Scotch abbot, who flourished in the sixth century,
and who is called sometimes by the foregoing appellations,
sometimes St. Blandano, or St. Blandanus. In the Martyr-
ology of the order of St. Augustine, he is said to have been
the patriarch of three thousand monks. About the middle
of the sixth century he accompanied his disciple, St. Mac-
lovio, or St. Malo, in search of certain islands possessing the
delights of paradise, which they were told existed in the midst
of the ocean, and were inhabited by infidels. These most
adventurous saints-errant wandered for a long time upon
the ocean, and at length landed upon an island called Ima.
Here St. Malo found the body of a giant lying in a sepulcher.
He resuscitated him, and had much interesting conversation
with him, the giant informing him that the inhabitants of
that island had some notions of the Trinity, and, moreover,
giving him a gratifying account of the torments which Jews
and Pagans suffered in the infernal regions. Finding the
giant so docile and reasonable, St. Malo expounded to him
the doctrines of the Christian religion, converted him, and
baptized him by the name of Mildum. The giant, however,
either through weariness of life or eagerness to enjoy the
benefits of his conversion, begged permission, at the end of
fifteen days, to die again, which was granted him.

According to another account, the giant told them he
knew of an island in the ocean, defended by walls of bur-
nished gold, so resplendent that they shone like crystal, but
to which there was no entrance. At their request he undertook to guide them to it, and taking the cable of their ship,
threw himself into the sea. He had not proceeded far, however, when a tempest rose, and obliged them all to return,
and shortly after the giant died.† A third legend makes the
saint pray to heaven on Easter day that they may be permitted to find land where they may celebrate the offices of
religion with becoming state. An island immediately appears, on which they land, perform a solemn mass and the
sacrament of the Eucharist; after which, re-embarking and

---

* Torre do Tombo. Lib. das Ylhas, f. 119.
† Fr. Gregorio Garcia, Origen de los Indios, lib. i., cap. 9.

making sail, they behold to their astonishment the supposed island suddenly plunge to the bottom of the sea, being nothing else than a monstrous whale.* When the rumor circulated of an island seen from the Canaries, which always eluded the search, the legends of St. Brandan were revived, and applied to this unapproachable land. We are told, also, that there was an ancient Latin manuscript in the archives of the cathedral church of the Grand Canary, in which the adventures of these saints were recorded. Through carelessness, however, this manuscript has disappeared.† Some have maintained that this island was known to the ancients, and was the same mentioned by Ptolemy among the Fortunate or Canary Islands, by the names of Aprositus,‡ or the Inaccessible; and which, according to friar Diego Philipo in his book on the Incarnation of Christ, shows that it possessed the same quality in ancient times of deluding the eye and being unattainable to the feet of mortals.§ But whatever belief the ancients may have had on this subject, it is certain that it took a strong hold on the faith of the moderns during the prevalent rage for discovery; nor did it lack abundant testimonials. Don Joseph de Viera y Clavijo says there never was a more difficult paradox nor problem in the science of geography; since to affirm the existence of this island is to trample upon sound criticism, judgment, and reason; and to deny it one must abandon tradition and experience, and suppose that many persons of credit had not the proper use of their senses.‖

The belief in this island has continued long since the time of Columbus. It was repeatedly seen, and by various persons at a time, always in the same place and of the same form. In 1526 an expedition set off for the Canaries in quest of it, commanded by Fernando de Troya and Fernando Alvarez. They cruised in the wonted direction, but in vain, and their failure ought to have undeceived the public. "The phantasm of the island, however," says Viera, "had such a secret enchantment for all who beheld it, that the public preferred doubting the good conduct of the explorers than their own senses." In 1570 the appearances were so repeated and clear that there was a universal fever of curiosity awakened

---

* Sigeberto, Epist. ad Tietmar. Abbat.
† Nuñez de la Pena. Conquist de la Gran Canaria.
‡ Ptolemy, lib. iv., tom. iv.
§ Fr. D. Philipo, lib. viii., fol. 25.
‖ Hist. Isl. Can., lib. i., cap. 28.

among the people of the Canaries, and it was determined to
send forth another expedition.

That they might not appear to act upon light grounds, an
exact investigation was previously made of all the persons of
talent and credibility who had seen these apparitions of land,
or who had other proofs of its existence.

Alonzo de Espinosa, governor of the island of Ferro, accordingly made a report, in which more than one hundred
witnesses, several of them persons of the highest respectabil-
ity, deposed that they had beheld the unknown island about
forty leagues to the northwest of Ferro; that they had contemplated it with calmness and certainty, and had seen the
sun set behind one of its points.

Testimonials of still greater force came from the islands
of Palma and Teneriffe. There were certain Portuguese who
affirmed that, being driven about by a tempest, they had
come upon the island of St. Borondon. Pedro Vello, who
was the pilot of the vessel, affirmed that, having anchored
in a bay, he landed with several of the crew. They drank
fresh water in a brook, and beheld in the sand the print of
footsteps, double the size of those of an ordinary man, and
the distance between them was in proportion. They found a
cross nailed to a neighboring tree; near to which were three
stones placed in form of a triangle, with signs of fire having
been made among them, probably to cook shellfish. Having
seen much cattle and sheep grazing in the neighborhood, two
of their party armed with lances went into the woods in pursuit of them. The night was approaching, the heavens began to lower, and a harsh wind arose. The people on board
the ship cried out that she was dragging her anchor, whereupon Vello entered the boat and hurried on board. In an
instant they lost sight of land, being, as it were, swept away
in the hurricane. When the storm had passed away, and
the sea and sky were again serene, they searched in vain for
the island; not a trace of it was to be seen, and they had to
pursue their voyage, lamenting the loss of their two companions who had been abandoned in the wood.*

A learned licentiate, Pedro Ortiz de Funez, inquisitor of
the Grand Canary, while on a visit at Teneriffe, summoned
several persons before him, who testified having seen the isl-
and. Among them was one Marcos Verde, a man well known

---

* Nuñez de la Pena, lib. i., cap. 1.   Viera, Hist. Isl. Can., tom. i.,
cap. 28.

in those parts. He stated that in returning from Barbary and arriving in the neighborhood of the Canaries, he beheld land, which, according to his maps and calculations, could not be any of the known islands. He concluded it to be the far-famed St. Borondon. Overjoyed at having discovered this land of mystery, he coasted along its spellbound shores until he anchored in a beautiful harbor formed by the mouth of a mountain ravine. Here he landed with several of his crew. It was now, he said, the hour of the "Ave Maria," or of vespers. The sun being set, the shadows began to spread over the land. The voyagers having separated, wandered about in different directions, until out of hearing of each other's shouts. Those on board, seeing the night approaching, made signal to summon back the wanderers to the ship. They re-embarked, intending to resume their investigations on the following day. Scarcely were they on board, however, when a whirlwind came rushing down the ravine with such violence as to drag the vessel from her anchor and hurry her out to sea, and they never saw anything more of this hidden and inhospitable island.

Another testimony remains on record in manuscript of one Abreu Galindo; but whether taken at this time does not appear. It was that of a French adventurer, who, many years before, making a voyage among the Canaries, was overtaken by a violent storm which carried away his masts. At length the furious winds drove him to the shores of an unknown island covered with stately trees. Here he landed with part of his crew, and choosing a tree proper for a mast cut it down, and began to shape it for his purpose. The guardian power of the island, however, resented as usual this invasion of his forbidden shores. The heavens assumed a dark and threatening aspect; the night was approaching, and the mariners, fearing some impending evil, abandoned their labor and returned on board. They were borne away as usual from the coast, and the next day arrived at the island of Palma.*

The mass of testimony collected by official authority in 1570 seemed so satisfactory that another expedition was fitted out in the same year in the island of Palma. It was commanded by Fernando de Villabolos, regidor of the island, but was equally fruitless with the preceding. St. Borondon seemed disposed only to tantalize the world with distant and serene

---

* Nuñez, Conquista le Gran Canaria. Viera, Hist., etc.

glimpses of his ideal paradise, or to reveal it amid storms to
tempest-tossed mariners, but to hide it completely from the
view of all who diligently sought it.   Still the people of Palma
adhered to their favorite chimera.   Thirty-four years afterward, in 1605, they sent another ship on the quest, commanded by Gaspar Perez de Acosta, an accomplished pilot,
accompanied by the padre Lorenzo Pinedo, a holy Franciscan
friar, skilled in natural science.   St. Borondon, however, refused to reveal his island to either monk or mariner.   After
cruising about in every direction, sounding, observing the
skies, the clouds, the winds, everything that could furnish
indications, they returned without having seen anything to
authorize a hope.

Upward of a century now elapsed without any new attempt to seek this fairy island.   Every now and then, it is
true, the public mind was agitated by fresh reports of its
having been seen.   Lemons and other fruits, and the green
branches of trees which floated to the shores of Gomera and
Ferro, were pronounced to be from the enchanted groves of
St. Borondon.   At length, in 1721, the public infatuation
again rose to such a height that a fourth expedition was
sent, commanded by Don Gaspar Dominguez, a man of probity and talent.   As this was an expedition of solemn and mysterious import, he had two holy friars as apostolical chap-
lains.   They made sail from the island of Teneriffe toward
the end of October, leaving the populace in an indescribable
state of anxious curiosity mingled with superstition.   The
ship, however, returned from its cruise as unsuccessful as all
its predecessors.

We have no account of any expedition being since undertaken, though the island still continued to be a subject of
speculation, and occasionally to reveal its shadowy mountains to the eyes of favored individuals.   In a letter written
from the island of Gomera, 1759, by a Franciscan monk, to
one of his friends, he relates having seen it from the village
of Alaxero at six in the morning of the third of May.   It appeared to consist of two lofty mountains, with a deep valley
between; and on contemplating it with a telescope, the valley or ravine appeared to be filled with trees.   He summoned
the curate Antonio Joseph Manrique, and upward of forty
other persons, all of whom beheld it plainly.*

Nor is this island delineated merely in ancient maps of

---

* Viera, Hist. Isl. Can., tom. i., cap. 28.

the time of Columbus. It is laid down as one of the Canary Islands in a French map published in 1704; and Mons. Gautier, in a geographical chart, annexed to his Observations on Natural History, published in 1755, places it five degrees to the west of the island of Ferro, in the 29th deg. of N. latitude.*

Such are the principal facts existing relative to the island of St. Brandan. Its reality was for a long time a matter of firm belief. It was in vain that repeated voyages and investigations proved its non-existence; the public, after trying all kinds of sophistry, took refuge in the supernatural, to defend their favorite chimera. They maintained that it was rendered inaccessible to mortals by Divine Providence, or by diabolical magic. Most inclined to the former. All kinds of extravagant fancies were indulged concerning it,† some confounded it with the fabled island of the Seven Cities situated somewhere in the bosom of the ocean, where in old times seven bishops and their followers had take refuge from the Moors. Some of the Portuguese imagined it to be the abode of their lost king Sebastian. The Spaniards pretended that Roderick, the last of their Gothic kings, had fled thither from the Moors after the disastrous battle of the Guadalete. Others suggested that it might be the seat of the terrestrial paradise, the place where Enoch and Elijah remained in a state of blessedness until the final day; and that it was made at times apparent to the eyes, but invisible to the search of mortals. Poetry, it is said, has owed to this popular belief one of its beautiful fictions, and the garden of Armida, where Rinaldo was detained enchanted, and which Tasso places in one of the Canary Islands, has been identified with the imaginary St. Borondon.‡

The learned father Feyjoo § has given a philosophical solution to this geographical problem. He attributes all these appearances, which have been so numerous and so well authenticated as not to admit of doubt, to certain atmospherical deceptions, like that of the Fata Morgana, seen at times in the straits of Messina, where the city of Reggio and its surrounding country is reflected in the air above the neighboring sea: a phenomenon which has likewise been witnessed in front of the city of Marseilles. As to the tales of the mariners who had landed on these forbidden shores, and been

---

* Viera, Hist. Isl. Can., tom. i., cap. 28.   † Ibid.
‡ Viera, ubi sup.   § Theatro Critico, tom. iv., d. x.

hurried thence in whirlwinds and tempests, he considers them as mere fabrications.

As the populace, however, reluctantly give up anything that partakes of the marvelous and mysterious, and as the same atmospherical phenomena, which first gave birth to the illusion, may still continue, it is not improbable that a belief in the island of St. Brandan may still exist among the ignorant and credulous of the Canaries, and that they at times behold its fairy mountains rising above the distant horizon of the Atlantic.

No. XXVI

THE ISLAND OF THE SEVEN CITIES

ONE of the popular traditions concerning the ocean, which were current during the time of Columbus, was that of the Island of the Seven Cities. It was recorded in an ancient legend that, at the time of the conquest of Spain and Portugal by the Moors, when the inhabitants fled in every direction to escape from slavery, seven bishops, followed by a great number of their people, took shipping and abandoned themselves to their fate on the high seas. After tossing about for some time they landed on an unknown island in the midst of the ocean. Here the bishops burned the ships to prevent the desertion of their followers, and founded seven cities. Various pilots of Portugal, it was said, had reached that island at different times, but had never returned to give any information concerning it, having been detained, according to subsequent accounts, by the successors of the bishops to prevent pursuit. At length, according to common report, at the time that Prince Henry of Portugal was prosecuting his discoveries, several seafaring men presented themselves one day before him, and stated that they had just returned from a voyage, in the course of which they had landed upon this island. The inhabitants, they said, spoke their language, and carried them immediately to church, to ascertain whether they were Catholics, and were rejoiced at finding them of the true faith. They then made earnest inquiries, to know whether the Moors still retained possession of Spain and Portugal. While part of the crew were at church, the rest gathered sand on the shore for the use of the kitchen, and found to their surprise that one third of it was gold. The islanders were anxious that the crew should remain with them a few days, until the return of their governor, who was absent; but the mariners, afraid of being detained, embarked and made sail. Such was the story they told to Prince Henry, hoping to receive reward for their intelligence. The prince expressed displeasure at their hasty departure from the island, and ordered them to return and procure further information; but the men, apprehensive, no doubt, of having the falsehood of their tale discovered, made their escape, and nothing more was heard of them.*

This story had much currency. The Island of the Seven Cities was identified with the island mentioned by Aristotle as having been discovered by the Carthaginians, and was put down in the early maps, about the time of Columbus, under the name of Antilla.

At the time of the discovery of New Spain, reports were brought to Hispaniola of the civilization of the country: that the people wore clothing; that their houses and temples were solid, spacious, and often magnificent; and that crosses were occasionally found among them. Juan de Grivalja, being dispatched to explore the coast of Yucatan, reported that in sailing along it he beheld, with great wonder, stately and beautiful edifices of lime and stone, and many high towers that shone at a distance.† For a time the old tradition of the Seven Cities was revived, and many thought that they were to be found in the same part of New Spain.

No. XXVII

DISCOVERY OF THE ISLAND OF MADEIRA

THE discovery of Madeira by Macham rests principally upon the authority of Francisco Alcaforado, an esquire of Prince Henry of Portugal, who composed an account of it for that prince. It does not appear to have obtained much faith among Portuguese historians. No mention is made of it in Barros; he attributes the first discovery of the island to Juan Gonzalez and Tristram Vaz, who he said descried it from Porto Santo, resembling a cloud on the horizon.‡

---

* Hist. del Almirante, cap. 10.
† Torquemada Monarquia Indiana, lib. iv., cap. 4. Origen de los Indios por Fr. Gregorio Garcia, lib. iv., cap. 20.
‡ Barros, Asia, decad. i., lib. i., cap. 3.

The abbé Provost, however, in his general history of voyages, vol. 6, seems inclined to give credit to the account of Alcaforado. "It was composed," he observes, "at a time when the attention of the public would have exposed the least falsities; and no one was more capable than Alcaforado of giving an exact detail of this event, since he was of the number of those who assisted at the second discovery." The narrative, as originally written, was overcharged with ornaments and digressions. It was translated into French and published in Paris in 1671. The French translator had retrenched the ornaments, but scrupulously retained the facts. The story, however, is cherished in the island of Madeira, where a painting in illustration of it is still to be seen. The following is the purport of the French translation: I have not been able to procure the original of Alcaforado.

During the reign of Edward the Third of England, a young man of great courage and talent, named Robert Macham, fell in love with a young lady of rare beauty, of the name of Anne Dorset. She was his superior in birth, and of a proud and aristocratic family; but the merit of Macham gained him the preference over all his rivals. The family of the young lady, to prevent her making an inferior alliance, obtained an order from the king to have Macham arrested and confined, until by arbitrary means they married his mistress to a man of quality. As soon as the nuptials were celebrated, the nobleman conducted his beautiful and afflicted bride to his seat near Bristol. Macham was now restored to liberty. Indignant at the wrongs he had suffered, and certain of the affections of his mistress, he prevailed upon several friends to assist him in a project for the gratification of his love and his revenge. They followed hard on the traces of the new-married couple to Bristol. One of the friends obtained an introduction into the family of the nobleman in quality of a groom. He found the young bride full of tender recollections of her lover, and of dislike to the husband thus forced upon her. Through the means of this friend, Macham had several communications with her, and concerted means for their escape to France, where they might enjoy their mutual love unmolested.

When all things were prepared, the young lady rode out one day, accompanied only by the fictitious groom, under pretense of taking the air. No sooner were they out of sight of the house than they galloped to an appointed place on the shore of the channel, where a boat awaited them. They were conveyed on board a vessel, which lay with anchor a-trip and sails unfurled, ready to put to sea. Here the lovers were once more united. Fearful of pursuit, the ship immediately weighed anchor; they made their way rapidly along the coast of Cornwall, and Macham anticipated the triumph of soon landing with his beautiful prize on the shores of gay and gallant France. Unfortunately an adverse and stormy wind arose in the night; at daybreak they found themselves out of sight of land. The mariners were ignorant and inexperienced; they knew nothing of the compass, and it was a time when men were unaccustomed to traverse the high seas. For thirteen days the lovers were driven about on a tempestuous ocean, at the mercy of wind and wave. The fugitive bride was filled with terror and remorse, and looked upon this uproar of the elements as the anger of Heaven directed against her. All the efforts of her lover could not remove from her mind a dismal presage of some approaching catastrophe.

At length the tempest subsided. On the fourteenth day, at dawn, the mariners perceived what appeared to be a tuft of wood rising out of the sea. They joyfully steered for it, supposing it to be an island. They were not mistaken. As they drew near, the rising sun shone upon noble forests, the trees of which were of a kind unknown to them. Flights of birds also came hovering about the ship, and perched upon the yards and rigging, without any signs of fear. The boat was sent on shore to reconnoiter, and soon returned with such accounts of the beauty of the country that Macham determined to take his drooping companion to the land, in hopes her health and spirits might be restored by refreshment and repose. They were accompanied on shore by the faithful friends who had assisted in their flight. The mariners remained on board to guard the ship.

The country was indeed delightful. The forests were stately and magnificent; there were trees laden with excellent fruits, others with aromatic flowers; the waters were cool and limpid, the sky was serene, and there was a balmy sweetness in the air. The animals they met with showed no signs of alarm or ferocity, from which they concluded that the island was uninhabited. On penetrating a little distance they found a sheltered meadow, the green bosom of which was bordered by laurels and refreshed by a mountain brook which ran sparkling over pebbles. In the center was a majestic tree, the wide branches of which afforded shade from the rays of the sun. Here Macham had bowers constructed and determined to pass a few days, hoping that the sweetness of the country and the serene tranquillity of this delightful solitude would recruit the drooping health and spirits of his companion. Three days, however, had scarcely passed when a violent storm arose from the northeast, and raged all night over the island. On the succeeding morning Macham repaired to the seaside, but nothing of his ship was to be seen, and he concluded that it had foundered in the tempest.

Consternation fell upon the little band, thus left in an uninhabited island in the midst of the ocean. The blow fell most severely on the timid and repentant bride. She reproached herself with being the cause of all their misfortunes, and, from the first, had been haunted by dismal forebodings. She now considered them about to be accomplished, and her horror was so great as to deprive her of speech; she expired in three days without uttering a word.

Macham was struck with despair at beholding the tragical end of this tender and beautiful being. He upbraided himself, in the transports of his grief, with tearing her from her home, her country, and her friends, to perish upon a savage coast. All the efforts of his companions to console him were in vain. He died within five days, broken-hearted; begging, as a last request, that his body might be interred beside that of his mistress, at the foot of a rustic altar which they had erected under the great tree. They set up a large wooden cross on the spot, on which was placed an inscription written by Macham himself, relating in a few words his piteous adventure, and praying any Christians who might arrive there to build a chapel in the place dedicated to Jesus the Saviour.

After the death of their commander, his followers consulted about means to escape from the island. The ship's boat remained on the shore. They repaired it and put it in a state to bear a voyage, and then made sail, intending to return to England. Ignorant of their situation, and carried about by the winds, they were cast upon the coast of Morocco, where, their boat being shattered upon the rocks, they were captured by the Moors and thrown into prison. Here they understood that their ship had shared the same fate, having been driven from her anchorage in the tempest, and carried to the same inhospitable coast, where all her crew were made prisoners.

The prisons of Morocco were in those days filled with captives of all nations, taken by their cruisers. Here the English prisoners met with an experienced pilot, a Spaniard of Seville, named Juan de Morales. He listened to their story with great interest; inquired into the situation and description of the island they had discovered; and, subsequently, on his redemption from prison, communicated the circumstances, it is said, to Prince Henry of Portugal.

There is a difficulty in the above narrative of Alcaforado in reconciling dates. The voyage is said to have taken place during the reign of Edward III., which commenced in 1327 and ended in 1378. Morales, to whom the English communicated their voyage, is said to have been in the service of the Portuguese, in the second discovery of Madeira, in 1418 and 1420. Even if the voyage and imprisonment had taken place in the last year of King Edward's reign, this leaves a space of forty years.

Hackluyt gives an account of the same voyage, taken from Antonio Galvano. He varies in certain particulars. It happened, he says, in the year 1344, in the time of Peter IV. of Aragon. Macham cast anchor in a bay since called after him Machio.

The lady being ill, he took her on shore, accompanied by some of his friends, and the ships sailed without them. After the death of the lady, Macham made a canoe out of a tree, and ventured to sea in it with his companions. They were cast upon the coast of Africa, where the Moors, considering it a kind of miracle, carried him to the king of their country, who sent him to the king of Castile. In consequence of the traditional accounts remaining of this voyage, Henry II. of Castile sent people, in 1395, to rediscover the island.

No. XXVIII

LAS CASAS

BARTHOLOMEW LAS CASAS, Bishop of Chiapa, so often cited in all histories of the New World, was born at Seville in 1474, and was of French extraction. The family name was Casaus. The first of the name who appeared in Spain served under the standard of Ferdinand III., surnamed the Saint, in his wars with the Moors of Andalusia. He was at the taking of Seville from the Moors, when he was rewarded

by the king, and received permission to establish himself
there. His descendants enjoyed the prerogatives of nobility,
and suppressed the letter *u* in their name, to accommodate it
to the Spanish tongue.

Antonio, the father of Bartholomew, went to Hispaniola
with Columbus in 1493, and returned rich to Seville in 1498.[*]
It has been stated by one of the biographers of Bartholomew
Las Casas that he accompanied Columbus in his third voyage in 1498, and returned with him in 1500.[†] This, however, is incorrect. He was, during that time, completing his
education at Salamanca, where he was instructed in Latin,
dialectics, logic, metaphysics, ethics, and physics, after the
supposed method and system of Aristotle. While at the university, he had, as a servant, an Indian slave, given him by
his father, who had received him from Columbus. When
Isabella, in her transport of virtuous indignation, ordered the
Indian slaves to be sent back to their country, this one was
taken from Las Casas. The young man was aroused by the
circumstance, and, on considering the nature of the case,
became inflamed with a zeal in favor of the unhappy Indians, which never cooled throughout a long and active life.
It was excited to tenfold fervor, when, at about the age of
twenty-eight years, he accompanied the commander Ovando
to Hispaniola in 1502, and was an eye-witness to many of
the cruel scenes which took place under his administration.
The whole of his future life, a space exceeding sixty years,
was devoted to vindicating the cause, and endeavoring to
meliorate the sufferings of the natives. As a missionary, he
traversed the wilderness of the New World in various direction, seeking to convert and civilize them; as a protector and
champion, he made several voyages to Spain, vindicated their
wrongs before courts and monarchs, wrote volumes in their
behalf, and exhibited a zeal and constancy and intrepidity
worthy of an apostle. He died at the advanced age of ninety-
two years, and was buried at Madrid, in the church of the
Dominican convent at Atocha, of which fraternity he was a
member.

Attempts have been made to decry the consistency, and
question the real philanthropy of Las Casas, in consequence
of one of the expedients to which he resorted to relieve the
Indians from the cruel bondage imposed upon them. This

---

[*] Navarrete, Colec. Viag., tom. i. Introd., p. lxx.
[†] T. A. Llorente, Œuvres de Las Casas, p. xi., Paris, 1822.

occurred in 1517, when he arrived in Spain, on one of his missions, to obtain measures in their favor from the government. On his arrival in Spain, he found Cardinal Ximenes, who had been left regent on the death of King Ferdinand, too ill to attend to his affairs. He repaired, therefore, to Valladolid, where he awaited the coming of the new monarch Charles, Archduke of Austria, afterward the Emperor Charles V. He had strong opponents to encounter in various persons high in authority, who, holding estates and repartimientos in the colonies, were interested in the slavery of the Indians. Among these, and not the least animated, was the Bishop Fonseca, President of the Council of the Indies.

At length the youthful sovereign arrived, accompanied by various Flemings of his court, particularly his grand chancellor, Dr. Juan de Selvagio, a learned and upright man, whom he consulted on all affairs of administration and justice. Las Casas soon became intimate with the chancellor, and stood high in his esteem; but so much opposition arose on every side that he found his various propositions for the relief of the natives but little attended to. In his doubt and anxiety he had now recourse to an expedient which he considered as justified by the circumstances of the case.* The chancellor Selvagio and other Flemings who had accompanied the youthful sovereign, had obtained from him, before quitting Flanders, licenses to import slaves from Africa to the colonies: a measure which had recently in 1516 been prohibited by a decree of Cardinal Ximenes while acting as regent. The chancellor, who was a humane man, reconciled it to his conscience by a popular opinion that one negro could perform, without detriment to his health, the labor of several Indians, and that therefore it was a great saving of human suffering. So easy is it for interest to wrap itself up in plausible argument! He might, moreover, have thought the welfare of the Africans but little affected by the change. They were accustomed to slavery in their own country, and they were said to thrive in the New World. "The Africans," observes Herrera, "prospered so much in the island of Hispaniola, that it was the opinion unless a negro should hap-

---

* Herrera clearly states this as an expedient adopted when others failed. "Bartolomé de las Casas, viendo que sus conceptos hallaban en todas partes dificultad, i que las opiniones que tenia, por mucha familiaridad que havia seguido i gran credito con el gran Canciller, no podian haber efecto, *se volvio a otros expedientes, etc.* Decad. ii., lib. ii., cap. 2.

pen to be hanged, he would never die; for as yet none had
been known to perish from infirmity. Like oranges, they
found their proper soil in Hispaniola, and it seemed ever
more natural to them than their native Guinea.''*

Las Casas, finding all other means ineffectual, endeavored
to turn these interested views of the grand chancellor to the
benefit of the Indians. He proposed that the Spaniards, resident in the colonies, might be permitted to procure negroes
for the labor of the farms and the mines, and other severe
toils, which were above the strength and destructive of the
lives of the natives.† He evidently considered the poor Africans as little better than mere animals; and he acted like
others, on an arithmetical calculation of diminishing human
misery, by substituting one strong man for three or four of
feebler nature. He, moreover, esteemed the Indians as a
nobler and more intellectual race of beings, and their preservation and welfare of higher importance to the general
interests of humanity.

It is this expedient of Las Casas which has drawn down
severe censure upon his memory. He has been charged with
gross inconsistency, and even with having originated this inhuman traffic in the New World. This last is a grievous
charge; but historical facts and dates remove the original
sin from his door, and prove that the practice existed in the
colonies, and was authorized by royal decree, long before he
took a part in the question.

Las Casas did not go to the New World until 1502. By
a royal ordinance passed in 1501, negro slaves were permitted
to be taken there, provided they had been born among Christians.‡ By a letter written by Ovando, dated 1503, it appears that there were numbers in the island of Hispaniola at
that time, and he entreats that no more might be permitted
to be brought.

In 1506 the Spanish government forbade the introduction
of negro slaves from the Levant, or those brought up with
the Moors; and stipulated that none should be taken to the
colonies but those from Seville, who had been instructed in
the Christian faith, that they might contribute to the conversion of the Indians.§ In 1510 King Ferdinand, being in-

---

* Herrera, Hist. Ind., lib. ii., decad. iii., cap. 4.
† Ibid., decad. ii., lib. ii., cap. 20.
‡ Ibid., d. ii., lib. iii., cap. 8.
§ Ibid., d. i., lib. vi., cap. 20.

formed of the physical weakness of the Indians, ordered fifty
Africans to be sent from Seville to labor in the mines.* In
1511 he ordered that a great number should be procured from
Guinea, and transported to Hispaniola, understanding that
one negro could perform the work of four Indians.† In 1512
and '13 he signed further orders relative to the same subject.
In 1516 Charles V. granted licenses to the Flemings to import negroes to the colonies. It was not until the year 1517
that Las Casas gave his sanction of the traffic. It already
existed, and he countenanced it solely with a view to having
the hardy Africans substituted for the feeble Indians. It
was advocated at the same time, and for the same reasons,
by the Jeronimite friars, who were missionaries in the colonies. The motives of Las Casas were purely benevolent,
though founded on erroneous notions of justice. He thought
to permit evil that good might spring out of it; to choose between two existing abuses, and to eradicate the greater by
resorting to the lesser. His reasoning, however fallacious
it may be, was considered satisfactory and humane by some
of the most learned and benevolent men of the age, among
whom was the Cardinal Adrian, afterward elevated to the
papal chair, and characterized by gentleness and humanity.
The traffic was permitted; inquiries were made as to the
number of slaves required, which was limited to four thousand, and the Flemings obtained a monopoly of the trade,
which they afterward farmed out to the Genoese.

Dr. Robertson, in noticing this affair, draws a contrast
between the conduct of the Cardinal Ximenes and that of
Las Casas, strongly to the disadvantage of the latter. "The
cardinal," he observes, "when solicited to encourage this
commerce, peremptorily rejected the proposition, because he
perceived the iniquity of reducing one race of men to slavery,
when he was consulting about the means of restoring liberty
to another; but Las Casas, from the inconsistency natural to
men who hurry with headlong impetuosity toward a favorite point, was incapable of making this distinction. In the
warmth of his zeal to save the Americans from the yoke, he
pronounced it to be lawful and expedient to impose one still
heavier on the Africans."‡

This distribution of praise and censure is not perfectly cor-

---

* Herrera, Hist. Ind., d. i., lib. viii., cap. 9.
† Ibid., d. i., lib. ix., cap. 5.
‡ Robertson, Hist. America, p. 3.

rect. Las Casas had no idea that he was imposing a heavier, nor so heavy, a yoke upon the Africans. The latter were considered more capable of labor, and less impatient of slavery. While the Indians sunk under their tasks, and perished by thousands in Hispaniola, the negroes, on the contrary, thrived there. Herrera, to whom Dr. Robertson refers as his authority, assigns a different motive, and one of mere finance, for the measures of Cardinal Ximenes. He says that he ordered that no one should take negroes to the Indies, because, as the natives were decreasing, and it was known that one negro did more work than four of them, there would probably be a great demand for African slaves, and a tribute might be imposed upon the trade, from which would result profit to the royal treasury.* This measure was presently after carried into effect, though subsequent to the death of the cardinal, and licenses were granted by the sovereign for pecuniary considerations. Flechier, in his Life of Ximenes, assigns another but a mere political motive for this prohibition. The cardinal, he says, objected to the importation of negroes into the colonies, as he feared they would corrupt the natives, and by confederacies with them render them formidable to government. De Marsolier, another biographer of Ximenes, gives equally politic reasons for this prohibition. He cites a letter written by the cardinal on the subject, in which he observed that he knew the nature of the negroes; they were a people capable, it was true, of great fatigue, but extremely prolific and enterprising; and that if they had time to multiply in America they would infallibly revolt, and impose on the Spaniards the same chains which they had compelled them to wear.†

These facts, while they take from the measure of the cardinal that credit for exclusive philanthropy which has been bestowed upon it, manifest the clear foresight of that able politician; whose predictions with respect to negro revolt have been so strikingly fulfilled in the island of Hispaniola.

Cardinal Ximenes, in fact, though a wise and upright statesman, was not troubled with scruples of conscience on these questions of natural right; nor did he possess more tol-

---

* Porque como iban faltando los Indios i se conocia que un negro trabajaba, mas que quatro, por lo qual habia gran demanda de ellos, parecia que se podia poner algun tributo en la saca, de que resultaria provecho á la Rl. Hacienda Herrera, decad. ii., lib. ii., cap. 8.

† De Marsolier, Hist. du Ministere Cardinal Ximenes, lib. vi. Toulouse, 1694.

eration than his contemporaries toward savage and infidel nations. He was grand inquisitor of Spain, and was very efficient during the latter years of Ferdinand in making slaves of the refractory Moors of Granada. He authorized, by express instructions, expeditions to seize and enslave the Indians of the Caribbee islands, whom he termed only suited to labor, enemies of the Christians, and cannibals. Nor will it be considered a proof of gentle or tolerant policy that he introduced the tribunal of the inquisition into the New World. These circumstances are cited not to cast reproach upon the character of Cardinal Ximenes, but to show how incorrectly he has been extolled at the expense of Las Casas. Both of them must be judged in connection with the customs and opinions of the age in which they lived.

Las Casas was the author of many works, but few of which have been printed. The most important is a general history of the Indies, from the discovery to the year 1520, in three volumes. It exists only in manuscript, but is the fountain from which Herrera, and most of the other historians of the New World, have drawn large supplies. The work, though prolix, is valuable, as the author was an eye-witness of many of the facts, had others from persons who were concerned in the transactions recorded, and possessed copious documents. It displays great erudition, though somewhat crudely and diffusely introduced. His history was commenced in 1527, at fifty-three years of age, and was finished in 1559, when eighty-five. As many things are set down from memory, there is occasional inaccuracy, but the whole bears the stamp of sincerity and truth. The author of the present work, having had access to this valuable manuscript, has made great use of it, drawing forth many curious facts hitherto neglected; but he has endeavored to consult it with caution and discrimination, collating it with other authorities, and omitting whatever appeared to be dictated by prejudice or overheated zeal.

Las Casas has been accused of high coloring and extravagant declamation in those passages which relate to the barbarities practiced on the natives; nor is the charge entirely without foundation. The same zeal in the cause of the Indians is expressed in his writings that shone forth in his actions, always pure, often vehement, and occasionally unseasonable. Still, however, where he errs it is on a generous and righteous side. If one-tenth part of what he says he "witnessed with his own eyes" be true, and his veracity is above all doubt, he would have been wanting in the natural feelings of humanity had he not expressed himself in terms of indignation and abhorrence.

In the course of his work, when Las Casas mentions the original papers lying before him, from which he drew many of his facts, it makes one lament that they should be lost to the world. Besides the journals and letters of Columbus, he says he had numbers of the letters of the adelantado, Don Bartholomew, who wrote better than his brother, and whose writings must have been full of energy. Above all, he had the map, formed from study and conjecture, by which Columbus sailed on his first voyage. What a precious document would this be for the world! These writings may still exist, neglected and forgotten among the rubbish of some convent in Spain. Little hope can be entertained of discovering them in the present state of degeneracy of the cloister. The monks of Atocha, in a recent conversation with one of the royal princes, betrayed an ignorance that this illustrious man was buried in their convent, nor can any of the fraternity point out his place of sepulture to the stranger.*

The publication of this work of Las Casas has not been permitted in Spain, where every book must have the sanction of a censor before it is committed to the press. The horrible picture it exhibits of the cruelties inflicted on the Indians would, it was imagined, excite an odium against their conquerors. Las Casas himself seems to have doubted the expediency of publishing it; for in 1560 he made a note with his own hand, which is preserved in the two first volumes of the original, mentioning that he left them in confidence to the college of the order of Predicators of St. Gregorio, in Valladolid, begging of its prelates that no secular person, nor even the collegians, should be permitted to read his history for the space of forty years; and that after that term it might be printed if consistent with the good of the Indies and of Spain.†

For the foregoing reason the work has been cautiously used by Spanish historians, passing over in silence, or with brief notice, many passages of disgraceful import. This feeling is natural, if not commendable; for the world is not

---

* In this notice the author has occasionally availed himself of the interesting memoir of Mon. J. A. Llorente, prefixed to his collection of the works of Las Casas, collating it with the history of Herrera, from which its facts are principally derived.

† Navarrete, Colec. de Viag., tom. i., p. lxxv.

prompt to discriminate between individuals and the nation of whom they are but a part. The laws and regulations for the government of the newly-discovered countries, and the decisions of the Council of the Indies on all contested points, though tinctured in some degree with the bigotry of the age, were distinguished for wisdom, justice, and humanity, and do honor to the Spanish nation. It was only in the abuse of them by individuals to whom the execution of the laws was intrusted, that these atrocities were committed. It should be remembered, also, that the same nation which gave birth to the sanguinary and rapacious adventurers who perpetrated these cruelties, gave birth likewise to the early missionaries, like Las Casas, who followed the sanguinary course of discovery, binding up the wounds inflicted by their countrymen; men who in a truly evangelical spirit braved all kinds of perils and hardships, and even death itself, not through a prospect of temporal gain or glory, but through a desire to meliorate the condition and save the souls of barbarous and suffering nations. The dauntless enterprises and fearful peregrinations of many of these virtuous men, if properly appreciated, would be found to vie in romantic daring with the heroic achievements of chivalry, with motives of a purer and far more exalted nature.

No. XXIX

PETER MARTYR

PETER MARTIR, or Martyr, of whose writings much use has been made in this history, was born at Anghierra, in the territory of Milan, in Italy, on the second of February, 1455. He is commonly termed Peter Martyr of *Angleria*, from the Latin name of his native place. He is one of the earliest historians that treat of Columbus, and was his contemporary and intimate acquaintance. Being at Rome in 1487, and having acquired a distinguished reputation for learning, he was invited by the Spanish embassador, the Count de Tendilla, to accompany him to Spain. He willingly accepted the invitation, and was presented to the sovereigns at Saragossa. Isabella, amid the cares of the war with Granada, was anxious for the intellectual advancement of her kingdom, and wished to employ Martyr to instruct the young nobility of the royal household. With her peculiar delicacy, however, she first made her confessor, Fernando de Talavera, inquire of Martyr in what capacity he desired to serve her. Contrary to her expectation, Martyr replied, "In the profession of arms." The queen complied, and he followed her in her campaigns, as one of her household and military suite, but without distinguishing himself, and perhaps without having any particular employ in a capacity so foreign to his talents. After the surrender of Granada, when the war was ended, the queen, through the medium of the grand cardinal of Spain, prevailed upon him to undertake the instruction of the young nobles of her court.

Martyr was acquainted with Columbus while making his application to the sovereigns, and was present at his triumphant reception by Ferdinand and Isabella in Barcelona, on his return from his first voyage. He was continually in the royal camp during the war with the Moors, of which his letters contain many interesting particulars. He was sent embassador extraordinary by Ferdinand and Isabella, in 1501, to Venice, and thence to the grand soldan of Egypt. The soldan, in 1490 or 1491, had sent an embassy to the Spanish sovereigns, threatening that, unless they desisted from the war against Granada, he would put all the Christians in Egypt and Syria to death, overturn all their temples, and destroy the holy sepulcher at Jerusalem. Ferdinand and Isabella pressed the war with tenfold energy, and brought it to a triumphant conclusion in the next campaign, while the soldan was still carrying on a similar negotiation with the pope. They afterward sent Peter Martyr embassador to the soldan to explain and justify their measure. Martyr discharged the duties of his embassy with great ability; obtained permission from the soldan to repair the holy places at Jerusalem, and an abolition of various extortions to which Christian pilgrims had been subjected. While on this embassy, he wrote his work De Legatione Babylonica, which includes a history of Egypt in those times.

On his return to Spain he was rewarded with places and pensions, and in 1524 was appointed a minister of the Council of the Indies. His principal work is an account of the discoveries of the New World, in eight decades, each containing ten chapters. They are styled Decades of the New World, or Decades of the Ocean, and, like all his other works, were originally written in Latin, though since translated into various languages. He had familiar access to letters, papers, journals, and narratives of the early discoverers, and was personally acquainted with many of them, gathering particulars from their conversation. In writing his Decades, he took great pains to obtain information from Columbus himself, and from others, his companions.

In one of his epistles (No. 153, January, 1494, to Pomponius Lætus), he mentions having just received a letter from Columbus, by which it appears he was in correspondence with him. Las Casas says that great credit is to be given to him in regard to those voyages of Columbus, although his Decades contain some inaccuracies relative to subsequent events in the Indies. Muñoz allows him great credit, as an author contemporary with his subject, grave, well cultivated, instructed in the facts of which he treats, and of entire probity. He observes, however, that his writings being composed on the spur or excitement of the moment, often related circumstances which subsequently proved to be erroneous; that they were written without method or care, often confusing dates and events, so that they must be read with some caution.

Martyr was in the daily habit of writing letters to distinguished persons, relating the passing occurrences of the busy court and age in which he lived. In several of these Columbus is mentioned, and also some of the chief events of his voyages, as promulgated at·the very moment of his return. These letters not being generally known or circulated, or frequently cited, it may be satisfactory to the reader to have a few of the main passages which relate to Columbus. They have a striking effect in carrying us back to the very time of the discoveries.

In one of his epistles, dated Barcelona, May 1, 1493, and addressed to C. Borromeo, he says: "Within these few days a certain Christopher Columbus has arrived from the western antipodes; a man of Liguria, whom my sovereigns reluctantly intrusted with three ships, to seek that region, for they thought that what he said was fabulous. He has returned and brought specimens of many precious things, but particularly gold, which those countries naturally produce."*

In another letter, dated likewise from Barcelona, in September following, he gives a more particular account. It is addressed to Count Tendilla, governor of Granada, and also to Fernando Talavera, archbishop of that diocese, and the same to whom the propositions of Columbus had been referred by the Spanish sovereigns. "Arouse your attention,

---

* Opus Epist. P. Martyris Anglerii, Epist. 131.

ancient sages," says Peter Martyr in his epistle; "listen to
a new discovery. You remember Columbus the Ligurian,
appointed in the camp by our sovereigns to search for a new
hemisphere of land at the western antipodes. You ought to
recollect, for you had some agency in the transaction; nor
would the enterprise, as I think, have been undertaken without your counsel. He has returned in safety, and relates the
wonders he has discovered. He exhibits gold as proofs of
the mines in those regions; Gossampine cotton, also, and
aromatics, and pepper more pungent than that from Cau-
casus. All these things, together with scarlet dye-woods,
the earth produces spontaneously. Pursuing the western
sun from Gades five thousand miles, of each a thousand
paces, as he relates, he fell in with sundry islands, and took
possession of one of them, of greater circuit, he asserts, than
the whole of Spain. Here he found a race of men living
contented, in a state of nature, subsisting on fruits and vegetables, and bread formed from roots. . . . These people
have kings, some greater than others, and they war occasionally among themselves, with bows and arrows, or lances
sharpened and hardened in the fire. The desire of command
prevails among them, though they are naked. They have
wives also. What they worship, except the divinity of
heaven, is not ascertained."*

In another letter, dated likewise in September, 1493, and
addressed to the cardinal and vice-chancellor Ascanius
Sforza, he says:

"So great is my desire to give you satisfaction, illustrious
prince, that I consider it a gratifying occurrence in the great
fluctuations of events, when anything takes place among us,
in which you may take an interest. The wonders of this
terrestrial globe, round which the sun makes a circuit in the
space of four and twenty hours, have, until our time, as you
are well aware, been known only in regard to one hemisphere, merely from the Golden Chersonesus to our Spanish
Gades. The rest has been given up as unknown by cos-
mographers, and if any mention of it has been made, it has
been slight and dubious. But now, O blessed enterprise!
under the auspices of our sovereigns, what has hitherto lain
hidden since the first origin of things has at length begun to
be developed. The thing has thus occurred—attend, illustrious prince! A certain Christopher Columbus, a Ligurian,

---

* Opus Epist. P. Martyris Anglerii, Epist. 184.

dispatched to those regions with three vessels by my sovereigns, pursuing the western sun above five thousand miles from Gades, achieved his way to the antipodes. Three and thirty successive days they navigated with naught but sky and water. At length from the masthead of the largest vessel, in which Columbus himself sailed, those on the lookout proclaimed the sight of land. He coasted along six islands, one of them, as all his followers declare, beguiled perchance by the novelty of the scene, is larger than Spain."

Martyr proceeds to give the usual account of the productions of the islands, and the manners and customs of the natives, particularly the wars which occurred among them; "as if *meum* and *tuum* had been introduced among them as among us, and expensive luxuries, and the desire of accumulating wealth; for what, you will think, can be the wants of naked men?" "What further may succeed," he adds, "I will hereafter signify. Farewell."*

In another letter, dated Valladolid, February 1st, 1494, to Fernando de Talavera, Archbishop of Granada, he observes, "The king and queen, on the return of Columbus to Barcelona, from his honorable enterprise, appointed him admiral of the ocean sea, and caused him, on account of his illustrious deeds, to be seated in their presence, an honor and a favor, as you know, the highest with our sovereigns. They have dispatched him again to those regions, furnished with a fleet of eighteen ships. There is prospect of great discoveries at the western antarctic antipodes. . . ." †

In a subsequent letter to Pomponius Lætus, dated from Alcala de Henares, December 9, 1494, he gives the first news of the success of this expedition.

"Spain," says he, "is spreading her wings, augmenting her empire, and extending her name and glory to the antipodes. . . . Of eighteen vessels dispatched by my sovereigns with the Admiral Columbus in his second voyage to the western hemisphere, twelve have returned and have brought Gossampine cotton, huge trees of dye-wood, and many other articles held with us as precious, the natural productions of that hitherto hidden world; and besides all other things, no small quantity of gold. O wonderful, Pomponius! Upon the surface of that earth are found rude masses of native gold, of a weight that one is afraid to mention. Some weigh two hundred and fifty ounces, and they

---

* Opus Epist. P. Martyris Anglerii, Epist. 135. † Ibid., Epist. 141.

hope to discover others of a much larger size, from what the naked natives intimate, when they extol their gold to our people. Nor are the Lestrigonians nor Polyphemi, who feed on human flesh, any longer doubtful. Attend—but beware! lest they rise in horror before thee! When he proceeded from the Fortunate Islands, now termed the Canaries, to Hispaniola, the island on which he first set foot, turning his prow a little toward the south, he arrived at innumerable islands of savage men, whom they call cannibals, or Caribbees; and these, though naked, are courageous warriors. They fight skillfully with bows and clubs, and have boats hollowed from a single tree, yet very capacious, in which they make fierce descents on neighboring islands, inhabited by milder people. They attack their villages, from which they carry off the men and devour them," etc.*

Another letter to Pomponius Lætus, on the same subject, has been cited at large in the body of this work. It is true these extracts give nothing that has not been stated more at large in the Decades of the same author, but they are curious, as the very first announcements of the discoveries of Columbus, and as showing the first stamp of these extraordinary events upon the mind of one of the most learned and liberal men of the age.

A collection of the letters of Peter Martyr was published in 1530, under the title of Opus Epistolarum, Petri Martyris Anglerii; it is divided into thirty-eight books, each containing the letters of one year. The same objections have been made to his letters as to his Decades, but they bear the same stamp of candor, probity, and great information. They possess peculiar value from being written at the moment, before the facts they record were distorted or discolored by prejudice or misrepresentation. His works abound in interesting particulars not to be found in any contemporary historian. They are rich in thought, but still richer in fact, and are full of urbanity, and of the liberal feeling of a scholar who has mingled with the world. He is a fountain from which others draw, and from which, with a little precaution, they may draw securely. He died in Valladolid, in 1526.

---

* Opus Epist. P. Martyris Anglerii, Epist. 147.

No. XXX

OVIEDO

GONZALO FERNANDEZ DE OVIEDO Y VALDES, commonly known as Oviedo, was born in Madrid in 1478, and died in Valladolid in 1557, aged seventy-nine years. He was of a noble Asturian family, and in his boyhood (in 1490) was appointed one of the pages to Prince Juan, heir apparent of Spain, the only son of Ferdinand and Isabella. He was in this situation at the time of the siege and surrender of Granada, was consequently at court at the time that Columbus made his agreement with the Catholic sovereigns, and was in the same capacity at Barcelona, and witnessed the triumphant entrance of the discoverer, attended by a number of the natives of the newly found countries.

In 1513, he was sent out to the New World by Ferdinand, to superintend the gold foundries. For many years he served there in various offices of trust and dignity, both under Ferdinand, and his grandson and successor Charles V. In 1535, he was made alcayde of the fortress of San Domingo in Hispaniola, and afterward was appointed historiographer of the Indies. At the time of his death, he had served the crown upward of forty years, thirty-four of which were passed in the colonies, and he had crossed the ocean eight times, as he mentions in various parts of his writings. He wrote several works; the most important is the chronicle of the Indies in fifty books, divided into three parts. The first part, containing nineteen books, was printed at Seville in 1535, and reprinted in 1547 at Salamanca, augmented by a twentieth book containing shipwrecks. The remainder of the work exists in manuscript. The printing of it was commenced at Valladolid in 1557, but was discontinued in consequence of his death. It is one of the unpublished treasures of Spanish colonial history.

He was an indefatigable writer, laborious in collecting and recording facts, and composed a multitude of volumes which are scattered through the Spanish libraries. His writings are full of events which happened under his own eye, or were communicated to him by eye-witnesses; but he was deficient in judgment and discrimination. He took his facts without caution, and often from sources unworthy of credit.

In his account of the first voyage of Columbus, he falls into several egregious errors, in consequence of taking the verbal information of a pilot named Hernan Perez Matteo, who was in the interest of the Pinzons, and adverse to the admiral. His work is not much to be depended upon in matters relative to Columbus. When he treats of a more advanced period of the New World, from his own actual observation, he is much more satisfactory, though he is accused of listening too readily to popular fables and misrepresentations. His account of the natural productions of the New World, and of the customs of its inhabitants, is full of curious particulars; and the best narratives of some of the minor voyages which succeeded those of Columbus are to be found in the unpublished part of his work.

No. XXXI

CURA DE LOS PALACIOS

ANDRES BERNALDES, or Bernal, generally known by the title of the curate of Los Palacios, from having been curate of the town of Los Palacios from about 1488 to 1513, was born in the town of Fuentes, and was for some time chaplain to Diego Deza, Archbishop of Seville, one of the greatest friends to the application of Columbus. Bernaldes was well acquainted with the admiral, who was occasionally his guest, and, in 1496, left many of his manuscripts and journals with him, which the curate made use of in a history of the reign of Ferdinand and Isabella, in which he introduced an account of the voyages of Columbus. In the narrative of the admiral's coasting along the southern side of Cuba, the curate is more minute and accurate than any other historian. His work exists only in manuscript, but is well known to historians, who have made frequent use of it. Nothing can be more simple and artless than the account which the honest curate gives of his being first moved to undertake his chronicle. "I who wrote these chapters of memoirs," he says, "being for twelve years in the habit of reading a register of my deceased grandfather, who was notary public of the town of Fuentes, where I was born, I found therein several chapters recording certain events and achievements which had taken place in his time; and my grandmother, his widow, who was very old, hearing me read them said to me, 'And thou, my son, since thou art not slothful in writing, why dost thou not write, in this manner, the good things which are happening at present in thy own day, that those who come hereafter may know them, and, marveling at what they read, may render thanks to God.'

"From that time," continues he, "I proposed to do so, and as I considered the matter, I said often to myself, 'If God gives me life and health I will continue to write until I behold the kingdom of Granada gained by the Christians;' and I always entertained a hope of seeing it and did see it: great thanks and praises be given to our Saviour Jesus Christ! And because it was impossible to write a complete and connected account of all things that happened in Spain, during the matrimonial union of the king Don Ferdinand, and the queen Dona Isabella, I wrote only about certain of the most striking and remarkable events, of which I had correct information, and of those which I saw or which were public and notorious to all men." *

The work of the worthy curate, as may be inferred from the foregoing statement, is deficient in regularity of plan; the style is artless and often inelegant, but it abounds in facts not to be met with elsewhere, often given in a very graphical manner, and strongly characteristic of the times. As he was contemporary with the events and familiar with many of the persons of his history, and as he was a man of probity and void of all pretension, his manuscript is a document of high authenticity. He was much respected in the limited sphere in which he moved, "yet," says one of his admirers, who wrote a short preface to his chronicle, "he had no other reward than that of the curacy of Los Palacios, and the place of chaplain to the archbishop Don Diego Deza."

In the possession of O. Rich, Esq., of Madrid, is a very curious manuscript chronicle of the reign of Ferdinand and Isabella already quoted in this work, made up from this history of the curate of Los Palacios, and from various other historians of the times, by some contemporary writer. In his account of the voyage of Columbus, he differs in some trivial particulars from the regular copy of the manuscript of the curate. These variations have been carefully examined by the author of this work, and wherever they appear to be for the better, have been adopted.

---

* Cura de los Palacios, cap. 7.

No. XXXII

"NAVIGATIONE DEL RE DE CASTIGLIA DELLE ISOLE E PAESE NUOVAMENTE RITROVATE"

"NAVIGATIO CHRISTOPHORI COLOMBI"

THE above are the titles, in Italian and in Latin, of the earliest narratives of the first and second voyages of Columbus that appeared in print. It was anonymous; and there are some curious particulars in regard to it. It was originally written in Italian by Montalbodo Fracanzo, or Fracanzano, or by Francapano de Montabaldo (for writers differ in regard to the name), and was published in Vicenza, in 1507, in a collection of voyages, entitled Mondo Novo, e Paese Nuovamente Ritrovate. The collection was republished at Milan, in 1508, both in Italian and in a Latin translation made by Archangelo Madrignano, under the title of Itinerarium Portugallensium; this title being given, because the work related chiefly to the voyages of Luigi Cadamosto, a Venetian in the service of Portugal.

The collection was afterward augmented by Simon Grinæus with other travels, and printed in Latin at Basle, in 1533,* by Hervagio, entitled Novus Orbis Regionum, etc. The edition of Basle, 1533, and the Italian edition of Milan, in 1508, have been consulted in the course of this work.

Peter Martyr (Decad. ii., cap. 7) alludes to this publication, under the first Latin title of the book, Itinerarium Portugallensium, and accuses the author, whom by mistake he terms Cadamosto, of having stolen the materials of his book from the three first chapters of his first Decade of the Ocean, of which, he says, he granted copies in manuscript to several persons, and in particular to certain Venetian embassadors. Martyr's Decades were not published until 1516, excepting the first three, which were published in 1511, at Seville.

This narrative of the voyages of Columbus is referred to by Gio. Batista Spotorno, in his historical memoir of Columbus, as having been written by a companion of Columbus.

---

* Bibliotheca Pinello.

It is manifest, from a perusal of the narrative, that though the author may have helped himself freely from the manuscript of Martyr, he must have had other sources of information. His description of the person of Columbus as a man tall of stature and large of frame, of a ruddy complexion and oblong visage, is not copied from Martyr, nor from any other writer. No historian had, indeed, preceded him, except Sabellicus, in 1504; and the portrait agrees with that subsequently given of Columbus in the biography written by his son.

It is probable that this narrative, which appeared only a year after the death of Columbus, was a piece of literary job-work, written for the collection of voyages published at Vicenza; and that the materials were taken from oral communication, from the account given by Sabellicus, and particularly from the manuscript copy of Martyr's first decade.

No. XXXIII

ANTONIO DE HERRERA

ANTONIO HERRERA DE TORDESILLAS, one of the authors most frequently cited in this work, was born in 1565, of Roderick Tordesillas, and Agnes de Herrera, his wife. He received an excellent education, and entered into the employ of Vespasian Gonzago, brother to the Duke of Mantua, who was Viceroy of Naples for Philip the Second of Spain. He was for some time secretary to this statesman, and intrusted with all his secrets. He was afterward grand historiographer of the Indies to Philip II., who added to that title a large pension. He wrote various books, but the most celebrated is a General History of the Indies, or American Colonies," in four volumes, containing eight decades. When he undertook this work all the public archives were thrown open to him, and he had access to documents of all kinds. He has been charged with great precipitation in the production of his two first volumes, and with negligence in not making sufficient use of the indisputable sources of information thus placed within his reach. The fact was, that he met with historical tracts lying in manuscript, which embraced a great part of the first discoveries, and he contented himself with stating events as he found them therein recorded. It is certain that a great part of his work is little more than a transcript of the manuscript history of the Indies by Las Casas, sometimes reducing and improving the language when tumid; omitting the impassioned sallies of the zealous father, when the wrongs of the Indians were in question; and suppressing various circumstances degrading to the character of the Spanish discoverers. The author of the present work has, therefore, frequently put aside the history of Herrera, and consulted the source of his information, the manuscript history of Las Casas.

Munoz observes that "in general Herrera did little more than join together morsels and extracts, taken from various parts, in the way that a writer arranges chronologically the materials from which he intends to compose a history"; he adds, that "had not Herrera been a learned and judicious man, the precipitation with which he put together these materials would have led to innumerable errors." The remark is just; yet it is to be considered that to select and arrange such materials judiciously, and treat them learnedly, was no trifling merit in the historian.

Herrera has been accused also of flattering his nation; exalting the deeds of his countrymen, and softening and concealing their excesses. There is nothing very serious in this accusation. To illustrate the glory of his nation is one of the noblest offices of the historian; and it is difficult to speak too highly of the extraordinary enterprises and splendid actions of the Spaniards in those days. In softening their excesses he fell into an amiable and pardonable error, if it were indeed an error for a Spanish writer to endeavor to sink them in oblivion.

Vossius passes a high eulogium on Herrera. "No one," he says, "has described with greater industry and fidelity the magnitude and boundaries of provinces, the tracts of sea, positions of capes and islands, of ports and harbors, the windings of rivers and dimensions of lakes; the situation and peculiarities of regions, with the appearance of the heavens, and the designation of places suitable for the establishment of cities." He has been called among the Spaniards the prince of the historians of America, and it is added that none have risen since his time capable of disputing with him that title. Much of this praise will appear exaggerated by such as examine the manuscript histories from which he transferred chapters and entire books, with very little alteration, to his volumes; and a great part of the eulogiums passed on him for his work on the Indies will be found really due to Las Casas, who has too long been eclipsed by his copyist. Still Herrera has left voluminous proofs of industrious research, extensive information, and great literary talent. His works bear the mark of candor, integrity, and a sincere desire to record the truth.

He died in 1625, at sixty years of age, after having obtained from Philip IV. the promise of the first charge of secretary of state that should become vacant.

No. XXXIV

BISHOP FONSECA

THE singular malevolence displayed by Bishop Juan Rodriguez de Fonseca toward Columbus and his family, and which was one of the secret and principal causes of their misfortunes, has been frequently noticed in the course of this work. It originated, as has been shown, in some dispute between the admiral and Fonseca at Seville in 1493, on account of the delay in fitting out the armament for the second voyage, and in regard to the number of domestics to form the household of the admiral. Fonseca received a letter from the sovereigns, tacitly reproving him, and ordering him to show all possible attention to the wishes of Columbus, and to see that he was treated with honor and deference. Fonseca never forgot this affront, and, what with him was the same thing, never forgave it. His spirit appears to have been of that unhealthy kind which has none of the balm of forgiveness; and in which, a wound once made, forever rankles. The hostility thus produced continued with increasing virulence throughout the life of Columbus, and at his death was transferred to his son and successor. This persevering animosity has been illustrated in the course of this work by facts and observations, cited from authors, some of them contemporary with Fonseca, but who were apparently restrained by motives of prudence from giving full vent to the indignation which they evidently felt. Even at the present day, a Spanish historian would be cautious of expressing his feelings freely on the subject, lest they should prejudice his work in the eyes of the ecclesiastical censors of the press. In this way Bishop Fonseca has in a great measure escaped the general odium his conduct merited.

This prelate had the chief superintendence of Spanish colonial affairs, both under Ferdinand and Isabella, and the Emperor Charles V. He was an active and intrepid, but selfish, overbearing, and perfidious man. His administration bears no marks of enlarged and liberal policy; but is full of traits of arrogance and meanness. He opposed the benevolent attempts of Las Casas to ameliorate the condition of the Indians, and to obtain the abolition of repartimientos; treating him with personal haughtiness and asperity.* The reason assigned is that Fonseca was enriching himself by those very abuses, retaining large numbers of the miserable Indians in slavery, to work on his possessions in the colonies.

To show that his character has not been judged with undue severity, it is expedient to point out his invidious and persecuting conduct toward Hernando Cortez. The bishop, while ready to foster rambling adventurers who came forward under his patronage, had never the head or the heart to appreciate the merits of illustrious commanders like Columbus and Cortez.

At a time when disputes arose between Cortez and Diego Velazquez, governor of Cuba, and the latter sought to arrest the conqueror of Mexico in the midst of his brilliant career, Fonseca, with entire disregard of the merits of the case, took a decided part in favor of Velazquez. Personal interest was at the bottom of this favor; for a marriage was negotiating between Velazquez and a sister of the bishop.† Complaints and misrepresentations had been sent to Spain by Velazquez of the conduct of Cortez, who was represented as a lawless and unprincipled adventurer, attempting to usurp absolute authority in New Spain. The true services of Cortez had already excited admiration at court, but such was the influence of Fonseca that, as in the case of Columbus, he succeeded in prejudicing the mind of the sovereign against one of the most meritorious of his subjects. One Christoval de Tapia, a man destitute of talent or character, but whose greatest recommendation was his having been in the employ of the bishop,‡ was invested with powers similar to those once given to Bobadilla to the prejudice of Columbus. He was to inquire into the conduct of Cortez, and in case he thought fit, to seize him, sequestrate his property, and super-

---

* Herrera, Hist. Ind., decad. ii., lib. ii., cap. 3.
† Ibid., decad. iii., lib. iv., cap. 3.
‡ Ibid., decad. iii., lib. i., cap. 15.

sede him in command. Not content with the regular official
letters furnished to Tapia, the bishop, shortly after his departure, sent out Juan Bono de Quexo with blank letters
signed by his own hand, and with others directed to various
persons, charging them to admit Tapia for governor, and
assuring them that the king considered the conduct of Cortez as disloyal. Nothing but the sagacity and firmness of
Cortez prevented this measure from completely interrupting,
if not defeating his enterprises; and he afterward declared
that he had experienced more trouble and difficulty from the
menaces and affronts of the ministers of the king than it cost
him to conquer Mexico.*

When the dispute between Cortez and Velazquez came to
be decided upon in Spain, in 1522, the father of Cortez, and
those who had come from New Spain as his procurators,
obtained permission from Cardinal Adrian, at that time
governor of the realm, to prosecute a public accusation of
the bishop. A regular investigation took place before the
Council of the Indies of their allegations against its president. They charged him with having publicly declared
Cortez a traitor and a rebel; with having intercepted and
suppressed his letters addressed to the king, keeping his
majesty in ignorance of their contents and of the important
services he had performed, while he diligently forwarded all
letters calculated to promote the interest of Velazquez; with
having prevented the representations of Cortez from being
heard in the Council of the Indies, declaring that they should
never be heard there while he lived; with having interdicted
the forwarding of arms, merchandise, and re-enforcements
to New Spain; and with having issued orders to the office of
the India House at Seville to arrest the procurators of Cortez
and all persons arriving from him, and to seize and detain
all gold that they should bring. These and various other
charges of similar nature were dispassionately investigated.
Enough were substantiated to convict Fonseca of the most
partial, oppressive and perfidious conduct, and the cardinal
consequently forbade him to interfere in the cause between
Cortez and Velazquez, and revoked all the orders which the
bishop had issued, in the matter, to the India House of
Seville. Indeed Salazar, a Spanish historian, says that
Fonseca was totally divested of his authority as president
of the council, and of all control of the affairs of New Spain,

---

* Herrera, Hist. Ind., decad. iii., lib. iv., cap. 8.

and adds that he was so mortified at the blow that it brought on a fit of illness which wellnigh cost him his life.[*]

The suit between Cortez and Velazquez was referred to a special tribunal, composed of the grand chancellor and other persons of note, and was decided in 1522. The influence and intrigues of Fonseca being no longer of avail, a triumphant verdict was given in favor of Cortez, which was afterward confirmed by the Emperor Charles V., and additional honors awarded him. This was another blow to the malignant Fonseca, who retained his enmity against Cortez until his last moment, rendered still more rancorous by mortification and disappointment.

A charge against Fonseca, of a still darker nature than any of the preceding, may be found lurking in the pages of Herrera, though so obscure as to have escaped the notice of succeeding historians. He points to the bishop as the instigator of a desperate and perfidious man, who conspired against the life of Hernando Cortez. This was one Antonio de Villafana, who fomented a conspiracy to assassinate Cortez, and elect Francisco Verdujo, brother-in-law of Velazquez, in his place. While the conspirators were waiting for an opportunity to poniard Cortez, one of them, relenting, apprised him of his danger. Villafana was arrested. He attempted to swallow a paper containing a list of the conspirators, but being seized by the throat, a part of it was forced from his mouth containing fourteen names of persons of importance. Villafana confessed his guilt, but tortures could not make him inculpate the persons whose names were on the list, whom he declared were ignorant of the plot. He was hanged by order of Cortez.[†]

In the investigation of the disputes between Cortez and Velazquez, this execution of Villafana was magnified into a cruel and wanton act of power; and in their eagerness to criminate Cortez the witnesses on the part of Alvarez declared that Villafana had been instigated to what he had done by letters from Bishop Fonseca! (Que se movio a lo que hizo con cartas del obispo de Burgos.[‡]) It is not probable that Fonseca had recommended assassination, but it shows the character of his agents, and what must have been the malignant nature of his instructions, when these men

---

[*] Salazar, Conq. de Mexico, lib. i., cap. 2.
[†] Herrera, Hist. Ind., decad. iii., lib. i., cap. 1.
[‡] Ibid., decad. iii., lib. iv., cap. 3.

thought that such an act would accomplish his wishes. Fonseca died at Burgos on the 4th of November, 1554, and was interred at Coca.

No. XXXV

OF THE SITUATION OF THE TERRESTRIAL PARADISE

THE speculations of Columbus on the situation of the terrestrial paradise, extravagant as they may appear, were such as have occupied many grave and learned men. A slight notice of their opinions on this curious subject may be acceptable to the general reader, and may take from the apparent wildness of the ideas expressed by Columbus.

The abode of our first parents was anciently the subject of anxious inquiry; and indeed mankind have always been prone to picture some place of perfect felicity, where the imagination, disappointed in the coarse realities of life, might revel in an Elysium of its own creation. It is an idea not confined to our religion, but is found in the rude creeds of the most savage nations, and it prevailed generally among the ancients.

The speculations concerning the situation of the garden of Eden resemble those of the Greeks concerning the garden of the Hesperides; that region of delight, which they forever placed at the most remote verge of the known world; which their poets embellished with all the charms of fiction; after which they were continually longing, and which they could never find. At one time it was in the Grand Oasis of Arabia. The exhausted travelers, after traversing the parched and sultry desert, hailed this verdant spot with rapture; they refreshed themselves under its shady bowers, and beside its cooling streams, as the crew of a tempest-tossed vessel repose on the shores of some green island in the deep; and from its being thus isolated in the midst of an ocean of sand, they gave it the name of the Island of the Blessed. As geographical knowledge increased, the situation of the Hesperian gardens was continually removed to a greater distance. It was transferred to the borders of the great Syrtis, in the neighborhood of Mount Atlas. Here, after traversing the frightful deserts of Barca, the traveler found himself in a fair and fertile country, watered by rivulets and gushing fountains. The oranges and citrons transported hence to Greece, where they were as yet unknown, delighted the Athenians by their golden beauty and delicious flavor, and they thought that none but the garden of the Hesperides could produce such glorious fruits. In this way the happy region of the ancients was transported from place to place, still in the remote and obscure extremity of the world, until it was fabled to exist in the Canaries, thence called the Fortunate or the Hesperian Islands. Here it remained, because discovery advanced no further, and because these islands were so distant, and so little known, as to allow full latitude to the fictions of the poet.*

In like manner the situation of the terrestrial paradise, or garden of Eden, was long a subject of earnest inquiry and curious disputation, and occupied the laborious attention of the most learned theologians. Some placed it in Palestine or the Holy Land; others in Mesopotamia, in that rich and beautiful tract of country embraced by the wanderings of the Tigris and the Euphrates; others in Armenia, in a valley surrounded by precipitous and inaccessible mountains, and imagined that Enoch and Elijah were transported thither, out of the sight of mortals, to live in a state of terrestrial bliss until the second coming of our Saviour. There were others who gave it situations widely remote, such as in the Trapoban of the ancients, at present known as the island of Ceylon; or in the island of Sumatra; or in the Fortunate or Canary Islands; or in one of the islands of Sunda; or in some favored spot under the equinoctial line.

Great difficulty was encountered by these speculators to reconcile the allotted place with the description given in Genesis of the garden of Eden; particularly of the great fountain which watered it, and which afterward divided itself into four rivers, the Pison or Phison, the Gihon, the Euphrates, and the Hiddekel. Those who were in favor of the Holy Land supposed that the Jordan was the great river which afterward divided itself into the Phison, Gihon, Tigris, and Euphrates, but that the sands have choked up the ancient beds by which these streams were supplied; that originally the Phison traversed Arabia Deserta and Arabia Felix, whence it pursued its course to the Gulf of Persia; that the Gihon bathed Northern or stony Arabia and fell into the Arabian Gulf or the Red Sea; that the Euphrates

---

* Gosselin, Recherches sur la Geog. des Anciens, tom. i.

and the Tigris passed by Eden to Assyria and Chaldea, whence they discharged themselves into the Persian Gulf.

By most of the early commentators the River Gihon is supposed to be the Nile. The source of this river was unknown, but was evidently far distant from the spots whence the Tigris and the Euphrates arose. This difficulty, however, was ingeniously overcome, by giving it a subterranean course of some hundreds of leagues from the common fountain, until it issued forth to daylight in Abyssinia.* In like manner, subterranean courses were given to the Tigris and the Euphrates, passing under the Red Sea, until they sprang forth in Armenia, as if just issuing from one common source. So also those who placed the terrestrial paradise in islands, supposed that the rivers which issued from it, and formed those heretofore named, either traversed the surface of the sea, as fresh water, by its greater lightness, may float above the salt; or that they flowed through deep veins and channels of the earth, as the fountain of Arethusa was said to sink into the ground in Greece, and rise in the island of Sicily, while the River Alpheus pursuing it, but with less perseverance, rose somewhat short of it in the sea.

Some contended that the deluge had destroyed the garden of Eden, and altered the whole face of the earth; so that the rivers had changed their beds, and had taken different directions from those mentioned in Genesis; others, however, among whom was St. Augustine, in his commentary upon the Book of Genesis, maintained that the terrestrial paradise still existed, with its original beauty and delights, but that it was inaccessible to mortals, being on the summit of a mountain of stupendous height, reaching into the third region of the air, and approaching the moon; being thus protected by its elevation from the ravages of the deluge.

By some this mountain was placed under the equinoctial line; or under that band of the heavens metaphorically called by the ancients "the table of the sun," † comprising the space between the tropics of Cancer and Capricorn, beyond which the sun never passed in his annual course. Here would reign a uniformity of nights and days and seasons, and the elevation of the mountain would raise it above the heats and storms of the lower regions. Others transported the garden beyond the equinoctial line, and placed it in the

---

* Feyjoo, Theatro Critico, lib. vii., § 2.
† Herodot., lib. iii. Virg. Georg. i. Pomp. Mela, lib. iii., cap. 10.

southern hemisphere; supposing that the torrid zone might be the flaming sword appointed to defend its entrance against mortals. They had a fanciful train of argument to support their theory. They observed that the terrestrial paradise must be in the noblest and happiest part of the globe; that part must be under the noblest part of the heavens; as the merits of a place do not so much depend upon the virtues of the earth as upon the happy influences of the stars and the favorable and benign aspect of the heavens. Now, according to philosophers, the world was divided into two hemispheres. The southern they considered the head, and the northern the feet, or under part; the right hand the east, whence commenced the movement of the primum mobile, and the left the west, toward which it moved. This supposed, they observed that as it was manifest that the head of all things, natural and artificial, is always the best and noblest part, governing the other parts of the body, so the south, being the head of the earth, ought to be superior and nobler than either east, or west, or north; and in accordance with this, they cited the opinion of various philosophers among the ancients, and more especially that of Ptolemy, that the stars of the southern hemisphere were larger, more resplendent, more perfect, and of course of greater virtue and efficacy than those of the northern: an error universally prevalent until disproved by modern discovery. Hence they concluded that in this southern hemisphere, in this head of the earth, under this purer and brighter sky, and these more potent and benignant stars, was placed the terrestrial paradise.

Various ideas were entertained as to the magnitude of this blissful region. As Adam and all his progeny were to have lived there, had he not sinned, and as there would have been no such thing as death to thin the number of mankind, it was inferred that the terrestrial paradise must be of great extent to contain them. Some gave it a size equal to Europe or Africa; others gave it the whole southern hemisphere. St. Augustine supposed that as mankind multiplied numbers would be translated without death to heaven; the parents, perhaps, when their children had arrived at mature age; or portions of the human race at the end of certain periods, and when the population of the terrestrial paradise had attained a certain amount.*

Others supposed that mankind, remaining in a state of

---

* St. August., lib. ix., cap. 6. Sup. Genesis.

primitive innocence, would not have required so much space as at present. Having no need of rearing animals for subsistence, no land would have been required for pasturage; and the earth not being cursed with sterility, there would have been no need of extensive tracts of country to permit of fallow land and the alternation of crops required in husbandry. The spontaneous and never-failing fruits of the garden would have been abundant for the simple wants of man. Still, that the human race might not be crowded, but might have ample space for recreation and enjoyment, and the charms of variety and change, some allowed at least a hundred leagues of circumference to the garden.

St. Basilius in his eloquent discourse on paradise * expatiates with rapture on the joys of this sacred abode, elevated to the third region of the air, and under the happiest skies. There a pure and never-failing pleasure is furnished to every sense. The eye delights in the admirable clearness of the atmosphere, in the verdure and beauty of the trees, and the never-withering bloom of the flowers. The ear is regaled with the singing of the birds, the smell with the aromatic odors of the land. In like manner the other senses have each their peculiar enjoyments. There the vicissitudes of the seasons are unknown, and the climate unites the fruitfulness of summer, the joyful abundance of autumn, and the sweet freshness and quietude of spring. There the earth is always green, the flowers are ever blooming, the waters limpid and delicate, not rushing in rude and turbid torrents, but swelling up in crystal fountains, and winding in peaceful and silver streams. There no harsh and boisterous winds are permitted to shake and disturb the air, and ravage the beauty of the groves, there prevails no melancholy, nor darksome weather, no drowning rain, nor pelting hail; no forked lightning, nor rending and resounding thunder; no wintry pinching cold, nor withering and panting summer heat; nor anything else that can give pain or sorrow or annoyance, but all is bland and gentle and serene; a perpetual youth and joy reigns throughout all nature, and nothing decays and dies.

The same idea is given by St. Ambrosius, in his book on Paradise†, an author likewise consulted and cited by Colum-

---

* St. Basilius was called the great. His works were read and admired by all the world, even by Pagans. They are written in an elevated and majestic style, with great splendor of idea and vast erudition.

† St. Ambrosius. Opera. Edit. Coignard. Parisiis. MDCXC.

bus. He wrote in the fourth century, and his touching eloquence, and graceful yet vigorous style, insured great popularity to his writings. Many of these opinions are cited by
Glanville, usually called Bartholomeus Anglicus, in his work
De Proprietatibus Rerum; a work with which Columbus
was evidently acquainted. It was a species of encyclopedia
of the general knowledge current at the time, and was likely
to recommend itself to a curious and inquiring voyager.
This author cites an assertion as made by St. Basilius and
St. Ambrosius, that the water of the fountain which proceeds
from the Garden of Eden falls into a great lake with such a
tremendous noise that the inhabitants of the neighborhood
are born deaf; and that from this lake proceed the four chief
rivers mentioned in Genesis.*

This passage, however, is not to be found in the Hexameron of either Basilius or Ambrosius, from which it is quoted;
neither is it in the oration on Paradise by the former, nor in
the letter on the same subject written by Ambrosius to Ambrosius Sabinus. It must be a misquotation by Glanville.
Columbus, however, appears to have been struck with it,
and Las Casas is of opinion that he derived thence his idea
that the vast body of fresh water which filled the Gulf of La
Ballena or Paria, flowed from the fountain of Paradise,
though from a remote distance; and that in this gulf, which
he supposed in the extreme part of Asia, originated the Nile,
the Tigris, the Euphrates, and the Ganges, which might be
conducted under the land and sea by subterranean channels,
to the places where they spring forth on the earth and assume their proper names.

I forbear to enter into various other of the voluminous
speculations which have been formed relative to the terrestrial paradise, and perhaps it may be thought that I have
already said too much on so fanciful a subject; but to illustrate clearly the character of Columbus, it is necessary to
elucidate those veins of thought passing through his mind

---

* Paradisus autem in Oriente, in altissimo monte, de cujus cacu-
mine cadentes aquæ, maximum faciunt lacum, que in suo casu tantum
faciunt strepitum et fragorem, quod omnes incolæ, juxta prædictum
lacum, nascunter surdi, ex immoderato sonitu seu fragore sensum audi-
tus in parvulis corrumpente. *Ut dicit Basilius in Hexameron, similiter
et Ambros.* Ex illo, lacu, velut ex uno fonte, procedunt illa flumina
quatuor, Phison, qui et Ganges, Gyon, qui et Nilus dicitur, et Tigris ac
Euphrates. Bart. Angl. de Proprietatibus rerum, lib. xv., cap. 112.
Francofurti, 1540.

while considering the singular phenomena of the unknown regions he was exploring, and which are often but slightly and vaguely developed in his journals and letters. These speculations, likewise, like those concerning fancied islands in the ocean, carry us back to the time, and make us feel the mystery and conjectural charm which reigned over the greatest part of the world, and have since been completely dispelled by modern discovery. Enough has been cited to show that in his observations concerning the terrestrial paradise, Columbus was not indulging in any fanciful and presumptuous chimeras, the offspring of a heated and disordered brain. However visionary his conjectures may seem, they were all grounded on written opinions held little less than oracular in his day; and they will be found on examination to be far exceeded by the speculations and theories of sages held illustrious for their wisdom and erudition in the school and cloister.

No. XXXVI

WILL OF COLUMBUS

In the name of the Most Holy Trinity, who inspired me with the idea, and afterward made it perfectly clear to me, that I could navigate and go to the Indies from Spain, by traversing the ocean westwardly; which I communicated to the king, Don Ferdinand, and to the queen, Dona Isabella, our sovereigns; and they were pleased to furnish me the necessary equipment of men and ships, and to make me their admiral over the said ocean, in all parts lying to the west of an imaginary line, drawn from pole to pole, a hundred leagues west of the Cape de Verde and Azore Islands; also appointing me their viceroy and governor over all continents and islands that I might discover beyond the said line westwardly; with the right of being succeeded in the said offices by my eldest son and his heirs forever; and a grant of the tenth part of all things found in the said jurisdiction; and of all rents and revenues arising from it; and the eighth of all the lands and everything else, together with the salary corresponding to my rank of admiral, viceroy, and governor, and all other emoluments accruing thereto, as is more fully expressed in the title and agreement sanctioned by their highnesses.

And it pleased the Lord Almighty, that in the year one thousand four hundred and ninety-two, I should discover the continent of the Indies and many islands, among them Hispaniola, which the Indians call Ayte, and the Monicongos, Cipango. I then returned to Castile to their highnesses, who approved of my undertaking a second enterprise for further discoveries and settlements; and the Lord gave me victory over the island of Hispaniola, which extends six hundred leagues, and I conquered it and made it tributary; and I discovered many islands inhabited by cannibals, and seven hundred to the west of Hispaniola, among which is Jamaica, which we call Santiago; and three hundred and thirty-three leagues of continent from south to west, besides a hundred and seven to the north, which I discovered in my first voyage, together with many islands, as may more clearly be seen by my letters, memorials, and maritime charts. And as we hope in God that before long a good and great revenue will be derived from the above islands and continent, of which, for the reasons aforesaid, belong to me the tenth and the eighth, with the salaries and emoluments specified above; and considering that we are mortal, and that it is proper for every one to settle his affairs, and to leave declared to his heirs and successors the property he possesses or may have a right to: Wherefore I have concluded to create an entailed estate (mayorazgo) out of the said eighth of the lands, places, and revenues, in the manner which I now proceed to state.

In the first place, I am to be succeeded by Don Diego, my son, who in case of death without children is to be succeeded by my other son Ferdinand; and should God dispose of him also without leaving children and without my having any other son, then my brother Don Bartholomew is to succeed; and after him his eldest son; and if God should dispose of him without heirs, he shall be succeeded by his sons from one to another forever; or, in the failure of a son, to be succeeded by Don Ferdinand, after the same manner, from son to son successively; or in their place by my brothers Bartholomew and Diego. And should it please the Lord that the estate, after having continued for some time in the line of any of the above successors, should stand in need of an immediate and lawful male heir, the succession shall then devolve to the nearest relation, being a man of legitimate birth, and bearing the name of Columbus derived from his father and his ancestors. This entailed estate shall in no wise be inherited by a woman, except in case that no male is to be found, either in this or any other quarter of the world, of my real lineage, whose name, as well as that of his ancestors, shall have always been Columbus. In such an event (which may God forefend), then the female of legitimate birth, most nearly related to the preceding possessor of the estate, shall succeed to it; and this is to be under the conditions herein stipulated at foot, which must be understood to extend as well to Don Diego, my son, as to the aforesaid and their heirs, every one of them, to be fulfilled by them; and failing to do so they are to be deprived of the succession, for not having complied with what shall herein be expressed; and the estate to pass to the person most nearly related to the one who held the right: and the person thus succeeding shall in like manner forfeit the estate, should he also fail to comply with said conditions; and another person, the nearest of my lineage, shall succeed, provided he abide by them, so that they may be observed forever in the form prescribed. This forfeiture is not to be incurred for trifling matters, originating in lawsuits, but in important cases, when the glory of God, or my own, or that of my family, may be concerned, which supposes a perfect fulfillment of all the things hereby ordained; all which I recommend to the courts of justice. And I supplicate his Holiness, who now is, and those that may succeed in the Holy Church, that if it should happen that this my will and testament has need of his holy order and command for its fulfillment, that such order be issued in virtue of obedience, and under penalty of excommunication, and that it shall not be in any wise disfigured. And I also pray the king and queen, our sovereigns, and their eldest-born, Prince Don Juan, our lord, and their successors, for the sake of the services I have done them, and because it is just, that it may please them not to permit this my will and constitution of my entailed estate to be any way altered, but to leave it in the form and manner which I have ordained, forever, for the greater glory of the Almighty, and that it may be the root and basis of my lineage, and a memento of the services I have rendered their highnesses; that, being born in Genoa, I came over to serve them in Castile, and discovered to the west of Terra Firma the Indies and islands before mentioned. I accordingly pray their highnesses to order that this my privilege and testament be held valid, and be executed summarily and without any opposition or demur, according to the letter. I also pray the grandees of the realm and the lords of the council, and all others having administration of justice, to be pleased not to suffer this my will and testament to be of no avail, but to cause it to be fulfilled as by me ordained; it being just that a noble, who has served the king and queen, and the kingdom, should be respected in the disposition of his estate by will, testament, institution of entail or inheritance, and that the same be not infringed either in whole or in part.

In the first place, my son Don Diego, and all my successors and descendants, as well as my brothers Bartholomew and Diego, shall bear my arms, such as I shall leave them after my days, without inserting anything else in them; and they shall be their seal to seal withal. Don Diego my son, or any other who may inherit this estate, on coming into possession of the inheritance, shall sign with the signature which I now make use of, which is an X with an S over it, and an M with a Roman A over it, and over that an S, and then a Greek Y, with an S over it, with its lines and points as is my custom, as may be seen by my signatures, of which there are many, and it will be seen by the present one.

He shall only write "the Admiral," whatever other titles the king may have conferred on him. This is to be understood as respects his signature, but not the enumeration of his titles, which he can make at full length if agreeable, only the signature is to be "the Admiral."

The said Don Diego, or any other inheritor of this estate, shall possess my offices of admiral of the ocean, which is to the west of an imaginary line, which his highness ordered to be drawn, running from pole to pole a hundred leagues beyond the Azores, and as many more beyond the Cape de Verde Islands, over all which I was made, by their order, their admiral of the sea, with all the pre-eminences held by Don Henrique in the admiralty of Castile, and they made me their governor and viceroy perpetually and forever, over all the islands and mainland discovered, or to be discovered, for myself and heirs, as is more fully shown by my treaty and privilege as above mentioned.

Item: The said Don Diego, or any other inheritor of this estate, shall distribute the revenue which it may please our Lord to grant him, in the following manner, under the above penalty:

First—Of the whole income of this estate, now and at all times, and of whatever may be had or collected from it, he shall give the fourth part annually to my brother Don Bartholomew Columbus, adelantado of the Indies; and this is to continue till he shall have acquired an income of a million of maravedis, for his support, and for the services he has rendered and will continue to render to this entailed estate; which million he is to receive, as stated, every year, if the said fourth amount to so much, and that he have nothing else; but if he possess a part or the whole of that amount in rents, that thenceforth he shall not enjoy the said million, nor any part of it, except that he shall have in the said fourth part unto the said quantity of a million, if it should amount to so much; and as much as he shall have of revenue beside this fourth part, whatever sum of maravedis of known rent from property or perpetual offices, the said quantity of rent or revenue from property or offices shall be discounted; and from the said million shall be reserved whatever marriage portion he may receive with any female he may espouse; so that whatever he may receive in marriage with his wife, no deduction shall be made on that account from said million, but only for whatever he may acquire, or may have, over and above his wife's dowry, and when it shall please God that he or his heirs and descendants shall derive from their property and offices a revenue of a million arising from rents, neither he nor his heirs shall enjoy any longer anything from the said fourth part of the entailed estate, which shall remain with Don Diego, or whoever may inherit it.

Item: From the revenues of the said estate, or from any other fourth part of it (should its amount be adequate to it), shall be paid every year to my son Ferdinand two millions, till such time as his revenue shall amount to two millions, in the same form and manner as in the case of Bartholomew, who, as well as his heirs, are to have the million or the part that may be wanting.

Item: The said Don Diego or Don Bartholomew shall make, out of the said estate, for my brother Diego, such provision as may enable him to live decently, as he is my brother, to whom I assign no particular sum, as he has attached himself to the church, and that will be given him which is right: and this to be given him in a mass, and before anything shall have been received by Ferdinand my son, or Bartholomew my brother, or their heirs, and also according to the amount of the income of the estate. And in case of discord, the case is to be referred to two of our relations, or other men of honor; and should they disagree among themselves, they will choose a third person as arbitrator, being virtuous and not distrusted by either party.

* * * 16—VOL. VII.

Item: All this revenue which I bequeath to Bartholomew, to Ferdinand, and to Diego, shall be delivered to and received by them as prescribed under the obligation of being faithful and loyal to Diego my son, or his heirs, they as well as their children; and should it appear that they, or any of them, had proceeded against him in anything touching his honor, or the prosperity of the family, or of the estate, either in word or deed, whereby might come a scandal and debasement to my family, and a detriment to my estate; in that case, nothing further shall be given to them or him, from that time forward, inasmuch as they are always to be faithful to Diego and to his successors.

Item: As it was my intention, when I first instituted this entailed estate, to dispose, or that my son Diego should dispose for me, of the tenth part of the income in favor of necessitous persons, as a tithe, and in commemoration of the Almighty and Eternal God; and persisting still in this opinion, and hoping that his High Majesty will assist me, and those who may inherit it, in this or the New World, I have resolved that the said tithe shall be paid in the manner following:

First—It is to be understood that the fourth part of the revenue of the estate which I have ordained and directed to be given to Don Bartholomew, till he have an income of one million, includes the tenth of the whole revenue of the estate; and that as in proportion as the income of my brother Don Bartholomew shall increase, as it has to be discounted from the revenue of the fourth part of the entailed estate, that the said revenue shall be calculated, to know how much the tenth part amounts to; and the part which exceeds what is necessary to make up the million for Don Bartholomew shall be received by such of my family as may most stand in need of it, discounting it from said tenth, if their income do not amount to fifty thousand maravedis; and should any of these come to have an income to this amount, such a part shall be awarded them as two persons, chosen for the purpose, may determine along with Don Diego, or his heirs. Thus, it is to be understood that the million which I leave to Don Bartholomew comprehends the tenth of the whole revenue of the estate; which revenue is to be distributed among my nearest and most needy relations in the manner I have directed; and when Don Bartholomew have an income of one million, and that nothing more shall be due to him on account of said fourth part, then, Don Diego my son, or the person who may be in possession of the estate, along with the two other persons which I shall herein point out, shall inspect the accounts, and so direct that the tenth of the revenue shall still continue to be paid to the most necessitous members of my family that may be found in this or any other quarter of the world, who shall be diligently sought out; and they are to be paid out of the fourth part from which Don Bartholomew is to derive his million; which sums are to be taken into account, and deducted from the said tenth, which, should it amount to more, the overplus, as it arises from the fourth part, shall be given to the most necessitous persons as aforesaid; and should it not be sufficient that Don Bartholomew shall have it until his own estate goes on increasing, leaving the said million in part or in the whole.

Item: The said Don Diego my son, or whoever may be the inheritor, shall appoint two persons of conscience and authority, and most nearly related to the family, who are to examine the revenue and its amount carefully, and to cause the said tenth to be paid out of the fourth from which Don Bartholomew is to receive his million, to the most necessitated members of my family that may be found here or elsewhere, whom they shall look for diligently upon their consciences; and as it might happen that said Don Diego, or others after him, for reasons which may concern their own welfare, or the credit and support of the estate, may be unwilling to make known the full amount of the income; nevertheless I charge him on his conscience to pay the sum aforesaid; and I charge them, on their souls and consciences, not to denounce or make it known, except with the consent of Don Diego, or the person that may succeed him; but let the above tithe be paid in the manner I have directed.

Item: In order to avoid all disputes in the choice of the two nearest relations who are to act with Don Diego or his heirs, I hereby elect Don Bartholomew my brother for one, and Don Fernando my son for the other; and when these two shall enter upon the business, they shall choose two others persons among the most trusty, and most nearly related, and these again shall elect two others when it shall be question of commencing the examination; and thus it shall be managed with diligence from one to the other, as well in this as in the other of government, for the service and glory of God, and the benefit of the said entailed estate.

Item: I also enjoin Diego, or any one that may inherit the estate, to have and maintain in the city of Genoa, one person of our lineage to reside there with his wife, and appoint him a sufficient revenue to enable him to live decently, as a person closely connected with the family, of which he is to be the root and basis in that city; from which great good may accrue to him, inasmuch as I was born there, and came from thence.

Item: The said Don Diego, or whoever shall inherit the estate, must remit in bills, or in any other way, all such sums as he may be able to save out of the revenue of the estate, and direct purchases to be made in his name, or that of his heirs, in a stock in the Bank of St. George, which gives an interest of six per cent and in secure money; and this shall be devoted to the purpose I am about to explain.

Item: As it becomes every man of property to serve God, either personally or by means of his wealth, and as all moneys deposited with St. George are quite safe, and Genoa is a noble city, and powerful by sea, and as at the time that I undertook to set out upon the discovery of the Indies, it was with the intention of supplicating the king and queen, our lords, that whatever moneys should be derived from the said Indies should be invested in the conquest of Jerusalem; and as I did so supplicate them; if they do this, it will be well; if not, at all events, the said Diego, or such person as may succeed him in this trust, to collect together all the money he can, and accompany the king our lord, should he go to the conquest of Jerusalem, or else go there himself with all the force he can command; and in pursuing this intention, it will please the Lord to assist toward the accomplishment of the plan; and should he not be able to effect the conquest of the whole, no doubt he will achieve it in part. Let him therefore collect and make a fund of all his wealth in St. George of Genoa, and let it multiply there till such time as it may appear to him that something of consequence may be effected as respects the project on Jerusalem; for I believe that when their highnesses shall see that this is contemplated, they will wish to realize it themselves, or will afford him, as their servant and vassal, the means of doing it for them.

Item: I charge my son Diego and my descendants, especially whoever may inherit this estate, which consists, as aforesaid, of the tenth of whatsoever may be had or found in the Indies, and the eighth part of the lands and rents, all which, together with my rights and emoluments as admiral, viceroy, and governor, amount to more than twenty-five per cent; I say that I require of him to employ all this revenue, as well as his person and all the means in his power, in well and faithfully serving and supporting their highnesses, or their successors, even to the loss of life and property; since it was their highnesses, next to God, who first gave me the means of getting and achieving this property, although, it is true, I came over to these realms to invite them to the enterprise, and that a long time elapsed before any provision was made for carrying it into execution; which, however, is not surprising, as this was an undertaking of which all the world was ignorant, and no one had any faith in it; wherefore I am by so much the more indebted to them, as well as because they have since also much favored and promoted me.

Item: I also require of Diego, or whomsoever may be in possession of the estate, that in the case of any schism taking place in the Church of God, or that any person of whatever class or condition should attempt to despoil it of its property and honors, they hasten to offer at the feet of his holiness, that is, if they are not heretics (which God forbid!), their persons, power, and wealth, for the purpose of suppressing such schism, and preventing any spoliation of the honor and property of the church.

Item: I command the said Diego, or whoever may possess the said estate, to labor and strive for the honor, welfare, and aggrandizement of the city of Genoa, and to make use of all his power and means in defending and enhancing the good and credit of that republic, in all things not contrary to the service of the church of God, or the high dignity of our king and queen, our lords, and their successors.

Item: The said Diego, or whoever may possess or succeed to the estate, out of the fourth part of the whole revenue, from which, as aforesaid, is to be taken the tenth, when Don Bartholomew or his heirs shall have saved the two millions, or part of them, and when the time shall come of making a distribution among our relations, shall apply and invest the said tenth in providing marriages for such daughters of our lineage as may require it, and in doing all the good in their power.

Item: When a suitable time shall arrive, he shall order a church to be built in the island of Hispaniola, and in the most convenient spot, to be called Santa Maria de la Concepcion; to which is to be annexed a hospital, upon the best possible plan, like those of Italy and Castile, and a chapel erected to say mass in for the good of my soul, and those of my ancestors and successors with great devotion, since no doubt it will please the Lord to give us a sufficient revenue for this and the aforementioned purposes.

Item: I also order Diego my son, or whomsoever may inherit after him, to spare no pains in having and maintaining in the island of Hispaniola, four good professors of theology, to the end and aim of their studying and laboring to convert to our holy faith the inhabitants of the Indies; and in proportion as, by God's will, the revenue of the estate shall increase, in the same degree shall the number of teachers and devout increase, who are to strive to make Christians of the natives; in attaining which no expense should be thought too great. And in commemoration of all that I hereby ordain, and of the foregoing, a monument of marble shall be erected in the said church of La Concepcion, in the most conspicuous place, to serve as a record of what I here enjoin on the said Diego, as well as to other persons who may look upon it; which marble shall contain an inscription to the same effect.

Item: I also require of Diego my son, and whomsoever may succeed him in the estate, that every time, and as often as he confesses, he first show this obligation, or a copy of it, to the confessor, praying him to read it through, that he may be enabled to inquire respecting its fulfillment; from which will redound great good and happiness to his soul.

S.

S. A. S.

X. M. Y.

EL ALMIRANTE.

No. XXXVII

SIGNATURE OF COLUMBUS

As everything respecting Columbus is full of interest, his signature has been a matter of some discussion. It partook of the pedantic and bigoted character of the age, and perhaps of the peculiar character of the man, who, considering himself mysteriously elected and set apart from among men for certain great purposes, adopted a correspondent formality and solemnity in all his concerns. His signature was as follows:

S.

S. A. S.

X. M. Y.

XPO FERENS.

The first half of the signature, XPO (for CHRISTO), is in Greek letters; the second, FERENS, is in Latin. Such was the usage of those days; and even at present both Greek and Roman letters are used in signatures and inscriptions in Spain.

The ciphers or initials above the signature are supposed to represent a pious ejaculation. To read them one must begin with the lower letters, and connect them with those above. Signor Gio. Batista Spotorno conjectures them to mean either Xristus (Christus) Sancta Maria Yosephus, or, Salve me, Xristus, Maria, Yosephus. The "North American Review," for April, 1827, suggests the substitution of Jesus for Josephus, but the suggestion of Spotorno is most probably correct, as a common Spanish ejaculation is "Jesus Maria y José."

It was an ancient usage in Spain, and it has not entirely gone by, to accompany the signature with some words of religious purport. One object of this practice was to show the writer to be a Christian. This was of some importance in a country in which Jews and Mohammedans were proscribed and persecuted.

Don Fernando, son to Columbus, says that his father, when he took his pen in hand, usually commenced by writing "Jesus cum Maria sit nobis in via"; and the book which the admiral prepared and sent to the sovereigns, containing the prophecies which he considered as referring to his discoveries, and to the rescue of the holy sepulcher, begins with the same words. This practice is akin to that of placing the initials of pious words above his signature, and gives great probability to the mode in which they have been deciphered.

END OF "LIFE AND VOYAGES OF COLUMBUS"

A TOUR ON THE PRAIRIES

INTRODUCTION

HAVING, since my return to the United States, made a
wide and varied tour, for the gratification of my curiosity,
it has been supposed that I did it for the purpose of writing
a book; and it has more than once been intimated in the
papers that such a work was actually in the press containing
scenes and sketches of the Far West.

These announcements, gratuitously made for me, before
I had put pen to paper, or even contemplated anything of the
kind, have embarrassed me exceedingly. I have been like
a poor actor, who finds himself announced for a part he had
no thought of playing, and his appearance expected on the
stage before he has committed a line to memory.

I have always had a repugnance, amounting almost to
disability, to write in the face of expectation; and, in the
present instance, I was expected to write about a region fruitful of wonders and adventures, and which had already been
made the theme of spirit-stirring narratives from able pens;
yet about which I had nothing wonderful or adventurous to
offer.

Since such, however, seems to be the desire of the public,
and that they take sufficient interest in my wanderings to
deem them worthy of recital, I have hastened, as promptly
as possible, to meet, in some degree, the expectation which
others have excited. For this purpose I have, as it were,
plucked a few leaves out of my memorandum book, containing a month's foray beyond the outposts of human habitation, into the wilderness of the Far West. It forms, indeed,

(369)

but a small portion of an extensive tour; but it is an episode
complete as far as it goes. As such, I offer it to the public,
with great diffidence. It is a simple narrative of every day
occurrences; such as happen to every one who travels the
prairies. I have no wonders to describe, nor any moving
accidents by flood or field to narrate; and as to those who
look for a marvelous or adventurous story at my hands, I
can only reply, in the words of the weary knife-grinder:
"Story! God bless you, I have none to tell, sir."

CHAPTER ONE

THE PAWNEE HUNTING GROUNDS—TRAVELING COMPANIONS —A COMMISSIONER—A VIRTUOSO—A SEEKER OF ADVENTURES—A GIL BLAS OF THE FRONTIER—A YOUNG MAN'S ANTICIPATIONS OF PLEASURE

IN the often vaunted regions of the Far West, several
hundred miles beyond the Mississippi, extends a vast tract
of uninhabited country, where there is neither to be seen the
log house of the white man nor the wigwam of the Indian.
It consists of great grassy plains, interspersed with forests
and groves, and clumps of trees, and watered by the Arkansas, the grand Canadian, the Red River, and their tributary streams. Over these fertile and verdant wastes still
roam the elk, the buffalo, and the wild horse, in all their
native freedom. These, in fact, are the hunting grounds of
the various tribes of the Far West. Hither repair the Osage,
the Creek, the Delaware and other tribes that have linked
themselves with civilization, and live within the vicinity of
the white settlements. Here resort, also, the Pawnees, the
Comanches, and other fierce, and as yet independent tribes,
the nomads of the prairies, or the inhabitants of the skirts of
the Rocky Mountains. The regions I have mentioned form
a debatable ground of these warring and vindictive tribes;

none of them presume to erect a permanent habitation within
its borders. Their hunters and "Braves" repair thither in
numerous bodies during the season of game, throw up their
transient hunting camps, consisting of light bowers covered
with bark and skins, commit sad havoc among the innumerable herds that graze the prairies, and having loaded themselves with venison and buffalo meat, warily retire from the
dangerous neighborhood. These expeditions partake, always,
of a warlike character; the hunters are all armed for action,
offensive and defensive, and are bound to incessant vigilance.
Should they, in their excursions, meet the hunters of an adverse tribe, savage conflicts take place. Their encampments,
too, are always subject to be surprised by wandering war
parties, and their hunters, when scattered in pursuit of game,
to be captured or massacred by lurking foes. Mouldering
skulls and skeletons, bleaching in some dark ravine, or near
the traces of a hunting camp, occasionally mark the scene of
a foregone act of blood, and let the wanderer know the dangerous nature of the region he is traversing. It is the purport of the following pages to narrate a month's excursion to
these noted hunting grounds, through a tract of country which
had not as yet been explored by white men.

It was early in October, 1832, that I arrived at Fort Gibson, a frontier post of the Far West, situated on the Neosho,
or Grand River, near its confluence with the Arkansas. I
had been traveling for a month past, with a small party from
St. Louis, up the banks of the Missouri, and along the frontier line of agencies and missions that extends from the Missouri to the Arkansas. Our party was headed by one of the
Commissioners appointed by the government of the United
States to superintend the settlement of the Indian tribes migrating from the east to the west of the Mississippi. In the
discharge of his duties, he was thus visiting the various outposts of civilization.

And here let me bear testimony to the merits of this worthy
leader of our little band. He was a native of one of the
towns of Connecticut, a man in whom a course of legal prac-

tice and political life had not been able to vitiate an innate
simplicity and benevolence of heart. The greater part of his
days had been passed in the bosom of his family and the
society of deacons, elders, and selectmen, on the peaceful
banks of the Connecticut; when suddenly he had been called
to mount his steed, shoulder his rifle, and mingle among
stark hunters, backwoodsmen, and naked savages, on the
trackless wilds of the Far West.

Another of my fellow-travelers was Mr. L., an English-
man by birth, but descended from a foreign stock; and who
had all the buoyancy and accommodating spirit of a native
of the Continent. Having rambled over many countries, he
had become, to a certain degree, a citizen of the world, easily
adapting himself to any change. He was a man of a thousand occupations; a botanist, a geologist, a hunter of beetles
and butterflies, a musical amateur, a sketcher of no mean
pretensions, in short, a complete virtuoso; added to which,
he was a very indefatigable, if not always a very successful,
sportsman. Never had a man more irons in the fire, and,
consequently, never was man more busy nor more cheerful.

My third fellow-traveler was one who had accompanied
the former from Europe, and traveled with him as his Tele-
machus; being apt, like his prototype, to give occasional perplexity and disquiet to his Mentor. He was a young Swiss
count, scarce twenty-one years of age, full of talent and
spirit, but galliard in the extreme, and prone to every kind
of wild adventure.

Having made this mention of my comrades, I must not
pass over unnoticed a personage of inferior rank, but of all-
pervading and prevalent importance: the squire, the groom,
the cook, the tent man, in a word, the factotum, and, I may
add, the universal meddler and marplot of our party. This
was a little swarthy, meager, French creole named Antoine,
but familiarly dubbed Tonish: a kind of Gil Blas of the frontier, who had passed a scrambling life, sometimes among
white men, sometimes among Indians; sometimes in the employ of traders, missionaries, and Indian agents; sometimes

mingling with the Osage hunters. We picked him up at St. Louis, near which he had a small farm, an Indian wife, and a brood of half-blood children. According to his own account, however, he had a wife in every tribe; in fact, if all this little vagabond said of himself were to believed, he was without morals, without caste, without creed, without country, and even without language; for he spoke a jargon of mingled French, English, and Osage. He was, withal, a notorious braggart, and a liar of the first water. It was amusing to hear him vapor and gasconade about his terrible exploits and hairbreadth escapes in war and hunting. In the midst of his volubility, he was prone to be seized by a spasmodic gasping, as if the springs of his jaws were suddenly unhinged; but I am apt to think it was caused by some falsehood that stuck in his throat, for I generally remarked that immediately afterward there bolted forth a lie of the first magnitude.

Our route had been a pleasant one, quartering ourselves, occasionally, at the widely separated establishments of the Indian missionaries, but in general camping out in the fine groves that border the streams, and sleeping under cover of a tent. During the latter part of our tour we had pressed forward, in hopes of arriving in time at Fort Gibson to accompany the Osage hunters on their autumnal visit to the buffalo prairies. Indeed the imagination of the young count had become completely excited on the subject. The grand scenery and wild habits of the prairies had set his spirits madding, and the stories that little Tonish told him of Indian braves and Indian beauties, of hunting buffaloes and catching wild horses, had set him all agog for a dash into savage life. He was a bold and hard rider, and longed to be scouring the hunting grounds. It was amusing to hear his youthful anticipations of all that he was to see, and do, and enjoy, when mingling among the Indians and participating in their hardy adventures; and it was still more amusing to listen to the gasconadings of little Tonish, who volunteered to be his faithful squire in all his perilous undertakings; to teach him how to catch the wild horse, bring down the buffalo, and win the smiles of Indian princesses—"And if we can only get sight of a prairie on fire!" said the young count—"By Gar, I'll set one on fire myself!" cried the little Frenchman.

CHAPTER TWO

ANTICIPATIONS DISAPPOINTED—NEW PLANS—PREPARATIONS TO JOIN AN EXPLORING PARTY—DEPARTURE FROM FORT GIBSON—FORDING OF THE VERDIGRIS—AN INDIAN CAVA-LIER

THE anticipations of a young man are prone to meet with disappointment. Unfortunately for the count's scheme of wild campaigning, before we reached the end of our journey, we heard that the Osage hunters had set forth upon their expedition to the buffalo grounds. The count still determined, if possible, to follow on their track and overtake them, and for this purpose stopped short at the Osage Agency, a few miles distant from Fort Gibson, to make inquiries and preparations. His traveling companion, Mr. L., stopped with him; while the commissioner and myself proceeded to Fort Gibson, followed by the faithful and veracious Tonish. I hinted to him his promises to follow the count in his campaignings, but I found the little varlet had a keen eye to self-interest. He was aware that the commissioner, from his official duties, would remain for a long time in the country, and be likely to give him permanent employment, while the sojourn of the count would be but transient. The gasconading of the little braggart was suddenly therefore at an end. He spake not another word to the young count about Indians, buffaloes, and wild horses, but putting himself tacitly in the train of the commissioner, jogged silently after us to the garrison.

On arriving at the fort, however, a new chance presented

itself for a cruise on the prairies. We learned that a company of mounted rangers, or riflemen, had departed but three days previous to make a wide exploring tour from the Arkansas to the Red River, including a part of the Pawnee hunting grounds where no party of white men had as yet penetrated. Here, then, was an opportunity of ranging over those dangerous and interesting regions under the safeguard of a powerful escort; for the commissioner, in virtue of his office, could claim the service of this newly raised corps of riflemen, and the country they were to explore was destined for the settlement of some of the migrating tribes connected with his mission.

Our plan was promptly formed and put into execution. A couple of Creek Indians were sent off express, by the commander of Fort Gibson, to overtake the rangers and bring them to a halt until the commissioner and his party should be able to join them. As we should have a march of three or four days through a wild country before we could overtake the company of rangers, an escort of fourteen mounted riflemen, under the command of a lieutenant, was assigned us.

We sent word to the young count and Mr. L. at the Osage Agency of our new plan and prospects, and invited them to accompany us. The count, however, could not forego the delights he had promised himself in mingling with absolutely savage life. In reply, he agreed to keep with us until we should come upon the trail of the Osage hunters, when it was his fixed resolve to strike off into the wilderness in pursuit of them; and his faithful Mentor, though he grieved at the madness of the scheme, was too stanch a friend to desert him. A general rendezvous of our party and escort was appointed, for the following morning, at the Agency.

We now made all arrangements for prompt departure. Our baggage had hitherto been transported on a light wagon, but we were now to break our way through an untraveled country, cut up by rivers, ravines, and thickets, where a vehicle of the kind would be a complete impediment. We were to travel on horseback, in hunter's style, and with as little encumbrance as possible. Our baggage, therefore, underwent a rigid and most abstemious reduction. A pair of saddle-bags, and those by no means crammed, sufficed for each man's scanty wardrobe, and, with his greatcoat, were to be carried upon the steed he rode. The rest of the baggage was placed on pack-horses. Each one had a bear-skin and a couple of blankets for bedding, and there was a tent to shelter us in case of sickness or bad weather. We took care to provide ourselves with flour, coffee, and sugar, together with a small supply of salt pork for emergencies; for our main subsistence we were to depend upon the chase.

Such of our horses as had not been tired out in our recent journey were taken with us as pack-horses, or supernumeraries; but as we were going on a long and rough tour, where there would be occasional hunting, and where, in case of meeting with hostile savages, the safety of the rider might depend upon the goodness of his steed, we took care to be well mounted. I procured a stout silver-gray; somewhat rough, but stanch and powerful; and retained a hardy pony which I had hitherto ridden, and which, being somewhat jaded, was suffered to ramble along with the pack-horses, to be mounted only in case of emergency.

All these arrangements being made, we left Fort Gibson, on the morning of the tenth of October, and crossing the river in the front of it, set off for the rendezvous at the Agency. A ride of a few miles brought us to the ford of the Verdigris, a wild rocky scene overhung with forest trees. We descended to the bank of the river and crossed in straggling file, the horses stepping cautiously from rock to rock, and in a manner feeling about for a foothold beneath the rushing and brawling stream.

Our little Frenchman, Tonish, brought up the rear with the pack-horses. He was in high glee, having experienced a kind of promotion. In our journey hitherto he had driven the wagon, which he seemed to consider a very inferior employ; now he was master of the horse.

He sat perched like a monkey behind the pack on one of

the horses; he sang, he shouted, he yelped like an Indian, and ever and anon blasphemed the loitering pack-horses in his jargon of mingled French, English and Osage, which not one of them could understand.

As we were crossing the ford we saw on the opposite shore a Creek Indian on horseback. He had paused to reconnoiter us from the brow of a rock, and formed a picturesque object, in unison with the wild scenery around him. He wore a bright blue hunting-shirt trimmed with scarlet fringe; a gayly colored handkerchief was bound round his head something like a turban, with one end hanging down beside his ear; he held a long rifle in his hand, and looked like a wild Arab on the prowl. Our loquacious and ever-meddling little Frenchman called out to him in his Babylonish jargon, but the savage, having satisfied his curiosity, tossed his hand in the air, turned the head of his steed, and galloping along the shore soon disappeared among the trees.

CHAPTER THREE

AN INDIAN AGENCY—RIFLEMEN—OSAGES, CREEKS, TRAP-
PERS, DOGS, HORSES, HALF-BREEDS—BEATTE,
THE HUNTSMAN

HAVING crossed the ford, we soon reached the Osage Agency, where Colonel Choteau has his offices and magazines, for the dispatch of Indian affairs, and the distribution of presents and supplies. It consisted of a few log houses on the banks of the river, and presented a motley frontier scene. Here was our escort awaiting our arrival; some were on horseback, some on foot, some seated on the trunks of fallen trees, some shooting at a mark. They were a heterogeneous crew; some in frock-coats made of green blankets; others in leathern hunting-shirts, but the most part in marvelously ill-cut garments, much the worse for wear, and evidently put on for rugged service.

Near by these was a group of Osages: stately fellows;
stern and simple in garb and aspect. They wore no ornaments; their dress consisted merely of blankets, leggings,
and moccasins. Their heads were bare; their hair was
cropped close, excepting a bristling ridge on the top, like
the crest of a helmet, with a long scalp lock hanging behind.
They had fine Roman countenances, and broad deep chests;
and, as they generally wore their blankets wrapped round
their loins, so as to leave the bust and arms bare, they looked
like so many noble bronze figures. The Osages are the finest
looking Indians I have ever seen in the West. They have
not yielded sufficiently, as yet, to the influence of civilization
to lay by their simple Indian garb, or to lose the habits of
the hunter and the warrior; and their poverty prevents their
indulging in much luxury of apparel.

In contrast to these was a gayly dressed party of Creeks.
There is something, at the first glance, quite Oriental in the
appearance of this tribe. They dress in calico hunting shirts,
of various brilliant colors, decorated with bright fringes, and
belted with broad girdles, embroidered with beads: they have
leggings of dressed deer skins, or of green or scarlet cloth,
with embroidered knee-bands and tassels: their moccasins
are fancifully wrought and ornamented, and they wear gaudy
handkerchiefs tastefully bound round their heads.

Besides these, there was a sprinkling of trappers, hunters,
half-breeds, creoles, negroes of every hue; and all that other
rabble rout of nondescript beings that keep about the frontiers, between civilized and savage life, as those equivocal
birds, the bats, hover about the confines of light and darkness.

The little hamlet of the Agency was in a complete bustle;
the blacksmith's shed, in particular, was a scene of preparation; a strapping negro was shoeing a horse; two half-breeds
were fabricating iron spoons in which to melt lead for bullets. An old trapper, in leathern hunting frock and moccasins, had placed his rifle against a work-bench, while he
superintended the operation, and gossiped about his hunting

exploits; several large dogs were lounging in and out of the shop, or sleeping in the sunshine, while a little cur, with head cocked on one side, and one ear erect, was watching, with that curiosity common to little dogs, the process of shoeing the horse, as if studying the art, or waiting for his turn to be shod.

We found the count and his companion, the virtuoso, ready for the march. As they intended to overtake the Osages, and pass some time in hunting the buffalo and the wild horse, they had provided themselves accordingly; having, in addition to the steeds which they used for traveling, others of prime quality, which were to be led when on the march, and only to be mounted for the chase.

They had, moreover, engaged the services of a young man named Antoine, a half-breed of French and Osage origin. He was to be a kind of Jack-of-all-work; to cook, to hunt, and to take care of the horses; but he had a vehement propensity to do nothing, being one of the worthless brood engendered and brought up among the missions. He was, moreover, a little spoiled by being really a handsome young fellow, an Adonis of the frontier, and still worse by fancying himself highly connected, his sister being concubine to an opulent white trader!

For our own parts, the commissioner and myself were desirous, before setting out, to procure another attendant well versed in woodcraft, who might serve us as a hunter; for our little Frenchman would have his hands full when in camp, in cooking, and on the march, in taking care of the pack-horses. Such a one presented himself, or rather was recommended to us, in Pierre Beatte, a half-breed of French and Osage parentage. We were assured that he was acquainted with all parts of the country, having traversed it in all directions, both in hunting and war parties; that he would be of use both as guide and interpreter, and that he was a first-rate hunter.

I confess I did not like his looks when he was first presented to me. He was lounging about, in an old hunting frock and metasses or leggings, of deer skin, soiled and greased, and almost japanned by constant use. He was apparently about thirty-six years of age, square and strongly built. His features were not bad, being shaped not unlike those of Napoleon, but sharpened up, with high Indian cheek bones. Perhaps the dusky greenish hue of his complexion aided his resemblance to an old bronze bust I had seen of the Emperor. He had, however, a sullen, saturnine expression, set off by a slouched woolen hat, and elf locks that hung about his ears.

Such was the appearance of the man, and his manners were equally unprepossessing He was cold and laconic; made no promises or professions; stated the terms he required for the services of himself and his horse, which we thought rather high, but showed no disposition to abate them, nor any anxiety to secure our employ. He had altogether more of the red than the white man in his composition; and, as I had been taught to look upon all half-breeds with distrust, as an uncertain and faithless race, I would gladly have dispensed with the services of Pierre Beatte. We had no time, however, to look out for any one more to our taste, and had to make an arrangement with him on the spot. He then set about making his preparations for the journey, promising to join us at our evening's encampment.

One thing was yet wanting to fit me out for the prairies —a thoroughly trustworthy steed: I was not yet mounted to my mind. The gray I had bought, though strong and serviceable, was rough. At the last moment I succeeded in getting an excellent animal; a dark bay; powerful, active, generous-spirited, and in capital condition. I mounted him with exultation, and transferred the silver gray to Tonish, who was in such ecstasies at finding himself so completely en Cavalier that I feared he might realize the ancient and well-known proverb of "a beggar on horseback."

CHAPTER FOUR

THE DEPARTURE

THE long-drawn notes of a bugle at length gave the signal for departure. The rangers filed off in a straggling line of march through the woods: we were soon on horseback and following on, but were detained by the irregularity of the pack-horses. They were unaccustomed to keep the line, and straggled from side to side among the thickets, in spite of all the pesting and bedeviling of Tonish; who, mounted on his gallant gray, with a long rifle on his shoulder, worried after them, bestowing a superabundance of dry blows and curses.

We soon, therefore, lost sight of our escort, but managed to keep on their track, thridding lofty forests and entangled thickets, and passing by Indian wigwams and negro huts, until toward dusk we arrived at a frontier farmhouse, owned by a settler of the name of Berryhill. It was situated on a hill, below which the rangers had encamped in a circular grove, on the margin of a stream. The master of the house received us civilly, but could offer us no accommodation, for sickness prevailed in his family. He appeared himself to be in no very thriving condition, for though bulky in frame he had a sallow, unhealthy complexion, and a whiffling double voice, shifting abruptly from a treble to a thorough-bass.

Finding his log house was a mere hospital, crowded with invalids, we ordered our tent to be pitched in the farmyard.

We had not been long encamped when our recently engaged attendant, Beatte, the Osage half-breed, made his appearance. He came mounted on one horse and leading another, which seemed to be well packed with supplies for the expedition. Beatte was evidently an "old soldier," as to the art of taking care of himself and looking out for emergencies. Finding that he was in government employ, being engaged by the commissioner, he had drawn rations of flour and bacon, and put them up so as to be weather-proof. In addition to the horse for the road, and for ordinary service, which was a rough, hardy animal, he had another for hunting. This was of a mixed breed like himself, being a cross of the domestic stock with the wild horse of the prairies; and a noble steed it was, of generous spirit, fine action, and admirable bottom. He had taken care to have his horses well shod at the Agency. He came prepared at all points for war or hunting: his rifle on his shoulder, his powder-horn and bullet-pouch at his side, his hunting-knife stuck in his belt, and coils of cordage at his saddle bow, which we were told were lariats, or noosed cords, used in catching the wild horse.

Thus equipped and provided, an Indian hunter on a prairie is like a cruiser on the ocean, perfectly independent of the world, and competent to self-protection and self-maintenance. He can cast himself loose from every one, shape his own course, and take care of his own fortunes. I thought Beatte seemed to feel his independence, and to consider himself superior to us all, now that we were launching into the wilderness. He maintained a half proud, half sullen look, and great taciturnity, and his first care was to unpack his horses and put them in safe quarters for the night. His whole demeanor was in perfect contrast to our vaporing, chattering, bustling little Frenchman. The latter, too, seemed jealous of this new-comer. He whispered to us that these half-breeds were a touchy, capricious people, little to be depended upon. That Beatte had evidently come prepared to take care of himself, and that, at any moment in the course of our tour, he would be liable to take some sudden disgust or affront, and abandon us at a moment's warning; having the means of shifting for himself, and being perfectly at home on the prairies.

CHAPTER FIVE

FRONTIER SCENES—A LYCURGUS OF THE BORDER—LYNCH'S
LAW—THE DANGER OF FINDING A HORSE—THE
YOUNG OSAGE

ON the following morning (October 11), we were on the march by half-past seven o'clock, and rode through deep rich bottoms of alluvial soil, overgrown with redundant vegetation, and trees of an enormous size. Our route lay parallel to the west bank of the Arkansas, on the borders of which river, near the confluence of the Red Fork, we expected to overtake the main body of rangers. For some miles the country was sprinkled with Creek villages and farmhouses; the inhabitants of which appeared to have adopted, with considerable facility, the rudiments of civilization, and to have thriven in consequence. Their farms were well stocked, and their houses had a look of comfort and abundance.

We met with numbers of them returning from one of their grand games of ball, for which their nation is celebrated. Some were on foot, some on horseback; the latter, occasionally, with gayly dressed females behind them. They are a well-made race, muscular and closely knit, with well-turned thighs and legs. They have a gypsy fondness for brilliant colors and gay decorations, and are bright and fanciful objects when seen at a distance on the prairies. One had a scarlet handkerchief bound round his head, surmounted with a tuft of black feathers like a cocktail. Another had a white handkerchief, with red feathers; while a third, for want of a plume, had stuck in his turban a brilliant bunch of sumach.

On the verge of the wilderness we paused to inquire our

way at a log house, owned by a white settler or squatter, a tall raw-boned old fellow, with red hair, a lank lantern visage, and an inveterate habit of winking with one eye, as if everything he said was of knowing import. He was in a towering passion. One of his horses was missing; he was sure it had been stolen in the night by a straggling party of Osages encamped in a neighboring swamp; but he would have satisfaction! He would make an example of the villains. He had accordingly caught down his rifle from the wall, that invariable enforcer of right or wrong upon the frontiers, and, having saddled his steed, was about to sally forth on a foray into the swamp; while a brother squatter, with rifle in hand, stood ready to accompany him.

We endeavored to calm the old campaigner of the prairies, by suggesting that his horse might have strayed into the neighboring woods; but he had the frontier propensity to charge everything to the Indians, and nothing could dissuade him from carrying fire and sword into the swamp.

After riding a few miles further we lost the trail of the main body of rangers, and became perplexed by a variety of tracks made by the Indians and settlers. At length coming to a log house, inhabited by a white man, the very last on the frontier, we found that we had wandered from our true course. Taking us back for some distance, he again brought us to the right trail; putting ourselves upon which, we took our final departure, and launched into the broad wilderness.

The trail kept on like a straggling footpath, over hill and dale, through brush and brake, and tangled thicket, and open prairie. In traversing the wilds it is customary for a party either of horse or foot to follow each other in single file like the Indians; so that the leaders break the way for those who follow, and lessen their labor and fatigue. In this way, also, the number of a party is concealed, the whole leaving but one narrow well-trampled track to mark their course.

We had not long regained the trail, when, on emerging from a forest, we beheld our raw-boned, hard-winking, hard-

riding knight-errant of the frontier, descending the slope of
a hill, followed by his companion in arms. As he drew
near to us, the gauntness of his figure and ruefulness of his
aspect reminded me of the description of the hero of La
Mancha, and he was equally bent on affairs of doughty
enterprise, being about to penetrate the thickets of the perilous swamp, within which the enemy lay ensconced.

While we were holding a parley with him on the slope of
the hill, we descried an Osage on horseback issuing out of
a skirt of wood about half a mile off, and leading a horse by
a halter. The latter was immediately recognized by our
hard-winking friend as the steed of which he was in quest.
As the Osage drew near, I was struck with his appearance.
He was about nineteen or twenty years of age, but well
grown, with the fine Roman countenance common to his
tribe, and as he rode with his blanket wrapped round his
loins, his naked bust would have furnished a model for a
statuary. He was mounted on a beautiful piebald horse, a
mottled white and brown, of the wild breed of the prairies,
decorated with a broad collar, from which hung in front a
tuft of horse-hair dyed of a bright scarlet.

The youth rode slowly up to us with a frank open air,
and signified, by means of our interpreter Beatte, that the
horse he was leading had wandered to their camp, and he
was now on his way to conduct him back to his owner.

I had expected to witness an expression of gratitude on
the part of our hard-favored cavalier, but to my surprise the
old fellow broke out into a furious passion. He declared
that the Indians had carried off his horse in the night, with
the intention of bringing him home in the morning, and
claiming a reward for finding him; a common practice, as
he affirmed, among the Indians. He was, therefore, for
tying the young Indian to a tree and giving him a sound
lashing; and was quite surprised at the burst of indignation
which this novel mode of requiting a service drew from us.
Such, however, is too often the administration of law on the
frontier, "Lynch's law," as it is technically termed, in which

the plaintiff is apt to be witness, jury, judge, and execu-
tioner, and the defendant to be convicted and punished on
mere presumption; and in this way, I am convinced, are
occasioned many of those heart-burnings and resentments
among the Indians, which lead to retaliation, and end in
Indian wars. When I compared the open, noble countenance
and frank demeanor of the young Osage with the sinister
visage and high-handed conduct of the frontiersman, I felt
little doubt on whose back a lash would be most meritoriously
bestowed.

Being thus obliged to content himself with the recovery
of his horse, without the pleasure of flogging the finder into
the bargain, the old Lycurgus, or rather Draco, of the frontier, set off growling on his return homeward, followed by
his brother squatter.

As for the youthful Osage, we were all prepossessed in
his favor; the young count especially, with the sympathies
proper to his age and incident to his character, had taken
quite a fancy to him. Nothing would suit but he must have
the young Osage as a companion and squire in his expedition
into the wilderness. The youth was easily tempted, and,
with the prospect of a safe range over the buffalo prairies
and the promise of a new blanket, he turned his bridle, left
the swamp and the encampment of his friends behind him,
and set off to follow the count in his wanderings in quest of
the Osage hunters.

Such is the glorious independence of man in a savage
state. This youth, with his rifle, his blanket, and his horse,
was ready at a moment's warning to rove the world; he carried all his worldly effects with him, and in the absence of
artificial wants possessed the great secret of personal freedom. We of society are slaves, not so much to others as to
ourselves; our superfluities are the chains that bind us, im-
peding every movement of our bodies and thwarting every
impulse of our souls. Such, at least, were my speculations
at the time, though I am not sure but that they took their
tone from the enthusiasm of the young count, who seemed

more enchanted than ever with the wild chivalry of the prairies, and talked of putting on the Indian dress and adopting the Indian habits during the time he hoped to pass with the Osages.

CHAPTER SIX

TRAIL OF THE OSAGE HUNTERS—DEPARTURE OF THE COUNT AND HIS PARTY—A DESERTED WAR CAMP—A VAGRANT DOG—THE ENCAMPMENT

In the course of the morning the trail we were pursuing was crossed by another, which struck off through the forest to the west in a direct course for the Arkansas River. Beatte, our half-breed, after considering it for a moment, pronounced it the trail of the Osage hunters; and that it must lead to the place where they had forded the river on their way to the hunting grounds.

Here then the young count and his companion came to a halt and prepared to take leave of us. The most experienced frontiersmen in the troop remonstrated on the hazard of the undertaking. They were about to throw themselves loose in the wilderness, with no other guides, guards, or attendants than a young ignorant half-breed and a still younger Indian. They were embarrassed by a pack-horse and two led horses, with which they would have to make their way through matted forests, and across rivers and morasses. The Osages and Pawnees were at war, and they might fall in with some warrior party of the latter, who are ferocious foes; besides, their small number, and their valuable horses, would form a great temptation to some of the straggling bands of Osages loitering about the frontier, who might rob them of their horses in the night, and leave them destitute and on foot in the midst of the prairies.

Nothing, however, could restrain the romantic ardor of the count for a campaign of buffalo hunting with the Osages,

and he had a game spirit that seemed always stimulated by
the idea of danger. His traveling companion, of discreeter
age and calmer temperament, was convinced of the rashness
of the enterprise; but he could not control the impetuous
zeal of his youthful friend, and he was too loyal to leave him
to pursue his hazardous scheme alone. To our great regret,
therefore, we saw them abandon the protection of our escort,
and strike off on their haphazard expedition. The old hunters of our party shook their heads, and our half-breed, Beatte,
predicted all kinds of trouble to them; my only hope was
that they would soon meet with perplexities enough to cool
the impetuosity of the young count and induce him to rejoin
us. With this idea we traveled slowly, and made a considerable halt at noon. After resuming our march, we came
in sight of the Arkansas. It presented a broad and rapid
stream, bordered by a beach of fine sand, overgrown with
willows and cotton-wood trees. Beyond the river, the eye
wandered over a beautiful champaign country, of flowery
plains and sloping uplands, diversified by groves and clumps
of trees, and long screens of woodland; the whole wearing
the aspect of complete and even ornamental cultivation, instead of native wildness. Not far from the river, on an open
eminence, we passed through the recently deserted camping
place of an Osage war party. The frames of the tents or
wigwams remained, consisting of poles bent into an arch,
with each end stuck into the ground; these are interwined
with twigs and branches, and covered with bark and skins.
Those experienced in Indian lore can ascertain the tribe, and
whether on a hunting or a warlike expedition, by the shape
and disposition of the wigwams. Beatte pointed out to us,
in the present skeleton camp, the wigwam in which the
chiefs had held their consultations around the council-fire;
and an open area, well trampled down, on which the grand
war-dance had been performed.

Pursuing our journey, as we were passing through a
forest we were met by a forlorn, half-famished dog, who
came rambling along the trail, with inflamed eyes and be-

wildered look. Though nearly trampled upon by the foremost rangers, he took notice of no one, but rambled heedlessly among the horses. The cry of "mad dog" was immediately raised, and one of the rangers leveled his rifle, but was stayed by the ever-ready humanity of the commissioner. "He is blind!" said he. "It is the dog of some poor Indian, following his master by the scent. It would be a shame to kill so faithful an animal." The ranger shouldered his rifle, the dog blundered blindly through the cavalcade unhurt, and, keeping his nose to the ground, continued his course along the trail, affording a rare instance of a dog surviving a bad name.

About three o'clock we came to a recent camping-place of the company of rangers: the brands of one of their fires were still smoking; so that, according to the opinion of Beatte, they could not have passed on above a day previously. As there was a fine stream of water close by, and plenty of pea-vines for the horses, we encamped here for the night.

We had not been here long when we heard a halloo from a distance, and beheld the young count and his party advancing through the forest. We welcomed them to the camp with heartfelt satisfaction; for their departure upon so hazardous an expedition had caused us great uneasiness. A short experiment had convinced them of the toil and difficulty of inexperienced travelers like themselves making their way through the wilderness with such a train of horses and such slender attendance. Fortunately, they determined to rejoin us before nightfall; one night's camping out might have cost them their horses. The count had prevailed upon his protege and esquire, the young Osage, to continue with him, and still calculated upon achieving great exploits, with his assistance, on the buffalo prairies.

CHAPTER SEVEN

NEWS OF THE RANGERS—THE COUNT AND HIS INDIAN SQUIRE
—HALT IN THE WOODS—WOODLAND SCENE—OSAGE VIL-
LAGE—OSAGE VISITORS AT OUR EVENING CAMP

IN the morning early (October 12th), the two Creeks who
had been sent express by the commander of Fort Gibson, to
stop the company of rangers, arrived at our encampment on
their return.   They had left the company encamped about
fifty miles distant, in a fine place on the Arkansas, abounding in game, where they intended to await our arrival.   This
news spread animation throughout our party, and we set out
on our march at sunrise with renewed spirit.

In mounting our steeds, the young Osage attempted to
throw a blanket upon his wild horse.   The fine, sensible
animal took fright, reared and recoiled.   The attitudes of
the wild horse and the almost naked savage would have
formed studies for a painter or a statuary.

I often pleased myself in the course of our march with
noticing the appearance of the young count and his newly
enlisted follower, as they rode before me.   Never was preux
chevalier better suited with an esquire.   The count was well
mounted, and, as I have before observed, was a bold and
graceful rider.   He was fond, too, of caracoling his horse,
and dashing about in the buoyancy of youthful spirits.   His
dress was a gay Indian hunting frock of dressed deer skin,
setting well to the shape, dyed of a beautiful purple, and
fancifully embroidered with silks of various colors; as if it
had been the work of some Indian beauty, to decorate a
favorite chief.   With this he wore leathern pantaloons and
moccasins, a foraging cap, and a double-barreled gun slung
by a bandoleer athwart his back: so that he was quite a

picturesque figure as he managed gracefully his spirited steed.

The young Osage would ride close behind him on his wild and beautifully mottled horse, which was decorated with crimson tufts of hair. He rode with his finely shaped head and bust naked; his blanket being girt round his waist. He carried his rifle in one hand, and managed his horse with the other, and seemed ready to dash off at a moment's warning, with his youthful leader, on any madcap foray or scamper. The count, with the sanguine anticipations of youth, promised himself many hardy adventures and exploits in company with his youthful "brave," when we should get among the buffaloes, in the Pawnee hunting grounds.

After riding some distance, we crossed a narrow, deep stream, upon a solid bridge, the remains of an old beaver dam; the industrious community which had constructed it had all been destroyed. Above us, a streaming flight of wild geese, high in the air, and making a vociferous noise, gave note of the waning year.

About half-past ten o'clock we made a halt in a forest, where there was abundance of the pea-vine. Here we turned the horses loose to graze. A fire was made, water procured from an adjacent spring, and in a short time our little Frenchman, Tonish, had a pot of coffee prepared for our refreshment. While partaking of it, we were joined by an old Osage, one of a small hunting party who had recently passed this way. He was in search of his horse, which had wandered away or been stolen. Our half-breed, Beatte, made a wry face on hearing of Osage hunters in this direction. "Until we pass those hunters," said he, "we shall see no buffaloes. They frighten away everything, like a prairie on fire."

The morning repast being over, the party amused themselves in various ways. Some shot with their rifles at a mark, others lay asleep half buried in the deep bed of foliage, with their heads resting on their saddles; others gossiped round the fire at the foot of a tree, which sent up wreaths of blue smoke among the branches. The horses banqueted luxuriously on the pea-vines, and some lay down and rolled among them.

We were overshadowed by lofty trees, with straight, smooth trunks, like stately columns; and as the glancing rays of the sun shone through the transparent leaves, tinted with the many-colored hues of autumn, I was reminded of the effect of sunshine among the stained windows and clustering columns of a Gothic cathedral. Indeed there is a grandeur and solemnity in our spacious forests of the West that awaken in me the same feeling I have experienced in those vast and venerable piles, and the sound of the wind sweeping through them supplies occasionally the deep breathings of the organ.

About noon the bugle sounded to horse, and we were again on the march, hoping to arrive at the encampment of the rangers before night; as the old Osage had assured us it was not above ten or twelve miles distant. In our course through a forest we passed by a lonely pool, covered with the most magnificent water-lilies I had ever beheld; among which swam several wood-ducks, one of the most beautiful of water-fowl, remarkable for the gracefulness and brilliancy of its plumage.

After proceeding some distance further, we came down upon the banks of the Arkansas, at a place where tracks of numerous horses, all entering the water, showed where a party of Osage hunters had recently crossed the river on their way to the buffalo range. After letting our horses drink in the river, we continued along its bank for a space, and then across prairies, where we saw a distant smoke, which we hoped might proceed from the encampment of the rangers. Following what we supposed to be their trail, we came to a meadow in which were a number of horses grazing: they were not, however, the horses of the troop. A little further on, we reached a straggling Osage village, on the banks of the Arkansas. Our arrival created quite a sensation. A number of old men came forward and shook hands with us all severally; while the women and children huddled together in groups, staring at us wildly, chattering and laughing among themselves. We found that all the young men of the village had departed on a hunting expedition, leaving the women and children and old men behind. Here the commissioner made a speech from on horseback; informing his hearers of the purport of his mission, to promote a general peace among the tribes of the West, and urging them to lay aside all warlike and bloodthirsty notions, and not to make any wanton attacks upon the Pawnees. This speech being interpreted by Beatte, seemed to have a most pacifying effect upon the multitude, who promised faithfully that, as far as in them lay, the peace should not be disturbed; and indeed their age and sex gave some reason to trust that they would keep their word.

Still hoping to reach the camp of the rangers before nightfall, we pushed on until twilight, when we were obliged to halt on the borders of a ravine. The rangers bivouacked under trees, at the bottom of the dell, while we pitched our tent on a rocky knoll near a running stream. The night came on dark and overcast, with flying clouds, and much appearance of rain. The fires of the rangers burned brightly in the dell, and threw strong masses of light upon the robber-looking groups that were cooking, eating, and drinking around them. To add to the wildness of the scene, several Osage Indians, visitors from the village we had passed, were mingled among the men. Three of them came and seated themselves by our fire. They watched everything that was going on around them in silence, and looked like figures of monumental bronze. We gave them food, and, what they most relished, coffee; for the Indians partake in the universal fondness for this beverage, which pervades the West. When they had made their supper, they stretched themselves, side by side, before the fire, and began a low nasal chant, drumming with their hands upon their breasts, by way of accompaniment. Their chant seemed to consist of regular staves, every one terminating, not in a melodious cadence, but in the abrupt interjection huh! uttered almost like a hiccup. This chant, we were told by our interpreter, Beatte, related to ourselves, our appearance, our treatment of them, and all that they knew of our plans. In one part they spoke of the young count, whose animated character and eagerness for Indian enterprise had struck their fancy, and they indulged in some waggery about him and the young Indian beauties, that produced great merriment among our half-breeds.

This mode of improvising is common throughout the savage tribes; and in this way, with a few simple inflections of the voice, they chant all their exploits in war and hunting, and occasionally indulge in a vein of comic humor and dry satire, to which the Indians appear to me much more prone than is generally imagined.

In fact, the Indians that I have had an opportunity of seeing in real life are quite different from those described in poetry. They are by no means the stoics that they are represented; taciturn, unbending, without a tear or a smile. Taciturn they are, it is true, when in company with white men, whose good-will they distrust, and whose language they do not understand; but the white man is equally taciturn under like circumstances. When the Indians are among themselves, however, there cannot be greater gossips. Half their time is taken up in talking over their adventures in war and hunting, and in telling whimsical stories. They are great mimics and buffoons, also, and entertain themselves excessively at the expense of the whites with whom they have associated, and who have supposed them impressed with profound respect for their grandeur and dignity. They are curious observers, noting everything in silence, but with a keen and watchful eye; occasionally exchanging a glance or a grunt with each other, when anything particularly strikes them: but reserving all comments until they are alone. Then it is that they give full scope to criticism, satire, mimicry, and mirth.

In the course of my journey along the frontier, I have had repeated opportunities of noticing their excitability and boisterous merriment at their games; and have occasionally noticed a group of Osages sitting round a fire until a late hour of the night, engaged in the most animated and lively conversation; and at times making the woods resound with peals of laughter. As to tears, they have them in abundance, both real and affected; at times they make a merit of them. No one weeps more bitterly or profusely at the death of a relative or friend; and they have stated times when they repair to howl and lament at their graves. I have heard doleful wailings at daybreak, in the neighboring Indian villages, made by some of the inhabitants, who go out at that hour into the fields, to mourn and weep for the dead: at such times, I am told, the tears will stream down their cheeks in torrents.

As far as I can judge, the Indian of poetical fiction is like the shepherd of pastoral romance, a mere personification of imaginary attributes.

The nasal chant of our Osage guests gradually died away; they covered their heads with their blankets and fell fast asleep, and in a little while all was silent, excepting the pattering of scattered rain drops upon our tent.

In the morning our Indian visitors breakfasted with us, but the young Osage who was to act as esquire to the count in his knight-errantry on the prairies was nowhere to be found. His wild horse, too, was missing, and, after many conjectures, we came to the conclusion that he had taken "Indian leave" of us in the night. We afterward ascertained that he had been persuaded so to do by the Osages we had recently met with; who had represented to him the perils that would attend him in an expedition to the Pawnee hunting grounds, where he might fall into the hands of the implacable enemies of his tribe; and, what was scarcely less to be apprehended, the annoyances to which he would be subjected from the capricious and overbearing conduct of the white men; who, as I have witnessed in my own short experience, are prone to treat the poor Indians as little better than brute animals. Indeed, he had had a specimen of it himself in the narrow escape he made from the infliction of "Lynch's law," by the hard-winking worthy of the frontier, for the flagitious crime of finding a stray horse.

The disappearance of the youth was generally regretted by our party, for we had all taken a great fancy to him from his handsome, frank, and manly appearance, and the easy grace of his deportment. He was indeed a native-born gentleman. By none, however, was he so much lamented as by the young count, who thus suddenly found himself deprived of his esquire. I regretted the departure of the Osage for his own sake, for we should have cherished him throughout the expedition, and I am convinced, from the munificent spirit of his patron, he would have returned to his tribe laden with wealth of beads and trinkets and Indian blankets.

CHAPTER EIGHT

THE HONEY CAMP

THE weather, which had been rainy in the night, having held up, we resumed our march at seven o'clock in the morning, in confident hope of soon arriving at the encampment of the rangers. We had not ridden above three or four miles when we came to a large tree which had recently been felled by an ax, for the wild honey contained in the hollow of its trunk, several broken flakes of which still remained. We now felt sure that the camp could not be far distant. About a couple of miles further some of the rangers set up a shout, and pointed to a number of horses grazing in a woody bottom. A few paces brought us to the brow of an elevated ridge, whence we looked down upon the encampment. It was a wild bandit, or Robin Hood, scene. In a beautiful open forest, traversed by a running stream, were booths of bark and branches, and tents of blankets, temporary shelters from the recent rain, for the rangers commonly bivouac in the open air. There were groups of rangers in every kind of uncouth garb. Some were cooking at large fires made at the feet of trees; some were stretching and dressing deer skins; some were shooting at a mark, and some lying about on the grass. Venison jerked, and hung on frames, was drying over the embers in one place; in another lay carcasses recently brought in by the hunters. Stacks of rifles were leaning against the trunks of the trees, and saddles, bridles, and powder-horns hanging above them, while the horses were grazing here and there among the thickets.

Our arrival was greeted with acclamation. The rangers crowded about their comrades to inquire the news from the fort; for our own part, we were received in frank simple hunter's style by Captain Bean, the commander of the company; a man about forty years of age, vigorous and active. His life had been chiefly passed on the frontier, occasionally in Indian warfare, so that he was a thorough woodsman, and a first-rate hunter. He was equipped in character; in leathern hunting shirt and leggings, and a leathern foraging cap.

While we were conversing with the captain, a veteran huntsman approached, whose whole appearance struck me. He was of the middle size, but tough and weather-proved; a head partly bald and garnished with loose iron-gray locks, and a fine black eye, beaming with youthful spirit. His dress was similar to that of the captain, a rifle shirt and leggings of dressed deer skin, that had evidently seen service; a powder-horn was slung by his side, a hunting-knife stuck in his belt, and in his hand was an ancient and trusty rifle, doubtless as dear to him as a bosom friend. He asked permission to go hunting, which was readily granted. "That's old Ryan," said the captain, when he had gone; "there's not a better hunter in the camp; he's sure to bring in game."

In a little while our pack-horses were unloaded and turned loose to revel among the pea-vines. Our tent was pitched; our fire made; the half of a deer had been sent to us from the captain's lodge; Beatte brought in a couple of wild turkeys; the spits were laden, and the camp kettle crammed with meat; and to crown our luxuries, a basin filled with great flakes of delicious honey, the spoils of a plundered bee-tree, was given us by one of the rangers.

Our little Frenchman, Tonish, was in an ecstasy, and tucking up his sleeves to the elbows, set to work to make a display of his culinary skill, on which he prided himself almost as much as upon his hunting, his riding, and his warlike prowess.

CHAPTER NINE

A BEE HUNT

THE beautiful forest in which we were encamped abounded in bee-trees; that is to say, trees in the decayed trunks of which wild bees had established their hives. It is surprising in what countless swarms the bees have overspread the Far West, within but a moderate number of years. The Indians consider them the harbinger of the white man, as the buffalo is of the red man; and say that, in proportion as the bee advances, the Indian and buffalo retire. We are always accustomed to associate the hum of the bee-hive with the farmhouse and flower-garden, and to consider those industrious little animals as connected with the busy haunts of man, and I am told that the wild bee is seldom to be met with at any great distance from the frontier. They have been the heralds of civilization, steadfastly preceding it as it advanced from the Atlantic borders, and some of the ancient settlers of the West pretend to give the very year when the honey-bee first crossed the Mississippi. The Indians with surprise found the mouldering trees of their forests suddenly teeming with ambrosial sweets, and nothing, I am told, can exceed the greedy relish with which they banquet for the first time upon this unbought luxury of the wilderness.

At present the honey-bee swarms in myriads, in the noble groves and forests which skirt and intersect the prairies, and extend along the alluvial bottoms of the rivers. It seems to me as if these beautiful regions answer literally to the description of the land of promise, "a land flowing with milk and honey"; for the rich pasturage of the prairies is calculated to sustain herds of cattle as countless as the sands upon the seashore, while the flowers with which they are enameled render them a very paradise for the nectar-seeking bee.

We had not been long in the camp when a party set out in quest of a bee-tree; and, being curious to witness the sport, I gladly accepted an invitation to accompany them. The party was headed by a veteran bee-hunter, a tall lank fellow in homespun garb that hung loosely about his limbs, and a straw hat shaped not unlike a bee-hive; a comrade, equally uncouth in garb, and without a hat, straddled along at his heels, with a long rifle on his shoulder. To these succeeded half a dozen others, some with axes and some with rifles, for no one stirs far from the camp without his firearms, so as to be ready either for wild deer or wild Indian.

After proceeding some distance we came to an open glade on the skirts of the forest. Here our leader halted, and then advanced quietly to a low bush, on the top of which I perceived a piece of honey-comb. This I found was the bait or lure for the wild bees. Several were humming about it, and diving into its cells. When they had laden themselves with honey they would rise into the air, and dart off in a straight line, almost with the velocity of a bullet. The hunters watched attentively the course they took, and then set off in the same direction, stumbling along over twisted roots and fallen trees, with their eyes turned up to the sky. In this way they traced the honey-laden bees to their hive, in the hollow trunk of a blasted oak, where, after buzzing about for a moment, they entered a hole about sixty feet from the ground.

Two of the bee-hunters now plied their axes vigorously at the foot of the tree to level it with the ground. The mere spectators and amateurs, in the meantime, drew off to a cautious distance, to be out of the way of the falling of the tree and the vengeance of its inmates. The jarring blows of the ax seemed to have no effect in alarming or disturbing this most industrious community. They continued to ply at their usual occupations, some arriving full freighted into port, others sallying forth on new expeditions, like so many merchantmen in a money-making metropolis, little suspicious of impending bankruptcy and downfall. Even a loud crack which announced the disrupture of the trunk failed to divert their attention from the intense pursuit of gain; at length down came the tree with a tremendous crash, bursting open from end to end, and displaying all the hoarded treasures of the commonwealth.

One of the hunters immediately ran up with a wisp of lighted hay as a defense against the bees. The latter, however, made no attack and sought no revenge; they seemed stupefied by the catastrophe and unsuspicious of its cause, and remained crawling and buzzing about the ruins without offering us any molestation. Every one of the party now fell to, with spoon and hunting-knife, to scoop out the flakes of honeycomb with which the hollow trunk was stored. Some of them were of old date and a deep brown color, others were beautifully white, and the honey in their cells was almost limpid. Such of the combs as were entire were placed in camp kettles to be conveyed to the encampment; those which had been shivered in the fall were devoured upon the spot. Every stark bee-hunter was to be seen with a rich morsel in his hand, dripping about his fingers, and disappearing as rapidly as a cream tart before the holiday appetite of a schoolboy.

Nor was it the bee-hunters alone that profited by the downfall of this industrious community; as if the bees would carry through the similitude of their habits with those of laborious and gainful man, I beheld numbers from rival hives, arriving on eager wing, to enrich themselves with the ruins of their neighbors. These busied themselves as eagerly and cheerfully as so many wreckers on an Indiaman that has been driven on shore; plunging into the cells of the broken honeycombs, banqueting greedily on the spoil, and then wing-ing their way full-freighted to their homes. As to the poor proprietors of the ruin, they seemed to have no heart to do anything, not even to taste the nectar that flowed around them; but crawled backward and forward, in vacant desolation, as I have seen a poor fellow with his hands in his pockets, whistling vacantly and despondingly about the ruins of his house that had been burned.

It is difficult to describe the bewilderment and confusion of the bees of the bankrupt hive who had been absent at the time of the catastrophe, and who arrived from time to time, with full cargoes from abroad. At first they wheeled about in the air, in the place where the fallen tree had once reared its head, astonished at finding it all a vacuum. At length, as if comprehending their disaster, they settled down in clusters on a dry branch of a neighboring tree, whence they seemed to contemplate the prostrate ruin, and to buzz forth doleful lamentations over the downfall of their republic. It was a scene on which the "melancholy Jacques" might have moralized by the hour.

We now abandoned the place, leaving much honey in the hollow of the tree. "It will all be cleared off by varmint," said one of the rangers. "What vermin?" asked I. "Oh, bears, and skunks, and raccoons, and 'possums. The bears is the knowingest varmint for finding out a bee tree in the world. They'll gnaw for days together at the trunk till they make a hole big enough to get in their paws, and then they'll haul out honey, bees and all."

CHAPTER TEN

AMUSEMENTS IN THE CAMP — CONSULTATIONS — HUNTERS'
FARE AND FEASTING—EVENING SCENES—CAMP MELODY
—THE FATE OF AN AMATEUR OWL

On returning to the camp, we found it a scene of the greatest hilarity. Some of the rangers were shooting at a mark.

others were leaping, wrestling, and playing at prison bars. They were mostly young men, on their first expedition, in high health and vigor, and buoyant with anticipations; and I can conceive nothing more likely to set the youthful blood into flow than a wild wood life of the kind, and the range of a magnificent wilderness, abounding with game and fruitful of adventure. We send our youth abroad to grow luxurious and effeminate in Europe; it appears to me that a previous tour on the prairies would be more likely to produce that manliness, simplicity, and self-dependence most in unison with our political institutions.

While the young men were engaged in these boisterous amusements, a graver set, composed of the captain, the doctor, and other sages and leaders of the camp, were seated or stretched out on the grass, round a frontier map, holding a consultation about our position and the course we were to pursue.

Our plan was to cross the Arkansas just above where the Red Fork falls into it, then to keep westerly, until we should pass through a grand belt of open forest, called the Cross Timber, which ranges nearly north and south from the Arkansas to Red River; after which we were to keep a southerly course toward the latter river.

Our half-breed, Beatte, being an experienced Osage hunter, was called into the consultation. "Have you ever hunted in this direction?" said the captain.

"Yes," was the laconic reply.

"Perhaps, then, you can tell us in which direction lies the Red Fork?"

"If you keep along yonder, by the edge of the prairie, you will come to a bald hill, with a pile of stones upon it."

"I have noticed that hill as I was hunting," said the captain.

"Well! those stones were set up by the Osages as a landmark: from that spot you may have a sight of the Red Fork."

"In that case," cried the captain, "we shall reach the Red Fork to-morrow; then cross the Arkansas above it, into the

Pawnee country, and then in two days we shall crack buffalo bones!"

The idea of arriving at the adventurous hunting grounds of the Pawnees, and of coming upon the traces of the buffaloes, made very eye sparkle with animation. Our further conversation was interrupted by the sharp report of a rifle at no great distance from the camp.

"That's old Ryan's rifle," exclaimed the captain; "there's a buck down, I'll warrant!" Nor was he mistaken; for, before long, the veteran made his appearance, calling upon one of the younger rangers to return with him, and aid in bringing home the carcass.

The surrounding country, in fact, abounded with game, so that the camp was overstocked with provisions, and, as no less than twenty bee-trees had been cut down in the vicinity, every one reveled in luxury. With the wasteful prodigality of hunters, there was a continual feasting, and scarce any one put by provision for the morrow. The cooking was conducted in hunter's style: the meat was stuck upon tapering spits of dogwood, which were thrust perpendicularly into the ground, so as to sustain the joint before the fire, where it was roasted or broiled with all its juices retained in it in a manner that would have tickled the palate of the most experienced gourmand. As much could not be said in favor of the bread. It was little more than a paste made of flour and water, and fried like fritters, in lard; though some adopted a ruder style, twisting it round the ends of sticks, and thus roasting it before the fire. In either way, I have found it extremely palatable on the prairies. No one knows the true relish of food until he has a hunter's appetite.

Before sunset, we were summoned by little Tonish to a sumptuous repast. Blankets had been spread on the ground near to the fire, upon which we took our seats. A large dish, or bowl, made from the root of a maple tree, and which we had purchased at the Indian village, was placed on the ground before us, and into it were emptied the contents of one of the camp kettles, consisting of a wild turkey hashed, together with slices of bacon and lumps of dough. Beside it was placed another bowl of similar ware, containing an ample supply of fritters. After we had discussed the hash, two wooden spits, on which the ribs of a fat buck were broiling before the fire, were removed and planted in the ground before us, with a triumphant air, by little Tonish. Having no dishes, we had to proceed in hunter's style, cutting off strips and slices with our hunting-knives, and dipping them in salt and pepper. To do justice to Tonish's cookery, however, and to the keen sauce of the prairies, never have I tasted venison so delicious. With all this, our beverage was coffee, boiled in a camp kettle, sweetened with brown sugar, and drunk out of tin cups: and such was the style of our banqueting throughout this expedition, whenever provisions were plenty, and as long as flour and coffee and sugar held out.

As the twilight thickened into night, the sentinels were marched forth to their stations around the camp; an indispensable precaution in a country infested by Indians. The encampment now presented a picturesque appearance. Camp fires were blazing and smoldering here and there among the trees, with groups of rangers round them; some seated or lying on the ground, others standing in the ruddy glare of the flames, or in shadowy relief. At some of the fires there was much boisterous mirth, where peals of laughter were mingled with loud ribald jokes and uncouth exclamations; for the troop was evidently a raw, undisciplined band, levied among the wild youngsters of the frontier, who had enlisted, some for the sake of roving adventure, and some for the purpose of getting a knowledge of the country. Many of them were the neighbors of their officers, and accustomed to regard them with the familiarity of equals and companions. None of them had any idea of the restraint and decorum of a camp, or ambition to acquire a name for exactness in a profession in which they had no intention of continuing.

While this boisterous merriment prevailed at some of the fires, there suddenly rose a strain of nasal melody from another, at which a choir of "vocalists" were uniting their voices in a most lugubrious psalm tune. This was led by one of the lieutenants; a tall, spare man, who we were informed had officiated as schoolmaster, singing-master, and occasionally as Methodist preacher, in one of the villages of the frontier. The chant rose solemnly and sadly in the night air, and reminded me of the description of similar canticles in the camps of the Covenanters; and, indeed, the strange medley of figures and faces and uncouth garbs, congregated together in our troop, would not have disgraced the banners of Praise-God Barebones.

In one of the intervals of this nasal psalmody, an amateur owl, as if in competition, began his dreary hooting. Immediately there was a cry throughout the camp of "Charley's owl! Charley's owl!" It seems this "obscure bird" had visited the camp every night, and had been fired at by one of the sentinels, a half-witted lad named Charley; who, on being called up for firing when on duty, excused himself by saying that he understood owls made uncommonly good soup.

One of the young rangers mimicked the cry of this bird of wisdom, who, with a simplicity little consonant with his character, came hovering within sight, and alighted on the naked branch of a tree, lighted up by the blaze of our fire. The young count immediately seized his fowling-piece, took fatal aim, and in a twinkling the poor bird of ill-omen came fluttering to the ground. Charley was now called upon to make and eat his dish of owl-soup, but declined, as he had not shot the bird.

In the course of the evening, I paid a visit to the captain's fire. It was composed of huge trunks of trees, and of sufficient magnitude to roast a buffalo whole. Here were a number of the prime hunters and leaders of the camp, some sitting, some standing, and others lying on skins or blankets before the fire, telling old frontier stories about hunting and Indian warfare.

As the night advanced, we perceived above the trees to the west a ruddy glow flushing up the sky.

"That must be a prairie set on fire by the Osage hunters," said the captain.

"It is at the Red Fork," said Beatte, regarding the sky. "It seems but three miles distant, yet it perhaps is twenty."

About half-past eight o'clock, a beautiful pale light gradually sprang up in the east, a precursor of the rising moon. Drawing off from the captain's lodge, I now prepared for the night's repose. I had determined to abandon the shelter of the tent, and henceforth to bivouac like the rangers. A bear-skin spread at the foot of a tree was my bed, with a pair of saddle-bags for a pillow. Wrapping myself in blankets, I stretched myself on this hunter's couch, and soon fell into a sound and sweet sleep, from which I did not awake until the bugle sounded at daybreak.

CHAPTER ELEVEN

BREAKING UP OF THE ENCAMPMENT—PICTURESQUE MARCH —GAME—CAMP SCENES—TRIUMPH OF A YOUNG HUNTER —ILL SUCCESS OF AN OLD HUNTER—FOUL MURDER OF A POLECAT

OCTOBER 14TH.—At the signal-note of the bugle the sentinels and patrols marched in from their stations around the camp and were dismissed. The rangers were roused from their night's repose, and soon a bustling scene took place. While some cut wood, made fires, and prepared the morning's meal, others struck their foul-weather shelters of blankets, and made every preparation for departure; while others dashed about, through brush and brake, catching the horses and leading or driving them into camp.

During all this bustle the forest rang with whoops and shouts, and peals of laughter; when all had breakfasted, packed up their effects and camp equipage, and loaded the pack-horses, the bugle sounded to saddle and mount. By eight o'clock the whole troop set off in a long straggling line, with whoop and halloo, intermingled with many an oath at the loitering pack-horses, and in a little while the forest, which for several days had been the scene of such unwonted bustle and uproar, relapsed into its primeval solitude and silence.

It was a bright sunny morning, with a pure transparent atmosphere that seemed to bathe the very heart with gladness. Our march continued parallel to the Arkansas, through a rich and varied country; sometimes we had to break our way through alluvial bottoms matted with redundant vegetation, where the gigantic trees were entangled with grapevines, hanging like cordage from their branches; sometimes we coasted along sluggish brooks, whose feebly trickling current just served to link together a succession of glassy pools, imbedded like mirrors in the quiet bosom of the forest, reflecting its autumnal foliage and patches of the clear blue sky. Sometimes we scrambled up broken and rocky hills, from the summits of which we had wide views stretching on one side over distant prairies diversified by groves and forests, and on the other ranging along a line of blue and shadowy hills beyond the waters of the Arkansas.

The appearance of our troop was suited to the country; stretching along in a line of upward of half a mile in length, winding among brakes and bushes, and up and down in the defiles of the hills, the men in every kind of uncouth garb, with long rifles on their shoulders, and mounted on horses of every color. The pack-horses, too, would incessantly wander from the line of march, to crop the surrounding herbage, and were banged and beaten back by Tonish and his half-breed compeers, with volleys of mongrel oaths. Every now and then the notes of the bugle, from the head of the column, would echo through the woodlands and along the hollow glens, summoning up stragglers, and announcing the line of march. The whole scene reminded me of the description given of bands of buccaneers penetrating the wilds of South America, on their plundering expeditions against the Spanish settlements.

At one time we passed through a luxuriant bottom or meadow bordered by thickets, where the tall grass was pressed down into numerous "deer beds," where those animals had couched the preceding night. Some oak trees also bore signs of having been clambered by bears, in quest of acorns, the marks of their claws being visible in the bark.

As we opened a glade of this sheltered meadow we beheld several deer bounding away in wild affright, until, having gained some distance, they would stop and gaze back, with the curiosity common to this animal, at the strange intruders into their solitudes. There was immediately a sharp report of rifles in every direction, from the young huntsmen of the troop, but they were too eager to aim surely, and the deer, unharmed, bounded away into the depths of the forest.

In the course of our march we struck the Arkansas, but found ourselves still below the Red Fork, and, as the river made deep bends, we again left its banks and continued through the woods until nearly eight o'clock, when we encamped in a beautiful basin bordered by a fine stream, and shaded by clumps of lofty oaks.

The horses were now hobbled, that is to say, their forelegs were fettered with cords or leathern straps, so as to impede their movements and prevent their wandering from the camp. They were then turned loose to graze. A number of rangers, prime hunters, started off in different directions in search of game. There was no whooping nor laughing about the camp as in the morning; all were either busy about the fires preparing the evening's repast or reposing upon the grass. Shots were soon heard in various directions. After a time a huntsman rode into the camp with the carcass of a fine buck hanging across his horse. Shortly afterward came in a couple of stripling hunters on foot, one of whom bore on his shoulders the body of a doe. He was evidently proud of his spoil, being probably one of his first achievements, though he and his companion were much bantered by their comrades, as young beginners who hunted in partnership.

Just as the night set in, there was a great shouting at one

end of the camp, and immediately afterward a body of young rangers came parading round the various fires, bearing one of their comrades in triumph on their shoulders. He had shot an elk for the first time in his life, and it was the first animal of the kind that had been killed on this expedition. The young huntsman, whose name was M'Lellan, was the hero of the camp for the night, and was the "father of the feast" into the bargain; for portions of his elk were seen roasting at every fire.

The other hunters returned without success. The captain had observed the tracks of a buffalo, which must have passed within a few days, and had tracked a bear for some distance until the footprints had disappeared. He had seen an elk, too, on the banks of the Arkansas, which walked out on a sand-bar of the river, but before he could steal round through the bushes to get a shot it had re-entered the woods.

Our own hunter, Beatte, returned silent and sulky, from an unsuccessful hunt. As yet he had brought us in nothing, and we had depended for our supplies of venison upon the captain's mess. Beatte was evidently mortified, for he looked down with contempt upon the rangers, as raw and inexperienced woodsmen, but little skilled in hunting; they, on the other hand, regarded Beatte with no very complacent eye, as one of an evil breed, and always spoke of him as "the Indian."

Our little Frenchman, Tonish, also, by his incessant boasting, and chattering, and gasconading, in his balderdashed dialect, had drawn upon himself the ridicule of many of the wags of the troop, who amused themselves at his expense in a kind of raillery by no means remarkable for its delicacy; but the little varlet was so completely fortified by vanity and self-conceit that he was invulnerable to every joke. I must confess, however, that I felt a little mortified at the sorry figure our retainers were making among these moss-troopers of the frontier. Even our very equipments came in for a share of unpopularity, and I heard many sneers at the double-barreled guns with which we were provided against smaller

* * * 18—VOL. VII.

game; the lads of the West holding "shotguns," as they call
them, in great contempt, thinking grouse, partridges, and
even wild turkeys as beneath their serious attention, and the
rifle the only firearm worthy of a hunter.

I was awakened before daybreak the next morning by
the mournful howling of a wolf, who was skulking about the
purlieus of the camp, attracted by the scent of venison.
Scarcely had the first gray streak of dawn appeared, when
a youngster at one of the distant lodges, shaking off his sleep,
crowed in imitation of a cock, with a loud clear note and prolonged cadence that would have done credit to the most veteran chanticleer. He was immediately answered from another quarter, as if from a rival rooster. The chant was
echoed from lodge to lodge, and followed by the cackling of
hens, quacking of ducks, gabbling of turkeys, and grunting
of swine, until we seemed to have been transported into the
midst of a farmyard, with all its inmates in full concert
around us.

After riding a short distance this morning, we came upon
a well-worn Indian track, and following it, scrambled to the
summit of a hill, whence we had a wide prospect over a country diversified by rocky ridges and waving lines of upland,
and enriched by groves and clumps of trees of varied tuft
and foliage. At a distance to the west, to our great satisfaction, we beheld the Red Fork rolling its ruddy current to the
Arkansas, and found that we were above the point of junction. We now descended and pushed forward, with much
difficulty, through the rich alluvial bottom that borders the
Arkansas. Here the trees were interwoven with grapevines,
forming a kind of cordage, from trunk to trunk and limb to
limb; there was a thick undergrowth, also, of bush and bram-
ble, and such an abundance of hops, fit for gathering, that it
was difficult for our horses to force their way through.

The soil was imprinted in many places with the tracks of
deer, and the claws of bears were to be traced on various
trees. Every one was on the lookout in the hope of starting
some game, when suddenly there was a bustle and a clamor

in a distant part of the line. A bear! a bear! was the cry. We all pressed forward to be present at the sport, when to my infinite, though whimsical chagrin, I found it to be our two worthies, Beatte and Tonish, perpetrating a foul murder on a polecat or skunk! The animal had ensconced itself beneath the trunk of a fallen tree, whence it kept up a vigorous defense in its peculiar style, until the surrounding forest was in a high state of fragrance.

Gibes and jokes now broke out on all sides at the expense of the Indian hunter, and he was advised to wear the scalp of the skunk as the only trophy of his prowess. When they found, however, that he and Tonish were absolutely bent upon bearing off the carcass as a peculiar dainty, there was a universal expression of disgust; and they were regarded as little better than cannibals.

Mortified at this ignominious debut of our two hunters I insisted upon their abandoning their prize and resuming their march. Beatte complied with a dogged, discontented air, and lagged behind muttering to himself. Tonish, however, with his usual buoyancy, consoled himself by vociferous eulogies on the richness and delicacy of a roasted polecat, which he swore was considered the daintiest of dishes by all experienced Indian gourmands. It was with difficulty I could silence his loquacity by repeated and peremptory commands. A Frenchman's vivacity, however, if repressed in one way, will break out in another, and Tonish now eased off his spleen by bestowing volleys of oaths and dry blows on the packhorses. I was likely to be no gainer in the end by my opposition to the humors of these varlets, for after a time, Beatte, who had lagged behind, rode up to the head of the line to resume his station as a guide, and I had the vexation to see the carcass of his prize, stripped of its skin, and looking like a fat sucking-pig, dangling behind his saddle. I made a solemn vow, however, in secret, that our fire should not be disgraced by the cooking of that polecat.

CHAPTER TWELVE

THE CROSSING OF THE ARKANSAS

WE had now arrived at the river, about a quarter of a
mile above the junction of the Red Fork; but the banks were
steep and crumbling, and the current was deep and rapid.
It was impossible, therefore, to cross at this place; and we
resumed our painful course through the forest, dispatching
Beatte ahead in search of a fording place. We had proceeded about a mile further, when he rejoined us, bringing
intelligence of a place hard by, where the river, for a great
part of its breadth, was rendered fordable by sand-bars, and
the remainder might easily be swum by the horses.

Here, then, we made a halt. Some of the rangers set to
work vigorously with their axes, felling trees on the edge of
the river, wherewith to form rafts for the transportation of
their baggage and camp equipage.   Others patroled the banks
of the river further up, in hopes of finding a better fording
place; being unwilling to risk their horses in the deep channel.

It was now that our worthies, Beatte and Tonish, had an
opportunity of displaying their Indian adroitness and resource.
At the Osage village which we had passed a day or two before, they had procured a dry buffalo skin.   This was now
produced; cords were passed through a number of small eye-
let-holes with which it was bordered, and it was drawn up,
until it formed a kind of deep trough.   Sticks were then
placed athwart it on the inside, to keep it in shape; our camp
equipage and a part of our baggage were placed within, and
the singular bark was carried down the bank and set afloat.
A cord was attached to the prow, which Beatte took between
his teeth, and throwing himself into the water, went ahead,
towing the bark after him; while Tonish followed behind, to

keep it steady and to propel it. Part of the way they had foothold, and were enabled to wade, but in the main current they were obliged to swim. The whole way, they whooped and yelled in the Indian style, until they landed safely on the opposite shore.

The commissioner and myself were so well pleased with this Indian mode of ferriage that we determined to trust ourselves in the buffalo hide. Our companions, the count and Mr. L., had proceeded with the horses, along the river bank, in search of a ford which some of the rangers had discovered, about a mile and half distant. While we were waiting for the return of our ferryman, I happened to cast my eyes upon a heap of luggage under a bush, and descried the sleek carcass of the polecat, snugly trussed up, and ready for roasting before the evening fire. I could not resist the temptation to plump it into the river, when it sunk to the bottom like a lump of lead; and thus our lodge was relieved from the bad odor which this savory viand had threatened to bring upon it.

Our men having recrossed with their cockle-shell bark, it was drawn on shore, half filled with saddles, saddlebags, and other luggage, amounting to a hundred weight; and being again placed in the water, I was invited to take my seat. It appeared to me pretty much like the embarkation of the wise men of Gotham, who went to sea in a bowl: I stepped in, however, without hesitation, though as cautiously as possible, and sat down on the top of the luggage, the margin of the hide sinking to within a hand-breadth of the water's edge. Rifles, fowling-pieces, and other articles of small bulk, were then handed in, until I protested against receiving any more freight. We then launched forth upon the stream, the bark being towed as before.

It was with a sensation half serious, half comic, that I found myself thus afloat, on the skin of a buffalo, in the midst of a wild river, surrounded by wilderness, and towed along by a half savage, whooping and yelling like a devil incarnate. To please the vanity of little Tonish, I discharged the double-barreled gun, to the right and left, when in the center of the stream.   The report echoed along the woody shores, and was answered by shouts from some of the rangers, to the great exultation of the little Frenchman, who took to himself the whole glory of this Indian mode of navigation.

Our voyage was accomplished happily; the commissioner was ferried across with equal success, and all our effects were brought over in the same manner.   Nothing could equal the vainglorious vaporing of little Tonish, as he strutted about the shore, and exulted in his superior skill and knowledge to the rangers.   Beatte, however, kept his proud, saturnine look, without a smile.   He had a vast contempt for the ignorance of the rangers, and felt that he had been undervalued by them.   His only observation was, "Dey now see de Indian good for someting, anyhow!"

The broad, sandy shore where we had landed was intersected by innumerable tracks of elk, deer, bears, raccoons, turkeys, and water-fowl.   The river scenery at this place was beautifully diversified, presenting long, shining reaches, bordered by willows and cottonwood trees; rich bottoms, with lofty forests; among which towered enormous plane trees, and the distance was closed in by high embowered promontories.   The foliage had a yellow autumnal tint, which gave to the sunny landscape the golden tone of one of the landscapes of Claude Lorraine.   There was animation given to the scene by a raft of logs and branches, on which the captain and his prime companion, the doctor, were ferrying their effects across the stream; and by a long line of rangers on horseback, fording the river obliquely, along a series of sandbars, about a mile and a half distant.

CHAPTER THIRTEEN

THE CAMP OF THE GLEN

CAMP GOSSIP—PAWNEES AND THEIR HABITS—A HUNTER'S
ADVENTURE—HORSES FOUND, AND MEN LOST

BEING joined by the captain and some of the rangers, we
struck into the woods for about half a mile, and then entered
a wild, rocky dell, bordered by two lofty ridges of limestone,
which narrowed as we advanced, until they met and united;
making almost an angle. Here a fine spring of water rose
among the rocks, and fed a silver rill that ran the whole
length of the dell, freshening the grass with which it was
carpeted.

In this rocky nook we encamped, among tall trees. The
rangers gradually joined us, straggling through the forest
singly or in groups; some on horseback, some on foot, driving their horses before them, heavily laden with baggage,
some dripping wet, having fallen into the river; for they had
experienced much fatigue and trouble from the length of the
ford, and the depth and rapidity of the stream. They looked
not unlike banditti returning with their plunder, and the
wild dell was a retreat worthy to receive them. The effect
was heightened after dark, when the light of the fires was
cast upon rugged looking groups of men and horses; with
baggage tumbled in heaps, rifles piled against the trees, and
saddles, bridles, and powder-horns hanging about their trunks.

At the encampment we were joined by the young count
and his companion, and the young half-breed, Antoine, who
had all passed successfully by the ford. To my annoyance,
however, I discovered that both of my horses were missing.
I had supposed them in the charge of Antoine; but he, with
characteristic carelessness, had paid no heed to them, and

they had probably wandered from the line on the opposite side of the river. It was arranged that Beatte and Antoine should recross the river at an early hour of the morning in search of them.

A fat buck and a number of wild turkeys being brought into the camp, we managed, with the addition of a cup of coffee, to make a comfortable supper; after which I repaired to the captain's lodge, which was a kind of council fire and gossiping place for the veterans of the camp.

As we were conversing together, we observed, as on former nights, a dusky, red glow in the west, above the summits of the surrounding cliffs. It was again attributed to Indian fires on the prairies; and supposed to be on the western side of the Arkansas. If so, it was thought they must be made by some party of Pawnees, as the Osage hunters seldom ventured in that quarter. Our half-breeds, however, pronounced them Osage fires; and that they were on the opposite side of the Arkansas.

The conversation now turned upon the Pawnees, into whose hunting grounds we were about entering. There is always some wild untamed tribe of Indians who form, for a time, the terror of a frontier, and about whom all kinds of fearful stories are told. Such, at present, was the case with the Pawnees, who rove the regions between the Arkansas and the Red River, and the prairies of Texas. They were represented as admirable horsemen, and always on horseback; mounted on fleet and hardy steeds, the wild race of the prairies. With these they roam the great plains that extend about the Arkansas, the Red River, and through Texas, to the Rocky Mountains; sometimes engaged in hunting the deer and buffalo, sometimes in warlike and predatory expedi- tions; for, like their counterparts, the sons of Ishmael, their hand is against every one, and every one's hand against them. Some of them have no fixed habitation, but dwell in tents of skin, easily packed up and transported, so that they are here to-day, and away, no one knows where, to-morrow.

One of the veteran hunters gave several anecdotes of their

mode of fighting. Luckless, according to his account, is the band of weary traders or hunters descried by them, in the midst of a prairie. Sometimes they will steal upon them by stratagem, hanging with one leg over the saddle, and their bodies concealed; so that their troop at a distance has the appearance of a gang of wild horses. When they have thus gained sufficiently upon the enemy, they will suddenly raise themselves in their saddles, and come like a rushing blast, all fluttering with feathers, shaking their mantles, brandishing their weapons, and making hideous yells. In this way, they seek to strike a panic into the horses, and put them to the scamper, when they will pursue and carry them off in triumph.

The best mode of defense, according to this veteran woodsman, is to get into the covert of some wood or thicket; or if there be none at hand, to dismount, tie the horses firmly head to head in a circle, so that they cannot break away and scatter, and resort to the shelter of a ravine, or make a hollow in the sand, where they may be screened from the shafts of the Pawnees. The latter chiefly use the bow and arrow, and are dexterous archers; circling round and round their enemy, and lanching their arrows when at full speed. They are chiefly formidable on the prairies, where they have free career for their horses, and no trees to turn aside their arrows. They will rarely follow a flying enemy into the forest.

Several anecdotes, also, were given, of the secrecy and caution with which they will follow, and hang about the camp of an enemy, seeking a favorable moment for plunder or attack.

"We must now begin to keep a sharp lookout," said the captain. "I must issue written orders that no man shall hunt without leave, or fire off a gun, on pain of riding a wooden horse with a sharp back. I have a wild crew of young fellows, unaccustomed to frontier service. It will be difficult to teach them caution. We are now in the land of a silent, watchful, crafty people, who, when we least suspect it, may be around us, spying out all our movements, and ready to pounce upon all stragglers."

"How will you be able to keep your men from firing, if they see game while strolling round the camp?" asked one of the rangers.

"They must not take their guns with them unless they are on duty, or have permission."

"Ah, captain!" cried the ranger, "that will never do for me. Where I go, my rifle goes. I never like to leave it behind; it's like a part of myself. There's no one will take such care of it as I, and there's nothing will take such care of me as my rifle."

"There's truth in all that," said the captain, touched by a true hunter's sympathy. "I've had my rifle pretty nigh as long as I have had my wife, and a faithful friend it has been to me."

Here the doctor, who is as keen a hunter as the captain, joined in the conversation: "A neighbor of mine says, next to my rifle, I'd as leave lend you my wife."

"There's few," observed the captain, "that take care of their rifles as they ought to be taken care of."

"Or of their wives either," replied the doctor, with a wink.

"That's a fact," rejoined the captain.

Word was now brought that a party of four rangers, headed by "Old Ryan," were missing. They had separated from the main body, on the opposite side of the river, when searching for a ford, and had straggled off, nobody knew whither. Many conjectures were made about them, and some apprehensions expressed for their safety.

"I should send to look after them," said the captain, "but old Ryan is with them, and he knows how to take care of himself and of them too. If it were not for him I would not give much for the rest; but he is as much at home in the woods or on a prairie as he would be in his own farmyard. He's never lost, wherever he is. There's a good gang of them to stand by one another; four to watch and one to take care of the fire."

"It's a dismal thing to get lost at night in a strange and wild country," said one of the younger rangers.

"Not if you have one or two in company," said an older one. "For my part, I could feel as cheerful in this hollow as in my own home, if I had but one comrade to take turns to watch and keep the fire going. I could lie here for hours, and gaze up to that blazing star there, that seems to look down into the camp as if it were keeping guard over it."

"Ay, the stars are a kind of company to one, when you have to keep watch alone. That's a cheerful star, too, some-how; that's the evening star, the planet Venus they call it, I think."

"If that's the planet Venus," said one of the council, who, I believe, was the psalm-singing schoolmaster, "it bodes us no good; for I recollect reading in some book that the Paw-nees worship that star, and sacrifice their prisoners to it. So I should not feel the better for the sight of that star in this part of the country."

"Well," said the sergeant, a thoroughbred woodsman, "star or no star, I have passed many a night alone in a wilder place than this, and slept sound too, I'll warrant you. Once, however, I had rather an uneasy time of it. I was belated in passing through a tract of wood, near the Tombigbee River; so I struck a light, made a fire, and turned my horse loose, while I stretched myself to sleep. By-and-by, I heard the wolves howl. My horse came crowding near me for protec-tion, for he was terribly frightened. I drove him off, but he returned, and drew nearer and nearer, and stood looking at me and at the fire, and dozing, and nodding, and tottering on his forefeet, for he was powerful tired. After a while, I heard a strange dismal cry. I thought at first it might be an owl. I heard it again, and then I knew it was not an owl, but must be a panther. I felt rather awkward, for I had no weapon but a double-bladed penknife. I, however, prepared for defense in the best way I could, and piled up small brands from the fire, to pepper him with, should he come nigh. The company of my horse now seemed a com-fort to me; the poor creature laid down beside me and soon fell asleep, being so tired. I kept watch, and nodded and

dozed, and started awake, and looked round, expecting to
see the glaring eyes of the panther close upon me; but some-
how or other fatigue got the better of me and I fell asleep
outright. In the morning I found the tracks of a panther
within sixty paces. They were as large as my two fists.
He had evidently been walking backward and forward, trying to make up his mind to attack me; but luckily he had
not courage."

October 16th.—I awoke before daylight. The moon was
shining feebly down into the glen, from among light drifting
clouds; the camp fires were nearly burned out, and the men
lying about them, wrapped in blankets. With the first streak
of day, our huntsman, Beatte, with Antoine, the young half-
breed, set off to recross the river, in search of the stray
horses, in company with several rangers who had left their
rifles on the opposite shore. As the ford was deep, and they
were obliged to cross in a diagonal line, against a rapid current, they had to be mounted on the tallest and strongest
horses.

By eight o'clock Beatte returned. He had found the
horses, but had lost Antoine. The latter, he said, was a boy,
a greenhorn, that knew nothing of the woods. He had wandered out of sight of him and got lost. However, there were
plenty more for him to fall in company with, as some of the
rangers had gone astray also, and old Ryan and his party
had not returned.

We waited until the morning was somewhat advanced,
in hopes of being rejoined by the stragglers, but they did not
make their appearance. The captain observed, that the
Indians on the opposite side of the river were all well disposed to the whites; so that no serious apprehensions need be
entertained for the safety of the missing. The greatest danger was, that their horses might be stolen in the night by
straggling Osages. He determined, therefore, to proceed,
leaving a rear-guard in the camp, to await their arrival.

I sat on a rock that overhung the spring at the upper part
of the dell, and amused myself by watching the changing

scene before me. First, the preparations for departure. Horses driven in from the purlieus of the camp; rangers riding about among rocks and bushes in quest of others that had strayed to a distance; the bustle of packing up camp equipage, and the clamor after kettles and frying-pans borrowed by one mess from another, mixed up with oaths and exclamations at restive horses, or others that had wandered away to graze after being packed, among which the voice of our little Frenchman, Tonish, was particularly to be distinguished.

The bugle sounded the signal to mount and march. The troop filed off in irregular line down the glen, and through the open forest, winding and gradually disappearing among the trees, though the clamor of voices and the notes of the bugle could be heard for some time afterward. The rearguard remained under the trees in the lower part of the dell, some on horseback, with their rifles on their shoulders; others seated by the fire or lying on the ground, gossiping in a low, lazy tone of voice, their horses unsaddled, standing and dozing around, while one of the rangers, profiting by this interval of leisure, was shaving himself before a pocket mirror stuck against the trunk of a tree.

The clamor of voices and the notes of the bugle at length died away, and the glen relapsed into quiet and silence, broken occasionally by the low murmuring tone of the group around the fire, or the pensive whistle of some laggard among the trees; or the rustling of the yellow leaves, which the lightest breath of air brought down in wavering showers, a sign of the departing glories of the year.

CHAPTER FOURTEEN

DEER-SHOOTING—LIFE ON THE PRAIRIES—BEAUTIFUL EN-
CAMPMENT—HUNTER'S LUCK—ANECDOTES OF THE
DELAWARES AND THEIR SUPERSTITIONS

HAVING passed through the skirt of woodland bordering
the river, we ascended the hills, taking a westerly course
through an undulating country of "oak openings," where
the eye stretched over wide tracts of hill and dale, diversified
by forests, groves, and clumps of trees. As we were proceeding at a slow pace, those who were at the head of the
line descried four deer grazing on a grassy slope about half
a mile distant. They apparently had not perceived our approach, and continued to graze in perfect tranquillity. A
young ranger obtained permission from the captain to go in
pursuit of them, and the troop halted in lengthened line,
watching him in silence. Walking his horse slowly and
cautiously, he made a circuit until a screen of wood intervened between him and the deer. Dismounting then, he
left his horse among the trees, and creeping round a knoll,
was hidden from our view. We now kept our eyes intently
fixed on the deer, which continued grazing, unconscious of
their danger. Presently there was the sharp report of a rifle;
a fine buck made a convulsive bound and fell to the earth;
his companion scampered off. Immediately our whole line
of march was broken; there was a helter-skelter galloping
of the youngsters of the troop, eager to get a shot at the
fugitives; and one of the most conspicuous personages in the
chase was our little Frenchman Tonish, on his silver-gray;
having abandoned his pack-horses at the first sight of the
deer. It was some time before our scattered forces could be
recalled by the bugle and our march resumed.

Two or three times in the course of the day we were interrupted by hurry-scurry scenes of the kind. The young
men of the troop were full of excitement on entering an unexplored country abounding in game, and they were too little
accustomed to discipline or restraint to be kept in order.
No one, however, was more unmanageable than Tonish.
Having an intense conceit of his skill as a hunter, and an
irrepressible passion for display, he was continually sallying
forth, like an ill-broken hound, whenever any game was
started, and had as often to be whipped back.

At length his curiosity got a salutary check. A fat doe
came bounding along in full view of the whole line. Tonish
dismounted, leveled his rifle, and had a fair shot. The doe
kept on. He sprang upon his horse, stood up on the saddle
like a posture master, and continued gazing after the animal
as if certain to see it fall. The doe, however, kept on its
way rejoicing; a laugh broke out along the line, the little
Frenchman slipped quietly into his saddle, began to belabor
and blaspheme the wandering pack-horses, as if they had
been to blame, and for some time we were relieved from his
vaunting and vaporing.

In one place of our march we came to the remains of an
old Indian encampment, on the banks of a fine stream, with
the moss-grown skulls of deer lying here and there about it.
As we were in the Pawnee country, it was supposed, of
course, to have been a camp of those formidable rovers; the
doctor, however, after considering the shape and disposition
of the lodges, pronounced it the camp of some bold Delawares,
who had probably made a brief and dashing excursion into
these dangerous hunting grounds.

Having proceeded some distance further, we observed a
couple of figures on horseback, slowly moving parallel to us
along the edge of a naked hill about two miles distant; and
apparently reconnoitering us. There was a halt, and much
gazing and conjecturing. Were they Indians? If Indians,
were they Pawnees? There is something exciting to the
imagination and stirring to the feelings, while traversing

these hostile plains, in seeing a horseman prowling along the horizon. It is like descrying a sail at sea in time of war, when it may be either a privateer or a pirate. Our conjectures were soon set at rest by reconnoitering the two horsemen through a small spyglass, when they proved to be two of the men we had left at the camp, who had set out to rejoin us, and had wandered from the track.

Our march this day was animating and delightful. We were in a region of adventure; breaking our way through a country hitherto untrodden by white men, excepting perchance by some solitary trapper. The weather was in its perfection, temperate, genial and enlivening; a deep blue sky with a few light feathery clouds, an atmosphere of perfect transparency, an air pure and bland, and a glorious country spreading out far and wide in the golden sunshine of an autumnal day; but all silent, lifeless, without a human habitation, and apparently without a human inhabitant! It was as if a ban hung over this fair but fated region. The very Indians dared not abide here, but made it a mere scene of perilous enterprise, to hunt for a few days, and then away.

After a march of about fifteen miles west we encamped in a beautiful peninsula, made by the windings and doublings of a deep, clear, and almost motionless brook, and covered by an open grove of lofty and magnificent trees. Several hunters immediately started forth in quest of game before the noise of the camp should frighten it from the vicinity. Our man, Beatte, also took his rifle and went forth alone, in a different course from the rest.

For my own part I laid on the grass under the trees, and built castles in the clouds, and indulged in the very luxury of rural repose. Indeed I can scarcely conceive a kind of life more calculated to put both mind and body in a healthful tone. A morning's ride of several hours diversified by hunting incidents; an encampment in the afternoon under some noble grove on the borders of a stream; an evening banquet of venison, fresh killed, roasted, or broiled on the coals; turkeys just from the thickets and wild honey from the trees;

and all relished with an appetite unknown to the gourmets of the cities. And at night—such sweet sleeping in the open air, or waking and gazing at the moon and stars, shining between the trees!

On the present occasion, however, we had not much reason to boast of our larder. But one deer had been killed during the day, and none of that had reached our lodge. We were fain, therefore, to stay our keen appetites by some scraps of turkey brought from the last encampment, eked out with a slice or two of salt pork. This scarcity, however, did not continue long. Before dark a young hunter returned well laden with spoil. He had shot a deer, cut it up in an artist like style, and, putting the meat in a kind of sack made of the hide, had slung it across his shoulder and trudged with it to camp.

Not long after, Beatte made his appearance with a fat doe across his horse. It was the first game he had brought in, and I was glad to see him with a trophy that might efface the memory of the polecat. He laid the carcass down by our fire without saying a word, and then turned to unsaddle his horse; nor could any questions from us about his hunting draw from him more than laconic replies. If Beatte, however, observed this Indian taciturnity about what he had done, Tonish made up for it by boasting of what he meant to do. Now that we were in a good hunting country he meant to take the field, and, if we would take his word for it, our lodge would henceforth be overwhelmed with game. Luckily this talking did not prevent his working, the doe was skillfully dissected, several fat ribs roasted before the fire, the coffee kettle replenished, and in a little while we were enabled to indemnify ourselves luxuriously for our late meager repast.

The captain did not return until late, and he returned empty handed. He had been in pursuit of his usual game, the deer, when he came upon the tracks of a gang of about sixty elk. Having never killed an animal of the kind, and the elk being at this moment an object of ambition among all the veteran hunters of the camp, he abandoned his pursuit of the deer, and followed the newly discovered track. After some time he came in sight of the elk, and had several fair chances of a shot, but was anxious to bring down a large buck which kept in the advance. Finding at length there was danger of the whole gang escaping him, he fired at a doe. The shot took effect, but the animal had sufficient strength to keep on for a time with its companions. From the tracks of blood he felt confident it was mortally wounded, but evening came on, he could not keep the trail, and had to give up the search until morning.

Old Ryan and his little band had not yet rejoined us, neither had our young half-breed Antoine made his appearance. It was determined, therefore, to remain at our encampment for the following day, to give time for all stragglers to arrive.

The conversation this evening, among the old huntsmen, turned upon the Delaware tribe, one of whose encampments we had passed in the course of the day; and anecdotes were given of their prowess in war and dexterity in hunting. They used to be deadly foes of the Osages, who stood in great awe of their desperate valor, though they were apt to attribute it to a whimsical cause. "Look at the Delawares," would they say, "dey got short leg—no can run—must stand and fight a great heap." In fact the Delawares are rather short legged, while the Osages are remarkable for length of limb.

The expeditions of the Delawares, whether of war or hunting, are wide and fearless; a small band of them will penetrate far into these dangerous and hostile wilds, and will push their encampments even to the Rocky Mountains. This daring temper may be in some measure encouraged by one of the superstitions of their creed. They believe that a guardian spirit, in the form of a great eagle, watches over them, hovering in the sky, far out of sight. Sometimes, when well pleased with them, he wheels down into the lower regions, and may be seen circling with wide spread wings against the white clouds; at such times the seasons are propitious, the corn grows finely, and they have great success in hunting. Sometimes, however, he is angry, and then he vents his rage in the thunder, which is his voice, and the lightning, which is the flashing of his eye, and strikes dead the object of his displeasure.

The Delawares make sacrifices to this spirit, who occasionally lets drop a feather from his wing in token of satisfaction. These feathers render the wearer invisible, and invulnerable. Indeed, the Indians generally consider the feathers of the eagle possessed of occult and sovereign virtues.

At one time a party of the Delawares, in the course of a bold excursion into the Pawnee hunting grounds, were surrounded on one of the great plains and nearly destroyed. The remnant took refuge on the summit of one of those isolated and conical hills which rise almost like artificial mounds, from the midst of the prairies. Here the chief warrior, driven almost to despair, sacrificed his horse to the tutelar spirit. Suddenly an enormous eagle, rushing down from the sky, bore off the victim in his talons, and, mounting into the air, dropped a quill feather from his wing. The chief caught it up with joy, bound it to his forehead, and, leading his followers down the hill, cut his way through the enemy with great slaughter, and without any one of his party receiving a wound.

CHAPTER FIFTEEN

THE SEARCH FOR THE ELK—PAWNEE STORIES

WITH the morning dawn, the prime hunters of the camp were all on the alert, and set off in different directions, to beat up the country for game. The captain's brother, Sergeant Bean, was among the first, and returned before breakfast with success, having killed a fat doe almost within the purlieus of the camp.

When breakfast was over, the captain mounted his horse, to go in quest of the elk which he had wounded on the preceding evening; and which, he was persuaded, had received its death-wound. I determined to join him in the search, and we accordingly sallied forth together, accompanied also by his brother, the sergeant, and a lieutenant. Two rangers followed on foot, to bring home the carcass of the doe which the sergeant had killed. We had not ridden far, when we came to where it lay, on the side of a hill, in the midst of a beautiful woodland scene. The two rangers immediately fell to work, with true hunters' skill, to dismember it, and prepare it for transportation to the camp, while we continued on our course. We passed along sloping hill-sides, among skirts of thicket and scattered forest trees, until we came to a place where the long herbage was pressed down with numerous elk beds. Here the captain had first roused the gang of elks, and, after looking about diligently for a little while, he pointed out their "trail," the footprints of which were as large as those of horned cattle. He now put himself upon the track, and went quietly forward, the rest of us following him in Indian file. At length he halted at the place where the elk had been when shot at. Spots of blood on the surrounding herbage showed that the shot had been effective. The wounded animal had evidently kept for some distance with the rest of the herd, as could be seen by sprinklings of blood here and there, on the shrubs and weeds bordering the trail. These at length suddenly disappeared. "Somewhere hereabout," said the captain, "the elk must have turned off from the gang. Whenever they feel themselves mortally wounded, they will turn aside and seek some out-of-the-way place to die alone."

There was something in this picture of the last moments of a wounded deer to touch the sympathies of one not hardened to the gentle disports of the chase; such sympathies, however, are but transient. Man is naturally an animal of prey; and, however changed by civilization, will readily relapse into his instinct for destruction. I found my ravenous and sanguinary propensities daily growing stronger upon the prairies.

After looking about for a little while, the captain succeeded in finding the separate trail of the wounded elk, which turned off almost at right angles from that of the herd, and entered an open forest of scattered trees. The traces of blood became more faint and rare, and occurred at greater distances; at length they ceased altogether, and the ground was so hard, and the herbage so much parched and withered, that the footprints of the animal could no longer be perceived.

"The elk must lie somewhere in this neighborhood," said the captain, "as you may know by those turkey-buzzards wheeling about in the air: for they always hover in that way above some carcass. However, the dead elk cannot get away, so let us follow the trail of the living ones: they may have halted at no great distance, and we may find them grazing, and get another crack at them."

We accordingly returned, and resumed the trail of the elks, which led us a straggling course over hill and dale, covered with scattered oaks. Every now and then we would catch a glimpse of a deer bounding away across some glade of the forest, but the captain was not to be diverted from his elk hunt by such inferior game. A large flock of wild turkeys, too, were roused by the trampling of our horses; some scampered off as fast as their long legs could carry them; others fluttered up into the trees, where they remained with outstretched necks, gazing at us. The captain would not allow a rifle to be discharged at them, lest it should alarm the elk, which he hoped to find in the vicinity. At length we came to where the forest ended in a steep bank, and the Red Fork wound its way below us, between broad sandy shores. The trail descended the bank, and we could trace it, with our eyes, across the level sands, until it terminated in the river, which, it was evident, the gang had forded on the preceding evening.

"It is needless to follow on any further," said the captain. "The elk must have been much frightened, and, after crossing the river, may have kept on for twenty miles without stopping."

Our little party now divided, the lieutenant and sergeant making a circuit in quest of game, and the captain and myself taking the direction of the camp. On our way, we came to a buffalo track, more than a year old. It was not wider than an ordinary footpath, and worn deep into the soil; for these animals follow each other in single file. Shortly afterward, we met two rangers on foot, hunting. They had wounded an elk, but he had escaped; and in pursuing him, had found the one shot by the captain on the preceding evening. They turned back and conducted us to it. It was a noble animal, as large as a yearling heifer, and lay in an open part of the forest, about a mile and a half distant from the place where it had been shot. The turkey-buzzards, which we had previously noticed, were wheeling in the air above it. The observation of the captain seemed verified. The poor animal, as life was ebbing away, had apparently abandoned its unhurt companions and turned aside to die alone.

The captain and the two rangers forthwith fell to work, with their hunting-knives, to flay and cut up the carcass. It was already tainted on the inside, but ample collops were cut from the ribs and haunches, and laid in a heap on the outstretched hide. Holes were then cut along the border of the hide, raw thongs were passed through them and the whole drawn up like a sack, which was swung behind the captain's saddle. All this while, the turkey-buzzards were soaring overhead, waiting for our departure to swoop down and banquet on the carcass.

The wreck of the poor elk being thus dismantled, the captain and myself mounted our horses, and jogged back to the camp, while the two rangers resumed their hunting.

On reaching the camp, I found there our young half-breed, Antoine. After separating from Beatte, in the search after the stray horses on the other side of the Arkansas, he had fallen upon a wrong track, which he followed for several miles, when he overtook old Ryan and his party, and found he had been following their traces.

They all forded the Arkansas about eight miles above our crossing place, and found their way to our late encampment in the glen, where the rear-guard we had left behind was waiting for them. Antoine, being well mounted, and somewhat impatient to rejoin us, had pushed on alone, following our trail, to our present encampment, and bringing the carcass of a young bear which he had killed.

Our camp, during the residue of the day, presented a mingled picture of bustle and repose. Some of the men were busy round the fires, jerking and roasting venison and bear's meat, to be packed up as a future supply. Some were stretching and dressing the skins of the animals they had killed; others were washing their clothes in the brook, and hanging them on the bushes to dry; while many were lying on the grass and lazily gossiping in the shade. Every now and then a hunter would return, on horseback or on foot, laden with game, or empty handed. Those who brought home any spoil deposited it at the captain's fire, and then filed off to their respective messes, to relate their day's exploits to their companions. The game killed at this camp consisted of six deer, one elk, two bears, and six or eight turkeys.

During the last two or three days, since their wild Indian achievement in navigating the river, our retainers had risen in consequence among the rangers; and now I found Tonish making himself a complete oracle among some of the raw and inexperienced recruits, who had never been in the wilderness. He had continually a knot hanging about him, and listening to his extravagant tales about the Pawnees, with whom he pretended to have had fearful encounters. His representations, in fact, were calculated to inspire his hearers with an awful idea of the foe into whose lands they were intruding. According to his accounts, the rifle of the white man was no match for the bow and arrow of the Pawnee. When the rifle was once discharged, it took time and trouble

to load it again, and in the meantime the enemy could keep
on lanching his shafts as fast as he could draw his bow.
Then the Pawnee, according to Tonish, could shoot with un-
erring aim, three hundred yards, and send his arrow clean
through and through a buffalo; nay, he had known a Pawnee
shaft pass through one buffalo and wound another. And
then the way the Pawnees sheltered themselves from the
shots of their enemy: they would hang with one leg over the
saddle, crouching their bodies along the opposite side of their
horse, and would shoot their arrows from under his neck,
while at full speed!

If Tonish was to be believed, there was peril at every step
in these debatable grounds of the Indian tribes. Pawnees
lurked unseen among the thickets and ravines. They had
their scouts and sentinels on the summit of the mounds which
command a view over the prairies, where they lay crouched
in the tall grass; only now and then raising their heads to
watch the movements of any war or hunting party that
might be passing in lengthened line below. At night, they
would lurk round an encampment; crawling through the
grass, and imitating the movements of a wolf, so as to deceive
the sentinel on the outpost, until, having arrived sufficiently
near, they would speed an arrow through his heart, and
retreat undiscovered. In telling his stories, Tonish would
appeal from time to time to Beatte, for the truth of what he
said; the only reply would be a nod or shrug of the shoulders;
the latter being divided in mind between a distaste for the
gasconading spirit of his comrade, and a sovereign contempt
for the inexperience of the young rangers in all that he considered true knowledge.

CHAPTER SIXTEEN

A SICK CAMP—THE MARCH—THE DISABLED HORSE—OLD
RYAN AND THE STRAGGLERS—SYMPTOMS OF CHANGE
OF WEATHER, AND CHANGE OF HUMORS

OCTOBER 18TH.—We prepared to march at the usual hour,
but word was brought to the captain that three of the rangers,
who had been attacked with the measles, were unable to proceed, and that another one was missing. The last was an
old frontiersman, by the name of Sawyer, who had gained
years without experience; and having sallied forth to hunt,
on the preceding day, had probably lost his way on the
prairies. A guard of ten men was, therefore, to take care
of the sick, and wait for the straggler. If the former recovered sufficiently in the course of two or three days, they were
to rejoin the main body, otherwise to be escorted back to the
garrison.

Taking our leave of the sick camp, we shaped our course
westward, along the heads of small streams, all wandering,
in deep ravines, toward the Red Fork. The land was high
and undulating, or "rolling," as it is termed in the West;
with a poor hungry soil mingled with the sandstone, which
is unusual in this part of the country, and checkered with
harsh forests of post-oak and black-jack.

In the course of the morning, I received a lesson on the
importance of being chary of one's steed on the prairies.
The one I rode on surpassed in action most horses of the
troop, and was of great mettle and a generous spirit. In
crossing the deep ravines, he would scramble up the steep
banks like a cat, and was always for leaping the narrow runs
of water. I was not aware of the imprudence of indulging
him in such exertions, until, in leaping him across a small
brook, I felt him immediately falter beneath me. He limped
* * * 19—VOL. VII.

forward a short distance, but soon fell stark lame, having sprained his shoulder. What was to be done? He could not keep up with the troop, and was too valuable to be abandoned on the prairie. The only alternative was to send him back to join the invalids in the sick camp, and to share their fortunes. Nobody, however, seemed disposed to lead him back, although I offered a liberal reward. Either the stories of Tonish about the Pawnees had spread an apprehension of lurking foes and imminent perils on the prairies; or there was a fear of missing the trail and getting lost. At length two young men stepped forward and agreed to go in company, so that, should they be benighted on the prairies, there might be one to watch while the other slept.

The horse was accordingly consigned to their care, and I looked after him with a rueful eye, as he limped off, for it seemed as if, with him, all strength and buoyancy had departed from me.

I looked round for a steed to supply his place, and fixed my eyes upon the gallant gray which I had transferred at the agency to Tonish. The moment, however, that I hinted about his dismounting and taking up with the supernumerary pony, the little varlet broke out into vociferous remonstrances and lamentations, gasping and almost strangling, in his eagerness to give vent to them. I saw that to unhorse him would be to prostrate his spirit and cut his vanity to the quick. I had not the heart to inflict such a wound, or to bring down the poor devil from his transient vainglory; so I left him in possession of his gallant gray, and contented myself with shifting my saddle to the jaded pony.

I was now sensible of the complete reverse to which a horseman is exposed on the prairies. I felt how completely the spirit of the rider depended upon his steed. I had hitherto been able to make excursions at will from the line, and to gallop in pursuit of any object of interest or curiosity. I was now reduced to the tone of the jaded animal I bestrode, and doomed to plod on patiently and slowly after my file leader. Above all, I was made conscious how unwise it is, on expeditions of the kind, where a man's life may depend upon the strength, and speed, and freshness of his horse, to task the generous animal by any unnecessary exertion of his powers.

I have observed that the wary and experienced huntsman and traveler of the prairies is always sparing of his horse, when on a journey; never, except in emergency, putting him off of a walk. The regular journeyings of frontiersmen and Indians, when on a long march, seldom exceed above fifteen miles a day, and are generally about ten or twelve, and they never indulge in capricious galloping. Many of those, however, with whom I was traveling were young and inexperienced, and full of excitement at finding themselves in a country abounding with game. It was impossible to retain them in the sobriety of a march, or to keep them to the line. As we broke our way through the coverts and ravines, and the deer started up and scampered off to the right and left, the rifle balls would whiz after them, and our young hunters dash off in pursuit. At one time they made a grand burst after what they supposed to be a gang of bears, but soon pulled up on discovering them to be black wolves, prowling in company.

After a march of about twelve miles we encamped, a little after midday, on the borders of a brook which loitered through a deep ravine. In the course of the afternoon old Ryan, the Nestor of the camp, made his appearance, followed by his little band of stragglers. He was greeted with joyful acclamations, which showed the estimation in which he was held by his brother woodsmen. The little band came laden with venison; a fine haunch of which the veteran hunter laid, as a present, by the captain's fire.

Our men, Beatte and Tonish, both sallied forth, early in the afternoon, to hunt. Toward evening the former returned with a fine buck across his horse. He laid it down, as usual, in silence, and proceeded to unsaddle and turn his horse loose. Tonish came back without any game, but with much more glory; having made several capital shots, though unluckily the wounded deer had all escaped him.

There was an abundant supply of meat in the camp; for, besides other game, three elk had been killed. The wary and veteran woodsmen were all busy jerking meat against a time of scarcity; the less experienced reveled in present abundance, leaving the morrow to provide for itself.

On the following morning (October 19th), I succeeded in changing my pony and a reasonable sum of money for a strong and active horse. It was a great satisfaction to find myself once more tolerably well mounted. I perceived, however, that there would be little difficulty in making a selection from among the troop, for the rangers had all that propensity for "swapping," or, as they term it, "trading," which pervades the West. In the course of our expedition there was scarcely a horse, rifle, powder-horn, or blanket, that did not change owners several times; and one keen "trader" boasted of having, by dint of frequent bargains, changed a bad horse into a good one, and put a hundred dollars in his pocket.

The morning was lowering and sultry, with low muttering of distant thunder. The change of weather had its effect upon the spirits of the troop. The camp was unusually sober and quiet; there was none of the accustomed farmyard melody of crowing and cackling at daybreak; none of the bursts of merriment, the loud jokes and banterings, that had commonly prevailed during the bustle of equipment. Now and then might be heard a short strain of a song, a faint laugh, or a solitary whistle; but, in general, every one went silently and doggedly about the duties of the camp, or the preparations for departure.

When the time arrived to saddle and mount, five horses were reported as missing; although all the woods and thickets had been beaten up for some distance round the camp. Several rangers were dispatched to "skir" the country round in quest of them. In the meantime, the thunder continued to growl, and we had a passing shower. The horses, like their riders, were affected by the change of weather. They stood here and there about the camp, some saddled and bridled, others loose, but all spiritless and dozing, with stooping head, one hind leg partly drawn up so as to rest on the point of the hoof, and the whole hide reeking with the rain and sending up wreaths of vapor. The men, too, waited in listless groups the return of their comrades who had gone in quest of the horses; now and then turning up an anxious eye to the drifting clouds, which boded an approaching storm. Gloomy weather inspires gloomy thoughts. Some expressed fears that we were dogged by some party of Indians, who had stolen the horses in the night. The most prevalent apprehension, however, was that they had returned on their traces to our last encampment or had started off on a direct line for Fort Gibson. In this respect, the instinct of horses is said to resemble that of the pigeon. They will strike for home by a direct course, passing through tracts of wilderness which they have never before traversed.

After delaying until the morning was somewhat advanced, a lieutenant with a guard was appointed to await the return of the rangers, and we set off on our day's journey, considerably reduced in numbers; much, as I thought, to the discomposure of some of the troop, who intimated that we might prove too weak-handed, in case of an encounter with the Pawnees.

CHAPTER SEVENTEEN

THUNDERSTORM ON THE PRAIRIES—THE STORM ENCAMP-
MENT—NIGHT SCENE—INDIAN STORIES—A
FRIGHTENED HORSE

OUR march for a part of the day lay a little to the south of west, through straggling forests of the kind of low scrubbed trees already mentioned, called "post-oaks" and "black-jacks." The soil of these "oak barrens" is loose and unsound; being little better at times than a mere quicksand, in which, in rainy weather, the horse's hoof slips from side to side, and now and then sinks in a rotten, spongy turf to the fetlock. Such was the case at present in consequence of successive thunder showers, through which we draggled along in dogged silence. Several deer were roused by our approach and scudded across the forest glades; but no one, as formerly, broke the line of march to pursue them. At one time, we passed the bones and horns of a buffalo, and at another time a buffalo track, not above three days old. These signs of the vicinity of this grand game of the prairies had a reviving effect on the spirits of our huntsmen; but it was of transient duration.

In crossing a prairie of moderate extent, rendered little better than a slippery bog by the recent showers, we were overtaken by a violent thunder gust. The rain came rattling upon us in torrents, and spattered up like steam along the ground; the whole landscape was suddenly wrapped in gloom that gave a vivid effect to the intense sheets of lightning, while the thunder seemed to burst over our very heads, and was reverberated by the groves and forests that checkered and skirted the prairie. Man and beast were so pelted, drenched, and confounded, that the line was thrown in complete confusion; some of the horses were so frightened as to be almost unmanageable, and our scattered cavalcade looked like a tempest-tossed fleet, driven hither and thither, at the mercy of wind and wave.

At length, at half-past two o'clock, we came to a halt, and gathering together our forces, encamped in an open and lofty grove, with a prairie on one side and a stream on the other. The forest immediately rang with the sound of the ax, and the crash of falling trees. Huge fires were soon blazing; blankets were stretched before them, by way of tents; booths were hastily reared of bark and skins; every fire had its group drawn close round it, drying and warming themselves, or preparing a comforting meal. Some of the rangers were discharging and cleaning their rifles, which had been exposed to the rain; while the horses, relieved from their saddles and burdens, rolled in the wet grass.

The showers continued from time to time, until late in the evening. Before dark, our horses were gathered in and tethered about the skirts of the camp, within the outposts, through fear of Indian prowlers, who are apt to take advantage of stormy nights for their depredations and assaults. As the night thickened, the huge fires became more and more luminous; lighting up masses of the overhanging foliage, and leaving other parts of the grove in deep gloom. Every fire had its goblin group around it, while the tethered horses were dimly seen, like specters, among the thickets; excepting that here and there a gray one stood out in bright relief.

The grove, thus fitfully lighted up by the ruddy glare of the fires, resembled a vast leafy dome, walled in by opaque darkness; but every now and then two or three quivering flashes of lightning in quick succession would suddenly reveal a vast champaign country, where fields and forests, and running streams, would start, as it were, into existence for a few brief seconds, and, before the eye could ascertain them, vanish again into gloom.

A thunderstorm on a prairie, as upon the ocean, derives grandeur and sublimity from the wild and boundless waste over which it rages and bellows. It is not surprising that these awful phenomena of nature should be objects of superstitious reverence to the poor savages, and that they should consider the thunder the angry voice of the Great Spirit. As our half-breeds sat gossiping round the fire, I drew from them some of the notions entertained on the subject by their Indian friends. The latter declare that extinguished thunderbolts are sometimes picked up by hunters on the prairies, who use them for the heads of arrows and lances, and that any warrior thus armed is invincible. Should a thunderstorm occur, however, during battle, he is liable to be carried away by the thunder, and never heard of more.

A warrior of the Konza tribe, hunting on a prairie, was overtaken by a storm, and struck down senseless by the thunder. On recovering, he beheld the thunderbolt lying on the ground, and a horse standing beside it. Snatching up the bolt, he sprang upon the horse, but found too late that he was astride of the lightning. In an instant he was whisked away over prairies and forests, and streams and deserts, until he was flung senseless at the foot of the Rocky Mountains; whence, on recovering, it took him several months to return to his own people.

This story reminded me of an Indian tradition, related by a traveler, of the fate of a warrior who saw the thunder lying upon the ground, with a beautifully wrought moccasin on each side of it. Thinking he had found a prize, he put on the moccasins; but they bore him away to the land of spirits, whence he never returned.

These are simple and artless tales, but they had a wild and romantic interest heard from the lips of half-savage narrators, round a hunter's fire, on a stormy night, with a forest on one side, and a howling waste on the other; and where, peradventure, savage foes might be lurking in the outer darkness.

Our conversation was interrupted by a loud clap of thunder, followed immediately by the sound of a horse galloping off madly into the waste. Every one listened in mute silence. The hoofs resounded vigorously for a time, but grew fainter and fainter, until they died away in remote distance.

When the sound was no longer to be heard, the listeners turned to conjecture what could have caused this sudden scamper. Some thought the horse had been startled by the thunder; others, that some lurking Indian had galloped off with him. To this it was objected that the usual mode with the Indians is to steal quietly upon the horse, take off his fetters, mount him gently, and walk him off as silently as possible, leading off others, without any unusual stir or noise to disturb the camp.

On the other hand, it was stated as a common practice with the Indians, to creep among a troop of horses when grazing at night, mount one quietly, and then start off suddenly at full speed. Nothing is so contagious among horses as a panic; one sudden break-away of this kind will sometimes alarm the whole troop, and they will set off, helter-skelter, after the leader.

Every one who had a horse grazing on the skirts of the camp was uneasy, lest his should be the fugitive; but it was impossible to ascertain the fact until morning. Those who had tethered their horses felt more secure; though horses thus tied up, and limited to a short range at night, are apt to fall off in flesh and strength, during a long march; and many of the horses of the troop already gave signs of being wayworn.

After a gloomy and unruly night, the morning dawned bright and clear, and a glorious sunrise transformed the whole landscape, as if by magic. The late dreary wilderness brightened into a fine open country, with stately groves, and clumps of oaks of a gigantic size, some of which stood singly, as if planted for ornament and shade, in the midst of rich meadows; while our horses, scattered about, and grazing under them, gave to the whole the air of a noble park. It was difficult to realize the fact that we were so far in the wilds beyond the residence of man. Our encampment, alone, had a savage appearance; with its rude tents of skins and blankets, and its columns of blue smoke rising among the trees.

The first care in the morning was to look after our horses. Some of them had wandered to a distance, but all were fortunately found; even the one whose clattering hoofs had caused such uneasiness in the night. He had come to a halt about a mile from the camp, and was found quietly grazing near a brook. The bugle sounded for departure about half-past eight. As we were in greater risk of Indian molestation the further we advanced, our line was formed with more precision than heretofore. Every one had his station assigned him, and was forbidden to leave it in pursuit of game, without special permission. The pack-horses were placed in the center of the line, and a strong guard in the rear.

CHAPTER EIGHTEEN

A GRAND PRAIRIE—CLIFF CASTLE—BUFFALO TRACKS— DEER HUNTED BY WOLVES—CROSS TIMBER

AFTER a toilsome march of some distance through a country cut up by ravines and brooks, and entangled by thickets, we emerged upon a grand prairie. Here one of the characteristic scenes of the Far West broke upon us. An immense extent of grassy, undulating, or, as it is termed, rolling country, with here and there a clump of trees, dimly seen in the distance like a ship at sea; the landscape deriving sublimity from its vastness and simplicity. To the southwest, on the summit of a hill, was a singular crest of broken rocks, resembling a ruined fortress. It reminded me of the ruin of some Moorish castle, crowning a height in the midst of a lonely Spanish landscape. To this hill we gave the name of Cliff Castle.

The prairies of these great hunting regions differed in the character of their vegetation from those through which I had hitherto passed. Instead of a profusion of tall flowering plants and long flaunting grasses, they were covered with a shorter growth of herbage called buffalo grass, somewhat coarse, but, at the proper seasons, affording excellent and abundant pasturage. At present it was growing wiry, and in many places was too much parched for grazing.

The weather was verging into that serene but somewhat arid season called the Indian Summer. There was a smoky haze in the atmosphere that tempered the brightness of the sunshine into a golden tint, softening the features of the landscape, and giving a vagueness to the outlines of distant objects. This haziness was daily increasing, and was attributed to the burning of distant prairies by the Indian hunting parties.

We had not gone far upon the prairie before we came to

where deeply worn footpaths were seen traversing the country: sometimes two or three would keep on parallel to each other, and but a few paces apart. These were pronounced to be traces of buffaloes, where large droves had passed. There were tracks also of horses, which were observed with some attention by our experienced hunters. They could not be the tracks of wild horses, as there were no prints of the hoofs of colts; all were full-grown. As the horses evidently were not shod, it was concluded they must belong to some hunting party of Pawnees. In the course of the morning, the tracks of a single horse, with shoes, were discovered. This might be the horse of a Cherokee hunter, or perhaps a horse stolen from the whites of the frontier. Thus, in traversing these perilous wastes, every footprint and dint of hoof becomes matter of cautious inspection and shrewd surmise; and the question continually is, whether it be the trace of friend or foe, whether of recent or ancient date, and whether the being that made it be out of reach, or liable to be encountered.

We were getting more and more into the game country: as we proceeded, we repeatedly saw deer to the right and left, bounding off for the coverts; but their appearance no longer excited the same eagerness to pursue. In passing along a slope of the prairie, between two rolling swells of land, we came in sight of a genuine natural hunting match. A pack of seven black wolves and one white one were in full chase of a buck, which they had nearly tired down. They crossed the line of our march without apparently perceiving us; we saw them have a fair run of nearly a mile, gaining upon the buck until they were leaping upon his haunches, when he plunged down a ravine. Some of our party galloped to a rising ground commanding a view of the ravine. The poor buck was completely beset, some on his flanks, some at his throat; he made two or three struggles and desperate bounds, but was dragged down, overpowered, and torn to pieces. The black wolves, in their ravenous hunger and fury, took no notice of the distant group of horsemen;

but the white wolf, apparently less game, abandoned the prey, and scampered over hill and dale, rousing various deer that were crouched in the hollows, and which bounded off likewise in different directions. It was altogether a wild scene, worthy of the "hunting grounds."

We now came once more in sight of the Red Fork, winding its turbid course between well-wooded hills, and through a vast and magnificent landscape. The prairies bordering on the rivers are always varied in this way with woodland, so beautifully interspersed as to appear to have been laid out by the hand of taste; and they only want here and there a village spire, the battlements of a castle, or the turrets of an old family mansion rising from among the trees, to rival the most ornamented scenery of Europe.

About midday we reached the edge of that scattered belt of forest land, about forty miles in width, which stretches across the country from north to south, from the Arkansas to the Red River, separating the upper from the lower prairies, and commonly called the "Cross Timber." On the skirts of this forest land, just on the edge of a prairie, we found traces of a Pawnee encampment of between one and two hundred lodges, showing that the party must have been numerous. The skull of a buffalo lay near the camp, and the moss which had gathered on it proved that the encampment was at least a year old. About half a mile off we encamped in a beautiful grove, watered by a fine spring and rivulet. Our day's journey had been about fourteen miles.

In the course of the afternoon we were rejoined by two of Lieutenant's King's party, which we had left behind a few days before, to look after stray horses. All the horses had been found, though some had wandered to the distance of several miles. The lieutenant, with seventeen of his companions, had remained at our last night's encampment to hunt, having come upon recent traces of buffalo. They had also seen a fine wild horse, which, however, had galloped off with a speed that defied pursuit.

Confident anticipations were now indulged that on the following day we should meet with buffalo, and perhaps with wild horses, and every one was in spirits. We needed some excitement of the kind, for our young men were growing weary of marching and encamping under restraint, and provisions this day were scanty. The captain and several of the rangers went out hunting, but brought home nothing but a small deer and a few turkeys. Our two men, Beatte and Tonish, likewise went out. The former returned with a deer athwart his horse, which, as usual, he laid down by our lodge, and said nothing. Tonish returned with no game, but with his customary budget of wonderful tales. Both he and the deer had done marvels. Not one had come within the lure of his rifle without being hit in a mortal part, yet, strange to say, every one had kept on his way without flinching. We all determined that, from the accuracy of his aim, Tonish must have shot with charmed balls, but that every deer had a charmed life. The most important intelligence brought by him, however, was that he had seen the fresh tracks of several wild horses. He now considered himself upon the eve of great exploits, for there was nothing upon which he glorified himself more than his skill in horse-catching.

CHAPTER NINETEEN

HUNTER'S ANTICIPATIONS—THE RUGGED FORD—A WILD HORSE

OCTOBER 21ST.—This morning the camp was in a bustle at an early hour: the expectation of falling in with buffalo in the course of the day roused every one's spirit. There was a continual cracking of rifles, that they might be reloaded: the shot was drawn off from double-barreled guns, and balls were substituted. Tonish, however, prepared chiefly for a campaign against wild horses. He took the field, with a coil of cordage hung at his saddle-bow, and a couple of white wands, something like fishing-rods, eight or ten feet in length, with forked ends. The coil of cordage thus used in hunting the wild horse is called a lariat, and answers to the lasso of South America. It is not flung, however, in the graceful and dexterous Spanish style. The hunter, after a hard chase, when he succeeds in getting almost head and head with the wild horse, hitches the running noose of the lariat over his head by means of the forked stick; then, letting him have the full length of the cord, plays him like a fish, and chokes him into subjection.

All this Tonish promised to exemplify to our full satisfaction; we had not much confidence in his success, and feared he might knock up a good horse in a headlong gallop after a bad one, for, like all the French creoles, he was a merciless hard rider. It was determined, therefore, to keep a sharp eye upon him, and to check his sallying propensities.

We had not proceeded far on our morning's march when we were checked by a deep stream, running along the bottom of a thickly wooded ravine. After coasting it for a couple of miles, we came to a fording place; but to get down to it was the difficulty, for the banks were steep and crumbling, and overgrown with forest trees, mingled with thickets, brambles, and grapevines. At length the leading horseman broke his way through the thicket, and his horse, putting his feet together, slid down the black crumbling bank to the narrow margin of the stream; then floundering across, with mud and water up to the saddle-girths, he scrambled up to the opposite bank, and arrived safe on level ground. The whole line followed pell-mell after the leader, and pushing forward in close order, Indian file, they crowded each other down the bank and into the stream. Some of the horsemen missed the ford, and were soused over head and ears; one was unhorsed, and plumped head foremost into the middle of the stream: for my own part, while pressed forward, and hurried over the bank by those behind me, I was interrupted by a grapevine, as thick as a cable, which hung in a festoon as low as the saddle-bow, and, dragging me from the saddle, threw me among the feet of the trampling horses. Fortunately, I escaped without injury, regained my steed, crossed the stream without further difficulty, and was enabled to join in the merriment occasioned by the ludicrous disasters.

It is at passes like this that occur the most dangerous ambuscades and sanguinary surprises of Indian warfare. A party of savages well placed among the thickets might have made sad havoc among our men, while entangled in the ravine.

We now came out upon a vast and glorious prairie, spreading out beneath the golden beams of an autumnal sun. The deep and frequent traces of buffalo showed it to be one of their favorite grazing grounds; yet none were to be seen. In the course of the morning we were overtaken by the lieutenant and seventeen men, who had remained behind, and who came laden with the spoils of buffaloes; having killed three on the preceding day. One of the rangers, however, had little luck to boast of; his horse having taken fright at sight of the buffaloes, thrown his rider, and escaped into the woods.

The excitement of our hunters, both young and old, now rose almost to fever height; scarce any of them having ever encountered any of this far-famed game of the prairies. Accordingly, when in the course of the day the cry of buffalo! buffalo! rose from one part of the line, the whole troop were thrown in agitation. We were just then passing through a beautiful part of the prairie, finely diversified by hills and slopes, and woody dells, and high, stately groves. Those who had given the alarm pointed out a large black-looking animal, slowly moving along the side of a rising ground, about two miles off. The ever-ready Tonish jumped up, and stood with his feet on the saddle, and his forked sticks in his hands, like a posture-master or scaramouch at a circus, just ready for a feat of horsemanship. After gazing at the animal for a moment, which he could have seen full as well without rising from his stirrups, he pronounced it a wild horse; and dropping again into his saddle was about to dash off full tilt in pursuit, when, to his inexpressible chagrin, he was called back, and ordered to keep to his post, in rear of the baggage horses.

The captain and two of his officers now set off to reconnoiter the game. It was the intention of the captain, who was an admirable marksman, to endeavor to crease the horse; that is to say, to hit him with a rifle ball in the ridge of the neck. A wound of this kind paralyzes a horse for a moment; he falls to the ground, and may be secured before he recovers. It is a cruel expedient, however, for an ill-directed shot may kill or maim the noble animal.

As the captain and his companions moved off laterally and slowly, in the direction of the horse, we continued our course forward; watching intently, however, the movements of the game. The horse moved quietly over the profile of the rising ground, and disappeared behind it. The captain and his party were likewise soon hidden by an intervening hill.

After a time the horse suddenly made his appearance to our right, just ahead of the line, emerging out of a small valley, on a brisk trot; having evidently taken the alarm. At sight of us he stopped short, gazed at us for an instant with surprise, then, tossing up his head, trotted off in fine style, glancing at us first over one shoulder, then over the other, his ample mane and tail streaming in the wind. Having dashed through a skirt of thicket, that looked like a hedgerow, he paused in the open field beyond, glanced back at us again, with a beautiful bend of the neck, snuffed the air, then, tossing his head again, broke into a gallop and took refuge in a wood.

It was the first time I had ever seen a horse scouring his native wilderness in all the pride and freedom of his nature. How different from the poor, mutilated, harnessed, checked, reined-up victim of luxury, caprice, and avarice, in our cities!

After traveling about fifteen miles we encamped about one o'clock, that our hunters might have time to procure a supply of provisions. Our encampment was in a spacious grove of lofty oaks and walnuts, free from underwood, on the border of a brook. While unloading the pack-horses, our little Frenchman was loud in his complaints at having been prevented from pursuing the wild horse, which he would certainly have taken. In the meantime, I saw our half-breed, Beatte, quietly saddle his best horse, a powerful steed of half-savage race, hang a lariat at the saddle-bow, take a rifle and forked stick in hand, and, mounting, depart from the camp without saying a word. It was evident he was going off in quest of the wild horse, but was disposed to hunt alone.

CHAPTER TWENTY

THE CAMP OF THE WILD HORSE

HUNTER'S STORIES — HABITS OF THE WILD HORSE — THE HALF-BREED AND HIS PRIZE — A HORSE CHASE — A WILD SPIRIT TAMED

WE had encamped in a good neighborhood for game, as the reports of rifles in various directions speedily gave notice. One of our hunters soon returned with the meat of a doe, tied up in the skin, and slung across his shoulders. Another brought a fat buck across his horse. Two other deer were brought in, and a number of turkeys. All the game was thrown down in front of the captain's fire, to be portioned out among the various messes. The spits and camp kettles were soon in full employ, and throughout the evening there was a scene of hunter's feasting and profusion.

We had been disappointed this day in our hopes of meeting with buffalo, but the sight of the wild horse had been a great novelty, and gave a turn to the conversation of the camp for the evening. There were several anecdotes told of a famous gray horse, which has ranged the prairies of this neighborhood for six or seven years, setting at naught every attempt of the hunters to capture him. They say he can pace and rack (or amble) faster than the fleetest horses can run. Equally marvelous accounts were given of a black horse on the Brazos, who grazed the prairies on that river's bank in Texas. For years he outstripped all pursuit. His fame spread far and wide; offers were made for him to the amount of a thousand dollars; the boldest and most hard-riding hunters tried incessantly to make prize of him, but in vain. At length he fell a victim to his gallantry, being decoyed under a tree by a tame mare, and a noose dropped over his head by a boy perched among the branches.

The capture of a wild horse is one of the most favorite achievements of the prairie tribes; and, indeed, it is from this source that the Indian hunters chiefly supply themselves. The wild horses which range those vast grassy plains, extending from the Arkansas to the Spanish settlements, are of various forms and colors, betraying their various descents. Some resemble the common English stock, and are probably descended from horses which have escaped from our border settlements. Others are of a low but strong make, and are supposed to be of the Andalusian breed, brought out by the Spanish discoverers.

Some fanciful speculatists have seen in them descendants of the Arab stock, brought into Spain from Africa, and thence transferred to this country; and have pleased themselves with the idea that their sires may have been of the pure coursers of the desert that once bore Mahomet and his warlike disciples across the sandy plains of Arabia.

The habits of the Arab seem to have come with the steed. The introduction of the horse on the boundless prairies of the Far West changed the whole mode of living of their inhabitants. It gave them that facility of rapid motion, and of sudden and distant change of place, so dear to the roving propensities of man. Instead of lurking in the depths of gloomy forests, and patiently threading the mazes of a tangled wilderness on foot, like his brethren of the North, the Indian of the West is a rover of the plain; he leads a brighter and more sunshiny life; almost always on horseback, on vast flowery prairies and under cloudless skies.

I was lying by the captain's fire, late in the evening, listening to the stories about those coursers of the prairies, and weaving speculations of my own, when there was a clamor of voices and a loud cheering at the other end of the camp; and word was passed that Beatte, the half-breed, had brought in a wild horse.

In an instant every fire was deserted; the whole camp crowded to see the Indian and his prize. It was a colt about two years old, well grown, finely limbed, with bright prominent eyes and a spirited yet gentle demeanor. He gazed about him with an air of mingled stupefaction and surprise, at the men, the horses, and the camp-fires; while the Indian stood before him with folded arms, having hold of the other end of the cord which noosed his captive, and gazing on him with a most imperturbable aspect. Beatte, as I have before observed, has a greenish olive complexion, with a strongly marked countenance, not unlike the bronze casts of Napoleon; and as he stood before his captive horse with folded arms and fixed aspect he looked more like a statue than a man.

If the horse, however, manifested the least restiveness, Beatte would immediately worry him with the lariat, jerking him first on one side, then on the other, so as almost to throw him on the ground; when he had thus rendered him passive, he would resume his statue-like attitude and gaze at him in silence.

The whole scene was singularly wild; the tall grove, partially illumined by the flashing fires of the camp, the horses tethered here and there among the trees, the carcasses of deer hanging around, and in the midst of all, the wild huntsman and his wild horse, with an admiring throng of rangers, almost as wild.

In the eagerness of their excitement, several of the young rangers sought to get the horse by purchase or barter, and even offered extravagant terms; but Beatte declined all their offers. "You give great price now," said he, "to-morrow you be sorry, and take back, and say d—d Indian!"

The young men importuned him with questions about the mode in which he took the horse, but his answers were dry and laconic; he evidently retained some pique at having been undervalued and sneered at by them; and at the same time looked down upon them with contempt as greenhorns, little versed in the noble science of woodcraft.

Afterward, however, when he was seated by our fire, I readily drew from him an account of his exploit; for, though taciturn among strangers, and little prone to boast of his actions, yet his taciturnity, like that of all Indians, had its times of relaxation.

He informed me that, on leaving the camp, he had returned to the place where we had lost sight of the wild horse. Soon getting upon its track, he followed it to the banks of the river. Here, the prints being more distinct in the sand, he perceived that one of the hoofs was broken and defective, so he gave up the pursuit.

As he was returning to the camp, he came upon a gang of six horses, which immediately made for the river. He pursued them across the stream, left his rifle on the river bank, and putting his horse to full speed, soon came up with the fugitives. He attempted to noose one of them, but the lariat hitched on one of his ears, and he shook it off. The horses dashed up a hill, he followed hard at their heels, when, of a sudden, he saw their tails whisking in the air, and they plunged down a precipice. It was too late to stop. He shut his eyes, held in his breath, and went over with them—neck or nothing. The descent was between twenty and thirty feet, but they all came down safe upon a sandy bottom.

He now succeeded in throwing his noose round a fine young horse. As he galloped alongside of him, the two horses passed each side of a sapling, and the end of the lariat was jerked out of his hand. He regained it, but an intervening tree obliged him again to let it go. Having once more caught it, and coming to a more open country, he was enabled to play the young horse with the line until he gradually checked and subdued him, so as to lead him to the place where he had left his rifle.

He had another formidable difficulty in getting him across the river, where both horses stuck for a time in the mire, and Beatte was nearly unseated from his saddle by the force of the current and the struggles of his captive. After much toil and trouble, however, he got across the stream, and brought his prize safe into camp.

For the remainder of the evening the camp remained in a high state of excitement; nothing was talked of but the capture of wild horses; every youngster of the troop was for this harum-scarum kind of chase; every one promised himself to return from the campaign in triumph, bestriding one of these wild coursers of the prairies. Beatte had suddenly risen to great importance; he was the prime hunter, the hero of the day. Offers were made him by the best mounted rangers to let him ride their horses in the chase, provided he would give them a share of the spoil. Beatte bore his honors in silence, and closed with none of the offers. Our stammering, chattering, gasconading little Frenchman, however, made up for his taciturnity by vaunting as much upon the subject as if it were he that had caught the horse. Indeed he held forth so learnedly in the matter, and boasted so much of the many horses he had taken, that he began to be considered an oracle; and some of the youngsters were inclined to doubt whether he were not superior even to the taciturn Beatte.

The excitement kept the camp awake later than usual. The hum of voices, interrupted by occasional peals of laughter, was heard from the groups around the various fires, and the night was considerably advanced before all had sunk to sleep.

With the morning dawn the excitement revived, and Beatte and his wild horse were again the gaze and talk of the camp. The captive had been tied all night to a tree among the other horses. He was again led forth by Beatte, by a long halter or lariat, and, on his manifesting the least restiveness, was, as before, jerked and worried into passive submission.   He appeared to be gentle and docile by nature, and had a beautifully mild expression of the eye.   In his strange and forlorn situation, the poor animal seemed to seek protection and companionship in the very horse which had aided to capture him.

Seeing him thus gentle and tractable, Beatte, just as we were about to march, strapped a light pack upon his back, by way of giving him the first lesson in servitude.   The native pride and independence of the animal took fire at this indignity.   He reared, and plunged, and kicked, and tried in every way to get rid of the degrading burden.   The Indian was too potent for him.   At every paroxysm he renewed the discipline of the halter, until the poor animal, driven to despair, threw himself prostrate on the ground, and lay motionless, as if acknowledging himself vanquished.   A stage hero, representing the despair of a captive prince, could not have played his part more dramatically.   There was absolutely a moral grandeur in it.

The imperturbable Beatte folded his arms, and stood for a time, looking down in silence upon his captive; until seeing him perfectly subdued, he nodded his head slowly, screwed his mouth into a sardonic smile of triumph, and, with a jerk of the halter, ordered him to rise.   He obeyed, and from that time forward offered no resistance.   During that day he bore his pack patiently, and was led by the halter; but in two days he followed voluntarily at large among the supernumerary horses of the troop.

I could not look without compassion upon this fine young animal, whose whole course of existence had been so suddenly reversed.   From being a denizen of these vast pastures, ranging at will from plain to plain and mead to mead, cropping of every herb and flower, and drinking of every stream, he was suddenly reduced to perpetual and painful servitude, to pass his life under the harness and the curb, amid, perhaps, the din and dust and drudgery of cities.   The transition in his lot was such as sometimes takes place in human affairs, and in the fortunes of towering individuals. One day, a prince of the prairies—the next day, a pack-horse!

CHAPTER TWENTY-ONE

THE FORDING OF THE RED FORK—THE DREARY FORESTS OF THE "CROSS TIMBER"—BUFFALO!

WE left the camp of the wild horse about a quarter before eight, and, after steering nearly south for three or four miles, arrived on the banks of the Red Fork, about seventy-five miles, as we supposed, above its mouth. The river was about three hundred yards wide, wandering among sand-bars and shoals. Its shores, and the long sandy banks that stretched out into the stream, were printed, as usual, with the traces of various animals that had come down to cross it or to drink its waters.

Here we came to a halt, and there was much consultation about the possibility of fording the river with safety, as there was an apprehension of quicksands. Beatte, who had been somewhat in the rear, came up while we were debating. He was mounted on his horse of the half-wild breed, and leading his captive by the bridle. He gave the latter in charge to Tonish, and without saying a word, urged his horse into the stream and crossed it in safety. Everything was done by this man in a similar way, promptly, resolutely, and silently, without a previous promise or an after vaunt.

The troop now followed the lead of Beatte, and reached the opposite shore without any mishap, though one of the pack-horses, wandering a little from the track, came near being swallowed up in a quicksand, and was with difficulty dragged to land.

After crossing the river, we had to force our way, for nearly a mile, through a thick cane-brake, which, at first sight, appeared an impervious mass of reeds and brambles. It was a hard struggle; our horses were often to the saddle-girths in mire and water, and both horse and horseman harassed and torn by bush and brier. Falling, however, upon a buffalo track, we at length extricated ourselves from this morass, and ascended a ridge of land, where we beheld a beautiful open country before us; while to our right, the belt of forest land, called "The Cross Timber," continued stretching away to the southward, as far as the eye could reach. We soon abandoned the open country, and struck into the forest land. It was the intention of the captain to keep on southwest by south, and traverse the Cross Timber diagonally, so as to come out upon the edge of the great western prairie. By thus maintaining something of a southerly direction, he trusted, while he crossed the belt of the forest, he would at the same time approach the Red River.

The plan of the captain was judicious; but he erred from not being informed of the nature of the country. Had he kept directly west, a couple of days would have carried us through the forest land, and we might then have had an easy course along the skirts of the upper prairies, to Red River; by going diagonally, we were kept for many weary days toiling through a dismal series of rugged forests.

The Cross Timber is about forty miles in breadth, and stretches over a rough country of rolling hills, covered with scattered tracts of post-oak and black-jack; with some intervening valleys, which, at proper seasons, would afford good pasturage. It is very much cut up by deep ravines, which, in the rainy seasons, are the beds of temporary streams, tributary to the main rivers, and these are called "branches." The whole tract may present a pleasant aspect in the fresh time of the year, when the ground is covered with herbage; when the trees are in their green leaf, and the glens are enlivened by running streams. Unfortunately, we entered it too late in the season. The herbage was parched; the foliage of the scrubby forests was withered; the whole woodland prospect, as far as the eye could reach, had a brown and arid hue. The fires made on the prairies by the Indian hunters had frequently penetrated these forests, sweeping in light transient flames along the dry grass, scorching and calcining the lower twigs and branches of the trees, and leaving them black and hard, so as to tear the flesh of man and horse that had to scramble through them. I shall not easily forget the mortal toil, and the vexations of flesh and spirit, that we underwent occasionally, in our wanderings through the Cross Timber. It was like struggling through forests of cast iron.

After a tedious ride of several miles, we came out upon an open tract of hill and dale, interspersed with woodland. Here we were roused by the cry of buffalo! buffalo! The effect was something like that of the cry of a sail! a sail! at sea. It was not a false alarm. Three or four of these enormous animals were visible to our sight grazing on the slope of a distant hill.

There was a general movement to set off in pursuit, and it was with some difficulty that the vivacity of the younger men of the troop could be restrained. Leaving orders that the line of march should be preserved, the captain and two of his officers departed at a quiet pace, accompanied by Beatte, and by the ever-forward Tonish; for it was impossible any longer to keep the little Frenchman in check, being half crazy to prove his skill and prowess in hunting the buffalo.

The intervening hills soon hid from us both the game and the huntsmen. We kept on our course in quest of a camping place, which was difficult to be found; almost all the channels of the streams being dry, and the country being destitute of fountain heads.

After proceeding some distance, there was again a cry of buffalo, and two were pointed out on a hill to the left. The captain being absent, it was no longer possible to restrain the ardor of the young hunters. Away several of them dashed, full speed, and soon disappeared among the ravines; the rest kept on, anxious to find a proper place for encampment.

* * * 20—Vol. VII.

Indeed we now began to experience the disadvantages of the season. The pasturage of the prairies was scanty and parched; the pea-vines which grew in the woody bottoms were withered, and most of the "branches" or streams were dried up. While wandering in this perplexity, we were overtaken by the captain and all his party, except Tonish. They had pursued the buffalo for some distance without getting within shot, and had given up the chase, being fearful of fatiguing their horses or being led off too far from camp. The little Frenchman, however, had galloped after them at headlong speed, and the last they saw of him, he was engaged, as it were, yardarm and yardarm, with a great buffalo bull, firing broadsides into him. "I tink dat little man crazy—somehow," observed Beatte, dryly.

CHAPTER TWENTY-TWO

THE ALARM CAMP

WE now came to a halt, and had to content ourselves with an indifferent encampment. It was in a grove of scrub oaks, on the borders of a deep ravine, at the bottom of which were a few scanty pools of water. We were just at the foot of a gradually-sloping hill, covered with half-withered grass, that afforded meager pasturage. In the spot where we had encamped the grass was high and parched. The view around us was circumscribed and much shut in by gently swelling hills.

Just as we were encamping, Tonish arrived, all glorious, from his hunting match; his white horse hung all round with buffalo meat. According to his own account, he had laid low two mighty bulls. As usual, we deducted one-half from his boastings; but, now that he had something real to vaunt about, there was no restraining the valor of his tongue.

After having in some measure appeased his vanity by

boasting of his exploit, he informed us that he had observed the fresh track of horses, which, from various circumstances, he suspected to have been made by some roving band of Pawnees. This caused some little uneasiness. The young men who had left the line of march in pursuit of the two buffaloes had not yet rejoined us; apprehensions were expressed that they might be waylaid and attacked. Our veteran hunter, old Ryan, also, immediately on our halting to encamp, had gone off on foot, in company with a young disciple. "Dat old man will have his brains knocked out by de Pawnees yet," said Beatte. "He tink he know everyting, but he don't know Pawnees, anyhow."

Taking his rifle, the captain repaired on foot to reconnoiter the country from the naked summit of one of the neighboring hills. In the meantime, the horses were hobbled and turned loose to graze; and wood was cut, and fires made, to prepare the evening's repast.

Suddenly there was an alarm of fire in the camp! The flame from one of the kindling fires had caught to the tall dry grass; a breeze was blowing; there was danger that the camp would soon be wrapped in a light blaze. "Look to the horses!" cried one. "Drag away the baggage!" cried another. "Take care of the rifles and powder-horns!" cried a third. All was hurry-scurry and uproar. The horses dashed wildly about; some of the men snatched away rifles and powder-horns, others dragged off saddles and saddle-bags. Meantime, no one thought of quelling the fire, nor indeed knew how to quell it. Beatte, however, and his comrades attacked it in the Indian mode, beating down the edges of the fire with blankets and horse cloths, and endeavoring to prevent its spreading among the grass; the rangers followed their example, and in a little while the flames were happily quelled.

The fires were now properly kindled on places from which the dry grass had been cleared away. The horses were scattered about a small valley, and on the sloping hill-side, cropping the scanty herbage. Tonish was preparing a sumptuous evening's meal from his buffalo meat, promising us a rich soup and a prime piece of roast beef, but we were doomed to experience another and more serious alarm.

There was an indistinct cry from some rangers on the summit of the hill, of which we could only distinguish the words, "The horses! the horses! get in the horses!"

Immediately a clamor of voices arose; shouts, inquiries, replies, were all mingled together, so that nothing could be clearly understood, and every one drew his own inference.

"The captain has started buffaloes," cried one, "and wants horses for the chase." Immediately a number of rangers seized their rifles and scampered for the hill-top. "The prairie is on fire beyond the hill," cried another; "I see the smoke—the captain means we shall drive the horses beyond the brook."

By this time a ranger from the hill had reached the skirts of the camp. He was almost breathless, and could only say that the captain had seen Indians at a distance.

"Pawnees! Pawnees!" was now the cry among our wild-headed youngsters. "Drive the horses into camp!" cried one. "Saddle the horses!" cried another. "Form the line!" cried a third. There was now a scene of clamor and confusion that baffles all description. The rangers were scampering about the adjacent field in pursuit of their horses. One might be seen tugging his steed along by a halter; another without a hat, riding bare-backed; another driving a hobbled horse before him, that made awkward leaps like a kangaroo.

The alarm increased. Word was brought from the lower end of the camp that there was a band of Pawnees in a neighboring valley. They had shot old Ryan through the head, and were chasing his companion! "No, it was not old Ryan that was killed—it was one of the hunters that had been after the two buffaloes." "There are three hundred Pawnees just beyond the hill," cried one voice. "More, more!" cried another.

Our situation, shut in among hills, prevented our seeing to any distance, and left us a prey to all these rumors. A cruel enemy was supposed to be at hand, and an immediate attack apprehended. The horses by this time were driven into the camp, and were dashing about among the fires, and trampling upon the baggage. Every one endeavored to prepare for action; but here was the perplexity. During the late alarm of fire the saddles, bridles, rifles, powder-horns, and other equipments, had been snatched out of their places, and thrown helter-skelter among the trees.

"Where is my saddle?" cried one. "Has any one seen my rifle?" cried another. "Who will lend me a ball?" cried a third, who was loading his piece. "I have lost my bullet pouch." "For God's sake help me to girth this horse!" cried another; "he's so restive I can do nothing with him." In his hurry and worry, he had put on the saddle the hind part before!

Some affected to swagger and talk bold; others said nothing, but went on steadily, preparing their horses and weapons, and on these I felt the most reliance. Some were evidently excited and elated with the idea of an encounter with Indians; and none more so than my young Swiss fellow traveler, who had a passion for wild adventure. Our man, Beatte, led his horses in the rear of the camp, placed his rifle against a tree, then seated himself by the fire in perfect silence. On the other hand, little Tonish, who was busy cooking, stopped every moment from his work to play the fanfaron, singing, swearing, and affecting an unusual hilarity, which made me strongly suspect that there was some little fright at bottom, to cause all this effervescence.

About a dozen of the rangers, as soon as they could saddle their horses, dashed off in the direction in which the Pawnees were said to have attacked the hunters. It was now determined, in case our camp should be assailed, to put our horses in the ravine in the rear, where they would be out of danger from arrow or rifle-ball, and to take our stand within the edge of the ravine. This would serve as a trench, and the trees and thickets with which it was bordered would be sufficient to turn aside any shaft of the enemy. The Pawnees, besides, are wary of attacking any covert of the kind; their warfare, as I have already observed, lies in the open prairie, where, mounted upon their fleet horses, they can swoop like hawks upon their enemy, or wheel about him and discharge their arrows. Still I could not but perceive, that, in case of being attacked by such a number of these well-mounted and warlike savages as were said to be at hand, we should be exposed to considerable risk from the inexperience and want of discipline of our newly raised rangers, and from the very courage of many of the younger ones who seemed bent on adventure and exploit.

By this time the captain reached the camp, and every one crowded round him for information. He informed us that he had proceeded some distance on his reconnoitering expedition, and was slowly returning toward the camp, along the brow of a naked hill, when he saw something on the edge of a parallel hill that looked like a man. He paused and watched it; but it remained so perfectly motionless that he supposed it a bush or the top of some tree beyond the hill. He resumed his course, when it likewise began to move in a parallel direction. Another form now rose beside it, of some one who had either been lying down or had just ascended the other side of the hill. The captain stopped and regarded them; they likewise stopped. He then lay down upon the grass, and they began to walk. On his rising, they again stopped, as if watching him. Knowing that the Indians are apt to have their spies and sentinels thus posted on the summit of naked hills, commanding extensive prospects, his doubts were increased by the suspicious movements of these men. He now put his foraging cap on the end of his rifle and waved it in the air. They took no notice of the signal. He then walked on, until he entered the edge of a wood which concealed him from their view. Stopping out of sight for a moment, he again looked forth, when he saw the two men passing swiftly forward. As the hill on which they were walking made a curve toward that on which he stood, it seemed as if they were endeavoring to head him before he should reach the camp. Doubting whether they might not belong to some large party of Indians, either in ambush or moving along the valley beyond the hill, the captain hastened his steps homeward, and, descrying some rangers on an eminence between him and the camp, he called out to them to pass the word to have the horses driven in, as these are generally the first objects of Indian depredation.

Such was the origin of the alarm which had thrown the camp in commotion. Some of those who heard the captain's narration, had no doubt that the men on the hill were Pawnee scouts, belonging to the band that had waylaid the hunters. Distant shots were heard at intervals, which were supposed to be fired by those who had sallied out to rescue their comrades. Several more rangers, having completed their equipments, now rode forth in the direction of the firing; others looked anxious and uneasy.

"If they are as numerous as they are said to be," said one, "and as well mounted as they generally are, we shall be a bad match for them with our jaded horses."

"Well," replied the captain, "we have a strong encampment, and can stand a siege."

"Ay, but they may set fire to the prairie in the night and burn us out of our encampment."

"We will then set up a counter fire!"

The word was now passed that a man on horseback approached the camp.

"It is one of the hunters! It is Clements! He brings buffalo meat!" was announced by several voices as the horseman drew near.

It was, in fact, one of the rangers who had set off in the morning in pursuit of the two buffaloes. He rode into the camp, with the spoils of the chase hanging round his horse, and followed by his companions, all sound and unharmed, and equally well laden. They proceeded to give an account of a grand gallop they had had after the two buffaloes, and how many shots it had cost them to bring one to the ground.

"Well, but the Pawnees—the Pawnees—where are the Pawnees?"

"What Pawnees?"

"The Pawnees that attacked you."

"No one attacked us."

"But have you seen no Indians on your way?"

"Oh, yes, two of us got to the top of a hill to look out for the camp, and saw a fellow on an opposite hill cutting queer antics, who seemed to be an Indian."

"Pshaw! that was I!" said the captain.

Here the bubble burst. The whole alarm had risen from this mutual mistake of the captain and the two rangers. As to the report of the three hundred Pawnees and their attack on the hunters, it proved to be a wanton fabrication, of which no further notice was taken; though the author deserved to have been sought out and severely punished.

There being no longer any prospect of fighting, every one now thought of eating; and here the stomachs throughout the camp were in unison. Tonish served up to us his promised regale of buffalo soup and buffalo beef. The soup was peppered most horribly, and the roast beef proved the bull to have been one of the patriarchs of the prairies; never did I have to deal with a tougher morsel. However, it was our first repast on buffalo meat, so we ate it with a lively faith; nor would our little Frenchman allow us any rest, until he had extorted from us an acknowledgment of the excellence of his cookery; though the pepper gave us the lie in our throats.

The night closed in without the return of old Ryan and his companion. We had become accustomed, however, to the aberrations of this old cock of the woods, and no further solicitude was expressed on his account.

After the fatigues and agitations of the day, the camp soon sunk into a profound sleep, excepting those on guard, who were more than usually on the alert; for the traces recently seen of Pawnees, and the certainty that we were in the midst of their hunting grounds, excited to constant vigilance. About half past ten o'clock we were all startled from sleep by a new alarm. A sentinel had fired off his rifle and run into camp, crying that there were Indians at hand.

Every one was on his legs in an instant. Some seized their rifles; some were about to saddle their horses; some hastened to the captain's lodge, but were ordered back to their respective fires. The sentinel was examined. He declared he had seen an Indian approach, crawling along the ground; whereupon he had fired upon him, and run into camp. The captain gave it as his opinion that the supposed Indian was a wolf; he reprimanded the sentinel for deserting his post, and obliged him to return to it. Many seemed inclined to give credit to the story of the sentinel; for the events of the day had predisposed them to apprehend lurking foes and sudden assaults during the darkness of the night. For a long time they sat round their fires, with rifle in hand, carrying on low, murmuring conversations, and listening for some new alarm. Nothing further, however, occurred; the voices gradually died away; the gossipers nodded and dozed, and sunk to rest; and, by degrees, silence and sleep once more stole over the camp.

CHAPTER TWENTY-THREE

BEAVER DAM—BUFFALO AND HORSE TRACKS—A PAWNEE
TRAIL—WILD HORSES—THE YOUNG HUNTER AND
THE BEAR—CHANGE OF ROUTE

ON mustering our forces in the morning (October 23d), old Ryan and his comrade were still missing; but the captain had such perfect reliance on the skill and resources of the veteran woodman, that he did not think it necessary to take any measures with respect to him.

Our march this day lay through the same kind of rough rolling country; checkered by brown dreary forests of post-oak, and cut up by deep dry ravines. The distant fires were evidently increasing on the prairies. The wind had been at northwest for several days; and the atmosphere had become so smoky, as in the height of Indian summer, that it was difficult to distinguish objects at any distance.

In the course of the morning we crossed a deep stream with a complete beaver dam, above three feet high, making a large pond, and doubtless containing several families of that industrious animal, though not one showed his nose above water. The captain would not permit this amphibious commonwealth to be disturbed.

We were now continually coming upon the tracks of buffaloes and wild horses; those of the former tended invariably to the south, as we could perceive by the direction of the trampled grass. It was evident we were on the great highway of these migratory herds, but that they had chiefly passed to the southward.

Beatte, who generally kept a parallel course several hundred yards distant from our line of march, to be on the lookout for game, and who regarded every track with the knowing eye of an Indian, reported that he had come upon a very suspicious trail. There were the tracks of men who wore Pawnee moccasins. He had scented the smoke of mingled sumach and tobacco, such as the Indians use. He had observed tracks of horses, mingled with those of a dog; and a mark in the dust where a cord had been trailed along; probably the long bridle, one end of which the Indian horsemen suffer to trail on the ground. It was evident, they were not the tracks of wild horses. My anxiety began to revive about the safety of our veteran hunter Ryan, for I had taken a great fancy to this real old Leatherstocking; every one expressed a confidence, however, that wherever Ryan was, he was safe, and knew how to take care of himself.

We had accomplished the greater part of a weary day's march, and were passing through a glade of the oak openings, when we came in sight of six wild horses, among which I especially noticed two very handsome ones, a gray and a roan. They pranced about, with heads erect, and long flaunting tails, offering a proud contrast to our poor, spiritless, travel-tired steeds. Having reconnoitered us for a moment, they set off at a gallop, passed through a woody dingle, and in a little while emerged once more to view, trotting up a slope about a mile distant.

The sight of these horses was again a sore trial to the vaporing Tonish, who had his lariat and forked stick ready, and was on the point of launching forth in pursuit, on his jaded horse, when he was again ordered back to the pack-horses.

After a day's journey of fourteen miles in a southwest direction, we encamped on the banks of a small clear stream, on the northern border of the Cross Timbers; and on the edge of those vast prairies that extend away to the foot of the Rocky Mountains. In turning loose the horses to graze, their bells were stuffed with grass to prevent their tinkling, lest it might be heard by some wandering horde of Pawnees.

Our hunters now went out in different directions, but without much success, as but one deer was brought into the camp. A young ranger had a long story to tell of his adventures. In skirting the thickets of a deep ravine he had wounded a buck, which he plainly heard to fall among the bushes. He stopped to fix the lock of his rifle, which was out of order, and to reload it; then advancing to the edge of the thicket, in quest of his game, he heard a low growling. Putting the branches aside, and stealing silently forward, he looked down into the ravine and beheld a huge bear dragging the carcass of the deer along the dry channel of a brook, and growling and snarling at four or five officious wolves, who seemed to have dropped in to take supper with him.

The ranger fired at the bear, but missed him. Bruin maintained his ground and his prize, and seemed disposed to make battle. The wolves, too, who were evidently sharp set, drew off to but a small distance. As night was coming on, the young hunter felt dismayed at the wildness and darkness of the place, and the strange company he had fallen in

with; so he quietly withdrew, and returned empty handed
to the camp, where, having told his story, he was heartily
bantered by his more experienced comrades.

In the course of the evening, old Ryan came straggling
into the camp, followed by his disciple, and as usual was
received with hearty gratulations. He had lost himself
yesterday, when hunting, and camped out all night, but had
found our trail in the morning, and followed it up. He had
passed some time at the beaver dam, admiring the skill and
solidity with which it had been constructed. "These bea-
vers," said he, "are industrious little fellows. They are the
knowingest varment as I know; and I'll warrant the pond
was stocked with them."

"Aye," said the captain, "I have no doubt most of the
small rivers we have passed are full of beaver. I would like
to come and trap on these waters all winter."

"But would you not run the chance of being attacked by
Indians?" asked one of the company.

"Oh, as to that, it would be safe enough here, in the
winter time. There would be no Indians here until spring.
I should want no more than two companions. Three persons
are safer than a large number for trapping beaver. They
can keep quiet, and need seldom fire a gun. A bear would
serve them for food for two months, taking care to turn
every part of it to advantage."

A consultation was now held as to our future progress.
We had thus far pursued a western course; and, having
traversed the Cross Timber, were on the skirts of the Great
Western Prairie. We were still, however, in a very rough
country, where food was scarce. The season was so far
advanced that the grass was withered, and the prairies
yielded no pasturage. The pea-vines of the bottoms, also,
which had sustained our horses for some part of the journey,
were nearly gone, and for several days past the poor animals
had fallen off wofully both in flesh and spirit. The Indian
fires on the prairies were approaching us from north, and
south, and west; they might spread also from the east, and

leave a scorched desert between us and the frontier, in which
our horses might be famished.

It was determined, therefore, to advance no further to
the westward, but to shape our course more to the east, so
as to strike the north fork of the Canadian as soon as possible, where we hoped to find abundance of young cane,
which, at this season of the year, affords the most nutritious
pasturage for the horses; and, at the same time, attracts
immense quantities of game. Here then we fixed the limits
of our tour to the Far West, being within little more than a
day's march of the boundary line of Texas.

CHAPTER TWENTY-FOUR

SCARCITY OF BREAD—RENCONTRE WITH BUFFALOES—WILD TURKEYS—FALL OF A BUFFALO BULL

THE morning broke bright and clear, but the camp had
nothing of its usual gayety. The concert of the farmyard
was at an end; not a cock crowed, nor dog barked; nor was
there either singing or laughing; every one pursued his
avocations quietly and gravely. The novelty of the expedition was wearing off. Some of the young men were getting
as way-worn as their horses; and most of them, unaccustomed to the hunter's life, began to repine at its privations.
What they most felt was the want of bread, their rations of
flour having been exhausted for several days. The old
hunters, who had often experienced this want, made light of
it; and Beatte, accustomed when among the Indians to live
for months without it, considered it a mere article of luxury.
"Bread," he would say scornfully, "is only fit for a child."

About a quarter before eight o'clock, we turned our backs
upon the Far West, and set off in a southeast course along a
gentle valley. After riding a few miles, Beatte, who kept
parallel with us, along the ridge of a naked hill to our right,
called out and made signals, as if something were coming

round the hill to intercept us. Some who were near me cried out that it was a party of Pawnees. A skirt of thickets hid the approach of the supposed enemy from our view. We heard a trampling among the brushwood. My horse looked toward the place, snorted and pricked up his ears, when presently a couple of large buffalo bulls, who had been alarmed by Beatte, came crashing through the brake, and making directly toward us. At sight of us they wheeled round and scuttled along a narrow defile of the hill. In an instant half a score of rifles cracked off; there was a universal whoop and halloo, and away went half the troop, helter-skelter in pursuit, and myself among the number. The most of us soon pulled up, and gave over a chase which led through birch and brier and break-neck ravines. Some few of the rangers persisted for a time; but eventually joined the line, slowly lagging one after another. One of them re-t. ned on foot; he had been thrown while in full chase; his rifle had been broken in the fall, and his horse, retaining the spirit of the rider, had kept on after the buffalo. It was a melancholy predicament to be reduced to; without horse or weapon in the midst of the Pawnee hunting grounds.

For my own part, I had been fortunate enough recently, by a further exchange, to get possession of the best horse in the troop; a full-blooded sorrel of excellent bottom, beautiful form, and most generous qualities.

In such a situation it almost seems as if a man changes his nature with his horse. I felt quite like another being, now that I had an animal under me, spirited yet gentle, docile to a remarkable degree, and easy, elastic, and rapid in all his movements. In a few days he became almost as much attached to me as a dog; would follow me when I dismounted, would come to me in the morning to be noticed and caressed; and would put his muzzle between me and my book, as I sat reading at the foot of a tree. The feeling I had for this my dumb companion of the prairies, gave me some faint idea of that attachment the Arab is said to entertain for the horse that has borne him about the deserts.

After riding a few miles further, we came to a fine meadow with a broad clear stream winding through it, on the banks of which there was excellent pasturage. Here we at once came to a halt, in a beautiful grove of elms, on the site of an old Osage encampment. Scarcely had we dismounted when a universal firing of rifles took place upon a large flock of turkeys scattered about the grove, which proved to be a favorite roosting-place for these simple birds. They flew to the trees, and sat perched upon their branches, stretching out their long necks, and gazing in stupid astonishment, until eighteen of them were shot down.

In the height of the carnage word was brought that there were four buffaloes in a neighboring meadow. The turkeys were now abandoned for nobler game. The tired horses were again mounted and urged to the chase. In a little while we came in sight of the buffaloes, looking like brown hillocks among the long green herbage. Beatte endeavored to get ahead of them and turn them toward us, that the inexperienced hunters might have a chance. They ran round the base of a rocky hill that hid us from the sight. Some of us endeavored to cut across the hill, but became entrapped in a thick wood, matted with grapevines. My horse, who, under his former rider, had hunted the buffalo, seemed as much excited as myself, and endeavored to force his way through the bushes. At length we extricated ourselves, and galloping over the hill, I found our little Frenchman, Tonish, curveting on horseback round a great buffalo which he had wounded too severely to fly, and which he was keeping employed until we should come up. There was a mixture of the grand and the comic, in beholding this tremendous animal and his fantastic assailant. The buffalo stood with his shaggy front always presented to his foe; his mouth open, his tongue parched, his eyes like coals of fire, and his tail erect with rage; every now and then he would make a faint rush upon his foe, who easily evaded his attack, capering and cutting all kinds of antics before him.

We now made repeated shots at the buffalo, but they

glanced into his mountain of flesh without proving mortal. He made a slow and grand retreat into the shallow river, turning upon his assailants whenever they pressed upon him; and when in the water, took his stand there as if prepared to sustain a siege. A rifle ball, however, more fatally lodged, sent a tremor through his frame. He turned and attempted to wade across the stream, but after tottering a few paces slowly fell upon his side and expired. It was the fall of a hero, and we felt somewhat ashamed of the butchery that had effected it; but, after the first shot or two, we had reconciled it to our feelings, by the old plea of putting the poor animal out of his misery.

Two other buffaloes were killed this evening, but they were all bulls, the flesh of which is meager and hard at this season of the year. A fat buck yielded us more savory meat for our evening's repast.

CHAPTER TWENTY-FIVE

RINGING THE WILD HORSE

WE left the buffalo camp about eight o'clock, and had a toilsome and harassing march of two hours, over ridges of hills, covered with a ragged meager forest of scrub-oaks, and broken by deep gullies. Among the oaks I observed many of the most diminutive size; some not above a foot high, yet bearing abundance of small acorns. The whole of the Cross Timber, in fact, abounds with mast. There is a pine-oak which produces an acorn pleasant to the taste and ripening early in the season.

About ten o'clock in the morning, we came to where this line of rugged hills swept down into a valley, through which flowed the north fork of the Red River. A beautiful meadow about half a mile wide, enameled with yellow autumnal flowers, stretched for two or three miles along the foot of the hills, bordered on the opposite side by the river, whose bank was fringed with cottonwood trees, the bright foliage of which refreshed and delighted the eye, after being wearied by the contemplation of monotonous wastes of brown forest.

The meadow was finely diversified by groves and clumps of trees, so happily dispersed that they seemed as if set out by the hand of art. As we cast our eyes over this fresh and delightful valley, we beheld a troop of wild horses, quietly grazing on a green lawn, about a mile distant to our right, while to our left, at nearly the same distance, were several buffaloes; some feeding, others reposing and ruminating among the high rich herbage, under the shade of a clump of cottonwood trees. The whole had the appearance of a broad beautiful tract of pasture land, on the highly ornamented estate of some gentleman farmer, with his cattle grazing about the lawns and meadows.

A council of war was now held, and it was determined to profit by the present favorable opportunity, and try our hand at the grand hunting maneuver, which is called ringing the wild horse. This requires a large party of horsemen, well mounted. They extend themselves in each direction, singly, at certain distances apart, and gradually form a ring of two or three miles in circumference, so as to surround the game. This has to be done with extreme care, for the wild horse is the most readily alarmed inhabitant of the prairie, and can scent a hunter at a great distance, if to windward.

The ring being formed, two or three ride toward the horses, who start off in an opposite direction. Whenever they approach the bounds of the ring, however, a huntsman presents himself and turns them from their course. In this way they are checked and driven back at every point; and kept galloping round and round this magic circle, until, being completely tired down, it is easy for the hunters to ride up beside them and throw the lariat over their heads. The prime horses of most speed, courage, and bottom, however, are apt to break through and escape, so that, in general, it is the second-rate horses that are taken.

Preparations were now made for a hunt of the kind. The pack-horses were taken into the woods and firmly tied to trees, lest, in a rush of the wild horses, they should break away with them. Twenty-five men were then sent, under the command of a lieutenant, to steal along the edge of the valley within the strip of wood that skirted the hills. They were to station themselves about fifty yards apart, within the edge of the woods, and not advance or show themselves until the horses dashed in that direction. Twenty-five men were sent across the valley, to steal in like manner along the river bank that bordered the opposite side, and to station themselves among the trees. A third party, of about the same number, was to form a line, stretching across the lower part of the valley, so as to connect the two wings. Beatte and our other half-breed, Antoine, together with the ever-officious Tonish, were to make a circuit through the woods so as to get to the upper part of the valley, in the rear of the horses, and to drive them forward into the kind of sack that we had formed, while the two wings should join behind them and make a complete circle.

The flanking parties were quietly extending themselves, out of sight, on each side of the valley, and the residue were stretching themselves, like the links of a chain, across it, when the wild horses gave signs that they scented an enemy; snuffing the air, snorting, and looking about. At length they pranced off slowly toward the river, and disappeared behind a green bank. Here, had the regulations of the chase been observed, they would have been quietly checked and turned back by the advance of a hunter from among the trees; unluckily, however, we had our wild-fire Jack-o'-lantern little Frenchman to deal with. Instead of keeping quietly up the right side of the valley, to get above the horses, the moment he saw them move toward the river, he broke out of the covert of woods, and dashed furiously across the plain in pursuit of them, being mounted on one of the led horses belonging to the count. This put an end to all system. The half-breeds and half a score of rangers joined in the chase.

Away they all went over the green bank; in a moment or two the wild horses reappeared, and came thundering down the valley, with Frenchman, half-breeds, and rangers galloping and yelling like devils behind them. It was in vain that the line drawn across the valley attempted to check and turn back the fugitives. They were too hotly pressed by their pursuers; in their panic they dashed through the line, and clattered down the plain. The whole troop joined in the headlong chase, some of the rangers without hats or caps, their hair flying about their ears, others with handkerchiefs tied round their heads. The buffaloes, who had been calmly ruminating among the herbage, heaved up their huge forms, gazed for a moment with astonishment at the tempest that came scouring down the meadow, then turned and took to heavy-rolling flight. They were soon overtaken; the promiscuous throng were pressed together by the contracting sides of the valley, and away they went, pell-mell, hurry-scurry, wild buffalo, wild horse, wild huntsman, with clang and clatter, and whoop and halloo, that made the forests ring.

At length the buffaloes turned into a green brake on the river bank, while the horses dashed up a narrow defile of the hills, with their pursuers close at their heels. Beatte passed several of them, having fixed his eye upon a fine Pawnee horse, that had his ears slit and saddle-marks upon his back He pressed him gallantly, but lost him in the woods. Among the wild horses was a fine black mare, far gone with foal. In scrambling up the defile, she tripped and fell. A young ranger sprang from his horse and seized her by the mane and muzzle. Another ranger dismounted, and came to his assistance. The mare struggled fiercely, kicking and biting, and striking with her forefeet, but a noose was slipped over her head, and her struggles were in vain. It was some time, however, before she gave over rearing and plunging and lashing out with her feet on every side. The two rangers then led her along the valley by two long lariats, which enabled them to keep at a sufficient distance on each side to be out of the reach of her hoofs, and whenever she struck out in one direction she was jerked in the other. In this way her spirit was gradually subdued.

As to little Scaramouch Tonish, who had marred the whole scene by his precipitancy, he had been more successful than he deserved, having managed to catch a beautiful cream-colored colt, about seven months old, which had not strength to keep up with its companions. The mercurial little Frenchman was beside himself with exultation. It was amusing to see him with his prize. The colt would rear and kick, and struggle to get free, when Tonish would take him about the neck, wrestle with him, jump on his back, and cut as many antics as a monkey with a kitten. Nothing surprised me more, however, than to witness how soon these poor animals, thus taken from the unbounded freedom of the prairie, yielded to the dominion of man. In the course of two or three days the mare and colt went with the led horses, and became quite docile.

CHAPTER TWENTY-SIX

FORDING OF THE NORTH FORK—DREARY SCENERY OF THE CROSS TIMBER—SCAMPER OF HORSES IN THE NIGHT— OSAGE WAR PARTY—EFFECTS OF A PEACE HARANGUE —BUFFALO—WILD HORSE

RESUMING our march, we forded the North Fork, a rapid stream, and of a purity seldom to be found in the rivers of the prairies. It evidently had its sources in high land, well supplied with springs. After crossing the river, we again ascended among hills, from one of which we had an extensive view over this belt of cross timber, and a cheerless prospect it was; hill beyond hill, forest beyond forest, all of one sad russet hue—excepting that here and there a line of green cottonwood trees, sycamores, and willows, marked the course

of some streamlet through a valley. A procession of buffaloes, moving slowly up the profile of one of those distant
hills, formed a characteristic object in the savage scene. To
the left, the eye stretched beyond this rugged wilderness of
hills, and ravines, and ragged forests, to a prairie about ten
miles off, extending in a clear blue line along the horizon. It
was like looking from among rocks and breakers upon a distant tract of tranquil ocean. Unluckily, our route did not
lie in that direction; we still had to traverse many a weary
mile of the "cross timber."

We encamped toward evening in a valley, beside a scanty
pool, under a scattered grove of elms, the upper branches of
which were fringed with tufts of the mystic mistletoe. In
the course of the night, the wild colt whinnied repeatedly;
and about two hours before day there was a sudden *stam-
pedo*, or rush of horses, along the purlieus of the camp, with
a snorting and neighing, and clattering of hoofs, that startled
most of the rangers from their sleep, who listened in silence,
until the sound died away like the rushing of a blast. As
usual, the noise was at first attributed to some party of ma-
rauding Indians; but as the day dawned, a couple of wild
horses were seen in a neighboring meadow, which scoured
off on being approached. It was now supposed that a gang
of them had dashed through our camp in the night. A general mustering of our horses took place, many were found
scattered to a considerable distance, and several were not to
be found. The prints of their hoofs, however, appeared deeply
dinted in the soil, leading off at full speed into the waste, and
their owners, putting themselves on the trail, set off in weary
search of them.

We had a ruddy daybreak, but the morning gathered up
gray and lowering, with indications of an autumnal storm.
We resumed our march silently and seriously, through a
rough and cheerless country, from the highest points of
which we could descry large prairies, stretching indefinitely
westward. After traveling for two or three hours, as we
were traversing a withered prairie, resembling a great brown

heath, we beheld seven Osage warriors approaching at a distance. The sight of any human being in this lonely wilderness was interesting; it was like speaking a ship at sea. One of the Indians took the lead of his companions, and advanced toward us with head erect, chest thrown forward, and a free and noble mien. He was a fine-looking fellow, dressed in scarlet frock and fringed leggings of deer skin. His head was decorated with a white tuft, and he stepped forward with something of a martial air, swaying his bow and arrows in one hand.

We held some conversation with him through our interpreter, Beatte, and found that he and his companions had been with the main part of their tribe hunting the buffalo, and had met with great success; and he informed us that, in the course of another day's march, we would reach the prairies on the banks of the Grand Canadian, and find plenty of game. He added that, as their hunt was over, and the hunters on their return homeward, he and his comrades had set out on a war party, to waylay and hover about some Pawnee camp, in hopes of carrying off scalps or horses.

By this time his companions, who at first stood aloof, joined him. Three of them had indifferent fowling-pieces; the rest were armed with bows and arrows. I could not but admire the finely shaped heads and busts of these savages, and their graceful attitudes and expressive gestures, as they stood conversing with our interpreter, and surrounded by a cavalcade of rangers. We endeavored to get one of them to join us, as we were desirous of seeing him hunt the buffalo with his bow and arrow. He seemed at first inclined to do so, but was dissuaded by his companions.

The worthy commissioner now remembered his mission as pacificator, and made a speech, exhorting them to abstain from all offensive acts against the Pawnees; informing them of the plan of their father at Washington, to put an end to all war among his red children; and assuring them that he was sent to the frontier to establish a universal peace. He told them, therefore, to return quietly to their homes, with the certainty that the Pawnees would no longer molest them, but would soon regard them as brothers.

The Indians listened to the speech with their customary silence and decorum; after which, exchanging a few words among themselves, they bade us farewell and pursued their way across the prairie.

Fancying that I saw a lurking smile in the countenance of our interpreter, Beatte, I privately inquired what the Indians had said to each other after hearing the speech. The leader, he said, had observed to his companions that, as their great father intended so soon to put an end to all warfare, it behooved them to make the most of the little time that was left them. So they had departed, with redoubled zeal, to pursue their project of horse stealing!

We had not long parted from the Indians before we discovered three buffaloes among the thickets of a marshy valley to our left. I set off with the captain and several rangers in pursuit of them. Stealing through a straggling grove, the captain, who took the lead, got within rifle-shot, and wounded one of them in the flank. They all three made off in headlong panic, through thickets and brushwood, and swamp and mire, bearing down every obstacle by their immense weight. The captain and rangers soon gave up a chase which threatened to knock up their horses; I had got upon the traces of the wounded bull, however, and was in hopes of getting near enough to use my pistols, the only weapons with which I was provided; but before I could effect it, he reached the foot of a rocky hill, covered with post-oak and brambles, and plunged forward, dashing and crashing along, with neck-or-nothing fury, where it would have been madness to have followed him.

The chase had led me so far on one side that it was some time before I regained the trail of our troop. As I was slowly ascending a hill, a fine black mare came prancing round the summit, and was close to me before she was aware. At sight of me she started back, then turning, swept at full speed down into the valley, and up the opposite hill, with flowing mane and tail, and action free as air. I gazed after her as long as she was in sight, and breathed a wish that so glorious an animal might never come under the degrading thraldom of whip and curb, but remain a free rover of the prairies.

CHAPTER TWENTY-SEVEN

FOUL WEATHER ENCAMPMENT—ANECDOTES OF BEAR HUNT-ING—INDIAN NOTIONS ABOUT OMENS—SCRUPLES RESPECTING THE DEAD

ON overtaking the troop, I found it encamping in a rich bottom of woodland, traversed by a small stream, running between deep crumbling banks. A sharp cracking off of rifles was kept up for some time in various directions, upon a numerous flock of turkeys, scampering among the thickets or perched upon the trees. We had not been long at a halt when a drizzling rain ushered in the autumnal storm that had been brewing. Preparations were immediately made to weather it; our tent was pitched, and our saddles, saddle-bags, packages of coffee, sugar, salt, and everything else that could be damaged by the rain, were gathered under its shelter. Our men, Beatte, Tonish, and Antoine, drove stakes with forked ends into the ground, laid poles across them for rafters, and thus made a shed or pent-house, covered with bark and skins, sloping toward the wind, and open toward the fire. The rangers formed similar shelters of bark and skins, or of blankets stretched on poles, supported by forked stakes, with great fires in front.

These precautions were well timed. The rain set in sullenly and steadily, and kept on, with slight intermissions, for two days. The brook which flowed peacefully on our arrival, swelled into a turbid and boiling torrent, and the forest became little better than a mere swamp. The men gathered under their shelters of skins and blankets, or sat cowering

rcund their fires; while columns of smoke curling up among
the trees, and diffusing themselves in the air, spread a blue
haze through the woodland.   Our poor, wayworn horses,
reduced by weary travel and scanty pasturage, lost all remaining spirit, and stood, with drooping heads, flagging
ears, and half-closed eyes, dozing and steaming in the rain,
while the yellow autumnal leaves, at every shaking of the
breeze, came wavering down around them.

Notwithstanding the bad weather, however, our hunters
were not idle, but during the intervals of the rain sallied
forth on horseback to prowl through the woodland.   Every
now and then the sharp report of a distant rifle boded the
death of a deer.   Venison in abundance was brought in.
Some busied themselves under the sheds, flaying and cutting
up the carcasses, or round the fires with spits and camp kettles, and a rude kind of feasting, or rather gormandizing,
prevailed throughout the camp.   The ax was continually at
work, and wearied the forest with its echoes.   Crash! some
mighty tree would come down; in a few minutes its limbs
would be blazing and crackling on the huge camp fires, with
some luckless deer roasting before it that had once sported
beneath its shade.

The change of weather had taken sharp hold of our little
Frenchman.   His meager frame, composed of bones and
whipcord, was racked with rheumatic pains and twinges.
He had the toothache—the earache—his face was tied up—
he had shooting pains in every limb; yet all seemed but to
increase his restless activity, and he was an incessant fidget
about the fire, roasting, and stewing, and groaning, and
scolding, and swearing.

Our man Beatte returned grim and mortified from hunting.   He had come upon a bear of formidable dimensions,
and wounded him with a rifle-shot.   The bear took to the
brook, which was swollen and rapid.   Beatte dashed after
him and assailed him in the rear with his hunting-knife.   At
every blow the bear turned furiously upon him, with a ter-
rific display of white teeth.   Beatte, having a foothold in the
* * * 21—VOL. VII.

brook, was enabled to push him off with his rifle, and, when he turned to swim, would flounder after, and attempt to hamstring him. The bear, however, succeeded in scrambling off among the thickets, and Beatte had to give up the chase.

This adventure, if it produced no game, brought up at least several anecdotes, round the evening fire, relative to bear hunting, in which the grizzly bear figured conspicuously. This powerful and ferocious animal is a favorite theme of hunter's story, both among red and white men; and his enormous claws are worn round the neck of an Indian brave as a trophy more honorable than a human scalp. He is now scarcely seen below the upper prairies and the skirts of the Rocky Mountains. Other bears are formidable when wounded and provoked, but seldom make battle when allowed to escape. The grizzly bear alone, of all the animals of our Western wilds, is prone to unprovoked hostility. His prodigious size and strength make him a formidable opponent; and his great tenacity of life often baffles the skill of the hunter, notwithstanding repeated shots of the rifle, and wounds of the hunting-knife.

One of the anecdotes related on this occasion gave a picture of the accidents and hard shifts to which our frontier rovers are inured. A hunter, while in pursuit of a deer, fell into one of those deep funnel-shaped pits, formed on the prairies by the settling of the waters after heavy rains, and known by the name of sink-holes. To his great horror, he came in contact, at the bottom, with a huge grizzly bear. The monster grappled him; a deadly contest ensued, in which the poor hunter was severely torn and bitten, and had a leg and an arm broken, but succeeded in killing his rugged foe. For several days he remained at the bottom of the pit, too much crippled to move, and subsisting on the raw flesh of the bear, during which time he kept his wounds open, that they might heal gradually and effectually. He was at length enabled to scramble to the top of the pit, and so out upon the open prairie. With great difficulty he crawled to a ravine, formed by a stream, then nearly dry. Here he took a delicious draught of water, which infused new life into him; then dragging himself along from pool to pool, he supported himself by small fish and frogs.

One day he saw a wolf hunt down and kill a deer in the neighboring prairie. He immediately crawled forth from the ravine, drove off the wolf, and, lying down beside the carcass of the deer, remained there until he made several hearty meals, by which his strength was much recruited.

Returning to the ravine, he pursued the course of the brook, until it grew to be a considerable stream. Down this he floated, until he came to where it emptied into the Mississippi. Just at the mouth of the stream he found a forked tree, which he launched with some difficulty, and, getting astride of it, committed himself to the current of the mighty river. In this way he floated along, until he arrived opposite the fort at Council Bluffs. Fortunately he arrived there in the daytime, otherwise he might have floated, unnoticed, past this solitary post, and perished in the idle waste of waters. Being descried from the fort, a canoe was sent to his relief, and he was brought to shore more dead than alive, where he soon recovered from his wounds, but remained maimed for life.

Our man Beatte had come out of his contest with the bear very much worsted and discomfited. His drenching in the brook, together with the recent change of weather, had brought on rheumatic pains in his limbs, to which he is subject. Though ordinarily a fellow of undaunted spirit, and above all hardship, yet he now sat down by the fire, gloomy and dejected, and for once gave way to repining. Though in the prime of life, and of a robust frame and apparently iron constitution, yet, by his own account he was little better than a mere wreck. He was, in fact, a living monument of the hardships of wild frontier life. Baring his left arm, he showed it warped and contracted by a former attack of rheumatism; a malady with which the Indians are often afflicted; for their exposure to the vicissitudes of the elements does not produce that perfect hardihood and insensibility to the changes of the seasons that many are apt to imagine. He bore the scars of various maims and bruises; some received in hunting, some in Indian warfare. His right arm had been broken by a fall from his horse; at another time his steed had fallen with him, and crushed his left leg.

"I am all broke to pieces and good for nothing," said he, "I no care now what happen to me any more. However," added he, after a moment's pause, "for all that, it would take a pretty strong man to put me down, anyhow."

I drew from him various particulars concerning himself, which served to raise him in my estimation. His residence was on the Neosho, in an Osage hamlet or neighborhood, under the superintendence of a worthy missionary from the banks of the Hudson, by the name of Requa, who was endeavoring to instruct the savages in the art of agriculture, and to make husbandmen and herdsmen of them. I had visited this agricultural mission of Requa in the course of my recent tour along the frontier, and had considered it more likely to produce solid advantages to the poor Indians than any of the mere praying and preaching missions along the border.

In this neighborhood, Pierre Beatte had his little farm, his Indian wife, and his half-breed children; and aided Mr. Requa in his endeavors to civilize the habits and meliorate the condition of the Osage tribe. Beatte had been brought up a Catholic, and was inflexible in his religious faith; he could not pray with Mr. Requa, he said, but he could work with him, and he evinced a zeal for the good of his savage relations and neighbors. Indeed, though his father had been French, and he himself had been brought up in communion with the whites, he evidently was more of an Indian in his tastes, and his heart yearned toward his mother's nation. When he talked to me of the wrongs and insults that the poor Indians suffered in their intercourse with the rough settlers on the frontiers; when he described the precarious and degraded state of the Osage tribe, diminished in numbers, broken in spirit, and almost living on sufferance in the land where they once figured so heroically, I could see his veins swell, and his nostrils distend with indignation; but he would check the feeling with a strong exertion of Indian self-command, and, in a manner, drive it back into his bosom.

He did not hesitate to relate an instance wherein he had joined his kindred Osages, in pursuing and avenging themselves on a party of white men who had committed a flagrant outrage upon them; and I found, in the encounter that took place, Beatte had shown himself the complete Indian.

He had more than once accompanied his Osage relations in their wars with the Pawnees, and related a skirmish which took place on the borders of these very hunting grounds, in which several Pawnees were killed. We should pass near the place, he said, in the course of our tour, and the unburied bones and skulls of the slain were still to be seen there. The surgeon of the troop, who was present at our conversation, pricked up his ears at this intelligence. He was something of a phrenologist, and offered Beatte a handsome reward if he would procure him one of the skulls.

Beatte regarded him for a moment with a look of stern surprise.

"No!" said he at length, "dat too bad! I have heart strong enough—I no care kill, but *let the dead alone!*"

He added that, once in traveling with a party of white men, he had slept in the same tent with a doctor, and found that he had a Pawnee skull among his baggage: he at once renounced the doctor's tent and his fellowship. "He try to coax me," said Beatte, "but I say no, we must part—I no keep such company."

In the temporary depression of his spirits, Beatte gave way to those superstitious forebodings to which Indians are prone. He had sat for some time, with his cheek upon his hand, gazing into the fire. I found his thoughts were wandering back to his humble home, on the banks of the Neosho; he was sure, he said, that he should find some one of his

family ill or dead on his return: his left eye had twitched
and twinkled for two days past; an omen which always
boded some misfortune of the kind.

Such are the trivial circumstances which, when magnified
into omens, will shake the souls of these men of iron. The
least sign of mystic and sinister portent is sufficient to turn
a hunter or a warrior from his course, or to fill his mind with
apprehensions of impending evil. It is this superstitious propensity, common to the solitary and savage rovers of the
wilderness, that gives such powerful influence to the prophet
and the dreamer.

The Osages, with whom Beatte had passed much of his
life, retain these superstitious fancies and rites in much of
their original force. They all believe in the existence of the
soul after its separation from the body, and that it carries
with it all its mortal tastes and habitudes. At an Osage village in the neighborhood of Beatte, one of the chief warriors
lost an only child, a beautiful girl, of a very tender age. All
her playthings were buried with her. Her favorite little
horse, also, was killed, and laid in the grave beside her, that
she might have it to ride in the land of spirits.

I will here add a little story, which I picked up in the
course of my tour through Beatte's country, and which illustrates the superstitions of his Osage kindred. A large party
of Osages had been encamped for some time on the borders
of a fine stream called the Nickanansa. Among them was
a young hunter, one of the bravest and most graceful of the
tribe, who was to be married to an Osage girl, who, for her
beauty, was called the Flower of the Prairies. The young
hunter left her for a time among her relatives in the encampment, and went to St. Louis, to dispose of the products of
his hunting, and purchase ornaments for his bride. After
an absence of some weeks, he returned to the banks of the
Nickanansa, but the camp was no longer there; and the bare
frames of the lodges and the brands of extinguished fires
alone marked the place. At a distance he beheld a female
seated, as if weeping, by the side of the stream. It was his

affianced bride. He ran to embrace her, but she turned mournfully away. He dreaded lest some evil had befallen the camp.

"Where are our people?" cried he.

"They are gone to the banks of the Wagrushka."

"And what art thou doing here alone?"

"Waiting for thee."

"Then let us hasten to join our people on the banks of the Wagrushka."

He gave her his pack to carry, and walked ahead, according to the Indian custom.

They came to where the smoke of the distant camp was seen rising from the woody margin of the stream. The girl seated herself at the foot of a tree. "It is not proper for us to return together," said she; "I will wait here."

The young hunter proceeded to the camp alone, and was received by his relations with gloomy countenances.

"What evil has happened," said he, "that ye are all so sad?"

No one replied.

He turned to his favorite sister, and bade her go forth, seek his bride, and conduct her to the camp.

"Alas!" cried she, "how shall I seek her? She died a few days since."

The relations of the young girl now surrounded him, weeping and wailing; but he refused to believe the dismal tidings. "But a few moments since," cried he, "I left her alone and in health: come with me, and I will conduct you to her."

He led the way to the tree where she had seated herself, but she was no longer there, and his pack lay on the ground. The fatal truth struck him to the heart; he fell to the ground dead.

I give this simple story almost in the words in which it was related to me, as I lay by the fire in an evening encampment on the banks of the haunted stream where it is said to have happened.

CHAPTER TWENTY-EIGHT

A SECRET EXPEDITION—DEER BLEATING—MAGIC BALLS

ON the following morning we were rejoined by the rangers who had remained at the last encampment to seek for the stray horses. They had tracked them for a considerable distance through bush and brake, and across streams, until they found them crooping the herbage on the edge of a prairie. Their heads were in the direction of the fort, and they were evidently grazing their way homeward, heedless of the unbounded freedom of the prairie so suddenly laid open to them.

About noon the weather held up, and I observed a mysterious consultation going on between our half-breeds and Tonish; it ended in a request that we would dispense with the services of the latter for a few hours, and permit him to join his comrades in a grand foray. We objected that Tonish was too much disabled by aches and pains for such an undertaking; but he was wild with eagerness for the mysterious enterprise, and, when permission was given him, seemed to forget all his ailments in an instant.

In a short time the trio were equipped and on horseback; with rifles on their shoulders and handkerchiefs twisted round their heads, evidently bound for a grand scamper. As they passed by the different lodges of the camp, the vainglorious little Frenchman could not help boasting to the right and left of the great things he was about to achieve; though the taciturn Beatte, who rode in advance, would every now and then check his horse, and look back at him with an air of stern rebuke. It was hard, however, to make the loquacious Tonish play "Indian."

Several of the hunters, likewise, sallied forth, and the

prime old woodman, Ryan, came back early in the afternoon, with ample spoil, having killed a buck and two fat does. I drew near to a group of rangers that had gathered round him as he stood by the spoil, and found they were discussing the merits of a stratagem sometimes used in deer hunting. This consists in imitating, with a small instrument called a bleat, the cry of the fawn, so as to lure the doe within reach of the rifle. There are bleats of various kinds, suited to calm or windy weather, and to the age of the fawn. The poor animal, deluded by them, in its anxiety about its young, will sometimes advance close up to the hunter. "I once bleated a doe," said a young hunter, "until it came within twenty yards of me, and presented a sure mark. I leveled my rifle three times, but had not the heart to shoot, for the poor doe looked so wistfully that it in a manner made my heart yearn. I thought of my own mother, and how anxious she used to be about me when I was a child; so to put an end to the matter, I gave a halloo, and started the doe out of rifle-shot in a moment."

"And you did right," cried honest old Ryan. "For my part, I never could bring myself to bleating deer. I've been with hunters who had bleats, and have made them throw them away. It is a rascally trick to take advantage of a mother's love for her young."

Toward evening our three worthies returned from their mysterious foray. The tongue of Tonish gave notice of their approach long before they came in sight; for he was vociferating at the top of his lungs, and rousing the attention of the whole camp. The lagging gait and reeking flanks of their horses gave evidence of hard riding; and, on nearer approach, we found them hung round with meat like a butcher's shambles. In fact, they had been scouring an immense prairie that extended beyond the forest, and which was covered with herds of buffalo. Of this prairie, and the animals upon it, Beatte had received intelligence a few days before, in his conversation with the Osages, but had kept the information a secret from the rangers, that he and his comrades might have the first dash at the game. They had contented themselves with killing four; though, if Tonish might be believed, they might have slain them by scores.

These tidings, and the buffalo meat brought home in evidence, spread exultation through the camp, and every one looked forward with joy to a buffalo hunt on the prairies. Tonish was again the oracle of the camp, and held forth by the hour to a knot of listeners, crouched round the fire, with their shoulders up to their ears. He was now more boastful than ever of his skill as a marksman. All his want of success in the early part of our march he attributed to being "out of luck," if not "spellbound"; and finding himself listened to with apparent credulity, gave an instance of the kind, which he declared had happened to himself, but which was evidently a tale picked up among his relations, the Osages.

According to this account, when about fourteen years of age, as he was one day hunting, he saw a white deer come out from a ravine. Crawling near to get a shot, he beheld another and another come forth, until there were seven, all as white as snow. Having crept sufficiently near, he singled one out and fired, but without effect; the deer remained unfrightened. He loaded and fired again and missed. Thus he continued firing and missing until all his ammunition was expended, and the deer remained without a wound. He returned home despairing of his skill as a marksman, but was consoled by an old Osage hunter. These white deer, said he, have a charmed life, and can only be killed by bullets of a particular kind.

The old Indian cast several balls for Tonish, but would not suffer him to be present on the occasion, nor inform him of the ingredients and mystic ceremonials.

Provided with these balls, Tonish again set out in quest of the white deer, and succeeded in finding them. He tried at first with ordinary balls, but missed as before. A magic ball, however, immediately brought a fine buck to the ground. Whereupon the rest of the herd immediately disappeared and were never seen again.

October 29th.—The morning opened gloomy and lowering; but toward eight o'clock the sun struggled forth and lighted up the forest, and the notes of the bugle gave signal to prepare for marching. Now began a scene of bustle, and clamor, and gayety. Some were scampering and brawling after their horses, some were riding in bare-backed and driving in the horses of their comrades. Some were stripping the poles of the wet blankets that had served for shelters; others packing up with all possible dispatch, and loading the baggage horses as they arrived, while others were cracking off their damp rifles and charging them afresh, to be ready for the sport.

About ten o'clock we began our march. I loitered in the rear of the troop as it forded the turbid brook, and defiled through the labyrinths of the forest. I always felt disposed to linger until the last straggler disappeared among the trees and the distant note of the bugle died upon the ear, that I might behold the wilderness relapsing into silence and solitude. In the present instance, the deserted scene of our late bustling encampment had a forlorn and desolate appearance. The surrounding forest had been in many places trampled into a quagmire. Trees felled and partly hewn in pieces, and scattered in huge fragments; tent-poles stripped of their covering; smoldering fires, with great morsels of roasted venison and buffalo meat, standing in wooden spits before them, hacked and slashed by the knives of hungry hunters; while around were strewed the hides, the horns, the antlers, and bones of buffaloes and deer, with uncooked joints, and unplucked turkeys, left behind with that reckless improvidence and wastefulness which young hunters are apt to indulge when in a neighborhood where game abounds. In the meantime a score or two of turkey-buzzards or vultures were already on the wing, wheeling their magnificent flight high in the high, and preparing for a descent upon the camp as soon as it should be abandoned.

CHAPTER TWENTY-NINE

THE GRAND PRAIRIE—A BUFFALO HUNT

AFTER proceeding about two hours in a southerly direction, we emerged toward midday from the dreary belt of the Cross Timber, and to our infinite delight beheld "the great Prairie" stretching to the right and left before us. We could distinctly trace the meandering course of the main Canadian, and various smaller streams, by the strips of green forest that bordered them. The landscape was vast and beautiful. There is always an expansion of feeling in looking upon these boundless and fertile wastes; but I was doubly conscious of it after emerging from our "close dungeon of innumerous boughs."

From a rising ground Beatte pointed out the place where he and his comrades had killed the buffaloes; and we beheld several black objects moving in the distance, which he said were part of the herd. The captain determined to shape his course to a woody bottom about a mile distant, and to encamp there for a day or two, by way of having a regular buffalo hunt, and getting a supply of provisions. As the troop defiled along the slope of the hill toward the camping ground, Beatte proposed to my messmates and myself that we should put ourselves under his guidance, promising to take us where we should have plenty of sport. Leaving the line of march, therefore, we diverged toward the prairie; traversing a small valley, and ascending a gentle swell of land. As we reached the summit, we beheld a gang of wild horses about a mile off. Beatte was immediately on the alert, and no longer thought of buffalo hunting. He was mounted on his powerful half-wild horse, with a lariat coiled at the saddle-bow, and set off in pursuit; while we remained

on a rising ground watching his maneuvers with great solicitude. Taking advantage of a strip of woodland, he stole
quietly along, so as to get close to them before he was perceived. The moment they caught sight of him a grand
scamper took place. We watched him skirting along the
horizon like a privateer in full chase of a merchantman; at
length he passed over the brow of a ridge and down into a
shallow valley; in a few moments he was on the opposite
hill, and close upon one of the horses. He was soon head
and head, and appeared to be trying to noose his prey; but
they both disappeared again below the hill, and we saw no
more of them. It turned out afterward that he had noosed
a powerful horse, but could not hold him, and had lost his
lariat in the attempt.

While we were waiting for his return, we perceived two
buffalo bulls descending a slope, toward a stream, which
wound through a ravine fringed with trees. The young
count and myself endeavored to get near them under covert
of the trees. They discovered us while we were yet three or
four hundred yards off, and, turning about, retreated up the
rising ground. We urged our horses across the ravine and
gave chase. The immense weight of head and shoulders
causes the buffalo to labor heavily up hill; but it accelerates
his descent. We had the advantage, therefore, and gained
rapidly upon the fugitives, though it was difficult to get our
horses to approach them, their very scent inspiring them
with terror. The count, who had a double-barreled gun,
loaded with ball, fired, but it missed. The bulls now altered
their course, and galloped down hill with headlong rapidity.
As they ran in different directions, we each singled out one
and separated. I was provided with a brace of veteran brass-
barreled pistols, which I had borrowed at Fort Gibson, and
which had evidently seen some service. Pistols are very
effective in buffalo hunting, as the hunter can ride up close
to the animal, and fire at it while at full speed; whereas the
long heavy rifles used on the frontier cannot be easily managed, nor discharged with accurate aim from horseback.

My object, therefore, was to get within pistol shot of the buffalo. This was no very easy matter. I was well mounted on a horse of excellent speed and bottom, that seemed eager for the chase, and soon overtook the game; but the moment he came nearly parallel, he would keep sheering off, with ears forked and pricked forward, and every symptom of aversion and alarm. It was no wonder. Of all animals, a buffalo, when close pressed by the hunter, has an aspect the most diabolical. His two short black horns curve out of a huge frontier of shaggy hair; his eyes glow like coals; his mouth is open, his tongue parched and drawn up into a half crescent; his tail is erect, and tufted and whisking about in the air. He is a perfect picture of mingled rage and terror.

It was with difficulty I urged my horse sufficiently near, when, taking aim, to my chagrin, both pistols missed fire. Unfortunately the locks of these veteran weapons were so much worn that, in the gallop, the priming had been shaken out of the pans. At the snapping of the last pistol I was close upon the buffalo, when, in his despair, he turned round with a sudden snort and rushed upon me. My horse wheeled about as if on a pivot, made a convulsive spring, and, as I had been leaning on one side with pistol extended, I came near being thrown at the feet of the buffalo.

Three or four bounds of the horse carried us out of the reach of the enemy; who, having merely turned in desperate self-defense, quickly resumed his flight. As soon as I could gather in my panic-stricken horse, and prime the pistols afresh, I again spurred in pursuit of the buffalo, who had slackened his speed to take breath. On my approach he again set off full tilt, heaving himself forward with a heavy rolling gallop, dashing with headlong precipitation through brakes and ravines, while several deer and wolves, startled from their coverts by his thundering career, ran helter-skelter to right and left across the waste.

A gallop across the prairies in pursuit of game is by no means so smooth a career as those may imagine who have only the idea of an open level plain. It is true, the prairies of the hunting ground are not so much entangled with flowering plants and long herbage as the lower prairies, and are principally covered with short buffalo grass; but they are diversified by hill and dale, and where most level are apt to be cut up by deep rifts and ravines, made by torrents after rains; and which, yawning from an even surface, are almost like pitfalls in the way of the hunter, checking him suddenly, when in full career, or subjecting him to the risk of limb and life. The plains, too, are beset by burrowing holes of small animals, in which the horse is apt to sink to the fetlock and throw both himself and his rider. The late rain had covered some parts of the prairie, where the ground was hard, with a thin sheet of water, through which the horse had to splash his way. In other parts there were innumerable shallow hollows, eight or ten feet in diameter, made by the buffaloes, who wallow in sand and mud like swine. These being filled with water, shone like mirrors, so that the horse was continually leaping over them or springing on one side. We had reached, too, a rough part of the prairie, very much broken and cut up; the buffalo, who was running for life, took no heed to his course, plunging down break-neck ravines, where it was necessary to skirt the borders in search of a safer descent. At length we came to where a winter stream had torn a deep chasm across the whole prairie, leaving open jagged rocks, and forming a long glen bordered by steep crumbling cliffs of mingled stone and clay. Down one of these the buffalo flung himself, half tumbling, half leaping, and then scuttled along the bottom; while I, seeing all further pursuit useless, pulled up, and gazed quietly after him from the border of the cliff, until he disappeared amid the windings of the ravine.

Nothing now remained but to turn my steed and rejoin my companions. Here at first was some little difficulty. The ardor of the chase had betrayed me into a long, heedless gallop. I now found myself in the midst of a lonely waste, in which the prospect was bounded by undulating swells of land, naked and uniform, where, from the deficiency of land-marks and distinct features, an inexperienced man may become bewildered, and lose his way as readily as in the wastes of the ocean. The day, too, was overcast, so that I could not guide myself by the sun; my only mode was to retrace the track my horse had made in coming, though this I would often lose sight of where the ground was covered with parched herbage.

To one unaccustomed to it, there is something inexpress-ibly lonely in the solitude of a prairie. The loneliness of a forest seems nothing to it. There the view is shut in by trees, and the imagination is left free to picture some livelier scene beyond. But here we have an immense extent of land-scape without a sign of human existence. We have the con-sciousness of being far, far beyond the bounds of human habitation; we feel as if moving in the midst of a desert world. As my horse lagged slowly back over the scenes of our late scamper, and the delirium of the chase had passed away, I was peculiarly sensible to these circumstances. The silence of the waste was now and then broken by the cry of a distant flock of pelicans, stalking like specters about a shal-low pool; sometimes by the sinister croaking of a raven in the air, while occasionally a scoundrel wolf would scour off from before me; and, having attained a safe distance, would sit down and howl and whine with tones that gave a dreari-ness to the surrounding solitude.

After pursuing my way for some time, I descried a horse-man on the edge of a distant hill, and soon recognized him to be the count. He had been equally unsuccessful with my-self; we were shortly after rejoined by our worthy comrade, the Virtuoso, who, with spectacles on nose, had made two or three ineffectual shots from horseback.

We determined not to seek the camp until we had made one more effort. Casting our eyes about the surrounding waste, we descried a herd of buffalo about two miles distant, scattered apart, and quietly grazing near a small strip of trees and bushes. It required but little stretch of fancy to picture

them so many cattle grazing on the edge of a common, and
that the grove might shelter some lowly farmhouse.

We now formed our plan to circumvent the herd, and by
getting on the other side of them, to hunt them in the direction where we knew our camp to be situated, otherwise the
pursuit might take us to such a distance as to render it impossible to find our way back before nightfall. Taking a wide
circuit, therefore, we moved slowly and cautiously, pausing
occasionally, when we saw any of the herd desist from
grazing. The wind fortunately set from them, otherwise they
might have scented us and have taken the alarm. In this
way we succeeded in getting round the herd without disturbing it. It consisted of about forty head, bulls, cows, and
calves. Separating to some distance from each other, we
now approached slowly in a parallel line, hoping by degrees
to steal near without exciting attention. They began, however, to move off quietly, stopping at every step or two to
graze, when suddenly a bull that, unobserved by us, had
been taking his siesta under a clump of trees to our left,
roused himself from his lair, and hastened to join his companions. We were still at a considerable distance, but the
game had taken the alarm. We quickened our pace, they
broke into a gallop, and now commenced a full chase.

As the ground was level, they shouldered along with
great speed, following each other in a line; two or three bulls
bringing up the rear, the last of whom, from his enormous
size and venerable frontlet, and beard of sunburned hair,
looked like the patriarch of the herd; and as if he might long
have reigned the monarch of the prairie.

There is a mixture of the awful and the comic in the look
of these huge animals, as they bear their great bulk forward,
with an up and down motion of the unwieldy head and
shoulders; their tail cocked up like the queue of Pantaloon
in a pantomime, the end whisking about in a fierce yet
whimsical style, and their eyes glaring venomously with an
expression of fright and fury.

For some time I kept parallel with the line, without being

able to force my horse within pistol shot, so much had he been alarmed by the assault of the buffalo in the preceding chase. At length I succeeded, but was again balked by my pistols missing fire. My companions, whose horses were less fleet, and more way-worn, could not overtake the herd; at length Mr. L., who was in the rear of the line, and losing ground, leveled his double-barreled gun, and fired a long raking shot. It struck a buffalo just above the loins, broke its backbone, and brought it to the ground. He stopped and alighted to dispatch his prey; when, borrowing his gun, which had yet a charge remaining in it, I put my horse to its speed, again overtook the herd which was thundering along, pursued by the count. With my present weapon there was no need of urging my horse to such close quarters; galloping along parallel, therefore, I singled out a buffalo, and by a fortunate shot brought it down on the spot. The ball had struck a vital part; it could not move from the place where it fell, but lay there struggling in mortal agony, while the rest of the herd kept on their headlong career across the prairie.

Dismounting, I now fettered my horse to prevent his straying, and advanced to contemplate my victim. I am nothing of a sportsman; I had been prompted to this unwonted exploit by the magnitude of the game and the excitement of an adventurous chase. Now that the excitement was over, I could not but look with commiseration upon the poor animal that lay struggling and bleeding at my feet. His very size and importance, which had before inspired me with eagerness, now increased my compunction. It seemed as if I had inflicted pain in proportion to the bulk of my victim, and as if it were a hundred-fold greater waste of life than there would have been in the destruction of an animal of inferior size.

To add to these after-qualms of conscience, the poor animal lingered in his agony. He had evidently received a mortal wound, but death might be long in coming. It would not do to leave him here to be torn piecemeal, while yet alive, by the wolves that had already snuffed his blood, and were skulking and howling at a distance, and waiting for my departure; and by the ravens that were flapping about, croaking dismally in the air. It became now an act of mercy to give him his quietus, and put him out of his misery. I primed one of the pistols, therefore, and advanced close up to the buffalo. To inflict a wound thus in cold blood, I found a totally different thing from firing in the heat of the chase. Taking aim, however, just behind the foreshoulder, my pistol for once proved true; the ball must have passed through the heart, for the animal gave one convulsive throe and expired.

While I stood meditating and moralizing over the wreck I had so wantonly produced, with my horse grazing near me, I was rejoined by my fellow-sportsman, the Virtuoso; who, being a man of universal adroitness, and withal more experienced and hardened in the gentle art of "venerie," soon managed to carve out the tongue of the buffalo, and delivered it to me to bear back to the camp as a trophy.

CHAPTER THIRTY

A COMRADE LOST—A SEARCH FOR THE CAMP—THE COM-
MISSIONER, THE WILD HORSE, AND THE BUFFALO—
A WOLF SERENADE

OUR solicitude was now awakened for the young count. With his usual eagerness and impetuosity he had persisted in urging his jaded horse in pursuit of the herd, unwilling to return without having likewise killed a buffalo. In this way he had kept on following them, hither and thither, and occasionally firing an ineffectual shot, until by degrees horseman and herd became indistinct in the distance, and at length swelling ground and strips of trees and thickets hid them entirely from sight.

By the time my friend, the amateur, joined me, the young

count had been long lost to view. We held a consultation on the matter. Evening was drawing on. Were we to pursue him, it would be dark before we should overtake him, granting we did not entirely lose trace of him in the gloom. We should then be too much bewildered to find our way back to the encampment; even now, our return would be difficult. We determined, therefore, to hasten to the camp as speedily as possible, and send out our half-breeds, and some of the veteran hunters, skilled in cruising about the prairies, to search for our companion.

We accordingly set forward in what we supposed to be the direction of the camp. Our weary horses could hardly be urged beyond a walk. The twilight thickened upon us; the landscape grew gradually indistinct; we tried in vain to recognize various landmarks which we had noted in the morning. The features of the prairies are so similar as to baffle the eye of any but an Indian, or a practiced woodman. At length night closed in. We hoped to see the distant glare of camp-fires; we listened to catch the sound of the bells about the necks of the grazing horses. Once or twice we thought we distinguished them; we were mistaken. Nothing was to be heard but a monotonous concert of insects, with now and then the dismal howl of wolves mingling with the night breeze. We began to think of halting for the night, and bivouacking under the lee of some thicket. We had implements to strike a light; there was plenty of firewood at hand, and the tongues of our buffaloes would furnish us with a repast.

Just as we were preparing to dismount, we heard the report of a rifle, and shortly after the notes of the bugle calling up the night guard. Pushing forward in that direction, the camp fires soon broke on our sight, gleaming at a distance from among the thick groves of an alluvial bottom.

As we entered the camp, we found it a scene of rude hunters' revelry and wassail. There had been a grand day's sport, in which all had taken a part. Eight buffaloes had been killed; roaring fires were blazing on every side; all hands were feasting upon roasted joints, broiled marrow-bones, and the juicy hump, far-famed among the epicures of the prairies. Right glad were we to dismount and partake of the sturdy cheer, for we had been on our weary horses since morning without tasting food.

As to our worthy friend, the commissioner, with whom we had parted company at the outset of this eventful day, we found him lying in a corner of the tent, much the worse for wear, in the course of a successful hunting match.

It seems that our man, Beatte, in his zeal to give the commissioner an opportunity of distinguishing himself, and gratifying his hunting propensities, had mounted him upon his half-wild horse, and started him in pursuit of a huge buffalo bull, that had already been frightened by the hunters. The horse, which was fearless as his owner, and, like him, had a considerable spice of devil in his composition, and who, besides, had been made familiar with the game, no sooner came in sight and scent of the buffalo than he set off full speed, bearing the involuntary hunter hither and thither, and whither he would not—up hill and down hill—leaping pools and brooks—dashing through glens and gullies, until he came up with the game. Instead of sheering off, he crowded upon the buffalo. The commissioner, almost in self-defense, discharged both barrels of a double-barreled gun into the enemy. The broadside took effect, but was not mortal. The buffalo turned furiously upon his pursuer; the horse, as he had been taught by his owner, wheeled off. The buffalo plunged after him. The worthy commissioner, in great extremity, drew his sole pistol from his holster, fired it off as a stern-chaser, shot the buffalo full in the breast, and brought him lumbering forward to the earth.

The commissioner returned to camp, lauded on all sides for his signal exploit; but grievously battered and way-worn. He had been a hard rider perforce, and a victor in spite of himself. He turned a deaf ear to all compliments and congratulations; had but little stomach for the hunter's fare placed before him, and soon retreated to stretch his limbs in the tent, declaring that nothing should tempt him again to mount that half devil Indian horse, and that he had had enough buffalo hunting for the rest of his life.

It was too dark now to send any one in search of the young count. Guns, however, were fired, and the bugle sounded from time to time, to guide him to the camp, if by chance he should straggle within hearing; but the night advanced without his making his appearance. There was not a star visible to guide him, and we concluded that wherever he was he would give up wandering in the dark and bivouac until daybreak.

It was a raw, overcast night. The carcasses of the buffaloes killed in the vicinity of the camp had drawn about it an unusual number of wolves, who kept up the most forlorn concert of whining yells, prolonged into dismal cadences and inflexions, literally converting the surrounding waste into a howling wilderness. Nothing is more melancholy than the midnight howl of a wolf on a prairie. What rendered the gloom and wildness of the night and the savage concert of the neighboring waste the more dreary to us was the idea of the lonely and exposed situation of our young and inexperienced comrade. We trusted, however, that on the return of daylight, he would find his way back to the camp, and then all the events of the night would be remembered only as so many savory gratifications of his passion for adventure.

CHAPTER THIRTY-ONE

A HUNT FOR A LOST COMRADE

THE morning dawned, and an hour or two passed without any tidings of the count. We began to feel uneasiness lest, having no compass to aid him, he might perplex himself and wander in some opposite direction. Stragglers are thus often lost for days; what made us the more anxious about him was, that he had no provisions with him, was totally unversed in "wood craft," and liable to fall into the hands of some lurking or straggling party of savages.

As soon as our people, therefore, had made their breakfast, we beat up for volunteers for a cruise in search of the count. A dozen of the rangers, mounted on some of the best and freshest horses, and armed with rifles, were soon ready to start; our half-breeds Beatte and Antoine also, with our little mongrel Frenchman, were zealous in the cause; so Mr. L. and myself taking the lead, to show the way to the scene of our little hunt where we had parted company with the count, we all set out across the prairie. A ride of a couple of miles brought us to the carcasses of the two buffaloes we had killed. A legion of ravenous wolves were already gorging upon them. At our approach they reluctantly drew off, skulking with a caitiff look to the distance of a few hundred yards, and there awaiting our departure, that they might return to their banquet.

I conducted Beatte and Antoine to the spot whence the young count had continued the chase alone. It was like putting hounds upon the scent. They immediately distinguished the track of his horse amid the trampings of the buffaloes, and set off at a round pace, following with the eye in nearly a straight course, for upward of a mile, when they came to where the herd had divided, and run hither and thither about a meadow. Here the track of the horse's hoofs wandered and doubled and often crossed each other; our half-breeds were like hounds at fault. While we were at a halt, waiting until they should unravel the maze, Beatte suddenly gave a short Indian whoop, or rather yelp, and pointed to a distant hill. On regarding it attentively, we perceived a horseman on the summit. "It is the count!" cried Beatte, and set off at full gallop, followed by the whole company. In a few moments he checked his horse. Another figure on horseback had appeared on the brow of the hill. This completely altered the case. The count had wandered off alone; no other person had been missing from the camp. If

one of these horsemen were indeed the count, the other must
be an Indian. If an Indian, in all probability a Pawnee.
Perhaps they were both Indians; scouts of some party lurking in the vicinity. While these and other suggestions were
hastily discussed, the two horsemen glided down from the
profile of the hill, and we lost sight of them. One of the
rangers suggested that there might be a straggling party of
Pawnees behind the hill, and that the count might have
fallen into their hands. The idea had an electric effect upon
the little troop. In an instant every horse was at full speed
the half-breeds leading the way; the young rangers as they
rode set up wild yelps of exultation at the thoughts of having
a brush with the Indians. A neck or nothing gallop brought
us to the skirts of the hill and revealed our mistake. In a
ravine we found the two horsemen standing by the carcass
of a buffalo which they had killed. They proved to be two
rangers, who, unperceived, had left the camp a little before
us, and had come here in a direct line, while we had made
a wide circuit about the prairie.

This episode being at an end, and the sudden excitement
being over, we slowly and coolly retraced our steps to the
meadow; but it was some time before our half-breeds could
again get on the track of the count. Having at length found
it, they succeeded in following it through all its doublings,
until they came to where it was no longer mingled with the
tramp of buffaloes, but became single and separate, wandering here and there about the prairies, but always tending in
a direction opposite to that of the camp. Here the count had
evidently given up the pursuit of the herd, and had endeavored to find his way to the encampment, but had become
bewildered as the evening shades thickened around him, and
had completely mistaken the points of the compass.

In all this quest our half-breeds displayed that quickness
of eye, in following up a track, for which Indians are so
noted. Beatte, especially, was as stanch as a veteran hound.
Sometimes he would keep forward on an easy trot; his eyes
fixed on the ground a little ahead of his horse, clearly dis-

tinguishing prints in the herbage which to me were invisible, excepting on the closest inspection. Sometimes he would pull up and walk his horse slowly, regarding the ground intensely, where to my eye nothing was apparent. Then he would dismount, lead his horse by the bridle, and advance cautiously step by step, with his face bent toward the earth, just catching, here and there, a casual indication of the vaguest kind to guide him onward. In some places where the soil was hard and the grass withered he would lose the track entirely, and wander backward and forward, and right and left, in search of it; returning occasionally to the place where he had lost sight of it, to take a new departure. If this failed he would examine the banks of the neighboring streams, or the sandy bottoms of the ravines, in hopes of finding tracks where the count had crossed. When he again came upon the track, he would remount his horse and resume his onward course. At length, after crossing a stream, in the crumbling banks of which the hoofs of the horse were deeply dented, we came upon a high dry prairie, where our half-breeds were completely baffled. Not a footprint was to be discerned, though they searched in every direction; and Beatte, at length coming to a pause, shook his head despondingly.

Just then a small herd of deer, roused from a neighboring ravine, came bounding by us. Beatte sprang from his horse, leveled his rifle, and wounded one slightly, but without bringing it to the ground. The report of the rifle was almost immediately followed by a long halloo from a distance. We looked around but could see nothing. Another long halloo was heard, and at length a horseman was descried emerging out of a skirt of forest. A single glance showed him to be the young count; there was a universal shout and scamper, every one setting off full gallop to greet him. It was a joyful meeting to both parties; for much anxiety had been felt by us all on account of his youth and inexperience, and for his part, with all his love of adventure, he seemed right glad to be once more among his friends.

As we supposed, he had completely mistaken his course on the preceding evening, and had wandered about until dark, when he thought of bivouacking. The night was cold, yet he feared to make a fire, lest it might betray him to some lurking party of Indians. Hobbling his horse with his pocket-handkerchief, and leaving him to graze on the margin of the prairie, he clambered into a tree, fixed his saddle in the fork of the branches, and placing himself securely with his back against the trunk, prepared to pass a dreary and anxious night, regaled occasionally with the howlings of the wolves. He was agreeably disappointed. The fatigue of the day soon brought on a sound sleep; he had delightful dreams about his home in Switzerland, nor did he wake until it was broad daylight.

He then descended from his roosting-place, mounted his horse, and rode to the naked summit of a hill, whence he beheld a trackless wilderness around him, but, at no great distance, the Grand Canadian, winding its way between borders of forest land. The sight of this river consoled him with the idea that, should he fail in finding his way back to the camp, or in being found by some party of his comrades, he might follow the course of the stream, which could not fail to conduct him to some frontier post or Indian hamlet. So closed the events of our haphazard buffalo hunt.

CHAPTER THIRTY-TWO

A REPUBLIC OF PRAIRIE DOGS

ON returning from our expedition in quest of the young count, I learned that a burrow, or village, as it is termed, of prairie dogs had been discovered on the level summit of a hill, about a mile from the camp. Having heard much of the habits and peculiarities of these little animals, I determined to pay a visit to the community. The prairie dog is, in fact, one of the curiosities of the Far West, about which travelers delight to tell marvelous tales, endowing him at times with something of the politic and social habits of a rational being, and giving him systems of civil government and domestic economy, almost equal to what they used to bestow upon the beaver.

The prairie dog is an animal of the coney kind, and about the size of a rabbit. He is of a sprightly mercurial nature; quick, sensitive, and somewhat petulant. He is very gregarious, living in large communities, sometimes of several acres in extent, where innumerable little heaps of earth show the entrances to the subterranean cells of the inhabitants, and the well beaten tracks, like lanes and streets, show their mobility and restlessness. According to the accounts given of them, they would seem to be continually full of sport, business, and public affairs; whisking about hither and thither, as if on gossiping visits to each other's houses, or congregating in the cool of the evening, or after a shower, and gamboling together in the open air. Sometimes, especially when the moon shines, they pass half the night in revelry, barking or yelping with short, quick, yet weak tones, like those of very young puppies. While in the height of their playfulness and clamor, however, should there be the least alarm, they all vanish into their cells in an instant, and the village remains blank and silent. In case they are hard pressed by their pursuers, without any hope of escape, they will assume a pugnacious air and a most whimsical look of impotent wrath and defiance.

The prairie dogs are not permitted to remain sole and undisturbed inhabitants of their own homes. Owls and rattlesnakes are said to take up their abodes with them; but whether as invited guests or unwelcome intruders is a matter of controversy. The owls are of a peculiar kind, and would seem to partake of the character of the hawk; for they are taller and more erect on their legs, more alert in their looks and rapid in their flight than ordinary owls, and do not confine their excursions to the night, but sally forth in broad day.

Some say that they only inhabit cells which the prairie dogs have deserted, and suffered to go to ruin, in consequence of the death in them of some relative; for they would make out this little animal to be endowed with keen sensibilities, that will not permit it to remain in the dwelling where it has witnessed the death of a friend. Other fanciful speculators represent the owl as a kind of housekeeper to the prairie dog; and, from having a note very similar, insinuate that it acts, in a manner, as family preceptor, and teaches the young litter to bark.

As to the rattlesnake, nothing satisfactory has been as certained of the part he plays in this most interesting household; though he is considered as little better than a sycophant and sharper, that winds himself into the concerns of the honest, credulous little dog, and takes him in most sadly. Certain it is, if he acts as toad-eater, he occasionally solaces himself with more than the usual perquisities of his order; as he is now and then detected with one of the younger members of the family in his maw.

Such are a few of the particulars that I could gather about the domestic economy of this little inhabitant of the prairies, who, with his pigmy republic, appears to be a subject of much whimsical speculation and burlesque remarks among the hunters of the Far West.

It was toward evening that I set out with a companion, to visit the village in question. Unluckily, it had been invaded in the course of the day by some of the rangers, who had shot two or three of its inhabitants, and thrown the whole sensitive community in confusion. As we approached we could perceive numbers of the inhabitants seated at the entrances of their cells, while sentinels seemed to have been posted on the outskirts to keep a lookout. At sight of us, the picket guards scampered in and gave the alarm; whereupon every inhabitant gave a short yelp, or bark, and dived into his hole, his heels twinkling in the air as if he had thrown a somersault.

We traversed the whole village, or republic, which covered an area of about thirty acres; but not a whisker of an inhabitant was to be seen. We probed their cells as far as the ramrods of our rifles would reach, but could unearth neither dog, nor owl, nor rattlesnake. Moving quietly to a little distance, we lay down upon the ground, and watched for a long time silent and motionless. By and by, a cautious old burgher would slowly put forth the end of his nose, but instantly draw it in again. Another, at a greater distance, would emerge entirely; but, catching a glance of us, would throw a somersault and plunge back again into his hole. At length, some who resided on the opposite side of the village, taking courage from the continued stillness, would steal forth, and hurry off to a distant hole, the residence possibly of some family connection, or gossiping friend, about whose safety they were solicitous, or with whom they wished to compare notes about the late occurrences.

Others, still more bold, assembled in little knots, in the streets and public places, as if to discuss the recent outrages offered to the commonwealth, and the atrocious murders of their fellow-burghers.

We rose from the ground and moved forward, to take a nearer view of these public proceedings, when yelp! yelp! yelp!—there was a shrill alarm passed from mouth to mouth; the meetings suddenly dispersed; feet twinkled in the air in every direction; and in an instant all had vanished into the earth.

The dusk of the evening put an end to our observations, but the train of whimsical comparisons produced in my brain by the moral attributes which I had heard given to these little politic animals, still continued after my return to camp; and late in the night, as I lay awake after all the camp was asleep, and heard in the stillness of the hour, a faint clamor of shrill voices from the distant village, I could not help picturing to myself the inhabitants gathered together in noisy assemblage and windy debate, to devise plans for the public safety, and to vindicate the invaded rights and insulted dignity of the republic.

CHAPTER THIRTY-THREE

A COUNCIL IN THE CAMP—REASONS FOR FACING HOME-
WARD—HORSES LOST — DEPARTURE WITH A DETACH-
MENT ON THE HOMEWARD ROUTE—SWAMP—WILD HORSE
—CAMP SCENES BY NIGHT—THE OWL, HARBINGER OF
DAWN

WHILE breakfast was preparing, a council was held as to
our future movements. Symptoms of discontent had appeared for a day or two past among the rangers, most of
whom, unaccustomed to the life of the prairies, had become
impatient of its privations, as well as the restraints of the
camp. The want of bread had been felt severely, and they
were wearied with constant travel. In fact, the novelty and
excitement of the expedition were at an end. They had
hunted the deer, the bear, the elk, the buffalo, and the wild
horse, and had no further object of leading interest to look
forward to. A general inclination prevailed, therefore, to
turn homeward.

Grave reasons disposed the captain and his officers to
adopt this resolution. Our horses were generally much
jaded by the fatigues of traveling and hunting, and had
fallen away sadly for want of good pasturage, and from
being tethered at night, to be protected from Indian depredations. The late rains, too, seemed to have washed
away the nourishment from the scanty herbage that remained; and since our encampment during the storm, our
horses had lost flesh and strength rapidly. With every possible care, horses, accustomed to grain, and to the regular
and plentiful nourishment of the stable and the farm, lose
heart and condition in traveling on the prairies. In all expeditions of the kind we were engaged in, the hardy Indian

horses, which are generally mustangs, or a cross of the wild breed, are to be preferred. They can stand all fatigues, hardships, and privations, and thrive on the grasses and wild herbage of the plains.

Our men, too, had acted with little forethought; galloping off whenever they had a chance, after the game that we encountered while on the march. In this way they had strained and wearied their horses, instead of husbanding their strength and spirits. On a tour of the kind, horses should as seldom as possible be put off of a quiet walk; and the average day's journey should not exceed ten miles.

We had hoped, by pushing forward, to reach the bottoms of the Red River, which abound with young cane, a most nourishing forage for cattle at this season of the year. It would now take us several days to arrive there, and in the meantime many of our horses would probably give out. It was the time, too, when the hunting parties of Indians set fire to the prairies; the herbage, throughout this part of the country, was in that parched state, favorable to combustion, and there was daily more and more risk that the prairies between us and the fort would be set on fire by some of the return parties of Osages, and a scorched desert left for us to traverse. In a word, we had started too late in the season, or loitered too much in the early part of our march, to accomplish our originally intended tour; and there was imminent hazard, if we continued on, that we should lose the greater part of our horses; and, besides suffering various other inconveniences, be obliged to return on foot. It was determined, therefore, to give up all further progress, and, turning our faces to the southeast, to make the best of our way back to Fort Gibson.

This resolution being taken, there was an immediate eagerness to put it into operation. Several horses, however, were missing, and among others those of the captain and the surgeon. Persons had gone in search of them, but the morning advanced without any tidings of them. Our party, in the meantime, being all ready for a march, the commissioner

determined to set off in the advance, with his original escort
of a lieutenant and fourteen rangers, leaving the captain to
come on at his convenience with the main body. At ten
o'clock we accordingly started, under the guidance of Beatte,
who had hunted over this part of the country and knew the
direct route to the garrison.

For some distance we skirted the prairie, keeping a southeast direction; and in the course of our ride we saw a variety
of wild animals, deer, white and black wolves, buffaloes,
and wild horses. To the latter, our half-breeds and Tonish
gave ineffectual chase, only serving to add to the weariness
of their already jaded steeds. Indeed it is rarely that any
but the weaker and least fleet of the wild horses are taken in
these hard racings; while the horse of the huntsman is prone
to be knocked up. The latter, in fact, risks a good horse to
catch a bad one. On this occasion, Tonish, who was a perfect imp on horseback, and noted for ruining every animal
he bestrode, succeeded in laming and almost disabling the
powerful gray on which we had mounted him at the outset
of our tour.

After proceeding a few miles, we left the prairie, and
struck to the east, taking what Beatte pronounced an old
Osage war-track. This led us through a rugged tract of
country, overgrown with scrubbed forests and entangled
thickets, and intersected by deep ravines, and brisk-running
streams, the sources of Little River. About three o'clock,
we encamped by some pools of water in a small valley, having come about fourteen miles. We had brought on a supply
of provisions from our last camp, and supped heartily upon
stewed buffalo meat, roasted venison, beignets, or fritters of
flour fried in bear's lard, and tea made of a species of the
golden-rod, which we had found, throughout our whole route,
almost as grateful a beverage as coffee. Indeed our coffee,
which, as long as it held out, had been served up with every
meal, according to the custom of the West, was by no means
a beverage to boast of. It was roasted in a frying-pan, without much care, pounded in a leathern bag, with a round

stone, and boiled in our prime and almost only kitchen utensil, the camp kettle, in "branch" or brook water; which, on the prairies, is deeply colored by the soil, of which it always holds abundant particles in a state of solution and suspension. In fact, in the course of our tour, we had tasted the quality of every variety of soil, and the draughts of water we had taken might vie in diversity of color, if not of flavor, with the tinctures of an apothecary's shop. Pure, limpid water is a rare luxury on the prairies, at least at this season of the year. Supper over, we placed sentinels about our scanty and diminished camp, spread our skins and blankets under the trees, now nearly destitute of foliage, and slept soundly until morning.

We had a beautiful daybreak. The camp again resounded with cheerful voices; every one was animated with the thoughts of soon being at the fort, and reveling on bread and vegetables. Even our saturnine man, Beatte, seemed inspired on this occasion; and as he drove up the horses for the march, I heard him singing, in nasal tones, a most forlorn Indian ditty. All this transient gayety, however, soon died away amid the fatigues of our march, which lay through the same kind of rough, hilly, thicketed country as that of yesterday. In the course of the morning we arrived at the valley of the Little River, where it wound through a broad bottom of alluvial soil. At present it had overflowed its banks and inundated a great part of the valley. The difficulty was to distinguish the stream from the broad sheets of water it had formed, and to find a place where it might be forded; for it was in general deep and miry, with abrupt crumbling banks. Under the pilotage of Beatte, therefore, we wandered for some time among the links made by this winding stream, in what appeared to us a trackless labyrinth of swamps, thickets, and standing pools. Sometimes our jaded horses dragged their limbs forward with the utmost difficulty, having to toil for a great distance with the water up to the stirrups, and beset at the bottom with roots and creeping plants. Sometimes we had to force our way through dense thickets of brambles and grapevines, which almost pulled us out of our saddles. In one place, one of the pack-horses sunk in the mire and fell on his side, so as to be extricated with great difficulty. Wherever the soil was bare, or there was a sand-bank, we beheld innumerable tracks of bears, wolves, wild horses, turkeys, and water-fowl; showing the abundant sport this valley might afford to the huntsman. Our men, however, were sated with hunting, and too weary to be excited by these signs, which in the outset of our tour would have put them in a fever of anticipation. Their only desire, at present, was to push on doggedly for the fortress.

At length we succeeded in finding a fording place, where we all crossed Little River, with the water and mire to the saddle-girths, and then halted for an hour and a half, to overhaul the wet baggage, and give the horses time to rest.

On resuming our march, we came to a pleasant little meadow, surrounded by groves of elms and cottonwood trees, in the midst of which was a fine black horse grazing. Beatte, who was in the advance, beckoned us to halt, and, being mounted on a mare, approached the horse gently, step by step, imitating the whinny of the animal with admirable exactness. The noble courser of the prairie gazed for a time, snuffed the air, neighed, pricked up his ears, and pranced round and round the mare in gallant style; but kept at too great a distance for Beatte to throw the lariat. He was a magnificent object, in all the pride and glory of his nature. It was admirable to see the lofty and airy carriage of his head; the freedom of every movement; the elasticity with which he trod the meadow. Finding it impossible to get within noosing distance, and seeing that the horse was receding and growing alarmed, Beatte slid down from his saddle, leveled his rifle across the back of his mare, and took aim, with the evident intention of creasing him. I felt a throb of anxiety for the safety of the noble animal, and called out to Beatte to desist. It was too late; he pulled the trigger as I spoke; luckily he did not shoot with his usual accuracy, and I had the satisfaction to see the coal-black steed dash off unharmed into the forest.

On leaving this valley, we ascended among broken hills and rugged, ragged forests, equally harassing to horse and rider. The ravines, too, were of red clay, and often so steep that, in descending, the horses would put their feet together and fairly slide down, and then scramble up the opposite side like cats. Here and there, among the thickets in the valleys, we met with sloes and persimmon, and the eagerness with which our men broke from the line of march, and ran to gather these poor fruits, showed how much they craved some vegetable condiment, after living so long exclusively on animal food.

About half-past three we encamped near a brook in a meadow, where there was some scanty herbage for our half-famished horses. As Beatte had killed a fat doe in the course of the day, and one of our company a fine turkey, we did not lack for provisions.

It was a splendid autumnal evening. The horizon, after sunset, was of a clear apple green, rising into a delicate lake which gradually lost itself in a deep purple blue. One narrow streak of cloud, of a mahogany color, edged with amber and gold, floated in the west, and just beneath it was the evening star, shining with the pure brilliancy of a diamond. In unison with this scene, there was an evening concert of insects of various kinds, all blended and harmonized into one sober and somewhat melancholy note, which I have always found to have a soothing effect upon the mind, disposing it to quiet musings.

The night that succeeded was calm and beautiful. There was a faint light from the moon, now in its second quarter, and after it had set, a fine starlight, with shooting meteors. The wearied rangers, after a little murmuring conversation round their fires, sank to rest at an early hour, and I seemed to have the whole scene to myself. It is delightful, in thus bivouacking on the prairies, to lie awake and gaze at the stars; it is like watching them from the deck of a ship at sea, when at one view we have the whole cope of heaven. One realizes, in such lonely scenes, that companionship with these beautiful luminaries which made astronomers of the Eastern shepherds, as they watched their flocks by night. How often, while contemplating their mild and benignant radiance, I have called to mind the exquisite text of Job: "Canst thou bind the secret influences of the Pleiades, or loose the bands of Orion?" I do not know why it was, but I felt this night unusually affected by the solemn magnificence of the firmament; and seemed, as I lay thus under the open vault of heaven, to inhale the pure untainted air, and exhilarating buoyancy of spirit, and, as it were, an ecstasy of mind. I slept and waked alternately; and when I slept, my dreams partook of the happy tone of my waking reveries. Toward morning, one of the sentinels, the oldest man in the troop, came and took a seat near me; he was weary and sleepy, and impatient to be relieved. I found he had been gazing at the heavens also, but with different feelings.

"If the stars don't deceive me," said he, "it is near daybreak."

"There can be no doubt of that," said Beatte, who lay close by. "I heard an owl just now."

"Does the owl, then, hoot toward daybreak?" asked I.

"Ay, sir, just as the cock crows."

This was a useful habitude of the bird of wisdom, of which I was not aware. Neither the stars nor owl deceived their votaries. In a short time there was a faint streak of light in the east.

CHAPTER THIRTY-FOUR

OLD CREEK ENCAMPMENT—SCARCITY OF PROVISIONS—BAD
WEATHER—WEARY MARCHING—A HUNTER'S BRIDGE

THE country through which we passed this morning (November 2d) was less rugged and of more agreeable aspect than that we had lately traversed. At eleven o'clock we came out upon an extensive prairie, and about six miles to our left beheld a long line of green forest, marking the course of the north fork of the Arkansas. On the edge of the prairie, and in a spacious grove of noble trees which overshadowed a small brook, were the traces of an old Creek hunting camp. On the bark of the trees were rude delineations of hunters and squaws, scrawled with charcoal; together with various signs and hieroglyphics, which our half-breeds interpreted as indicating that from this encampment the hunters had returned home.

In this beautiful camping ground we made our midday halt. While reposing under the trees, we heard a shouting at no great distance, and presently the captain and the main body of rangers, whom we had left behind two days since, emerged from the thickets, and, crossing the brook, were joyfully welcomed into the camp. The captain and the doctor had been unsuccessful in the search after their horses, and were obliged to march for the greater part of the time on foot; yet they had come on with more than ordinary speed.

We resumed our march about one o'clock, keeping easterly, and approaching the north fork obliquely; it was late before we found a good camping place; the beds of the streams were dry, the prairies, too, had been burned in various places by Indian hunting parties. At length we found water in a small alluvial bottom, where there was tolerable pasturage.

On the following morning there were flashes of lightning in the east, with low, rumbling thunder, and clouds began to gather about the horizon. Beatte prognosticated rain, and that the wind would veer to the north. In the course of our march a flock of brant were seen overhead, flying from the north. "There comes the wind!" said Beatte; and, in fact, it began to blow from that quarter almost immediately, with occasional flurries of rain. About half-past nine o'clock we forded the north fork of the Canadian, and encamped about one, that our hunters might have time to beat up the neighborhood for game; for a serious scarcity began to prevail in the camp. Most of the rangers were young, heedless, and inexperienced, and could not be prevailed upon, while provisions abounded, to provide for the future, by jerking meat, or carrying away any on their horses. On leaving an encampment, they would leave quantities of meat lying about, trusting to Providence and their rifles for a future supply. The consequence was that any temporary scarcity of game, or ill-luck in hunting, produced almost a famine in the camp. In the present instance, they had left loads of buffalo meat at the camp on the great prairie; and having ever since been on a forced march, leaving no time for hunting, they were now destitute of supplies and pinched with hunger. Some had not eaten anything since the morning of the preceding day. Nothing would have persuaded them, when reveling in the abundance of the buffalo encampment, that they would so soon be in such famishing plight.

The hunters returned with indifferent success. The game had been frightened away from this part of the country by Indian hunting parties which had preceded us. Ten or a dozen wild turkeys were brought in, but not a deer had been seen. The rangers began to think turkeys and even prairie hens deserving of attention; game which they had hitherto considered unworthy of their rifles.

The night was cold and windy, with occasional sprinklings of rain; but we had roaring fires to keep us comfortable. In the night, a flight of wild geese passed over the camp, making a great cackling in the air; symptoms of approaching winter.

We set forward at an early hour the next morning, in a northeast course, and came upon the trace of a party of Creek Indians, which enabled our poor horses to travel with more ease. We entered upon a fine champaign country. From a rising ground we had a noble prospect, over extensive prairies, finely diversified by groves and tracts of woodland, and bounded by long lines of distant hills, all clothed with the rich mellow tints of autumn. Game, too, was more plenty. A fine buck sprang up from among the herbage on our right and dashed off at full speed; but a young ranger by the name of Childers, who was on foot, leveled his rifle, discharged a ball that broke the neck of the bounding deer, and sent him tumbling head over heels forward. Another buck and a doe, besides several turkeys, were killed before we came to a halt, so that the hungry mouths of the troop were once more supplied.

About three o'clock we encamped in a grove after a forced march of twenty-five miles, that had proved a hard trial to the horses. For a long time after the head of the line had encamped, the rest kept straggling in, two and three at a time; one of our pack-horses had given out, about nine miles back, and a pony belonging to Beatte shortly after. Many of the other horses looked so gaunt and feeble that doubts were entertained of their being able to reach the fort. In the night there was heavy rain, and the morning dawned cloudy and dismal. The camp resounded, however, with something of its former gayety. The rangers had supped well, and were renovated in spirits, anticipating a speedy arrival at the garrison. Before we set forward on our march, Beatte returned, and brought his pony to the camp with great difficulty. The pack-horse, however, was completely knocked up and had to be abandoned. The wild mare, too, had cast her foal, through exhaustion, and was not in a state to go forward. She and the pony, therefore, were left at this encampment, where there was water and good pasturage; and where there would be a chance of their reviving, and being afterward sought out and brought to the garrison.

We set off about eight o'clock, and had a day of weary and harassing travel; part of the time over rough hills, and part over rolling prairies. The rain had rendered the soil slippery and plashy, so as to afford unsteady foothold. Some of the rangers dismounted, their horses having no longer strength to bear them. We made a halt in the course of the morning, but the horses were too tired to graze. Several of them laid down, and there was some difficulty in getting them on their feet again. Our troop presented a forlorn appearance, straggling slowly along, in a broken and scattered line that extended over hill and dale, for three miles and upward, in groups of three and four, widely apart; some on horseback, some on foot, with a few laggards far in the rear. About four o'clock we halted for the night in a spacious forest, beside a deep narrow river called the Little North Fork, or Deep Creek. It was late before the main part of the troop straggled into the encampment, many of the horses having given out. As this stream was too deep to be forded we waited until the next day to devise means to cross it; but our half-breeds swam the horses of our party to the other side in the evening, as they would have better pasturage, and the stream was evidently swelling. The night was cold and unruly; the wind sounding hoarsely through the forest and whirling about the dry leaves. We made long fires of great trunks of trees, which diffused something of consolation if not cheerfulness around.

The next morning there was general permission given to hunt until twelve o'clock; the camp being destitute of provisions. The rich woody bottom in which we were encamped abounded with wild turkeys, of which a considerable number were killed. In the meantime, preparations were made for crossing the river, which had risen several feet during the night; and it was determined to fell trees for the purpose, to serve as bridges.

The captain and doctor, and one or two other leaders of the camp, versed in woodcraft, examined, with learned eye, the trees growing on the river bank, until they singled out a couple of the largest size and most suitable inclinations. The ax was then vigorously applied to their roots, in such a way as to insure their falling directly across the stream. As they did not reach to the opposite bank, it was necessary for some of the men to swim across and fell trees on the other side, to meet them. They at length succeeded in making a precarious footway across the deep and rapid current, by which the baggage could be carried over; but it was necessary to grope our way, step by step, along the trunks and main branches of the trees, which for a part of the distance were completely submerged, so that we were to our waists in water. Most of the horses were then swum across, but some of them were too weak to brave the current, and evidently too much knocked up to bear any further travel. Twelve men, therefore, were left at the encampment to guard these horses, until, by repose and good pasturage, they should be sufficiently recovered to complete their journey; and the captain engaged to send the men a supply of flour and other necessaries as soon as we should arrive at the fort.

CHAPTER THIRTY-FIVE

A LOOKOUT FOR LAND—HARD TRAVELING AND HUNGRY
HALTING—A FRONTIER FARMHOUSE—ARRIVAL
AT THE GARRISON

IT was a little after one o'clock when we again resumed our weary wayfaring. The residue of that day and the whole of the next were spent in toilsome travel. Part of the way was over stony hills, part across wide prairies, rendered spongy and miry by the recent rain, and cut up by brooks swollen into torrents. Our poor horses were so feeble that it was with difficulty we could get them across the deep ravines and turbulent streams. In traversing the miry plains, they slipped and staggered at every step, and most of us were obliged to dismount and walk for the greater part of the way. Hunger prevailed throughout the troop; every one began to look anxious and haggard, and to feel the growing length of each additional mile. At one time, in crossing a hill, Beatte climbed a high tree, commanding a wide prospect, and took a lookout, like a mariner from the masthead at sea. He came down with cheering tidings. To the left he had beheld a line of forest stretching across the country, which he knew to be the woody border of the Arkansas; and at a distance he had recognized certain landmarks, from which he concluded that we could not be above forty miles distant from the fort. It was like the welcome cry of land to tempest-tossed mariners.

In fact we soon after saw smoke rising from a woody glen at a distance. It was supposed to be made by a hunting-party of Creek or Osage Indians from the neighborhood of the fort, and was joyfully hailed as a harbinger of man. It was now confidently hoped that we would soon arrive among the frontier hamlets of Creek Indians, which are scattered along the skirts of the uninhabited wilderness; and our hungry rangers trudged forward with reviving spirit, regaling themselves with savory anticipations of farmhouse luxuries, and enumerating every article of good cheer, until their mouths fairly watered at the shadowy feasts thus conjured up.

A hungry night, however, colsed in upon a toilsome day. We encamped on the border of one of the tributary streams of the Arkansas, amid the ruins of a stately grove that had been riven by a hurricane. The blast had torn its way through the forest in a narrow column, and its course was marked by enormous trees shivered and splintered, and upturned, with their roots in the air; all lay in one direction, like so many brittle reeds broken and trodden down by the hunter.

Here was fuel in abundance, without the labor of the ax; we had soon immense fires blazing and sparkling in the frosty air, and lighting up the whole forest; but, alas! we had no meat to cook at them. The scarcity in the camp almost amounted to famine. Happy was he who had a morsel of jerked meat, or even the half-picked bones of a former repast. For our part, we were more lucky at our mess than our neighbors; one of our men having shot a turkey. We had no bread to eat with it, nor salt to season it withal. It was simply boiled in water; the latter was served up as soup, and we were fain to rub each morsel of the turkey on the empty salt-bag, in hopes some saline particle might remain to relieve its insipidity.

The night was biting cold; the brilliant moonlight sparkled on the frosty crystals which covered every object around us. The water froze beside the skins on which we bivouacked, and in the morning I found the blanket in which I was wrapped covered with a hoar frost; yet I had never slept more comfortably.

After a shadow of a breakfast, consisting of turkey bones and a cup of coffee without sugar, we decamped at an early hour; for hunger is a sharp quickener on a journey. The prairies were all gemmed with frost, that covered the tall weeds and glistened in the sun. We saw great flights of prairie-hens or grouse, that hovered from tree to tree, or sat in rows along the naked branches, waiting until the sun should melt the frost from the weeds and herbage. Our rangers no longer despised such humble game, but turned from the ranks in pursuit of a prairie-hen as eagerly as they formerly would go in pursuit of a deer.

Every one now pushed forward, anxious to arrive at some human habitation before night. The poor horses were urged beyond their strength, in the thought of soon being able to indemnify them for present toil, by rest and ample provender. Still the distances seemed to stretch out more than ever, and the blue hills, pointed out as landmarks on the horizon, to recede as we advanced. Every step became a labor; every now and then a miserable horse would give out and lie down. His owner would raise him by main strength, force him forward to the margin of some stream, where there might be a scanty border of herbage, and then abandon him to his fate. Among those that were thus left on the way was one of the led horses of the count; a prime hunter, that had taken the lead of everything in the chase of the wild horses. It was intended, however, as soon as we should arrive at the fort, to send out a party provided with corn, to bring in such of the horses as should survive.

In the course of the morning we came upon Indian tracks, crossing each other in various directions, a proof that we must be in the neighborhood of human habitations. At length, on passing through a skirt of wood, we beheld two or three log houses, sheltered under lofty trees on the border of a prairie, the habitations of Creek Indians, who had small farms adjacent. Had they been sumptuous villas, abounding with the luxuries of civilization, they could not have been hailed with greater delight.

Some of the rangers rode up to them in quest of food; the greater part, however, pushed forward in search of the habitation of a white settler, which we were told was at no great distance. The troop soon disappeared among the trees, and I followed slowly in their track; for my once fleet and generous steed faltered under me, and was just able to drag one foot after the other, yet I was too weary and exhausted to spare him.

In this way we crept on, until, on turning a thick clump of trees, a frontier farmhouse suddenly presented itself to view. It was a low tenement of logs, overshadowed by great forest trees, but it seemed as if a very region of Cocaigne prevailed around it. Here was a stable and barn, and granaries teeming with abundance, while legions of grunting swine, gobbling turkeys, cackling hens and strutting roosters, swarmed about the farmyard.

My poor jaded and half-famished horse raised his head and pricked up his ears at the well-known sights and sounds. He gave a chuckling inward sound, something like a dry laugh; whisked his tail, and made great leeway toward a corn-crib, filled with golden ears of maize, and it was with some difficulty that I could control his course, and steer him up to the door of the cabin. A single glance within was sufficient to raise every gastronomic faculty. There sat the captain of the rangers and his officers, round a three-legged table, crowned by a broad and smoking dish of boiled beef and turnips. I sprang off my horse in an instant, cast him loose to make his way to the corn-crib, and entered this palace of plenty. A fat good-humored negress received me at the door. She was the mistress of the house, the spouse of the white man, who was absent. I hailed her as some swart fairy of the wild, that had suddenly conjured up a banquet in the desert; and a banquet was it in good sooth. In a twinkling she lugged from the fire a huge iron pot, that might have rivaled one of the famous flesh-pots of Egypt, or the witches' caldron in "Macbeth." Placing a brown earthen dish on the floor, she inclined the corpulent caldron on one side, and out leaped sundry great morsels of beef, with a regiment of turnips tumbling after them, and a rich cascade of broth overflowing the whole. This she handed me with an ivory smile that extended from ear to ear; apologizing for our humble fare, and the humble style in which it was served up. Humble fare! humble style! Boiled beef and turnips, and an earthen dish to eat them from! To think of apologizing for such a treat to a half-starved man from the prairies; and then such magnificent slices of bread and butter! Head of Apicius, what a banquet!

"The rage of hunger" being appeased, I began to think of my horse. He, however, like an old campaigner, had taken good care of himself. I found him paying assiduous attention to the crib of Indian corn, and dexterously drawing forth and munching the ears that protruded between the bars. It was with great regret that I interrupted his repast, which he abandoned with a heavy sigh, or rather a rumbling groan. I was anxious, however, to rejoin my traveling companions, who had passed by the farmhouse without stopping, and proceeded to the banks of the Arkansas; being in hopes of arriving before night at the Osage Agency. Leaving the captain and his troop, therefore, amid the abundance of the farm, where they had determined to quarter themselves for the night, I bade adieu to our sable hostess, and again pushed forward.

A ride of about a mile brought me to where my comrades were waiting on the banks of the Arkansas, which here poured along between beautiful forests. A number of Creek Indians, in their brightly colored dresses, looking like so many gay tropical birds, were busy aiding our men to transport the baggage across the river in a canoe. While this was doing, our horses had another regale from two great cribs heaped up with ears of Indian corn, which stood near the edge of the river. We had to keep a check upon the poor half-famished animals, lest they should injure themselves by their voracity.

The baggage being all carried to the opposite bank, we embarked in the canoe, and swum our horses across the river I was fearful lest in their enfeebled state they should not be able to stem the current; but their banquet of Indian corn had already infused fresh life and spirit into them, and it would appear as if they were cheered by the instinctive consciousness of their approach to home, where they would soon be at rest, and in plentiful quarters; for no sooner had we landed and resumed our route than they set off on a hand-gallop, and continued so for a great part of seven miles that we had to ride through the woods.

It was an early hour in the evening when we arrived at the Agency, on the banks of the Verdigris River, whence we had set off about a month before. Here we passed the night comfortably quartered; yet, after having been accustomed to sleep in the open air, the confinement of a chamber was, in some respects, irksome. The atmosphere seemed close, and destitute of freshness; and when I woke in the night and gazed about me upon complete darkness, I missed the glorious companionship of the stars.

The next morning, after breakfast, I again set forward, in company with the worthy commissioner, for Fort Gibson, where we arrived much tattered, travel-stained, and weather-beaten, but in high health and spirits; and thus ended my foray into the Pawnee Hunting Grounds.

END OF VOLUME SEVEN